The Art of Veiled Speech

THE ART OF VEILED SPEECH

Self-Censorship from Aristophanes to Hobbes

Edited by

Han Baltussen and Peter J. Davis

PENN

UNIVERSITY OF PENNSYLVANIA PRESS

PHILADELPHIA

Published by
University of Pennsylvania Press
Philadelphia, Pennsylvania 19104-4112
www.upenn.edu/pennpress

Printed in the United States of America on acid-free paper
1 3 5 7 9 10 8 6 4 2

A Cataloging-in-Publication record is available from the
Library of Congress

The art of veiled speech : self-censorship from Aristophanes
to Hobbes / edited by Han Baltussen and Peter J. Davis.
pages cm
Includes bibliographical references and index.
ISBN 978-0-8122-4735-0 (alk. paper)
1. Classical literature—History and criticism. 2. Politics
and literature—History. 3. Freedom of speech in literature—
History. 4. Freedom of speech—History. 5. Censorship—
History. I. Baltussen, Han, editor, author. II. Davis, Peter J.,
editor, author.
PA3015.P63A78 2015
363.31—dc23

2015005388

Contents

Chapter 1. *Parrhêsia*, Free Speech, and Self-Censorship 1
Han Baltussen and Peter J. Davis

Chapter 2. Self-Censorship in Ancient Greek Comedy 18
Andrew Hartwig

Chapter 3. *Parrhêsia* and Censorship in the *Polis* and the Symposium: An Exploration of Hyperides *Against Philippides* 3 42
Lara O'Sullivan

Chapter 4. A Bark Worse Than His Bite? Diogenes the Cynic and the Politics of Tolerance in Athens 74
Han Baltussen

Chapter 5. Censorship for the Roman Stage? 94
Gesine Manuwald

Chapter 6. The Poet as Prince: Author and Authority Under Augustus 115
Ioannis Ziogas

Chapter 7. "*Quae quis fugit damnat*": Outspoken Silence in Seneca's *Epistles* 137
Marcus Wilson

Chapter 8. Argo's Flavian Politics: The Workings of Power in Valerius Flaccus 157
Peter J. Davis

Chapter 9. Compulsory Freedom: Literature in Trajan's Rome 176
John Penwill

Chapter 10. Christian Correspondences: The Secrets of Letter-Writers and Letter-Bearers 209
Pauline Allen

Chapter 11. "Silence Is Also Annulment": Veiled and Unveiled Speech in Seventh-Century Martyr Commemorations 233
Bronwen Neil

Chapter 12. "*Dixit quod nunquam vidit hereticos*": Dissimulation and Self-Censorship in Thirteenth-Century Inquisitorial Testimonies 251
Megan Cassidy-Welch

Chapter 13. Inquisition, Art, and Self-Censorship in the Early Modern Spanish Church, 1563–1834 269
François Soyer

Chapter 14. Thomas Hobbes and the Problem of Self-Censorship 293
Jonathan Parkin

Epilogue 318
Han Baltussen and Peter J. Davis

List of Contributors 321

Index 323

Acknowledgments 329

Chapter 1

Parrhêsia, Free Speech, and Self-Censorship

Han Baltussen and Peter J. Davis

Prologue

Jocasta: What is hard for exiles?
Polynices: One thing is biggest: he has no *parrhêsia.*
Jocasta: Not saying what you think, that's typical of a slave.
Jocasta: That is painful, being foolish with the foolish.
Polynices: For the sake of gain you have to be a slave against your nature.

—Euripides, *Phoenician Women*

In this brief exchange between a mother and her exiled son, Euripides has Jocasta and Polynices discuss the place of *parrhêsia* in fifth-century Athenian thinking.[1] First, *parrhêsia* is the property of a free citizen: it characterizes a man who is free (i.e., he is not a slave) and who participates in the affairs of his native city (i.e., he is not an exile). Second, *parrhêsia* is defined not as "free speech" as commonly understood in the twenty-first century, as a universal human right, but as "frank speech," the ability to "say what you think." In the view of Jocasta and Polynices, slaves and exiles must hide their true thoughts. The tension between "frank speech," typical of the ideal free citizen, and the art of "veiled speech," that is, the methods of expression adopted by the less-than-free, is this book's central theme.

This opening chapter both sets out the broader conceptual framework we use for this collection and clarifies the ways in which subsequent chapters share this common theme of veiled speech and self-censorship. One point in need of clarification is *why* we focus on veiled speech as a form of subversion. Another is what the common thread is in the selection of authors ranging "from Aristophanes to Hobbes," despite their chronological spread and range of different historical and literary contexts.

We have taken a broad sweep at the evidence because censorship is a phenomenon that seems to have no temporal or geographical boundaries: it characterizes both totalitarian dictatorships and liberal democracies from ancient Athens to the twentieth century and is still with us in the twenty-first. While the centralized forms of censorship practiced in countries like China and Iran are notorious, we should not forget that even states with a constitutional commitment to freedom of speech impose limits on that freedom; *nowhere* is the right absolute. And this is not by any means a bad thing.[2] How to balance the right to free speech against other legitimate concerns is a perennial issue. The most extreme form of free speech is no doubt frank speech, *parrhêsia*, which etymologically originates in *pan* ("everything") and *rhêsia* ("speaking"): in other words, the freedom to "say all." But it will be obvious that in practice this is hardly ever possible. Cultural and social conventions impose limits on what we can say, whether in interactions between private persons (family, friends, colleagues) or in the public sphere between individuals and the state. In general terms, censorship can be defined as the regulation of a person's political and moral expression by the imposition of limits on the free circulation of ideas, images, and information.[3] All democratic states recognize that there is an inherent tension between the individual's right to free speech and the public's interest in such matters as privacy, security, the administration of justice, and the protection of community standards.

The collection's chronological spread of essays was chosen to cover a number of flashpoints in classical and later periods, ending just before the modern age when the concept was about to change (BCE: fifth, fourth to third, and first centuries; CE: first, second, fourth to sixth, seventh, thirteenth, sixteenth to seventeenth, and eighteenth centuries). It should be kept in mind that the selection is also in part a result of the availability of good material, especially in periods when the tension around free speech (and attempts to control it) intensified, as for instance in imperial Rome or the Christian era. Furthermore, the essays cover not only different literary genres (that is, poetic texts as well as historical, epistolary, and philosophical prose) and many periods in history, but also many modes of expression (the collection is "multimodal" in that it makes use of examples from oral culture and theater, written sources, and images to illustrate the persistent presence of self-regulating measures by writers and creative artists of a variety of works).

These three aspects of the topic under scrutiny (diversity in chronology, theme, and medium) raise another issue regarding the theoretical framework of this collection. These considerations about the ubiquity of self-censorship not only help to *illustrate* that this is a perennial problem, but also help to *define* self-regulation as a social and cultural phenomenon. While traditional treatments tend to position the discourse on censorship solely within the political environment, there is as yet little debate on self-regulation in antiquity. In other words, these essays are taking the first steps to study this aspect based on carefully selected samples, and the volume as a whole puts forward a number of claims that we hope will change the focus and widen the scope regarding the debate on *parrhêsia* and the limits different groups choose to impose on it.

While it would go too far to claim that our investigations will produce a "theory" of self-censorship, the chapters clearly emphasize the many ways in which the (potentially) oppressed respond to the threat of controlling authorities. As a result a picture emerges that throws light on the dynamics of the subtle subversion in different kinds of context. By carefully defining the core terms such as *parrhêsia*, *libertas*, and (self-)censorship, we aim to ensure that our perspective is built on clear principles and distinctive from the standard one, in which the censoring party is often central and regularly subjected to a modern (negative) judgment.

The evidence also justifies the importance of antiquity—which is why the weight of chapters leans toward classical and late antique/medieval times. The inclusion of two chapters relating to the early modern period puts us in a position to add a further dimension to the discussion (the religious censure of images), and to sketch the views of a theorist about self-censorship based on his own experience (suppression of his work).[4] Combined, the chapters show how the concrete situations that are analyzed underscore the social origin of subversion and censorship. Thus each chapter shores up the broader thesis we articulate. We hope that this will eventually allow for a theoretical framework that clarifies the dynamics between "oppressors" and "the oppressed," even if (1) we use these terms not just in a political sense, (2) we privilege the perspective of the oppressed (and those under the threat of oppression), and (3) we allow for some gaps in coverage—it is impossible to cover all historical periods in one volume—but offer a considered selection of cases. Some of the *thematic* links and common threads of the essays will be highlighted in the epilogue.

In terms of its more specific objectives, the volume aims to show, first, that limitations on free speech have prompted creative responses that often require subtle and sophisticated decoding;[5] second, that the tension between "frank speech" and the art of veiled speech is the result of a wider human need for expressing opinions—one that unavoidably leads to disagreement and dispute; and third, that examination of such an omnipresent theme across different historical periods is possible, provided that we use a cautious and even-handed method of analysis in order to avoid projecting modern notions of free speech onto the evidence. These three objectives are intended to serve the broader objective we have set ourselves, namely to approach the theme of subversion and censorship "from below" (bottom-up) instead of the more common "from above" (top-down) perspective. The resulting diachronic and cross-cultural vista on the dynamics of censorship will begin to give us a more fine-grained understanding of the creative choices made by those who felt limited in their expression of views and were forced to "self-regulate" in some form or other, whether they attempted to evade political, cultural, religious, or social restrictions.

Censorship and Veiled Speech in Antiquity

It is a remarkable fact that in the last decade of the sixth century BCE (at least as dated by tradition) political revolutions took place in two of the most important cities of the ancient Mediterranean world, revolutions that led to the centrality of the concept of free speech in contemporary (and not just Western) political discourse, for this was the decade that saw the introduction of democratic reforms associated with Cleisthenes in Athens and the overthrow of monarchy at Rome and the creation of the Roman Republic. But if these societies gave birth to "free" or "frank" speech (*parrhêsia*, *libertas*), they also began the exploration of the limits of free speech, for it is too often ignored that the history of censorship in the West has its origins in ancient Greece and Rome. Some writers (e.g., Coetzee 1996) suggest that systematic censorship was brought into being by the invention of printing, because it centralized the process of publication and so enabled governments to impose greater controls. By contrast, in scribal cultures, like those of classical antiquity and the European Middle Ages, where books and ideas were disseminated by handwritten copies, the power of publication was widely dispersed. As a result the situation that faces us today is very similar to that before the invention of printing: on the Internet thoughts and ideas can be published without the kinds of controls traditionally exerted by governments and great publishing houses. Yet the problems arising from regimes under authoritarian leaders are of all ages; dissent and censorship were as widespread in antiquity as they are today. Athens and Rome provide examples of pretechnological societies in which issues of freedom of thought and speech were, nevertheless, of pressing concern. Similar to many other periods in history, they provide two contexts in which freedom of speech was acknowledged as the "right" of every citizen. Both societies experienced difficulties in clearly defining and defending these "rights," in particular when political circumstances changed so that the right to freedom of speech became more precarious and more dangerous for its practitioners (e.g., imperial Rome as authoritarian state). We pursue the theme into the Christian and early modern eras because doing so allows us to shift focus from contexts driven by social and political concerns to one determined by a religious ideology.

Existing work on censorship and subversion in antiquity is quickly summarized, since it is either absent or piecemeal. Very little work has been done that assists in charting and analyzing the kind of subversive strategies we have assembled here under the common heading "veiled speech." In other words, a full and comprehensive study for the important periods of classical Greece (fifth and fourth centuries) and republican and imperial Rome is still to be written. This volume takes a first step in that direction. The evolution of the struggle between arbitrary suppression and free speech in classical and medieval times offers a fascinating dossier of untapped stories on power abuse, intellectual courage, and subversive action.

The scholarship on these conflicts over political and moral ideas between rulers and their subjects from the specific angle of *self-censorship* is clearly limited and of variable scope.[6] After the two useful (but incomplete) surveys on book burning (Forbes 1936; Cramer 1945) and the pioneering article by Ahl (1984), little was published in English with a clear focus on censorship or free speech in antiquity until Sluiter and Rosen (2004) and Konstan (2012). A recent surge in historical surveys on book destruction has not really filled that void.[7] Book burning is only one strategy of oppressive regimes, but more often than not the analysis on ancient sources is too much dominated by twentieth-century events, in particular the famous 1933 book burning in

Berlin organized by students—half-heartedly endorsed, but not led by, the National Socialists.[8] The images of books on a pyre have haunted the discussion ever since. Of course this was an iconic event, but there are very few parallels for this kind of systematic destruction of the physical carriers of intellectual capital associated with one particular group.[9] Book burning is a recurrent and much used method to settle disputes over issues of intellectual or religious importance: often "the book is the double of the man, and burning it is the equivalent of killing him."[10] But modern treatments of book destruction suffer from an overly narrow approach, apart from having other flaws (Báez 2008 is unsatisfactory in terms of analysis; Bosmajian 2006 does not cover antiquity sufficiently).[11] We grant that Bosmajian offers a useful model to categorize cases of book burning: heresy, obscenity, or sedition.[12] His scheme basically covers the most important areas (religious, moral, political), but still leaves room for improvement, given that these are the more traditional categories used in scholarship on the subject.[13]

In ancient Greece the notion of frank speech (*parrhêsia*) was *both political and social*. We find it in the context of the city assembly,[14] but also in historical and philosophical writings.[15] Intellectuals interacting with men in power had to know their place or they might suffer from it. One helpful example is what happened to Callisthenes, Aristotle's cousin: when introduced at the court of Alexander, he "did not take his own advice" and spoke "with too much freedom to the king" (παρρησιαστικώτερον λαλοῦντα D.L. 5.4–5), upon which Aristotle allegedly remarked that he would "be short-lived by what he said" (ibid.). Callisthenes died miserably after a period of isolated imprisonment. The incident even made Aristotle unwelcome at the court. Not only does this anecdote reveal the sensitive nature of the relationship between a monarch and his entourage, but it also illustrates that those close to the king were aware of the need for tact and social agility.

Among orators and ancient historians "frank speech" was also a much-used element in their work. We know of the sometimes rowdy circumstances in assemblies, in which the shouting and protesting could be used to subdue a speaker into silence.[16] Comments on the proper task of a historian and the right method reflect great self-awareness of the genre and its role. Lucian offers an interesting judgment on this issue in his *On How to Write History* (*Hist. conscr.* 59): "eulogy and censure should be careful and considered, free from slander, supported by evidence, cursory and relevant to the occasion for those involved are not in court; otherwise *you* will be censured just like Theopompus who made a business of impeaching everyone in a quarrelsome spirit, acting as a prosecutor rather than a recorder of events."[17] It was quite common to use "robust" language in historical writings: Theopompus the historian was famously condemned by Polybius for his abusive account of Philip of Macedon.[18] Yet Dionysius of Halicarnassus "defended Theopompus' attack against Polybius criticism as a praiseworthy example of παρρησία" (Walbank 1962, 2). In this assessment Walbank does not expand on the meaning of the term, but both its etymology and the context suggest that we can interpret it as frank speech, or more literally, "speaking without reservations." Dionysus clearly believed that Theopompus was right to speak freely and not hold back. Behind such a view is not the idea of a legal *right* to speak freely, but rather the fact that there was no impediment to doing so. Dionysus also disagreed with Polybius's reasons, which concern the appropriate use of the genre (historical biography). The example shows that ancient authors did not always discuss these matters from an ethical point of view or even with a concern about etiquette.

What all three examples show is that censorship in its broadest possible meaning is part of a continuous debate about boundaries within different spheres of human interaction: in these cases it concerns debate about (sometimes implicit) rules of social interaction or conventions of a literary genre. On a grander scale a whole society will be in the business of determining what its boundaries are—ethically, politically, and culturally. This is why we can speak of self-regulation or self-censorship. It is a core component of human behavior playing a role in the private and public spheres, and expanding in ever widening circles of human interaction. Individuals form groups, and sociologists and anthropologists refer to the outcomes of the process that includes or excludes others from a group as "in-groups" and "out-groups."[19] These terms convey the central notions underpinning our use of censorship in a broad sense: it refers to the mechanism of social groups, which have implicit or explicit "rules" about whom the core members will admit into their midst.

Clearly this is not the meaning that people normally attach to the word "censorship." In the twentieth century the term became a byword for the excessive use of power by evil regimes and is closely associated with fascism and communism. That use of the term makes it almost exclusively political. In this study we want to emphasize the strong social dimension attached to the notion of selecting one view over another; when this leads to suppressing a view by forceful means it is one mode of censorship, played out in the political arena. In short, we consider the social dimension as more important than the political one.

One further study should be mentioned in this context. In her book *Free Speech and Democracy in Ancient Athens*, Arlene Saxonhouse offers an original and insightful analysis of *parrhêsia*. Her perspective emphasizes the break from the Homeric age characterized by shame and deference. The loss of shame would lead to the "shameless [and shaming] speech" of Socrates and introduce a new paradigm in Athenian society. What we can learn from this approach is how the annulment of the cohesive power of shame (a *social* constraint) triggered a new *political* discourse of "fearless speech."[20] In its most extreme form Athenian democracy represents a radical stance to political participation, without the aristocratic limits, but with the liberties of speaking freely. This is the reason why Saxonhouse defines *parrhêsia* as "the democratic practice of shamelessness."[21]

Précis of the Volume

In this book we have brought together experts in a deliberately diverse range of areas. Together they explore the creative strategies to get around the threat of censorship and illustrate how such approaches to self-expression and self-regulation are of all times. The diachronic arrangement supports the broader argument that aims to illustrate the *ubiquity* of subtle subversion. At the same time there is a *thematic coherence* in the analyses of these chapters that also reinforces the chronological progression.

In Athens, the city in the classical world that we most closely associate with freedom of expression, *parrhêsia* was not without its complexities and limitations. After all, this is the city that executed Socrates. But it will not do to focus on one infamous case, because this outcome was determined not only by attitudes toward, and views about, the limits of free speech, but also by the peculiar historical circumstances and the long buildup of Socrates' life and practice—that is, if we can trust Plato's account of these.[22] It will be useful to explore both the conceptual and historical aspects of the issue at hand in order to understand fully what was (and is) at stake, when we try to ascertain the dynamics of censorship.

One reason for Athens's reputation for *parrhêsia* is that it was here that comedy, a form of drama centrally concerned with mocking the follies and foibles of the city's politicians, was invented and first flourished. Boundaries were imposed, however, even upon this famously free space. For this reason Chapter 2 begins by exploring the limitations imposed upon comic playwrights in classical Athens and the extent to which dramatists like Aristophanes and Eupolis practiced self-censorship in order to protect themselves from prosecution. While rejecting the possibility of censorship by the archons, Andrew Hartwig finds that certain intellectual positions were likely to attract legal action (denial of the existence of the gods, for example) and that greater freedom of political comment was allowed at the Lenaia, a festival with a primarily local audience, than at the City Dionysia, which attracted foreign spectators as well.

Chapter 3 takes up the issue of *parrhêsia* and self-censorship in classical Athens again, but in a different cultural and political context, that of the symposium. Lara O'Sullivan argues that while *parrhêsia* and *isêgoria* (equality of access to speech) were viewed as characteristic of Athenian democracy, "*parrhêsia* also had a place in the private domain of the symposium." O'Sullivan argues for parallelism between the public and private spheres, contending that the few restrictions upon freedom of speech in the *dêmos* also applied in the symposium (i.e., that participants in a symposium practiced self-censorship), because unfettered freedom had the potential for producing civil discord. She concludes that the restrictions applicable in the symposium mirror not only those found in the *dêmos*, but also those characteristic of the comic stage.

Chapter 4 explores the case of one of classical Athens's more extreme exponents of *parrhêsia*, Diogenes the Cynic, and poses a provocative question: why did he not suffer the same fate as Socrates? Central to this discussion is the concept of tolerance, for despite his eccentricity Diogenes was tolerated, even loved, by the Athenians. Han Baltussen is concerned to examine the boundaries of social tolerance applicable not to an institution, such as comedy or the symposium, but to an extreme individual who chose to reject conventional values in the most public way possible and did not get suppressed for it. His analysis teases out new insights from the responses by Diogenes' audience recorded in ancient sources, and makes use of modern sociological perspectives on in-groups and out-groups.

When we turn to the Romans, we discover that the Latin language has no precise equivalent for the Greek *parrhêsia*. It does not follow, however, that Romans did not value the ability to employ "frank speech." *Libertas*, "freedom," covered the same semantic ground as the Greek *eleutheria* and *parrhêsia* combined, for it included both "the civil status of a free man" (*OLD* §1) and "frankness of speech" (*OLD* §7). Similarly, the cognate adjective *liber* meant both "possessing the social and legal status of a free man" (*OLD* §1) and "open, frank, candid" (*OLD* §11). And if writers wished to make it clear that they were referring specifically to free or frank speech as opposed to freedom in general, they could, like speakers of English, resort to such periphrases as *oratio libera* ("free/frank speech"), Quintilian's preferred translation of *parrhêsia* (9.2.27). And so we should not be surprised if a writer like Cicero prizes the ability to speak his thoughts freely (e.g., *Phil.* 3.5.9, 3.37.2, *Brut.* 256.6, *Fam.* 10.5.3, *Att.* 14.14.2). It is also worth noting that Cicero, like the Euripidean Jocasta and Polynices, considers it slavish to accept restrictions upon free speech: "'It is tyranny to speak against anyone you want and to defend anyone you want.' No, it is slavery not to speak against anyone you want and not to defend anyone you want" (*Sull.* 48).

As in Athens, the theater in republican Rome was a place for contesting the limits of speech. In Chapter 5 Gesine Manuwald argues that there was "no complete freedom for the content and tone of dramas." She contends that while there were no laws governing what could be said on stage, the Romans viewed the stage as an inappropriate place for comments on an individual's conduct because of the medium's one-sidedness. On the other hand, there is abundant evidence to suggest, first, that playwrights did engage with contemporary moral and political issues; second, that dramatic performances became increasingly politicized in the last century of the republic and in the early imperial period; and third, that although there was no formal censorship in the first century CE, there was "control of literature by 'the powerful' . . . who might interfere if they suspected anything subversive in literary works."

While the ability to speak one's thoughts frankly was still prized in the early empire (e.g., Tac. *Hist.* 1.1.20), the opportunities for free expression were far more restricted, primarily because of Augustus's extension of the law on treason to cover words as well as deeds (Tac. *Ann.* 1.72). Ovid's banishment to Tomis in 8 CE is only the best known attempt to control free expression under the principate. And Augustus was not the only culprit. Writers continued to be exiled or executed and their books destroyed under the Julio-Claudian and Flavian emperors (e.g., Tac. *Ann.* 4.34–35, Suet. *Dom.* 10). *Parrhêsia* became impossible, veiled speech a necessity.

In Chapter 6 we have the first of three case studies of individual writers attempting to negotiate these new, more restrictive conditions. Ioannis Ziogas takes up the examples of Virgil and Ovid, poets who compete with the emperor "to shape artistic creation, define its meaning, and make it known to the Roman world." Thus the author (*auctor*) of the *Aeneid* was unable to compete with the author of the principate when he wished to practice self-censorship and have his poem destroyed. Rather the poem was preserved, as the *Life of Virgil* has it, *auctore Augusto*, and so became, Ovid claimed, Augustus's own poem. Ovid, by contrast, claims that he himself tried to destroy *Metamorphoses*, but that the work survived. This act of self-censorship also failed, thus proving the claim at the end of book 15 that fire could not destroy the poet's work.

Seneca, a figure central to the history of both politics and philosophy under the early principate, is the focus of Chapter 7. Hence it is appropriate that Marcus Wilson both examines growing political censorship under the Julio-Claudians and places Seneca's conspicuous silence about politics in the *Moral Epistles* within the context of late Neronian Rome. He pays particular attention to Seneca's philosophical eclecticism (most notably his frequent references to the Epicurean ideal of withdrawal from public life) and concludes that Seneca faced a "censorship regime that necessitated philosophical eclecticism on pain of death."

Chapter 8 brings us to the Flavians and the *Argonautica* of Valerius Flaccus. The most prestigious of all literary genres in Rome, epic was a primary vehicle for reflection upon Roman power and identity and so an object of imperial scrutiny since Augustus and "his" *Aeneid*. Even under Vespasian, an emperor famous for his leniency, the practice of *parrhêsia* could lead to execution. Peter J. Davis argues that Valerius, in writing mythological epic, attempted "a strategy of complex indirection," a strategy that allowed reflection on contemporary issues such as the Roman propensity to civil war and the problems posed by the principate for the display of aristocratic *uirtus*. For Valerius Flaccus "indirection was the safest way of avoiding censorship."

Chapter 9 takes a different approach, offering an overview not of an author but of literature under the reigns of Nerva and Trajan, an era that, at least at first, proclaimed "liberty" as its watchword. For John Penwill the key to understanding the literature of this era (most notably Martial, Juvenal, Tacitus, and Pliny) is its emphasis on the temporary nature of the freedom offered, its awareness of freedom's dependence on the character of the *princeps*, and its concentration on methods of expressing political dissent.

From the Roman Empire at the height of its power we move to the Christian world of late antiquity and beyond. The rise of the church introduced a new field for censorship, because ecclesiastical authorities, both Catholic and Orthodox, were concerned to enforce theological conformity through the suppression of variant forms of Christian belief which they labeled "heresy." In the late antique, medieval, and early modern worlds, rulers of both church and state were no less anxious than some emperors of the first and second centuries to prevent the communication of ideas of which they disapproved. Particularly striking is the fact that although the religion had changed, responses to suppressing freedom of thought and expression did not.

In Chapter 10 Pauline Allen takes up the case of Christian letter-writers in the fourth, fifth, and sixth centuries and the means they adopted in order to circumvent various forms of civil and ecclesiastical censorship. She underlines the importance of self-censorship as a means of avoiding exile or prosecution for treason and of the careful selection of diplomatic letter-bearers, who might well carry an oral message to accompany the written letter, and whose instructions commonly insisted upon secrecy and veiled speech.

The concept of heresy is central to Chapter 11, for that was one of the charges laid in the 640s by censors against those who resisted the Byzantine emperor's attempted suppression of debate on the nature of Jesus Christ. Bronwen Neil focuses on the cases of Maximus, who failed to practice self-censorship, openly comparing his accusers to heretics of previous times, and so suffered flogging as well as the amputation of his tongue and right hand, and Pope Martin, whose letters from exile (his death sentence was commuted) constitute clear examples of self-censorship, since he refrains from naming both his persecutors and his addressees.

Chapter 12 also considers attempts to suppress heresy, this time in thirteenth-century France. The massive and detailed records produced by the inquisitors enable Megan Cassidy-Welch to explore the responses not of senior churchmen to accusations of heresy (as in Chapter 11), but of ordinary inhabitants of the Languedoc. She finds that the accused adopted a variety of strategies of self-censorship before the tribunal: claims that they could not remember, that they had no knowledge, or that remarks were made in jest. Outside the tribunal inquisitors met other forms of resistance: the destruction of inquisitorial records, violent protest, and even murder.

Chapter 13 takes up the questions of heresy and self-censorship in the context of the visual arts in early modern Spain, where the Inquisition, enforcing rules laid down by the Council of Trent (concluded 1563), insisted on the policing of images in churches. François Soyer notes that artists themselves practiced self-censorship, with some publishing guidelines for the appropriate treatment of religious subjects, and presents three case studies in which clergymen denounced works of art to the Inquisition in order to prevent the propagation of heresy before it occurred. In these cases self-censorship

was the product not of resistance, as in the Languedoc, but of .
torial prosecution.

Chapter 14 closes the volume appropriately enough with an essay on Thomas Hobbes, the English philosopher who both practiced self-censorship and reflected upon it. Jonathan Parkin argues that Hobbes concealed his own political, religious, and scientific views for the sake of self-preservation and made self-censorship a centerpiece of his political theory, one task of the sovereign in *Leviathan* being to limit individuals to expressions of thought and belief that did not endanger social cohesion. In the context of the present volume, it is striking that Hobbes's views coincide exactly with those of the ancient Athenians examined in Chapters 2–4, for they too viewed unfettered freedom of expression as likely to produce civil discord.

To sum up, the volume places the notions of *parrhêsia* and self-regulation (expressed as veiled speech or self-censorship) at its core, while the individual topics and texts should be seen as a carefully selected set of case studies. Combined, the chapters attempt to bring out the common features of oral and written reports that reflect the interaction between individual points of view as well as conventional views within certain communities of various sizes: since the authors were not in a position to "speak frankly," they chose ways to speak less frankly, but speak nonetheless. This form of self-regulation becomes self-censorship, in particular in the public sphere. Thus "frank speech" may mean different things in different contexts, but it hardly means a *right*; rather we may call it a "privilege" or "entitlement" arising from a particular situation.[23]

The historical progression reflected in the chapters is intended to show how the dynamic between an oppressive social or political framework and creative attempts to subvert such a framework is present in all historical periods under examination. During Athenian democracy, in imperial Rome, during the Christian era, and beyond, human beings attempted to speak up, and the use of veiled speech frequently gave them a chance to do so with impunity.

NOTES

This volume offers newly commissioned essays on the theme of self-censorship in antiquity and after, with a particular focus on how we can identify strategies of self-regulation in a wide range of writings across time. The volume is part of a larger examination of subversion and censorship in antiquity within the "Banning Ideas, Burning Books: The Dynamics of Censorship in Antiquity" project, funded by the Australian Research Council (DP 110100915; 2011–13). Standard abbreviations for authors and works are used throughout the book.

1. For discussion of this passage, see Mastronarde (1994) 259. Mastronarde notes important parallel passages, including Democritus B226, Plato *Rep.* 557b4–5, Eur. *Hipp.* 422, *Ion* 672–75, *Or.* 905, [Xen.] *Ath. Pol.* 1.6, Ar. *Frogs* 948–55, Isocr. 8.14.

2. Compare Stanley Fish's (1994) book title: *There Is No Such Thing as Free Speech . . . and It's a Good Thing Too.*

3. While dealing with a modern case of self-censorship in publishing, Cook and Heilman (2010) speak of the very common constraints imposed by "taste, civility and morality."

4. For instance, Hobbes's *Leviathan* was banned and burned during the Interregnum (1649–60); see Collins (2007) 478, who reminds us (481) that Hobbes wrote the work in France, where he angered the Stuart court, while the book was printed at a time when the Stationers' Company, which regulated prepublication censorship, was close to collapsing.

5. For an example of "decoding" a (classical) text produced under a (modern) oppressive regime, see Baltussen (2014).

6. E.g., Ahl (1984), Gruen (2002), Naddaf (2002), Ober (1999), Rudich (1993), Rutledge (2001).

7. Raven (2004), Polastron (2007), Báez (2008); but see Thiem (1979), Wallace (1996).

8. It is no coincidence that Forbes (1936), Cramer (1945), and Pease (1946) wrote their articles just before and during World War II. For the intriguing reconstruction of the actual prime movers of this event (and its consequences), see Weidermann (2008). The best overview on book burning is still Speyer (1981), but see now also Werner (2007) on the medieval period.

9. At least in the West. For the book burning in China by the first emperor, Qin, in c. 213 BCE, see Wood (2007) 40–41, 78–88; for similar cases (but on a smaller scale) in Jewish and Christian history, see Speyer (1981).

10. Polastron (2007) x.

11. Báez (2008) aims for comprehensiveness—a format that achieves its goal at the expense of precision—while Bosmajian's (2006) focus on rhetorical aspects of the process is one-sided. Both have an interest in the history of the book rather than providing an account of censorship.

12. Heresy is of course unknown in pagan antiquity, but fits medieval practices; sedition also fits a number of ancient examples (alongside libel and abuse), but obscenity will be more difficult to apply, presumably since it arises out of a particular view on sexual behavior and its transgressions.

13. Others (Fishburn 2008, Weidermann 2008) have concentrated on the twentieth century only (Nazi Germany and the aftermath, 1933–53). This period is not within the scope of our project.

14. Saxonhouse (2006). More on this below.

15. Konstan et al. (1998) produced a translation of Philodemus's *Peri Parrhêsias.*

16. Roisman (2004) esp. 264–68.

17. Walbank (1962) 1.

18. Ibid., 2.

19. Barclay (1995). See also Chapter 4.

20. Saxonhouse (2006) 28, 86–87. Compare Foucault's *Fearless Speech* (English edition 2001; original 1983).

21. Saxonhouse (2006) 89.

22. For a recent persuasive analysis of the factors involved in the execution of Socrates, see Waterfield (2009). Another emerging trend is the renewed study of Xenophon as a source for Socrates' life and thought, see, e.g., Danzig (2010), *Apologizing for Socrates.*

23. "Privilege" is how Konstan (2012: 1) describes the notion, or "license to express one's views, whatever the context" (4). Konstan also has some useful comments on private and public contexts.

REFERENCES

Ahl, F. M. 1984. "The Art of Safe Criticism in Greece and Rome." *American Journal of Philology* 105: 174–208.

Báez, F. 2008. *A Universal History of the Destruction of Books: From Ancient Sumer to Modern Iraq*. Barcelona: Ediciones Destino, 2004 [in Spanish]. Reprint, New York: Atlas.

Baltussen, H. 2014. "A 'Homeric' Hymn to Stalin: Safe Criticism in Ancient Greek?" *Classical Receptions Journal* 7: 1–19. http://crj.oxfordjournals.org/crj/clu008.pdf.

Barclay, J. M. G. 1995. "Deviance and Apostasy: Some Applications of Deviance Theory to First-Century Judaism and Christianity." In *Modelling Early Christianity. Social-Scientific Studies of the New Testament in Its Context*, ed. P. F. Esler, 114–27. London: Routledge.

Bosmajian, H. A. 2006. *Burning Books*. Jefferson, NC: McFarland.

Coetzee, J. M. 1996. *Giving Offence: Essays on Censorship*. Chicago: University of Chicago Press.

Collins, J. R. 2007. "Silencing Thomas Hobbes: The Presbyterians and Leviathan." In *The Cambridge Companion to Hobbes' Leviathan*, ed. P. Springborg, 478–500. Cambridge: Cambridge University Press.

Cook, P. and C. Heilman. 2010. "Censorship and Two Types of Self-Censorship: Public and Private." Social Science Research Network, March 20. http://ssrn.com/abstract=1575662.

Cramer, F. H. 1945. "Bookburning and Censorship in Ancient Rome: A Chapter in the History of Freedom of Speech." *Journal of the History of Ideas* 6: 157–96.

Danzig, G. 2010. *Apologizing for Socrates: How Plato and Xenophon Created Our Socrates.* Lanham, MD: Lexington Books.

Fish, S. 1994. *There Is No Such Thing as Free Speech . . . and It's a Good Thing Too.* New York: Oxford University Press.

Fishburn, M. 2008. *Burning Books.* Basingstoke: Palgrave Macmillan.

Forbes, C. 1936. "Books for the Burning." *Transactions of the American Philological Association* 67: 114–25.

Foucault, M. 2001. *Fearless Speech.* Los Angeles: Semiotexte(s).

Gruen, Erich S. 2002. *Diaspora: Jews Amidst Greeks and Romans.* Cambridge, MA: Harvard University Press.

Konstan, D. 2012. "The Two Faces of *Parrhêsia*: Free Speech and Self-Expression in Ancient Greece." *Antichthon* 46: 1–13.

Konstan, D., D. Clay, and C. E. Glad, tr. and eds. 1998. *Philodemus: On Frank Criticism.* Atlanta, GA: Scholars Press.

MacMullen, R. 1967. *Enemies of the Roman Order: Treason, Unrest, and Alienation in the Empire.* Cambridge, MA: Harvard University Press.

Mastronarde, D. J., ed. 1994. *Euripides: Phoenissae.* Cambridge: Cambridge University Press.

Naddaf, R. A. 2002. *Exiling the Poets: The Production of Censorship in Plato's Republic.* Chicago: University of Chicago Press.

Ober, J. 1999. *Political Dissent in Democratic Athens: Intellectual Critics of Popular Rule.* Princeton: Princeton University Press.

Pease, A. S. 1946. "Notes on Book-Burning." In *Munera Studiosa: Studies in Honor of W.H.P. Hatch*, ed. Massey Hamilton Shepherd Jr. and Sherman Eldridge Johnson, 145–60. Cambridge, MA: Episcopal Theological School.

Polastron, L. X. 2007. *Books on Fire: The Destruction of Libraries Throughout History.* Tr. Jon Graham. Rochester, VT: Inner Traditions.

Raven, J., ed. 2004. *Lost Libraries: The Destruction of Great Book Collections Since Antiquity.* Houndmills: Palgrave Macmillan.

Roisman, J. 2004. "Speaker-Audience Interaction in Athens: A Power Struggle." In *Free Speech in Classical Antiquity*, ed. I. Sluiter and R. M. Rosen, 261–78. Leiden: Brill.

Rudich, V. 1993. *Political Dissidence Under Nero: The Price of Dissimulation.* London: Routledge.

Rutledge, S. H. 2001. *Imperial Inquisitions: Prosecutors and Informants from Tiberius to Domitian.* London: Routledge.

Saxonhouse, A. W. 2006. *Free Speech and Democracy in Ancient Athens.* Cambridge: Cambridge University Press.

Sluiter, I. and R. M. Rosen, eds. 2004. *Free Speech in Classical Antiquity.* Leiden: Brill.

Sommerstein, A. H. 2004. "Harassing the Satirist: The Alleged Attempts to Prosecute Aristophanes." In *Free Speech in Classical Antiquity*, ed. I. Sluiter and R. M. Rosen, 145–74. Leiden: Brill.

Speyer, W. 1981. *Büchervernichtung und Zensur des Geistes bei Heiden, Juden und Christen.* Stuttgart: A. Hiersemann Verlag.

Thiem, J. 1979. "The Great Library of Alexandria Burnt: Towards the History of a Symbol." *Journal of the History of Ideas* 40: 507–26.

Walbank, F. W. 1962. "Polemic in Polybius." *Journal of Roman Studies* 52: 1–12.
Wallace, R. W. 1996. "Book Burning in Ancient Athens." In *Transitions to Empire: Essays in Greco-Roman History, 360–146 B.C., in Honor of E. Badian*, ed. R. W. Wallace and E. M. Harris, 226–40. Norman: University of Oklahoma Press.
Waterfield, R. 2009. *Why Socrates Died: Dispelling the Myths*. London: Faber.
Weidermann, V. 2008. *Das Buch der verbrannten Bücher*. Cologne: Kiepenheuer & Witsch.
Werner, T. 2007. *Den Irrtum liquidieren: Bücherverbrennungen im Mittelalter*. Göttingen: Vandenhoeck & Ruprecht.
Wood, F. 2007. *The First Emperor of China*. London: Profile Books.

Chapter 2

Self-Censorship in Ancient Greek Comedy

Andrew Hartwig

The phenomenon of self-censorship in ancient Greek comedy has been underexplored in studies of the relationship between politics and the stage. In this chapter I argue that this form of self-regulation can shed valuable light on comic practice in political comedy. The idea of self-censorship necessarily presupposes conditions where comic poets were at risk, a point of contention in itself. To help identify such conditions this chapter first analyzes two cases where comic poets were ostensibly accused of harming the interests of the state: first, the notorious dispute between the comic poet Aristophanes and the demagogue Kleon, and second the remarkably similar clash between the comic poet Philippides and the politician Stratokles more than a century later. The first case could be considered a watershed moment in comedy that consequently prompted forms of self-censorship when engaging in political subject matter. The latter, which rarely receives even token acknowledgment in standard discussions of comedy and politics, is treated here in much greater detail for the important parallels it provides on the latent risks of political comedy within fraught political environments. Both cases demonstrate how these topics could be turned against poets when taken out of their original comic context, and how individuals could exploit a gray area in Athenian law if a poet ventured beyond personal mockery into satire of domestic politics and foreign policy. The very real risk of repercussions, as these cases exemplify, required caution. One of the more striking consequences, I suggest, is the uneven spread of political content between the two major dramatic festivals of Athens, the City

Dionysia and the Lenaia, a phenomenon that, surprisingly, has not been considered from the perspective of self-censorship.

Comic Boundaries

There is much debate in scholarship over the "license" of ancient Greek comedy, whether comic poets faced the same legal restrictions as ordinary citizens, or whether the festival context allowed them to speak with absolute freedom, especially when it came to personal abuse and slander.[1] This, to a large extent, is impossible to determine when we consider that comedy seems to have had, if not a legal, then at least some level of cultural immunity when mocking individuals, as determined by the festival context. Indeed this, together with generic expectations and the ritualistic nature of comic abuse, often conceals whether it was serious in intent or not. Personal satire is par for the course, and may wildly exaggerate faults in the target or overstate supposed enmities.[2] An offshoot of this is that we can never be certain how serious a comic poet may be when presenting political content, since forays into politics may not necessarily reflect a personal political agenda or beliefs.[3] Observations of this kind have allowed greater focus on the "poetics" of political comedy, where apparently serious political advice and poets boasting of having taken great personal risks are seen largely as shaped by literary and generic concerns.[4] While this approach should be kept in mind, applied strictly it risks a retreat into a kind of agnostic solipsism that excludes other potential influences on comic practice, not least of all historical, legal, and political factors.[5] One recent strand of scholarship on Athenian drama, for example, emphasizes the politically charged atmosphere of the City Dionysia festival in the late fifth century, indicated not only by the presence of Athens's allies who brought tribute for display in the theater, a sensitive issue in itself, but also by the presentation of orphans of the Athenian war dead, the public crowning of foreign benefactors, the pouring of libations by the ten generals, the announcement of prodemocratic propaganda immediately before and during the festival, not to mention the festival's convenience as a time of diplomacy, when peace agreements could be made and ratified (Thuc. 5.23.4–6).[6] Such contexts would have influenced poetic behavior and public attitudes. Historical currents too, such as the Peloponnesian War with its ever-present problem of revolt and shifting alliances, threats of oligarchy, and compromised democracies, can also shape the unwritten rules for comic behavior. Given these changeable dynamics, political comedy, whether offered in seriousness or not, was not necessarily immune from controversy if it was thought to conflict with or compromise Athens's larger political aims.

We have some evidence that comedy, even if largely considered harmless fun, nevertheless might have bred resentment among audience members. We know of at least one temporary imposition of censorship. Athens appears to have issued a decree in the archonship of Morychides (440/39) lasting until 437/6 that restricted certain forms of comic humor, perhaps jokes pertaining to the Samian War.[7] We also hear, although admittedly our sources are the comic poets themselves, of politicians attempting to interfere with comedy. Aristophanes' *Frogs* 367–68 mentions politicians attempting to reduce the comic poets' pay because they were ridiculed in comedy, while Plato Comicus in *Skeuai* (fr. 141) and Sannyrion in *Danae* (fr. 9) satirize Archinos and Agyrrhios for meddling in comic poets' affairs, probably in relation to the same matter raised by Aristophanes (so Scholion Ar. *Frogs* 367). The fact that three separate sources mention this suggests a degree of objective truth to the incident. Eupolis in *Demoi* fr. 99.29 (c. 412) also mentions a demagogue interfering with comedy.[8] Even allowing for exaggeration, there is at least the underlying premise that comedy could be highly provocative. It was possible for comic targets to take offense and seek redress—if not on a personal level, which legal or socioreligious grounds may have discouraged, then certainly by roundabout means, whether undermining the institution through political channels, or bringing more serious charges of public importance if such an offense could be identified.

The latter response is of particular interest here. When comic poets ventured beyond the standard personal abuse expected of the genre into apparent satire of the political system, this, it seems, could be twisted against them and represented as abuse of the state and its democracy. Under such circumstances, at least, comedy might be exposed to severe legal action, as the following examples suggest.

Aristophanes and Kleon

While details of the dispute, ostensibly a legal action, between Aristophanes and Kleon are occasionally doubted as literary exaggeration,[9] it is these very details that lend it authenticity. Aristophanes' *Acharnians* recounts a legal dispute played out in public, more specifically before the council, with the specific charge of slandering the *dêmos*. The audience members themselves were witnesses to this dispute, as Aristophanes reminds them, and were unsympathetic or indifferent at the time.[10] To invent such details, as Pelling notes, would "pose a puzzle to the audience which is simply distracting, and will make a joke which the audience will not get."[11] Not only would it cause confusion, such a fabrication would also invite ridicule from rival comic poets. We also have some reason to believe that Aristophanes' animosity toward Kleon was genuine, and not entirely the product of a poetic agenda. This is strongly implied, certainly, by his continued abuse of Kleon after his death, as distinct from the usual benign treatment of former comic targets.[12] The incident with Kleon is also of a piece with his often satirized tendency to bring accusations of antidemocratic behavior before the council on the slightest pretext.[13] Rather than borrowing this comic cliché to exaggerate what we might assume was only a minor incident with Kleon, Aristophanes probably based much of this humor in later comedies on his own disquieting experience. While he may embellish the particulars, there are good reasons to accept that a legal process was initiated against him.

What offense did Aristophanes supposedly commit? *Acharnians* 502–3 recounts that Kleon accused him of speaking ill of the city, particularly when foreigners were in the audience:

> *οὐ γάρ με νῦν γε διαβαλεῖ Κλέων ὅτι*
> *ξένων παρόντων τὴν πόλιν κακῶς λέγω.*

> For Kleon will not slander me now at least, on the grounds that
> I speak ill of the city while foreigners are present.

Later in the same play he rephrases this as "making comedy of the city and insulting the *dêmos*" (631: *ὡς κωμῳδεῖ τὴν πόλιν ἡμῶν καὶ τὸν δῆμον καθυβρίζει*).[14] More specifically, in his comedy *Babylonians*, produced the previous year in 426, Aristophanes insulted several current Athenian office holders (Scholion Ar. *Ach.* 378 = Ar. *Babylonians* test. iv. K.-A.): "He means the *Babylonians* . . . in which he insulted many people. For he made fun of the allotted and elected offices (*κληρωτὰς καὶ χειροτονητὰς ἀρχὰς*) and Kleon while foreigners were present."[15]

Surviving fragments from *Babylonians* give further clues.[16] Fragment 84 describes the politician Peisandros and another unnamed individual (or individuals) receiving bribes (*δωροδοκῆσαι*) and providing an "office of war" or a "beginning of war" (ἀρχὴν πολέμου) in return. Another fragment (fr. 75) describes the god Dionysos accosted by demagogues on his way to a trial and told to hand over drinking cups.[17] This may be an attack on the demagogue Kleon for claiming large taxes from foreign traders, or even claiming too much tribute from the allies.[18] The additional detail of Dionysos on his way to a trial may even suggest political blackmail of the allies (i.e., "sycophancy") where one extorts "hush money" in return for dropping a dishonest lawsuit. This is a frequent complaint against Kleon in comedy and most likely featured in *Babylonians* too.[19]

Aristophanes also appears to criticize the treatment of Athens's allies in this play. There is justification for thinking that the chorus—nominally composed of Babylonian slaves[20]—was an allegorical representation of the allies. The fragments suggest as much: fragment 71 compares the chorus with the "Samian *dêmos*,"[21] a key member of the Delian League; fragment 90 compares them with the Istrians,[22] most likely a member of the Delian League, given that they were a sea power that changed from oligarchy to democracy around the mid-fifth century.[23] Fragment 72 depicts what is probably the chorus in military formation equipped with shields,[24] while other fragments allude to runaway slaves—a probable allusion to revolt by Athens's allies—and their punishment by being branded with stigmata or forced to work in the mill.[25] Comparisons between the allies and slaves were already familiar. Mytilene, which revolted from Athens in 428/7 BCE, justified its stance by claiming Athens treated its tribute-paying allies as slaves.[26] Aristophanes' ironic claim in *Acharnians* that he "showed the people in the cities (i.e., the allies) how they are 'democratically' governed" (*Ach.* 642: καὶ τοὺς δήμους ἐν ταῖς πόλεσιν δείξας ὡς δημοκρατοῦνται)[27] would also suggest he depicted them as the subjects of Athens, indeed no different from Persian vassal states.

Although critical of Athenian foreign policy, *Babylonians* apparently won first prize.[28] Kleon, on the other hand, saw grounds for serious charges, accusing the poet of insulting the *dêmos* in the presence of foreigners, and, as Aristophanes' description of the dispute suggests, initiated legal proceedings known as *eisangelia* ("impeachment").[29] This is implied by the specific charge of slandering the *dêmos*, as well as Aristophanes' claim that Kleon dragged him into the *bouleutêrion* or "council house" (*Ach.* 379). *Eisangeliai* could be heard either before the assembly for serious cases of treason (i.e., "destroying the *dêmos*"),[30] or else—as in the case of Aristophanes—before the council for magistrates or citizens who perform a public charge and abuse that position.[31] This is what Pollux 8.51 appears to refer to when he says that *eisangelia* was appointed not only for cases of treason, but also for "wrongful acts against the *dêmos* which are not written down" (ἀγράφων δημοσίων ἀδικημάτων). That a comic poet could be exposed to impeachment suggests they were regarded as performing a public duty, certainly insofar as they were appointed a chorus by the archon, received pay from the state, and were granted a platform before a significant public audience.

Aristophanes was thought to have abused this position by bad-mouthing the *dêmos*; although Aristophanes himself may have counterargued that he merely abused officials within the city, rather than the city itself (see *Ach.* 515–16).[32] The fact that he did this before an international audience is presented as a key factor. Many of Athens's allies present at the festival were less than content with the alliance. The chief sore point was the question of tribute, which would be more than doubled in the course of 425/4.[33] Revolt was an ever-present issue that affected Athens's coffers. Kleon had earlier advocated the brutal treatment of the Mytileneans as a deterrent to any states wishing to change sides,[34] and anything that compromised this tenuous union might therefore readily be considered hostile to the *dêmos*. Aristophanes himself appears to answer an implicit charge that *Babylonians* threatened future tribute and fomented revolt when he cheekily counterargues that the allies will now be even more eager to bring tribute during the City Dionysia, since they will want to see the poet who "dares to say among the Athenians what is right" (*Ach.* 643–45). The potential of Aristophanes' comedy to disaffect many already disgruntled allies and threaten future tribute, then, must have played a significant role in any impeachment by Kleon.[35]

Of the trial itself and its outcome we can glimpse a few details without resorting to the often untrustworthy accounts of ancient commentators. Aristophanes tells us that Kleon dragged him into the *bouleutêrion* and proceeded to slander him (Ar. *Ach.* 379–80). During the proceedings themselves Aristophanes suggests he received little public sympathy. At *Acharnians* 630 he complains that the Athenians were "overly quick to judge matters" (ταχυβούλοις) while his enemies slandered him.[36] He may be referring to the same incident in *Wasps* when he describes how the public showed little interest in his plight while Kleon was denouncing him (1287–89): "those outside began to laugh, watching him roar loudly, without any concern for me, except to see if I would throw out a little joke at some point while being squeezed."[37] One further passage suggests, on the surface, that Aristophanes came close to conviction, with Kleon's rhetoric and forceful delivery more convincing than the substance of his accusation (cf. *Knights* 626–38). He says that Kleon roared so much and washed him over like the Kykloboros stream "such that I was nearly destroyed" (Ar. *Ach.* 381–82: *ὥστ' ὀλίγου πάνυ ἀπωλόμην*).[38] Heath has suggested Kleon's suit may have spectacularly failed and that Aristophanes' depiction of a close call was intended ironically to rub Kleon's nose in it.[39] This, however, does not adequately explain Aristophanes' defensive attitude throughout *Acharnians* toward the audience and public. Not only does he depict them as capricious, quick to judge, and antagonistic, but he makes repeated pleas that they not misunderstand his intentions on the present occasion.[40] We would have to understand all this as ironic too. Passages such as line 562, where the chorus complains that comedy has no right discussing political matters, seem rather to reflect the antagonistic attitude among some members of the public, many of whom probably had little interest in comedy or the specific details of Aristophanes' supposed crime, but were easily swayed by what popular demagogues like Kleon had to say. If Aristophanes came close to conviction, the *boulê* might have imposed a fine of up to five hundred drachmas; if more, the case had to be referred to the courts.[41] It seems Aristophanes at least avoided the more serious consequences of the latter.

The effect of this episode on Aristophanes and on comedy more generally during the last quarter of the fifth century will be considered below. It demonstrated that political comedy could be risky business, fostering significant anxieties and prompting safeguards and self-censorship among the comic poets.

Philippides and Stratokles

At the end of the fourth century we find a remarkably similar incident between a comic poet and a politician. A passage by the Athenian comic poet Philippides—well known for his active political engagement with Athens (cf. *IG* II^2 657) and for his friendship with the Macedonian "King" Lysimachos, rival of Demetrios the Besieger—famously attacked the Athenian politician Stratokles for the excessive honors bestowed on Demetrios after he helped restore democracy at Athens in 307 BCE.

ὁ τὸν ἐνιαυτὸν συντεμὼν εἰς μῆν' ἕνα,
ὁ τὴν ἀκρόπολιν πανδοκεῖον ὑπολαβὼν
καὶ τὰς ἑταίρας εἰσαγαγὼν τῇ παρθένῳ,
δι' ὃν ἀπέκαυσεν ἡ πάχνη τὰς ἀμπέλους,

δι' ὃν ἀσεβοῦνθ' ὁ πέπλος ἐρράγη μέσος,
τὰς τῶν θεῶν τιμὰς ποιοῦντ' ἀνθρωπίνας·
ταῦτα καταλύει δῆμον, οὐ κωμῳδία.

The one who reduced the year into a single month,
The one who took over the acropolis as a hotel
And introduced prostitutes to the Virgin,
Because of whom the frost burned the vines,
Because of whose impiety, the robe was torn in the middle,
Making honors that belong to the gods fit for mortals:
These things, not comedy, destroy the *dêmos*. (Philippides fr. 25)

Of particular interest are the implications of the final line. Philippides is apparently repudiating an earlier attack against him by Stratokles for having compromised the democracy, turning the same accusation back against him.[42] It is difficult to conceive this attack as an elaborate ironic joke, or as a fabrication in the service of Philippides' desired comic persona (if indeed he had one as a poet of New Comedy). The charge itself was not insignificant, and the allusive reference to it suggests it was a matter of public knowledge. The serious tone, rhetoric, and defensiveness of the passage, especially in relation to a powerful politician like Stratokles, also hint at more grave circumstances. Philippides, it seems, had been outspoken in an earlier comedy that Stratokles deemed dangerous to the democracy. The particular language used here (καταλύει δῆμον) indicates he even threatened the poet with an *eisangelia* before the assembly. Whether he formally pushed ahead with such a charge, however, is uncertain.[43]

We can date fragment 25 to either the Lenaia or the City Dionysia of 301 since it mentions events that took place after the dramatic festivals of 302.[44] Philippides left Athens soon after—just before the Battle of Ipsus in 301—and took up residence at the court of Lysimachos, very likely in self-imposed exile as a result of the escalating dispute.[45] After his eventual return to Athens many years later Philippides was publicly honored in 283/2 for, among other things, having "never opposed the democracy, either in word or in action" (*IG* II^2 657.48–50 = Philipp. test. 3 K.-A.): κα[ὶ οὐ]θὲν ὑπεναντίον πρὸ[ς δ]ημοκρατίαν οὐδεπώποτε [ἐποίησ]ε[ν ο]ὔτ[ε λόγωι οὔτ'] ἔργωι. Although largely formulaic, this decree absolved the poet of any suspected antidemocratic activity in the past, and is especially poignant in light of Stratokles' accusations many years earlier.

What, then, had offended Stratokles? And what can we reconstruct of this fascinating episode in the history of comic drama? Our best evidence for a preexisting quarrel lies in Philippides fragment 26. Scholars typically lump this together with fragment 25 and assume both come from the same comedy. But fragment 26 just as likely came from an earlier and different comedy. Plutarch preserves the fragment in his *Amatorius* in a passage describing men who put up with ill-natured women for the sake of sex: Plut. *Amat.* 750e–f: "for there is nothing more enamored than this: a man who, not for profit, but for the sake of love and sex endures a troublesome and unaffectionate woman, just as Philippides the comic poet wrote, laughing at the politician Stratokles." Plutarch then quotes a line from this unnamed comedy describing a woman who turns away her head when someone—apparently Stratokles—tries to kiss her: "ἀποστρεφομένης τὴν κορυφὴν φιλεῖς μόλις" ("When she turns away her head, you struggle to kiss her"; Philippides fr. 26). Philippides, it appears, featured Stratokles in a relationship with this unidentified woman in a comedy. The woman rejecting his attempted kisses, moreover, seems most likely an *hetaira*, a favorite character of Middle and New Comedy. While this may have caused Stratokles personal offense, it certainly did not threaten the Athenian democracy or give grounds for an impeachment. Philippides must have ventured into riskier and more politically sensitive territory.

There is good reason to suspect that his depiction of the *hetaira* is in fact a thinly veiled representation of Demetrios the Besieger.[46] Stratokles seems to have fawned over her excessively, despite her general indifference and apparent concern only for the perks she received. Other evidence also supports this identification with Demetrios. In 1900 Frantz suggested that an anecdote on Stratokles in Plutarch's *Life of Demetrios* may have been lifted from the same nexus of comedies by Philippides.[47] Plutarch reports that Stratokles took up an *hetaira* named Phylakion and recounts an episode when she came home from the market with expensive delicacies: Plut. *Dem.* 11.3: "he had taken up the *hetaira* Phylakion, and one day when she had bought for him brains and neck joints from the agora for dinner, he exclaimed, 'Wow! You've bought the sort of delicacies we politicians play ball with!'" Plutarch's use of direct speech, and the exclamation "wow!" (παπαῖ)[48] immediately raise suspicions about the source of this anecdote. So too does the punning joke on politicians playing ball with "brains" and "necks."[49] These features, not to mention the tendency among ancient writers to source biographical information directly or indirectly from comedy, suggest the anecdote is comic in origin.

Of further interest is the *hetaira* "Phylakion" who might plausibly be identified with the woman in fragment 26. Apart from the diminutive form, the name is somewhat unusual for an *hetaira*, since it contains no obvious allusion to the profession.[50] Instead the stem φυλακ- suggests a "guardian" or "protector." This would certainly provide a pertinent allusion to Demetrios in his capacity as foreign patron and protector of Athens. If we are correct to see a close connection between these passages, Philippides, it would seem, alluded to Demetrios as a hired prostitute of Stratokles with the comically apt name "little" or "beloved" guardian. The relevance of the name would not be lost on an Athenian audience. The patronage of the Antigonids played an important role in ensuring the survival of democracy in Athens. They had expelled the oligarchic regime of Demetrios of Phaleron, were granted divine honors as the "saviors" (*Soteres*) of Athens, and, most symbolically of all, granted the exceptional honor of statues alongside those of the tyrannicides Harmodios and Aristogeiton.[51] They also secured Athens against the ever-present threat of Kassandros whom the Athenians feared would enslave the city if he captured it.[52] Athens, under the leadership of Stratokles, effectively bought their continued support, indulging Demetrios's profligate behavior to prevent this eventuality.[53]

A comedian who mocked this political relationship under such circumstances might conceivably be accused of jeopardizing the frail existence of Athens's democracy. Anything that prospectively weakened Demetrios's already hard-won patronage, including insults in a comedy, compromised the existence of democracy itself. How frivolous Philippides' original comedy may have been is beside the point. His retreat behind the broader banner of "comedy" may indeed emphasize this. It also summons any inherent religious protection the festival context might offer, whether actual or not, depicting Stratokles' attack as a further example of his supposed antireligious agenda, and as one deserving of expulsion to purify the city. In any event, the fact that an accusation usually reserved for politicians could be attached to a comic poet hints at how the comic stage might be regarded little differently from the politicians' *bema* if it aired anything resembling a political view.

Comic Anxieties and Self-Censorship After *Babylonians*

The evidence discussed above gives us some framework for understanding professed comic anxieties and indications of self-censorship in the comic poets. Even allowing for distortion and exaggerated claims of heroics,[54] there is some underlying truth to claims by Aristophanes, especially in light of Kleon's reported actions, that he "took a risk *beyond*" (*Ach.* 645: παρεκινδύνευσ') to say what was right. Indeed, much of *Acharnians* appears to reflect anxieties resulting from the response to *Babylonians*.

One topic now fraught with anxiety was the "city." At *Acharnians* 497–99 Aristophanes pointedly asks the audience not to be aggrieved if he should talk about the city in a comedy:

> μή μοι φθονήσητ', ἄνδρες οἱ θεώμενοι,
> εἰ πτωχὸς ὢν ἔπειτ' ἐν Ἀθηναίοις λέγειν
> μέλλω περὶ τῆς πόλεως, τρυγῳδίαν ποιῶν.
>
> Don't begrudge me, Spectators,
> If, being a beggar, I intend to speak among the Athenians
> About the city, although making a "trugedy" (i.e., comedy).

Later Aristophanes pedantically distinguishes for the audience the difference between attacking the city and attacking individuals within it, a confusion that likely played a role in Kleon's earlier accusation:

> ἡμῶν γὰρ ἄνδρες, κοὐχὶ τὴν πόλιν λέγω,
> μέμνησθε τοῦθ', ὅτι οὐχὶ τὴν πόλιν λέγω.
>
> For men among us, and I don't mean the city,
> Remember this, that I don't mean the city. (Ar. *Ach.* 515–16)

Hair splitting of this kind might also be seen in *Knights* where Aristophanes carefully distinguishes the character of "Demos" from corrupt servants like "Paphlagon."[55] At *Birds* 36 Aristophanes also appears to preempt any potential misunderstanding that he is critical of the city per se when the main characters, fed up with the problems in Athens, explain why they have decided to settle elsewhere.[56] Sensitivity in relation to the "city" may also partly explain why the goddess Athena, unlike most other gods, is virtually absent from the comic tradition.[57] There may have been some reluctance among comic poets to treat the patron goddess of Athens frivolously, especially if this might be interpreted as an insult to the city and its democracy. Comedy, at any rate, generally invokes Athena in a civic or more serious political context.[58] Its avoidance of Athena might therefore be considered a symptom of anxiety and self-censorship.

One phenomenon, which the following discussion will argue was a product of self-censorship, is the strong concentration of politically tinged comedies at the Lenaia festival, and their relative absence from the City Dionysia. Our evidence here comes mostly from the production records. These are otherwise free from the distortions present in literary and scholastic sources, therefore providing us with independent testimony, and suggest that political content was treated with some discrimination by the comic poets.

Among the so-called demagogue comedies of the late fifth century, which targeted the leading popular politicians of the time,[59] those for which production details survive were all notably performed at the Lenaia. These comedies are Aristophanes' *Knights* (424), which targeted Kleon; Eupolis's *Marikas* (421), which targeted Hyperbolos; and Plato's *Kleophon* (405), which abused the politician of the same name. Other known comedies of this type, such as Hermippos's *Bread Sellers* and Plato's *Hyperbolos*, both roughly datable between 420 and 415, unfortunately cannot be placed at a specific festival.[60] Nevertheless, other "political" themed comedies, including *Acharnians* (425) and *Wasps* (422), are Lenaian. To these we can add the unnamed Lenaian comedy by Aristophanes in 423, possibly his *Merchant Ships*, which reportedly attacked Kleon and other sycophants.[61]

A good example of discrimination between the two festivals, where a poet seems deliberately to have favored the Lenaia over the more politically sensitive City Dionysia for presenting certain material, is the *Frogs* of Aristophanes (405). While this play is otherwise "literary-critical" in theme, it can be included here on the basis of its *parabasis*. There Aristophanes had proposed that any citizens exiled or partially disenfranchised after the short-lived oligarchy of 411 should have their full citizen rights restored:

τὸν ἱερὸν χορὸν δίκαιόν ἐστι χρηστὰ τῇ πόλει
ξυμπαραινεῖν καὶ διδάσκειν. πρῶτον οὖν ἡμῖν δοκεῖ
ἐξισῶσαι τοὺς πολίτας κἀφελεῖν τὰ δείματα.
κεἴ τις ἥμαρτε σφαλείς τι Φρυνίχου παλαίσμασιν,
ἐγγενέσθαι φημὶ χρῆναι τοῖς ὀλισθοῦσιν τότε
αἰτίαν ἐκθεῖσι λῦσαι τὰς πρότερον ἁμαρτίας.
εἶτ' ἄτιμόν φημι χρῆναι μηδέν' εἶν' ἐν τῇ πόλει.

It is right that the sacred chorus join in advising and teaching
The city what is useful. First, then, we think it a good idea
To make the citizens equal and remove their fears.

And if someone erred, tripped up at all by Phrynichos's maneuvers,
I say it ought to be permitted to those who slipped up then,
To put aside blame and resolve their previous wrongs.
Next I say that no one in the city should be without full rights.
(Ar. *Frogs* 686–92)

The seriousness of the poet in raising this matter is sometimes doubted.[62] But broader contexts suggest otherwise. There are hints elsewhere in *Frogs* that this advice was offered with some anxiety, since it had considerable potential to offend. The poet is compelled to emphasize the sacred aspect of the chorus that delivers the advice, not only in their comic persona as initiates but also as a festival chorus with a sacrosanct "right" (δίκαιον) to address the city.[63] Comments in the earlier choral songs, such as line 368, emphasize comedy's Dionysian connection (ἐν ταῖς πατρίοις τελεταῖς ταῖς τοῦ Διονύσου), as if to exploit any religious scruples to their advantage. Soon after (385–90) they ask Demeter to stand alongside and protect them, announcing their intention not only to tell jokes (γέλοια) but also to say "many serious things" (πολλὰ δὲ σπουδαῖα).[64]

The specific topic of the oligarchy was particularly sensitive after the events of 411. One of Aristophanes' comedies from that year, *Thesmophoriazusae*, is notable for its relative lack of personal abuse and overt political content,[65] but also for its apprehensive subtle comments on Athens's compromised democracy at the time.[66] This is not surprising considering the uncertain atmosphere just prior to the oligarchy, and suggests a prudent measure of self-censorship at a time when political comment could be dangerous. Now that democracy was restored, to suggest that former oligarchs be granted amnesty might easily be construed as antidemocratic. It is a brave declaration, mitigated partly by the choral statements beforehand, but also by the fact Aristophanes delivered it at the Lenaia festival.

To do so at the City Dionysia was far more risky. Less than four years earlier, in 409, Athens had instituted the practice of publicly awarding gold crowns to foreign benefactors immediately before the tragic contest of the City Dionysia. The first recipients of this honor were Thrasyboulos of Kalydon and Apollodoros of Megara, for assassinating the oligarch Phrynichos (*IG* I^3 102).[67] In the same year the citizens of Athens swore the oath of Demophantos "before the Dionysia" (πρὸ Διονυσίων), pledging to kill anyone who destroyed the democracy, and setting up an inscribed copy of the oath in the agora for future reference.[68] The orphaned sons of those who died fighting the oligarchy may also have been presented there in similar fashion to the war orphans.[69] Furthermore, on the very day of the comic competition at the City Dionysia, a proclamation had traditionally been read out to reward a talent to anyone killing a tyrant.[70] With such an antityrannical, antioligarchical ethos pervading the festival at the time, Aristophanes' delivery of this advice at the Lenaia would seem purposely calculated. That it was received in a serious spirit by the audience, and not as a joke, is also indicated by the report—which we have reason to trust—that Aristophanes was granted a second production of *Frogs* for this advice, and was awarded a crown of sacred olive.[71] Athens's response might potentially have been far different.

While the Lenaia was prominent for political themes, the City Dionysia, by contrast, avoided them. This is true of the comedies we know were produced at the City Dionysia of 423. Kratinos's *Pytine* was an "autobiographical" parody of the poet's alleged alcohol abuse; Ameipsias's *Konnos* satirized philosophers and parasites; while Aristophanes' *Clouds* similarly attacked Socrates and philosophy, a noticeable change from his earlier politically tinged comedies.[72] At the City Dionysia of 421 Eupolis satirized the hangers-on of the wealthy Kallias in his *Flatterers*. Aristophanes' *Peace* is noticeably political, but Kleon had recently died, and its theme corresponded with the peace deal that would be agreed with Sparta immediately after the festival (see Thuc. 5.20.1). In general, while these plays may contain occasional sideswipes at political targets, this is usually not a predominant theme.

The difference between both festivals is significantly highlighted by examples where a poet produced two plays in the same year. Here we see a preference for allocating politically themed plays to the Lenaia, and other styles of comedy to the City Dionysia. In 423, for example, Aristophanes produced an aggressively political play at the Lenaia,[73] while reserving his *Clouds*—which chose a softer target in the philosopher Socrates—for the City Dionysia. In 421 Eupolis produced the politically charged *Marikas* at the Lenaia, while reserving his social comedy on philosophers and parasites, the *Flatterers*, for the City Dionysia. A similar phenomenon is discernible in Aristophanes' comedies of 411, if their festival assignation is correct: the *Lysistrata*, with its topic of peace with Sparta was Lenaian, while the largely apolitical *Thesmophoriazusae* was reserved for the City Dionysia. In all there appears to be a deliberate division of content based on the particular festival.

Expressions of sympathy for Sparta, interestingly, seem only to occur in Lenaian plays.[74] Most comic references to Sparta are overwhelmingly negative, and Aristophanes suggests that positive sentiments might even provoke some sections of the public.[75] Avoiding positive sentiments at the City Dionysia, however, might have had more to do with the presence of the allies and the putative risk of weakening these relationships through anything resembling pro-Spartan attitudes. The composition of the audience at each festival, after all, would have been considerably different.[76] As noted earlier, the City Dionysia not only fell in spring around the beginning of the sailing season,[77] but also occurred when Athens's allies brought their tribute.[78] The Lenaia, by contrast, was celebrated in the winter. Aristophanes' claim that foreigners were absent during the Lenaia (*Ach.* 504–5) would appear generally true; indeed he goes out of his way to acknowledge their presence in his City Dionysia plays, adapting his texts to reflect this.[79]

When we consider the reasons for this discriminating habit between the two festivals, self-censorship emerges as the most likely candidate. Comic poets certainly do not appear to have avoided political comedy at the City Dionysia as a courtesy to foreign guests. Comedies produced at the City Dionysia are often highly parochial in other ways, with Athenocentric settings, characters, themes, and institutions that were potentially puzzling to foreign audience members.[80] One should also not assume that Athens's allies were uninterested in the city's politics. As members of the Delian League, subject to Athens, they most undoubtedly were. Political content, then, was unlikely to have been excluded on the grounds it might be unappealing to foreigners.

Could these divisions have been determined instead by external censorship? One possibility here is that the archon who granted choruses to the poets played a censorship role. What we know of this process, unfortunately, is very little. Plato's ideal state as presented at *Laws* 817d gives the impression that the archons exercised censorship powers after close scrutiny of a poet's completed text.[81] But this more likely reflects how Plato wanted things to be done rather than how they actually were. Instead archons appear to have awarded choruses largely on the basis of a poet's previous reputation and success,[82] with obvious concessions in the case of less experienced poets. They also awarded them early in the year, long before a dramatic script might be completed.[83] Whether the poets offered a play title or synopsis at this stage is uncertain, but even this would not have given sufficient reason for rejecting a play on politically sensitive grounds. Poets were free to insert any such material into a play long after a chorus was awarded. Censorship by the archons, then, seems very unlikely.[84]

The most likely reason for avoiding political content at the City Dionysia thus remains self-censorship. Aristophanes himself effectively admits as much in *Acharnians* when he claims that Kleon will now be unable to charge him for insulting the city in the presence of foreigners since he is presenting his ideas at the Lenaia (*Ach.* 502–3). Kleon's prosecution not only had an immediate effect on Aristophanes' behavior, but likely influenced comic practice as a whole, as the production records suggest. The *Babylonians* of 426, then, would appear to mark a significant moment when comedy became conscious of the dangers of political material, whether offered in seriousness or not, and more sensitive to the sociopolitical contexts of the two major Athenian dramatic festivals. Paradoxically, comedy also appears to have become more politically aggressive around this time,[85] but we see numerous checks and balances emerge to offset this new brand of comedy. Although free to discuss political material at the City Dionysia, comic poets deliberately minimized the prospect of unexpected reprisals by exercising self-censorship and reserving this material mostly for the less charged atmosphere of the Lenaia instead.

NOTES

I would like to thank Eric Csapo, Sebastiana Nervegna, and Peter Wilson, who gave insightful comments on sections of this chapter, as well as the anonymous reader, and especially the editors, Han Baltussen and Peter Davis, for their guidance and for inviting me to participate.

1. Contrast, for example, Sommerstein (2004a) 216: "neither in theory nor in practice was comedy above the law: its freedom of speech was no greater and no less than that of every Athenian," with Halliwell (1991; cf. 2008, 243–44), who leans toward the legal immunity of comedy.

2. Cf. Halliwell (1984), (2004) 135–41, (2008) 206–14; Heath (1987); Rosen (1988) 59–82, (2007) 27–32. For obscenity (*aischrologia*) at Greek festivals, see Arist. *Pol.* 1336b3–23; and Fluck (1931). For the idea that mockery even honored the target, see Bierl (2002).

3. An observation first emphasized by Gomme (1938).

4. Cf. Heath (1990) 237.

5. Important here are the introductory comments of Henderson (1990) 271–75. Cf. also the balanced assessment of Carey (1994).

6. See Goldhill (1990); Henderson (1990) 285–87; and more recently Wilson (2009), with relevant bibliography on the issue at 8n2.

7. Scholion to Ar. *Ach.* 67. For its possible connection with the Samian War, see, e.g., Halliwell (1991) 58–59; Sommerstein (2004a) 208–9; Wallace (1994) 114 and (2005) 362–63. Another possible decree is the so-called decree of Syrakosios of 415/14 (Scholion to Ar. *Birds* 1297), although Halliwell (1991) 62–63 doubts its authenticity. Sommerstein (1986), Atkinson (1992) 62, and Henderson (1998) 262 connect it with the scandals of the Mysteries and Herms. MacDowell (1978) 128 and Wallace (2005) 367 suggest it instituted a

general law against slandering individuals in a comedy, although there is no evidence such a law ever existed.

8. Possibly Kleophon according to Kyriakidi (2007) 26–28. Storey (2003) 155–60 identifies other possible candidates. For politicians hostile to comedy, see Henderson (1998) 263.

9. So Rosen (1988) 63–64, Rosen (2010) 233–35. Cf. Lefkowitz (2012) 107–8.

10. Ar. *Ach.* 630; *Wasps* 1287–88.

11. See Pelling (2000) 150. Cf. also Hubbard (1991) 46n18; Olson (1998) on *Peace* 47–48; Brockmann (2003) 154–56; Sommerstein (2004a) 209–10, and especially the comments in (2004b) 152–53. It is unclear how Rosen's suggestion (2010, 234) that Aristophanes wished to create "the persona of a comically oppressed poet, marshalling a vote of sympathy" would work here if Aristophanes fabricated the legal action for this purpose. The audience would have known it was false, having themselves supposedly taken part in the incident, and the attempt would have backfired or come across as ironic. This does not, of course, preclude such a strategy being applied elsewhere to better effect (cf. Rosen 2014).

12. See Ar. *Peace* 47–48, 268–73, 313–15, 647–56, 753–60 (cf. Olson 1998, on *Peace* 47–48). Abusing the dead itself had its risks: cf. Plut. *Sol.* 21.1; Dem. 20.104, 40.49; scholion Ar. *Peace* 648b. Contrast the favorable treatment for the deceased Kratinos at Ar. *Frogs* 357; Lamachos at *Thesm.* 839–41 and *Frogs* 1039; and note Eupolis's posthumous praise of Perikles (fr. 102), a popular comic target in his lifetime.

13. E.g., Ar. *Knights* 257, 452, 475–79, 624–82, 860–63; *Wasps* 417, 463–507. While comedy depicts these accusations as based on trivial grounds, the real danger, as the Sausage-Seller suggests at *Knights* 626–38, is that Kleon could be formidably persuasive before the Council.

14. The claim by the Old Oligarch in Pseudo-Xenophon's *Ath. Pol.* 2.18 that Athens did not tolerate comic abuse of the *dêmos* (κωμῳδεῖν δ' αὖ καὶ κακῶς λέγειν τὸν μὲν δῆμον οὐκ ἐῶσιν; "They do not allow one to make comedy and speak badly of the *dêmos*") was probably inferred from this celebrated example.

15. That the commentator was evidently acquainted with the text of *Babylonians*, see Brockmann (2003) 148.

16. For discussion of this comedy, see Welsh (1983), and more recently Starkey (2013).

17. Cf. Ar. fr. 68, which may be dialogue from this scene.

18. The Dionysia marked not only the arrival of the allies, but also the beginning of the sailing season and the arrival of traders to Athens (cf. Hermippos fr. 63.1–3). For Kleon's tight control of the harbors, cf. Ar. *Knights* 165, 171.

19. Kleon is explicitly called a sycophant at Ar. *Peace* 653. Apparent instances of blackmailing allies are suggested at Ar. *Knights* 361 (Miletos), 438–39 (Potideia), and 832–85 (Mytilene. See Thuc. 3.11.7). See also *Knights* 65–70, 237–39, 802, 839–40; and *Birds* 1422–31 and 1454–60 where a sycophant who harasses the allies appears on stage.

20. See Ar. frr. 71, 89, 90, 95, 99 (cf. 77 and 100). At fr. 81 the chorus is said to speak in a "barbaric manner."

21. Ar. fr. 71: "Someone says in Aristophanes, upon seeing the Babylonians from the mill: 'It's the people of Samos. How multi-lettered they are!'"

22. Ar. fr. 90: "Aristophanes in *Babylonians* says that the foreheads of the slaves are Istrian, since they are tattooed."

23. See Hansen and Nielsen (2004) 932–33 no. 685.

24. Cf. also Ar. frr. 73 and 81.

25. Ar. frr. 71 and 90 mention tattooed slaves (Samos attempted revolt in 440). Stigmata and punishment at the mill are mentioned at frr. 95 and 99. The altar of Kore and Demeter, which offered asylum to runaway slaves, is mentioned at fr. 89. And fr. 97 refers to someone "Lakedaimonizing," most likely an allusion to revolt.

26. Thuc. 3.10.3; 3.10.4; and 3.10.5. Cf. Kleon's heavy-handed views on managing the allies during the Mytilenean debate (Thuc. 3.37). See also Sommerstein and Bayliss (2013) 207–11 on the "enslavement" of the allies.

27. So Welsh (1983) 139; and Olson (2002) on *Ach.* 642.

28. Cf. Millis and Olson (2012) 157 with n. 17.

29. Cf. Sommerstein (2004b) 153.

30. The law was originally Solonic: [Arist.] *Ath. Pol.* 8.4: "and [the Areopagos] judged those who conspire to destroy the *dêmos* (τοὺς ἐπὶ καταλύσει τοῦ δήμου συνισταμένους), after Solon passed a law of *eisangelia* concerning them." Cf. Poll. 8.51 which says it applied to politicians who attempted to "destroy the *dêmos*" (καταλυόντων τὸν δῆμον); Hansen (1975) 69–111.

31. Cf. Hansen (1975) 28, 112–20. The *boulê* or "Council" took over responsibility for *eisangeliai* from the Areopagos probably during the reforms of Ephialtes in the late 460s: see Rhodes (1972) 199–201; Hansen (1975) 22–23; and cf. Isocr. 15.314 and 16.6.

32. This too was ordinarily a criminal offence: [Arist.] *Prob.* 952b28–32; Dem. 21.32–34; Lys. 9.6; Plut. *Sol.* 21.1. See Sommerstein (2004a) 206–8.

33. Plut. *Arist.* 24.3. Kleon himself may have played a role in this increase, but cf. Gomme (1956) 500–505. Isocrates 8.82 criticizes the practice of displaying tribute in the theater, which bred resentment among the allies. For financial pressure on Athens around this time, see Samons (2000) 172–73.

34. Thuc. 3.39.7. Revolts also prompted the armistice between Athens and Sparta in March 423 (Thuc. 4.117.1).

35. Cf. also Olson (2010) 42. Starkey (2013, 510) suggests that *Babylonians* ridiculed the state of the Athenian navy, a considerable source of pride, in the presence of the allies.

36. *Acharnians* itself is presented as an opportunity to win back their favor, hinting that their characteristic inclination to "change opinion" (632: μεταβούλους) would now be welcome in his present attempts to win them over, not least of all from a competitive standpoint.

37. Contrast Storey (1995), Pelling (2000) 132–33, and Sommerstein (2004b) 151 with n. 17, who raise the possibility this refers to a second lawsuit by Kleon.

38. Sommerstein (2004b) 147 discusses the range of possible meanings of ἀπωλόμην.

39. Heath (1987) 17–18.

40. See esp. *Ach.* 497–99, 515–16, and 562.

41. Harrison (1971) 56; Rhodes (1972) 164, 171; MacDowell (1978) 183.

42. O'Sullivan (2009) 67, in a detailed discussion of these matters suggests Stratokles may not be reacting to a comedy specifically by Philippides, but that Philippides takes up the comic cause nonetheless.

43. *Eisangelia* was regularly abused by the democracy, prompting the introduction of a 1000 drachma fine c. 333–330 BCE if the prosecutor failed to secure more than one fifth of the vote (Poll. 8.52; MacDowell 1978, 419; Harrison 1971, 51 with n. 3; Hansen 1975, 29–31). Nevertheless Stratokles and his associates regularly used it: cf. Philoch. *FGrHist* 328 F 66; Dion. Hal. *De Din.* 2. This extended to infighting between democrats. He had his political rival Demochares—in circumstances apparently quite similar to Philippides—exiled as an enemy of the democracy (c. 303–302 BCE) after Demochares helped repeal a decree granting Demetrios excessive powers to "govern by letter": Plut. *Mor.* 851e; *Demetr.* 24.10–11; and Shear (1978) 48–49.

44. Philippides' complaint that Stratokles "reduced the year into a single month" refers to the return of Demetrios to Athens in Mounychion (April/May) of 302 BCE when he wanted to be initiated immediately into the Lesser and Greater Mysteries, despite the fact they were held in Anthesterion and Boedromion, respectively. The damage to the *peplos* (or "tapestry") mentioned in line 5 took place either at the Great Panathenaia of 306 or 302. The latter date is suggested by the fact that Philippides, although not living in Athens at the time, helped purchase a new yard arm for the *peplos* in 299/8, in time for the next Panathenaia (*IG* II^2 657.13–16).

45. Cf. Ferguson (1911) 124–26. On the date and extent of Philippides' absence, see the comments of Shear (1978) 49 on *IG* II^2 657.10.

46. For Demetrios in comedy, see Lape (2004) 61–63.

47. Frantz (1900) 671. Kassel and Austin include it at *PCG* VII, 352 (below Philippides fr. 41).

48. Here expressing surprise, even joy or excitement. Cf. Ar. *Lys.* 924; *Thesm.* 1191; Eur. *Cycl.* 153.

49. It most likely alludes to the Athenian defeat at Amorgos when Stratokles infamously deceived the Athenian public, reporting victory and holding a celebratory feast at his own expense. See Plut. *Dem.* 11.3; Plut. *Prae. ger. reip.* 799f.

50. For *hetaira* names, see Schneider (1913) 1358–60; cf. Cox (1998) 175–77.

51. Plut. *Dem.* 9.1, 10.3; Diod. 20.46.2. Cf. Bayliss (2011) 120–21, who notes the Antigonids were virtually synonymous with democracy itself.

52. Cf. Habicht (1997) 75; Bayliss (2011) 120, 169; *IG* II^2 469.9–10 and *SEG* 25 (1971) 141.7–8 (= *Agora* 16 114).

53. Cf. Bayliss (2011) 117–19 and 182.

54. Cf. Rosen (2014).

55. Cf. Henderson (1990) 310. For "Demos" as a comic character criticizing his own politicians, see also Plat. Com. fr. 201.

56. Pelling (2000) 158. Cf. also Sommerstein (2009) 219, who notes that plays such as *Birds* and *Ecclesiazusae*, which present alternatives to democracy, take place only in fantasy settings.

57. Cf. Nock (1972) 543; Bakola (2010) 286–87. Hermippos's *Birth of Athena* (late fifth century BCE) is a notable exception.

58. E.g., Ar. *Knights* 581–94; *Thesm.* 1136–47; see Anderson (1995).

59. On "demagogue" comedies, see Lind (1990) 235–52.

60. We might also include Plato's *Peisandros* (see Sommerstein 2000, 439–40), perhaps produced at the Lenaia of 419 (see Hartwig 2010, 29n57). Lind (1990) 239n3, expresses doubts whether this was a "demagogue" comedy at all.

61. See Ar. *Wasps* 1037–42. Ar. *Peace* Hyp. III.36–40 (Wilson) reports that *Merchant Ships* ridiculed Kleon. The "sycophant" theme would also seem to suit that comedy.

62. Cf. Rosen (2010) 275–77.

63. For political comedy and τὰ δίκαια, see also Ar. *Ach.* 500–501, 645, 655, 661, cf. 562; *Knights* 510. Note also the name "Dikaiopolis" (clearly derived from *Ach.* 499–500), who often represents Aristophanes' voice in *Acharnians* (cf. Hubbard 1991, 45–46).

64. Halliwell (2008) 212–13 argues that these comments are relevant only to the chorus of "initiates" within the play. The line, however, between festival and fictional personae is constantly blurred in comedy, and the reference to "serious matters" may very easily apply to the comic poet's advice.

65. Aristophanes' comedies of 411 both claim they will not abuse any individuals: *Lys.* 1043–45; *Thesm.* 964.

66. Ar. *Thesm.* 317–19, 335–39, 365–68, 1136–47. Cf. Thuc. 8.53 for the political situation in Athens.

67. See Wilson (2009); Wilson and Hartwig (2009); Shear (2011) 141–46.

68. Andoc. 1.96–98; Lycurg. *Leocr.* 125–27. See Shear (2007) and (2011) 136–41; Wilson (2009) 15–16, 23–25.

69. Cf. *SEG* 28.46; Lys. fr. 129.26–47; and Shear (2011) 317.

70. Ar. *Birds* 1072–75. See Wilson (2009) 26; Shear (2011) 151.

71. The source of this information was very likely the Peripatetic Dikaiarchos, who certainly could not have inferred it from literary evidence alone. See Sommerstein (2009) 254–62.

72. It is possible *Clouds* marked Aristophanes' return to the Dionysia since *Babylonians*, this time with a far less provocative comedy. Paradoxically, it was also his first dramatic disappointment.

73. See Ar. *Wasps* 1038–43.

74. E.g., Ar. *Ach.* 509–14; *Merchant Ships* (probably Lenaia 423: frr. 415 and 420); and *Lysistrata*.

75. See Ar. *Ach.* 315–16, 514. Note also the poet's risk of going to the "chopping block" for saying anything that might be construed as pro-Spartan at *Ach.* 355–56 and 366–69.

76. Contrast Pelling (2000) 149–50, who is skeptical it was much different at all.

77. See Theophr. *Char.* 3.3 with Diggle (2004) 201; Cf. Hermippos fr. 63.

78. Isocr. *De Pace* 82; Scholion to Ar. *Ach.* 504a; Raubitschek (1941) 356–62; Olson (1998) on *Peace* 45–46.

79. See Ar. *Clouds* 609; *Peace* 45–48, 296–98, and esp. 759–60: an adaptation of *Wasps* 1036–37 that originally addressed only the Athenians, but is now adjusted to include the allies as well.

80. See Revermann (2006) 166. Cf. Pelling (2000) 149–50.

81. Cf. also Plato *Rep.* 385b–c.

82. See Suda χ 408; cf. also Ar. fr. 590.27–29, which seems to complain about the eponymous archon not taking into consideration Lenaian success when awarding choruses for the City Dionysia.

83. Cf. the anecdote on Menander (Plut. *Mor.* 347e–f = Men. test. 70 K.-A.), who left writing his play until quite late.

84. Cf. also Revermann (2006) 164.

85. Cf. Ar. *Knights* 507–11 where, boasting aside, Aristophanes claims to have introduced a more aggressive approach toward politicians as comic targets.

REFERENCES

Anderson, C. A. 1995. *Athena's Epithets: Their Structural Significance in Plays of Aristophanes.* Stuttgart: Teubner.

Atkinson, J. E. 1992. "Curbing the Comedians: Cleon Versus Aristophanes and Syracosius' Decree." *Classical Quarterly* 42: 56–64.

Bakola, E. 2010. *Cratinus and the Art of Comedy.* Oxford: Oxford University Press.

Bayliss, A. J. 2011. *After Demosthenes: The Politics of Early Hellenistic Athens.* London: Continuum.

Bierl, A. 2002. "Viel Spott, viel Ehr!—Die Ambivalenz des ὀνομαστὶ κωμῳδεῖν im festlichen und generischen Kontext." In *Spoudaiogeloion. Form und Funktion der Verspottung in der aristophanischen Komödie, Drama*, vol. 11, ed. A. Ercolani, 169–87. Stuttgart: Metzler.

Brockmann, C. 2003. *Aristophanes und die Freiheit der Komödie.* Munich: De Gruyter.

Carey, C. 1994. "Comic Ridicule and Democracy." In *Ritual, Finance, Politics: Athenian Democratic Accounts Presented to D. M. Lewis*, ed. R. Osborne and S. Hornblower, 69–84. Oxford: Oxford University Press.

Cox, C. A. 1998. *Household Interests: Property, Marriage Strategies, and Family Dynamics in Ancient Athens.* Princeton: Princeton University Press.

Diggle, J. 2004. *Theophrastus: Characters.* Cambridge: Cambridge University Press.

Ferguson, W. S. 1911. *Hellenistic Athens: An Historical Essay.* London: Macmillan.

Fluck, H. 1931. *Skurrile Riten in griechischen Kulten.* Endigen: Wild.

Frantz, W. 1900. "Ein Fragment des Komikers Philippides." *Hermes* 35: 671.

Goldhill, S. 1990. "The Great Dionysia and Civic Ideology." In *Nothing to Do with*

Dionysos? Athenian Drama in Its Social Context, ed. J. J. Winkler and F. I. Zeitlin, 97–129. Princeton: Princeton University Press.

Gomme, A. W. 1938. "Aristophanes and Politics." *Classical Review* 52: 97–109.

———. 1956. *A Historical Commentary on Thucydides*. Vol. 3. Oxford: Oxford University Press.

Habicht, C. 1997. *Athens from Alexander to Antony*. Tr. D. L. Schneider. Cambridge, MA: Harvard University Press.

Halliwell, S. 1984. "Aristophanic Satire." *Yearbook of English Studies* 14: 6–20.

———. 1991. "Comic Satire and Freedom of Speech in Classical Athens." *Journal of Hellenic Studies* 111: 48–70.

———. 2004. "Aischrology, Shame, and Comedy." In *Free Speech in Classical Antiquity*, ed. I. Sluiter and R. M. Rosen, 115–44. Leiden: Brill.

———. 2008. *Greek Laughter: A Study of Cultural Psychology from Homer to Early Christianity*. Cambridge: Cambridge University Press.

Hansen, M. H. 1975. *Eisangelia: The Sovereignty of the People's Court in Athens in the Fourth Century B.C. and the Impeachment of Generals and Politicians*. Odense: Odense Universitetsforlag.

Hansen, M. H. and T. H. Nielsen. 2004. *An Inventory of Archaic and Classical Poleis*. Oxford: Oxford University Press.

Harrison, A. R. W. 1971. *The Law of Athens*. Vol. 2. Oxford: Oxford University Press.

Hartwig, A. 2010. "The Date of the *Rhabdouchoi* and the Early Career of Plato Comicus." *Zeitschrift für Papyrologie und Epigraphik* 174: 19–31.

Heath, M. 1987. *Political Comedy in Aristophanes*. Göttingen: Vandenhoeck & Ruprecht.

———. 1990. "Some Deceptions in Aristophanes." *Papers of the Leeds International Latin Seminar* 6: 229–40.

Henderson, J. 1990. "The *Dēmos* and the Comic Competition." In *Nothing to Do with Dionysos? Athenian Drama in Its Social Context*, ed. J. J. Winkler and F. I. Zeitlin, 271–313. Princeton: Princeton University Press.

———. 1998. "Attic Old Comedy, Frank Speech, and Democracy." In *Democracy, Empire, and the Arts in Fifth Century Athens*, ed. D. Boedeker and K. A. Raaflaub, 255–73. Cambridge, MA: Harvard University Press.

Hubbard, T. K. 1991. *The Mask of Comedy: Aristophanes and the Intertextual Parabasis*. Ithaca, NY: Cornell University Press.

Kassel, R. and C. Austin. 1983–2001. *Poetae Comici Graeci*. Berlin: De Gruyter.

Kyriakidi, N. 2007. *Aristophanes und Eupolis: Zur Geschichte einer dichterischen Rivalität*. Berlin: De Gruyter.

Lape, S. 2004. *Reproducing Athens: Menander's Comedy, Democratic Culture, and the Hellenistic City*. Princeton: Princeton University Press.

Lefkowitz, M. R. 2012. *The Lives of the Greek Poets*. 2nd ed. London: Duckworth.

Lind, H. 1990. *Der Gerber Kleon in den "Rittern" des Aristophanes*. Frankfurt: Peter Lang.

MacDowell, D. M. 1978. *The Law in Classical Athens*. London: Thames and Hudson.

Millis, B. W. and S. D. Olson. 2012. *Inscriptional Records for the Dramatic Festivals at Athens*. Leiden: Brill.

Nock, A. D. 1972. *Essays on Religion and the Ancient World*. Vol. 2. Oxford: Oxford University Press.

Olson, S. D. 1998. *Aristophanes: Peace*. Oxford: Oxford University Press.

———. 2002. *Aristophanes: Acharnians*. Oxford: Oxford University Press.

———. 2010. "Comedy, Politics, and Society." In *Brill's Companion to the Study of Greek Comedy*, ed. G. W. Dobrov, 35–69. Leiden: Brill.

O'Sullivan, L. 2009. "History from Comic Hypotheses: Stratocles, Lachares, and *P.Oxy.* 1235." *Greek, Roman and Byzantine Studies* 49: 53–79.

Pelling, C. B. R. 2000. *Literary Texts and the Greek Historian*. London: Routledge.

Raubitschek, A. E. 1941. "Two Notes on Isocrates." *Transactions of the American Philological Association* 72: 356–64.

Revermann, M. 2006. *Comic Business: Theatricality, Dramatic Technique, and Performance Contexts of Aristophanic Comedy*. Oxford: Oxford University Press.

Rhodes, P. J. 1972. *The Athenian Boule*. Oxford: Oxford University Press.

Rosen, R. M. 1988. *Old Comedy and the Iambographic Tradition*. Atlanta, GA: Scholars Press.

———. 1989. "Trouble in the Early Career of Plato Comicus: Another Look at POxy. 2737.44–51 (*PCG* III 2, 590)." *Zeitschrift für Papyrologie und Epigraphik* 76: 223–28.

———. 2007. *Making Mockery: The Poetics of Ancient Satire*. Oxford: Oxford University Press.

———. 2010. "Aristophanes." In *Brill's Companion to the Study of Greek Comedy*, ed. G. W. Dobrov, 227–78. Leiden: Brill.

———. 2014. "Comic Parrhesia and the Paradoxes of Repression." In *Ancient Comedy and Reception: Essays in Honor of Jeffrey Henderson*, ed. S. D. Olson, 13–28. Berlin: De Gruyter.

Samons, L. J. 2000. *Empire of the Owl: Athenian Imperial Finance*. Stuttgart: Steiner.

Schneider, K. 1913. "Hetairai." In *Paulys Realencyclopädie der classischen Altertumswissenschaft*, vol. 8, cols. 1331–72. Stuttgart: A. Druckenmüller.

Shear, J. L. 2007. "The Oath of Demophantos and the Politics of Athenian Identity." In *Horkos: The Oath in Greek Society*, ed. A. H. Sommerstein and J. Fletcher, 148–60. Exeter: Bristol Phoenix Press.

———. 2011. *Polis and Revolution: Responding to Oligarchy in Classical Athens*. Cambridge: Cambridge University Press.

Shear, T. L. 1978. *Kallias of Sphettos and the Revolt of Athens in 286 BC*. Princeton: American School of Classical Studies at Athens.

Sommerstein, A. H. 1986. "The Decree of Syrakosios." *Classical Quarterly* 36: 101–8.

———. 2000. "Platon, Eupolis and the 'Demagogue-Comedy.'" In *The Rivals of Aristophanes: Studies in Athenian Old Comedy*, ed. F. D. Harvey and J. Wilkins, 437–51. London: Duckworth.

———. 2004a. "Comedy and the Unspeakable." In *Law, Rhetoric, and Comedy in*

Classical Athens: Essays in Honour of Douglas M. MacDowell, ed. D. L. Cairns and R. A. Knox, 205–22. Llandysul: Classical Press of Wales.
———. 2004b. "Harassing the Satirist: The Alleged Attempts to Prosecute Aristophanes." In *Free Speech in Classical Antiquity*, ed. I. Sluiter and R. M. Rosen, 145–74. Leiden: Brill.
———. 2009. *Talking About Laughter and Other Studies in Greek Comedy*. Oxford: Oxford University Press.
Sommerstein, A. H. and A. J. Bayliss. 2013. *Oath and State in Ancient Greece*. Berlin: De Gruyter.
Starkey, J. S. 2013. "Soldiers and Sailors in Aristophanes' *Babylonians*." *Classical Quarterly* 63: 501–10.
Storey, I. C. 1995. "*Wasps* 1284–91 and the Portrait of Kleon in *Wasps*." *Scholia* 4: 3–23.
———. 2003. *Eupolis: Poet of Old Comedy*. Oxford: Oxford University Press.
Wallace, R. W. 1994. "The Athenian Laws Against Slander." In *Symposion 1993: Vorträge zur griechischen und hellenistischen Rechtsgeschichte*, ed. G. Thür, 109–24. Cologne: Böhlau.
———. 2005. "Law, Attic Comedy, and the Regulation of Comic Speech." In *The Cambridge Companion to Ancient Greek Law*, ed. M. Gagarin and D. Cohen, 357–73. Cambridge: Cambridge University Press.
Welsh, D. 1983. "The Chorus of Aristophanes' *Babylonians*." *Greek, Roman and Byzantine Studies* 24: 137–50.
Wilson, P. 2009. "Tragic Honours and Democracy: Neglected Evidence for the Politics of the Athenian Dionysia." *Classical Quarterly* 59: 8–29.
Wilson, P. and A. Hartwig. 2009. "*IG* I^3 102 and the Tradition of Proclaiming Honours at the Tragic *Agon* of the Athenian City Dionysia." *Zeitschrift für Papyrologie und Epigraphik* 169: 17–27.

Chapter 3

Parrhêsia and Censorship in the *Polis* and the Symposium: An Exploration of Hyperides *Against Philippides* 3

Lara O'Sullivan

Alongside their famed *isonomia* (equality under the law) and their *isêgoria* (equality of access to speech, most particularly to speech before the *dêmos*),[1] Athenians of the classical age laid claim to *parrhêsia*—an access to a freedom and frankness in what they said. While not a formalized "right" (in the sense that the liberty to speak frankly was not enshrined in law), *parrhêsia* is indeed cast as an essential quality of Athenian democracy itself, making it a fitting inclusion for celebration in pseudo-Demosthenes' state funeral oration.[2] Democracy and *parrhêsia* are even at times rendered virtually synonymous by the Attic orators of the fourth century,[3] while Plato includes *parrhêsia*, alongside that fundamental quality of freedom (*eleutheria*), as a key characteristic of citizens under democracy: "*οὐκοῦν πρῶτον μὲν δὴ ἐλεύθεροι, καὶ ἐλευθερίας ἡ πόλις μεστὴ καὶ παρρησίας γίγνεται, καὶ ἐξουσία ἐν αὐτῇ ποιεῖν ὅτι τις βούλεται*" ("Firstly, are they not free? And is not the city sated with liberty and freedom of speech? And has not every man license to do whatever he likes?"; *Rep.* 557b). Laws restricting speech were, in consequence, famously few at Athens. There was a prohibition, amply attested and apparently of Solonian origin, against speaking ill (*κακῶς λέγειν*) of the dead, and restrictions too against the abuse of a serving magistrate;[4] of other claimed instances of legal impediments, however, many apply to the regulation of comic abuse and are historically suspect.[5] Given the apparent reluctance of the Athenians to restrict speech through legislation, Hyperides' allusion in the fourth-century speech *Against Philippides* to a measure curbing denigration of those democratic icons, the tyrannicides, is thus of particular note.[6] Hyperides claims that "*ἐν νόμῳ γράψας [ὁ] δῆμος ἀπεῖπεν μήτε [λ]έγειν ἐξεῖναι [μηδενὶ] κακῶς Ἁρμόδιον καὶ Ἀρ[ισ]τογείτονα, μήτ' ᾆσα[ι ἐ]πὶ τὰ κακίονα*" ("the *dêmos* wrote a prohibition in law, forbidding anyone to say or sing things to the detriment of Harmodius and Aristogeiton"; Hyp. 2.3). The symposium must be a prime target here,[7] for the engagement of the symposium with the figures of the tyrannicides is well attested. Numerous *skolia*, or sympotic drinking songs, are preserved in the Attic corpus celebrating Harmodius and Aristogeiton.[8] Athenaeus cites a number of them, of which the following may serve as an example:

> *ἐν μύρτου κλαδὶ τὸ ξίφος φορήσω,*
> *ὥσπερ Ἁρμόδιος καὶ Ἀριστογείτων,*
> *ὅτε τὸν τύραννον κτανέτην*
> *ἰσονόμους τ' Ἀθήνας ἐποιησάτην.*
>
> I shall carry my sword in a myrtle branch,
> Just as Harmodius and Aristogeiton did,
> When they slew the tyrant
> And gave equality to Athens. (Ath. 15.695a)

Given the prevalence of such *skolia*, it is clear that the singing of derogatory verses about this pair is to be located principally in the same sympotic setting, and this is in fact confirmed by Hyperides' following comment that the law "made it impossible *for even a drunkard* to slander [the tyrannicides]" (Hyp. 2.3).

It is the purpose of this chapter to contextualize this prohibition by exploring the scope of *parrhêsia* in democratic Athens. What follows is an exploration of the "saying and singing of bad things" in the differing cultural contexts of public spaces of the democratic *polis* on the one hand (that is, the law courts, assembly, and agora), and, on the other, of the symposium, a space that enjoyed a complex relationship with the *polis*. We will tease out some of the tensions between the *parrhêsia* of the *polis* and the symposium, and look at how such tension might have been mediated by the wider political context. These cultural and political approaches to the construction of frank speech in the symposium may offer another dimension to our perspectives on issues of censorship and free speech in Greek antiquity and more specifically in Athens.

Saying Bad Things Among the *Dêmos* and in the Symposium

The willingness of Athenians to indulge in abuse in public forums such as the law courts is a trait well known to those who study Athenian culture. The propensity for personal insults no doubt stems in large measure from the recognized entertainment value of invective: Demosthenes identifies it as part of human nature to find pleasure in listening to abuse and accusations (*loidoriai, katêgoriai*: so Dem. 18.3). On a more serious note, the willingness to criticize could be given a political cast. Demosthenes, indeed, would laud the Athenians' freedom to shame their fellow Athenians publicly as one of the safeguards and strengths of the city, for fear of shame (and its converse, the desire for praise) serves to encourage noble behavior.

> *αἱ μὲν γὰρ διὰ τῶν ὀλίγων δυναστεῖαι δέος μὲν ἐνεργάζονται τοῖς πολίταις, αἰσχύνην δ' οὐ παριστᾶσιν. ἡνίκ' ἂν οὖν ὁ ἀγὼν ἔλθῃ τοῦ πολέμου, πᾶς τις εὐχερῶς ἑαυτὸν σῴζει, συνειδὼς ὅτι . . . κἂν τὰ δεινότατ' ἀσχημονήσῃ, μικρὸν ὄνειδος τὸ λοιπὸν αὐτῷ καταστήσεται. αἱ δὲ δημοκρατίαι πολλά τ' ἄλλα καὶ καλὰ καὶ δίκαι' ἔχουσιν, ὧν τὸν εὖ φρονοῦντ' ἀντέχεσθαι δεῖ, καὶ τὴν παρρησίαν ἐκ τῆς ἀληθείας ἠρτημένην οὐκ ἔστι τἀληθὲς δηλοῦν ἀποτρέψαι. . . . ἃ φοβούμενοι πάντες εἰκότως τῇ τῶν μετὰ ταῦτ' ὀνειδῶν αἰσχύνῃ τόν τε προσιόντ' ἀπὸ τῶν ἐναντίων κίνδυνον εὐρώστως ὑπέμειναν, καὶ θάνατον καλὸν εἵλοντο μᾶλλον ἢ βίον αἰσχρόν.*
>
> For though absolute governments dominated by a few create fear in their citizens, they fail to awaken the sense of shame. Consequently, when the test of war comes, everyone lightheartedly proceeds to save himself, knowing full well that . . . even though he becomes guilty of the most revolting conduct, only slight reproach will attach to him thereafter. Democracies, however, possess many other just and noble features, to which right-minded men should hold fast, and in particular it is impossible to deter freedom of speech, which depends upon speaking the truth, from exposing the truth. . . . Through fear of such condemnation, all these men, as

> was to be expected, for shame at the thought of subsequent reproaches, manfully faced the threat arising from our foes and chose a noble death in preference to life and disgrace. (ps.-Dem. 60.25–26)

Yet despite *parrhêsia*'s associations with democracy and its perceived advantages to the *polis* itself, the free and frank speech claimed for all citizens of the Athenian *dêmos* generated social anxieties that might, at times, see the praxis of *parrhêsia* moderated by self-censorship.[9] Despite the realities of the abusiveness of much court oratory, social mores and rhetorical teaching nevertheless urged against indulgence in *aischrologia* (a notion which might range across obscenity, personal vilification and direct reference to religiously sanctioned subjects) within public democratic forums such as the law courts; as a result, the indulgence in abusive speech and in *aischrologia* is not infrequently prefaced by some form of self-conscious preamble. Orators might thus explicitly advertise their own avoidance of offensive speech, as does the speaker of Demosthenes' *Against Conon* when detailing his alleged abuse at the hands of drunken assailants:[10] "*κείμενος δ' αὐτῶν ἤκουον πολλὰ καὶ δεινὰ λεγόντων. καὶ τὰ μὲν ἄλλα καὶ βλασφημίαν ἔχει τινὰ καὶ ὀνομάζειν ὀκνήσαιμ' ἂν ἐν ὑμῖν ἔνια*" ("As I lay there [beaten up], I heard [the accused] utter much outrageous language, much of which was most abusive, and some of it I would shrink from repeating before you"; Dem. 54.8–9). The defense of his own abusiveness by Theophrastus's "bad-mouther" (*ὁ κακολόγος*), on the grounds that his offensive talk is actually "frankness and democracy and freedom" (*παρρησίαν καὶ δημοκρατίαν καὶ ἐλευθερίαν*: *Char.* 28.6), implies a more usual circumscription of free speech through self-censorship, and betrays too the danger that *aischrologia* could be defended through disingenuous appeal to the notion of democratic *parrhêsia*.

The anxieties about the possibility of *parrhêsia* generating shameful speech, and the resulting tendency toward self-censorship in public forums, we may suspect to be in part a lingering product of an earlier social moderation of the right to speak. As has long been acknowledged, access to the right to speak and the liberty to speak frankly were, in many Greek communities, largely mediated by hierarchies, particularly hierarchies of social prestige and wealth. The *locus classicus* for this nexus between speech and status is found in the Homeric exchange in the *Iliad* (2.211–77) between Odysseus and the lowly Thersites (a man whose lesser rank is implied by his lack of patronymic).[11] Thersites's outspoken criticism of his overlord, Agamemnon, draws down the wrath of Odysseus in part because of his failure to observe the conventions of proper speech (his words, which are explicitly "insults," are "without measure" and "disorderly," and spoken "in a reckless way," with "no proper arrangement"),[12] but perhaps more fundamentally because Thersites himself had no social right to speak up in the presence of his superior. The hierarchical aspect of the reprisal against Thersites is evident through an implicit contrast with Achilles. As noted already in antiquity,[13] the substance of Thersites' remarks against Agamemnon echoes complaints already lodged by Achilles, and the form of his speech (at *Il.* 2.225–42) hardly merits the preceding description of the speaker as being of "disorderly mind." Yet only Thersites is assailed, and his assault by Odysseus is one that Homer's audience is well primed to condone.[14]

In classical Athens, by contrast, the emergence of democracy had seen this restrictive quality of social prestige considerably undermined. In her influential analysis of Athenian free speech, Saxonhouse formulates the change as fundamentally linked to the evolution of democracy: "The transition to democracy in the fifth and fourth centuries in Athens is marked by the purgings of the hierarchies so evident [in earlier contexts]. There, in democratic Athens, there will be no limits on who can speak, on what they can say, on the insults that they can hurl at their supposed superiors."[15] No Odysseus would chide an Athenian Thersites for daring to address the assembly or smite him for verbal abuse of his social superiors.[16] While liberation from such fear may have been at the heart of the concept of *parrhêsia* (indeed *parrhêsia* at Athens may be conceived as being less about freedom from censorship or from any active coercion as such, and more as a freedom from one's own sense of fear or shame about speaking frankly),[17] it is clear that the assumption of *parrhêsia* as a quality of democracy did not destroy this cultural connection between *aischrologia* and social inferiority. The association remained useful as a weapon for denigrating political opponents (witness Demosthenes' stigmatization of Aeschines as both salesman and slanderer: Dem. 19.121; 18.126; 18.180). More particularly, it remained current as a point of attack by detractors of democracy. Thucydides' Cleon is notably like Thersites in both his social inferiority and his guilt in speaking abusively in the assembly. Indeed Thucydides' characterization of this Athenian politician owes much to Homer, with the base Cleon echoing the words of the noble Pericles in a way that serves to evoke the Homeric Thersites/Achilles pairing.[18] *Aischrologia* and social inferiority thus remained potentially intertwined: *aischrologia* is a marker of vulgarity, feared because its use risks betraying the social inferiority of the speaker.[19]

While the Athenian *dêmos* may have adopted *isêgoria* and *parrhêsia* as qualities of public discourse generally, *parrhêsia* also had a place in the more elite and private domain of the symposium. *Parrhêsia* is claimed as a characteristic of the symposium by the early third-century BCE Attic historian Philochorus, who writes that "*οἱ πίνοντες οὐ μόνον ἑαυτοὺς ἐμφανίζουσιν οἵτινές εἰσιν, ἀλλὰ τῶν ἄλλων ἕκαστον ἀνακαλύπτουσι παρρησίαν ἄγοντες*" ("Those drinking reveal not only their own true natures but also that of others, since they engage in *parrhêsia*"; *FGrH* 328 F170).[20] In the light of the historical differentiation of free speech by social hierarchies noted above, the praxis of free and frank speech within the symposium itself is hardly surprising; within the symposium there existed, at least nominally, an equality among the participants of the drinking party which mirrored the equality among the *dêmos* at large, but which was a product not of equality of citizen status but of aristocratic equality and friendship. The equality and unusual degree of license engendered within the symposium is at the heart of the entertaining and irreverent anecdote that Xenophon offers in the *Cyropaedia*, where the young Cyrus, after describing his father's rowdiness and disorderly dancing after taking wine, claims,

> *ἐπελέλησθε δὲ παντάπασι σύ τε ὅτι βασιλεὺς ἦσθα, οἵ τε ἄλλοι ὅτι σὺ ἄρχων. τότε γὰρ δὴ ἔγωγε καὶ πρῶτον κατέμαθον ὅτι τοῦτ᾽ ἄρ᾽ ἦν ἡ ἰσηγορία ὃ ὑμεῖς τότ᾽ ἐποιεῖτε: οὐδέποτε γοῦν ἐσιωπᾶτε.*
>
> And all of you quite forgot: you, that you were king, and the rest, that you were their sovereign. It was then that I for my part also discovered, and for the first time, that what you were practicing was your "equal freedom of speech"—at any rate, never were any of you silent. (*Cyrop.* 1.3.10)

This equality imposed by the bonds of friendship within the setting of the symposium imparted an enduring quality to the free speech there practiced—one that survived beyond the circumscription of democratic *isonomia* and *parrhêsia* at the public, *polis*-level that the influence of the regal courts brought about in the Hellenistic period.[21]

In an environment somewhat distanced from those open democratic forums where social anxieties were focalized, the symposium could offer a manifestation of *parrhêsia* that was in some ways more absolute than the *parrhêsia* of the *polis*. Drunken sympotic revelry among elites could, in particular, permit an indulgence in the kind of abusive and shameful language that caused both delight and yet anxiety with the *dêmos* at large. (One might note in particular here that the abusive tirade that the speaker of Demosthenes' *Against Conon* pretends to shy away from repeating to his audience of jurors—above, p. 45—is delivered by the drunken participants of a post-symposium processional revel, or *kômos*.) The location of the performance of iambic mockery, with all its attendant transgressions into *aischrologia* and abuse, within the archaic symposium is a clear indication of this frankness of discourse,[22] and the tendency of sympotic discourse to degenerate into outright abuse is clearly isolated by the warning issued by one of Eubulus's comic characters that sensible people go home after the third mixing bowl has been emptied; for those who stay on, the fourth bowl is "for insult" (ὁ δὲ τέταρτος οὐκ ἔτι ἡμέτερός ἐστ' ἀλλ' ὕβρεος: Eubulus F93 KA). With this may be compared the following revealing description from a fourth-century elegiac poem, which situates abusive raillery before more serious entertainment within the symposium:

> χρὴ δ', ὅταν εἰς τοιοῦτο συνέλθωμεν φίλοι ἄνδρες
> πρᾶγμα, γελᾶν παίζειν χρησαμένους ἀρετῇ,
> ἥδεσθαί τε συνόντας, ἐς ἀλλήλους τε φ[λ]υαρεῖν
> καὶ σκώπτειν τοιαῦθ' οἷα γέλωτα φέρειν.
> ἡ δὲ σπουδὴ ἑπέσθω, ἀκούωμέν [τε λ]εγόντων
> ἐν μέρει· ἥδ' ἀρετὴ συμποσίου πέλεται..
>
> And whenever we friends come together for this sort of an affair, we should laugh and sport in accordance with *aretê*, take pleasure as we assemble, and insult and jeer in such as way as to bring laughter. Let seriousness follow after, and let us listen to people speaking in their turn: this is the *aretê* of the symposium. (*Elegiaca Adespota IEG* 27)

Even the Spartan public messes, or *syssitia*, encouraged (within limits) the practice of playful mockery among participants, if Plutarch is to be trusted: so *Lycurgus* 12.6, where it is reported of Spartan boys attending the *syssitia* that "they became accustomed to sport and joke without coarse buffoonery" (αὐτοί τε παίζειν εἰθίζοντο καὶ σκώπτειν ἄνευ βωμολοχίας).[23] Such practices may be discerned at work in our most plentifully attested historical symposia, namely those of the Macedonian courts of Philip II and Alexander III.[24] These famed symposia also encouraged abusive discourse, if we can trust Aeschines' vignette of Alexander the Great as a youngster playing the cithara and attacking another boy through the medium of his song at a symposium.[25] The experienced and high-ranking Macedonian general Cleitus may have looked to such conventions of sympotic *parrhêsia* for license to criticize his king, Alexander, as we are told he did in a fateful drinking party at Maracanda in 328 BCE. In an exchange that culminated in his death at Alexander's hand,[26] Cleitus launched jibes against his king's pretensions to divine filiation (Heracles-like, Alexander had begun to claim Zeus as his father), and against his implicit repudiation of the part played by the Macedonian rank and file in his victories (victories that Alexander was crediting instead to the favor of his divine sire Zeus).

Such *sympotic* indulgence in abusive speech may have been encouraged not only by aristocratic equalities and by the liberating influence of wine,[27] but also by the proximity of the symposium itself to those other cultural contexts—notably comedy, and also those festivals of Demeter and Dionysus in which iambic abuse featured—in which ritual license permitted abusive *parrhêsia*.[28] The similarity between abusive raillery in the symposium and the ritual abuse that accompanied a number of the festivals of Demeter and Dionysus is alluded to in the Homeric hymn dedicated to Hermes, in which Hermes hails a tortoise as "comrade of the feast" (χοροιτύπε, δαιτὸς ἑταίρη: 4.31) and, having fashioned the lyre from its shell, proceeds to engage in scurrilous banter and to sing in mocking fashion of Zeus himself and his adulterous liaison with Hermes' mother, Maia:[29]

ἣ δ' ὑπὸ χειρὸς
σμερδαλέον κονάβησε: θεὸς δ' ὑπὸ καλὸν ἄειδεν
ἐξ αὐτοσχεδίης πειρώμενος, ἠύτε κοῦροι
ἡβηταὶ θαλίῃσι παραιβόλα κερτομέουσιν,
ἀμφὶ Δία Κρονίδην καὶ Μαιάδα καλλιπέδιλον,
ὡς πάρος ὠρίζεσκον ἑταιρείῃ φιλότητι,
ἣν τ' αὐτοῦ γενεὴν ὀνομακλυτὸν ἐξονομάζων.

At the touch of his hand it sounded marvelously; and, as he tried it, the god sang sweet random snatches, even as youths bandy scandalous mockery at festivals. He sang of Zeus the son of Cronos and neat-shod Maia, the converse that they had before in the comradeship of love, telling all the glorious tale of his own begetting.

The abuse indulged in within the symposium is further linked to the abuse performed in that other great Dionysian setting, the dramatic stage, by their joint "artificiality"—that is, by their adherence to certain cultural and generic conventions,[30] and the fact that the speaker does not always speak in propria persona but through an assumed "mask" of literary recitation.[31] Alexander's symposium at Maracanda in 328 BCE saw featured the mockery of a group of Macedonian generals, mockery that Plutarch claims to have been delivered in song: "*πότου δὲ νεανικοῦ συρραγέντος ᾔδετο ποιήματα Πρανίχου τινός, ὡς δέ φασιν ἔνιοι, Πιερίωνος, εἰς τοὺς στρατηγοὺς πεποιημένα τοὺς ἔναγχος ἡττημένους ὑπὸ τῶν βαρβάρων ἐπ' αἰσχύνῃ καὶ γέλωτι*" ("Once the serious drinking was underway, verses by a certain Pranichus [or as some say, Pierion] were sung, which had been composed to insult and mock the generals who had recently been humiliated by the barbarians"; Plut. *Alex.* 50.3). Potentially sensitive criticisms of Alexander himself were also delivered in a sympotic setting through the recitation by fellow symposiasts of carefully selected passages of tragedy. The philosopher Anaxarchus delivered carefully veiled critiques of Alexander's divine aspirations by quoting to him lines from Euripides, and Cleitus himself similarly expressed some of his own anger toward the king through quotation of the Macedonians' favorite tragedian.[32] (Similar sympotic patterns may be discerned in the Roman context: Claudius's son Britannicus, for instance, voiced implicit criticism of his stepbrother Nero at a banquet by performing a song that was readily understood by its audience as alluding to Britannicus's displacement from his paternal inheritance.)[33]

While individuals might react badly to the abusive performances of their fellow symposiasts (Britannicus indeed was poisoned by Nero as a result of his song, and Cleitus slain by Alexander),[34] the use of such devices to distance the speaker from what he has said may normally have encouraged a greater tolerance than permitted to speech delivered in most other key sites for rhetoric in the classical Greek world, such as the law courts, the assembly, and the agora. A tantalizing glimpse of the difference that the social setting of the symposium might make to the perception of abuse is offered by what seems to have been the presentation of the outspokenness of Thersites in the *Aethiopis* (the fragmentary poem of the Epic cycle known now largely from references in Proclus's *Chrestomathia*). Just as in the *Iliad*, Thersites in the *Aethiopis* is again the purveyor of abuse, this time mocking Achilles for his rumored love of Penthesilea,[35] but in the *Aethiopis* Thersites' abusiveness is likely to have been cast within a sympotic context rather than in the open assembly of the

Thersites episode in the *Iliad*.[36] This is a setting in which his attempts to elicit laughter through abuse (as described at *Il.* 2.214–15) would have been much more appropriate;[37] it is notable too that, at least in Quintus Smyrnaeus's later version of his quarrel about Penthesilea (*Posthom.* 1. 774–78), Thersites is given a pedigree (with familial links to Diomedes) that makes his presence among the aristocratic symposium *philoi* less incongruent. Rosen suggests that these differences in Thersites' context and status between the *Iliad* and the *Aethiopis* condition how the listener is meant to respond to the violence that Thersites' outspoken mockery elicits; when Achilles kills Thersites in the *Aethiopis*, there does seem to be some ambivalence about Achilles' response, and he is made to atone ritually for his slaying of his detractor. Against the conventions of sympotic *parrhêsia*, the violence that met the abusiveness of Thersites and of Cleitus was thus disturbing.[38]

Sympotic abusiveness did, however, have its dangers. While the conventions of sympotic blame poetry seem to have encouraged the direction of abuse at fellow *hetairoi* rather than at targets outside the sympotic group,[39] there existed a potential for abusive speech to act as a stimulus to political antagonism—a potential made all the more potent by the very nature of the symposium, which, with its closely knit cohorts and its iambic discourse, had an inherent potential to act as a site for remembering factional discord, for forging partisan allegiances, and thus for breeding civic strife.[40] This potential for stasis is recognized within some sympotic literature, where the concern is so great that it prompts urgings of sympotic self-censorship. Xenophanes sets forth (in what are admittedly difficult and disputed lines of his best-preserved elegy) an idealized template for behavior, in which he delineates the appropriate limitations of sympotic discussion (1.19ff.):

> *ἀνδρῶν δ' αἰνεῖν τοῦτον ὃς ἐσθλὰ πιὼν ἀναφαίνει,*
> *ὡς ἧι μνημοσύνη καὶ τόνος ἀμφ' ἀρετῆς,*
> *οὔ τι μάχας διέπων Τιτήνων οὐδὲ Γιγάντων*
> *οὐδέ <τι> Κενταύρων, πλάσμα<τα> τῶν προτέρων,*
> *ἢ στάσιας σφεδανάς (τοῖς οὐδὲν χρηστὸν ἔνεστιν).*

Praise the man who, when he has taken drink, brings noble deeds to light, as memory and a striving for virtue bring to him, while avoiding to deal with the battles of Titans or Giants or Centaurs, fictions of our forebears, or furious conflicts, for there is no use in these.[41]

Similar regulation is encouraged by Anacreon, who states that he does not respect the man who, in the symposium, "talks of civil strife and tearful war" (νείκεα καὶ πόλεμον δακρυόεντα λέγει: Anacreon *IEG* 2.1–2). The very fact that Xenophanes and Anacreon feel the need to warn against stasis as a topic for discussion at the symposium should alert us to the possibility that it was felt to be particularly widespread (and for some confirmatory evidence we can, of course, think of Alcaeus's surviving *stasiotika*, his polemics against the tyrant Pittacus).[42] Such counsel of self-censorship from Anacreon and Xenophanes may have a more serious motivation than the social snobbery that underscores the parody of sympotic conversational guidelines delivered by Aristophanes' young Bdelycleon to Philocleon in the *Wasps*, where the son urges his father to avoid the kind of vulgarly humorous mythological topics that the old man himself favors (and in which a flatulent Lamia figures prominently). It is not merely fabulous mythology that Xenophanes isolates: rather, the mythical topics he prohibits—Centauromachies, Gigantomachies—are those that deal with stasis.

The declarations by Xenophanes, Anacreon, and Bdelycleon are themselves informed by the generic interplay of praise and blame within the sympotic space; in this dichotomy, strife seems to function as one of the variables able to act as an equivalent to blame, as the counterpoint to praise.[43] Given their literary contexts, the above passages thus should not be taken as straightforward expressions of real concern for political upheaval fueled by abuse uttered within the confines of the symposium. The cautions expressed in them nonetheless highlight the possibility that abusive discourse in the symposium might be perceived to have an inflammatory political effect, and this is something that needs to be taken into account when we return to our consideration of the Athenians' legislation against the saying and singing of "bad things" about the tyrannicides.

A Clash of Frankness: Symposium and *Polis*

The discussion above has explored some differences in the realities of the *parrhêsia* claimed by the *dêmos* within democratic Athens and that of the aristocratic symposium. In broad terms, the vulgarity and abuse that might occasion social anxiety within the *dêmos* were a central feature of the *parrhêsia* of the symposium.[44] The expression of such abuse within the symposium could, in turn, raise the specter of stasis within the *polis*. The underlying tensions that result between the *parrhêsia* of democratic Athens and of sympotic groups do find expression in a number of contexts. For example, the distinction between sympotic license and the norms regulating speech in the democracy is at the heart of a very interesting fragment from Critias preserved by Aelian (88 B44 DK). Critias implicitly draws attention to the contravention of censorship provisions in the sympotic poetry of that most archetypal of "blame" poets, Archilochus.[45] By deploying the standard identification of the poet himself with the poetic first person, Critias criticizes Archilochus for revealing in his own poetry that he (Archilochus) was born of a slave mother, that he was driven by poverty from Paros to Thasos and that on Thasos he fell foul of the inhabitants, that he was an adulterer, and (to crown it all) that he threw away his shield.[46] Critias here draws attention to Archilochus's explicit statements, within the sympotic performance of his verses, of personal details that would have rendered his very citizenship illegitimate in Athenian society; the last of Archilochus's stated offenses, that of throwing away his shield (based on the infamous Archilochus 5W), would render Archilochus under Athenian law either *atimos* and debarred from speaking before the assembly,[47] or (if his allegation against himself is admitted to be false, a mere literary fiction) guilty under Athens's own law against slander, which is known to have made actionable accusations that one had thrown away one's shield (so Lys. 10.9). Critias's implicit application of the *dêmos'* norms of public discourse to Archilochus's sympotic *parrhêsia* serves to emphasize the dissonance between these two speech contexts. The interplay of contexts may be amplified if Critias's denunciation of Archilochus itself took the form of sympotic poetry (a plausible but unprovable hypothesis, given that it survives only in Aelian's paraphrase).[48]

It is probable, moreover, that Critias's attack on Archilochus should be understood in a highly politicized light. Critias himself was, of course, an arch-oligarch, who met his death as one of the Thirty Tyrants who had ruled briefly with Spartan backing in 404. His antidemocratic agenda is well known, and (as we shall see again presently) oligarchic tendencies have been identified in his writings for and about the symposium.[49] A suspicion of an antidemocratic subtext extends to his lines about Archilochus, a poet who had been adopted as something of an icon in democratic circles;[50] in pointing to Archilochus's supposed unfitness for democratic society and/or his flouting of the *dêmos'* restraints on speech, Critias pokes fun at the *dêmos'* hero, at the *dêmos* itself, and at its norms.

The coexistence of competing notions of *parrhêsia* is also thrown into high relief in a historical anecdote. Diodorus (16.87) reports a clash between one of Athens's own notoriously frank democratic politicians, the orator Demades, and Philip II of Macedon.[51] In the wake of his momentous victory over the Greek allies at Chaeronea, Philip celebrated with a wine-fueled symposium and *kômos*, during which he heaped derision and abuse on his hapless prisoners of war. Demades stopped Philip short with his response. "O King," he asked, "when Fortune has cast you in the role of Agamemnon, are you not ashamed to act the part of Thersites?" Whether apocryphal or not,[52] the exchange operates around contrasting conceptualizations of *parrhêsia*. Demades functions as its democratic embodiment. His frankness allows him to speak out, even as a prisoner and thus a man with no rights, as an Athenian citizen against a king at his height of victory; importantly, his *parrhêsia* secures benefits for Athens, for Philip responds to Demades' challenge by restoring not only his freedom but also that of the other Athenian prisoners. Philip himself exhibits *parrhêsia*, but his is the lack of restraint that enjoins inappropriate abusiveness, and which serves to demean the speaker himself. Hence Demades' appeal to the old Homeric distinctions of rank; it is the lowness of Philip's speech that renders him, although a king, a Thersites-like object of shame. Philip's frankness is, moreover, a frankness engendered by a sympotic setting. His jeering at the unfortunate prisoners is set firmly in the context of drunkenness and *kômos*; the nature of his jibes, reported elsewhere, adheres to the iambic witticism expected of the drinking party;[53] the immediate and sobering effect of Demades' jibe is to cause Philip to discard his garland, the token of the symposium.

Sympotic Speech and Political Contexts

The potential for tension noted above between the speech of the symposium and the wider *polis* will have been constant, and exacerbated further by the inherent tensions in the relationship between the democracy and the symposium more broadly. The complexities of the dynamics between the Athenian *polis* and the symposium cannot be denied. The sympotic space could be at times a metaphor for the city itself (as it is for Solon *IEG* 4. 9–10, where civil strife is equated with discord within the drinking group), and its practices emulated in the daily *syssitia* of the state magistrates in the heart of the democratic agora and perhaps even adapted for the cultivation of a "democratic identity" within some sympotic circles.[54] Despite these factors, however, the aristocratic origins of the symposium, the "political training ground" for the young "gentleman" or *kaloskagathos*,[55] made it a site particularly prey to democratic suspicion, and its luxuries a target for democratic criticism.[56] Witness in particular the centering of suspicions around sympotic groups in the oligarchic uprisings of late fifth-century Athens.[57]

While firm evidence is regrettably lacking, it may nonetheless be possible to posit temporal connections between the indicators of Athens's interest in regulating sympotic speech and periods of heightened political anxiety. The two exemplars of the tensions noted above, from Critias and Diodorus, certainly belong to periods of very real apprehension about the stability of Athenian democracy: thus the oligarchic revolutions of the late fifth century, and the period of Philip II's ascendancy in which the imposition of an oligarchy was deemed a real threat. In the former context, we can certainly trace further the performance in sympotic speech of antidemocratic material, material conducive indeed to stasis and material that will have given the *polis* sound basis for concern. Critias again is vital here. The sympotic poetry of this tyrant is at times patently engaged with the politics of his day, albeit in ways impossible to discern with clarity. In DK 88 B5 he purports to remind Alcibiades of his instrumental role in the latter's recall from exile, and he does so in a piece that has been interpreted as "nothing less than a call to coup d'état."

> *γνώμη δ' ἥ σε κατήγαγ', ἐγὼ ταύτην ἐν ἅπασιν*
> *εἶπον καὶ γράψας τοὖργον ἔδρασα τόδε.*
> *σφραγὶς δ' ἡμετέρης γλώττης ἐπὶ τοῖσδεσι κεῖται.*

> As for the proposal that brought you home, I was the one who
> spoke for it among all the people, and by my motion I accom-
> plished this deed. The seal of my tongue is set on these words.

Alcibiades is again the focus of Critias's attention in verses that combine, in revolutionary fashion, the meters of elegy and iambics. So 88 B4 DK:

> *καὶ νῦν Κλεινίου υἱὸν Ἀθηναῖον στεφανώσω*
> *Ἀλκιβιάδην νέοισιν ὑμνήσας τρόποις·*
> *οὐ γάρ πως ἦν τοὔνομ' ἐφαρμόζειν ἐλεγείωι·*
> *νῦν δ' ἐν ἰαμβείωι κείσεται οὐκ ἀμέτρως.*

> And now I shall crown the Athenian son of Cleinias,
> Alcibiades, with a song in a new manner.

For it was not possible in any way to fit the name into elegy;
but now it will lie, not without measure, in an iambic line.

It has been argued that Critias's purpose in these fragments is to recall Alcibiades to the allegiances proper to a man of his wealth and breeding—that is, to a renunciation of his collaboration with the *dêmos* and the assumption of a more fitting commitment to his aristocratic *philoi*. For a man like Critias, for whom poetic meter functions as simile for politics (witness in particular the existence of his work titled Πολιτείας ἐμμέτρους—*Well-Balanced Constitutions* or *Constitutions in Meter*), the demagogic Alcibiades cannot "fit" into the elegiac meter of the aristocratic symposium; it is the iambic trimeter, arguably more demotic because of its association both with Solon's verse and with the theatrical stage, that Alcibiades "fits." By juxtaposing the meters, Critias creates something new to accommodate him, but the intent may not be to promote a "reconciliation" or "fusion" but perhaps to highlight the tension. Dragging Alcibiades' name forcibly into the world of sympotic poetry, Critias appeals to a man who ought be a sympotic *philos* to show "more of the 'measure' suited to his kind."[58] The subtext is not that different from Critias's take on Archilochus, the poet who must be lampooned for betraying his aristocratic origins to become an icon of the *dêmos*.

History demonstrates, of course, that Critias's politics were no mere literary conceit played out in the confines of the symposium. The oligarchic tendencies of his sympotic utterances (assuming, as is likely, that the lines cited above were designed for such performance)[59] were matched by actual revolutionary behavior. It is worth noting the possibility that Critias also matched his sympotic poetry with the expression of antidemocratic views in literature of potentially wider audience, particularly if the *Constitution of Athens* that circulates variously under the names of Xenophon and "the Old Oligarch" is indeed attributable to Critias, as some would maintain.[60] This wider context may be important, for within it the expression of politically inflammatory ideas within the world of the *hetaireiai* will less easily have been dismissed as simply private discourse, or regarded as less threatening because contained within the culturally transgressive space of the symposium and framed within the literary conventions of sympotic expression.

The law with which our discussion began, namely the prohibition against saying and singing bad things about the tyrannicides, may itself be located in close proximity to this Critias material in the aftermath of the oligarchic revolutions of the late fifth century, when sympotic groups had indeed been perceived to be at the heart of antidemocratic behavior and when the restored democracy was particularly sensitive about potential attacks upon the pair.[61] The tyrannicides were, after all, figureheads of Athenian democratic identity, with their act idealized in popular Athenian ideology as the foundational act of democracy itself; in the late fifth century, their importance was being affirmed in legislation that looked to the very refoundation and protection of democracy itself.[62] Denigration of this pair thus had the potential to be perceived as an expression of oligarchic sympathies, and as an implicit rejection of the democratic regime.

I have suggested elsewhere that the law prohibiting their abuse may be seen as a response to the kind of view of the tyrannicides that we find reflected in Thucydides (and to a lesser extent also in Herodotus)—tyrannicides whose actions sprang not from repudiation of tyranny as much as from the *eros* of aristocratic and homoerotic passion, and whose act of "tyrannicide" produced not the birth of democracy but a period of stasis ended only by the armed intervention of Sparta; a kind of image of which there are traces too in sympotic material.[63] (Some elements of the representation of the tyrannicides as aristocratic symposiasts rather than politically motivated democratic heroes need not have been a challenge to their democratic identity,[64] but others may well: politically provocative in its iconographic undertones, for example, is a *skyphos* on which the Athenian tyrannicides are depicted in a pose derived from a distinctly *un*democratic tyrant-slayer, Orestes—one whose Laconic heritage may well have evoked very uncomfortable recollections of the part played by Spartan troops in the real ouster of Athens's tyrants.[65]) The contested image of Harmodius and Aristogeiton could thus act as an implicit political challenge to democratic identity, an evocation of and indeed enticement to the kind of stasis that their murder of Hipparchus had actually unleashed; hence the potential sensitivity about representations of these figures in this period.

The concern for controlling the image of tyrannicides need not, however, be confined to a single period. As noted above, the only explicit attestation of the law censoring the symposium comes in fact from a speech (*Against Philippides*) in the corpus of Hyperides. This too coincides with a time of intense political instability, and a period in which the politics of sympotic behavior seems to have come under particular scrutiny. The speech itself belongs somewhere in the tense years of 338 to 336 BCE,[66] when tyranny at Athens was again perceived in some quarters as a real prospect; this threat was particularly palpable after the defeat of the Greek forces at Chaeronea, when the proximity of the Macedonian army combined with the existence of pockets of sympathizers within Athens elevated the possibility of Macedonian intervention in Athenian domestic affairs.[67]

The prosecution of Philippides, the target of Hyperides' speech, is part of the democratic backlash against the threat of revolution. Philippides himself was facing an indictment for illegal proposals, the proposal in question being his move to honor a board of *proedroi*, but this formal charge is not the central concern of Hyperides' speech. The prosecution was clearly political, and Philippides is cast as a Macedonian sympathizer and implicated in antidemocratic machinations. (Such suspicions were well founded, if Philippides' later activity is anything to go by: he was honored [*IG* II^2 649] for his long political career in 292 BCE, a year in which the city was in the thrall of an oligarchy backed by the Macedonian Demetrius Poliorcetes.) At issue is thus not so much any technical infringement by Philippides in honoring the *proedroi*; the case was rather a challenge to some of the honorific decrees earlier put to the vote by those presiding officers themselves in their terms of office—honors perhaps directly for Philip of Macedon himself, but just as possibly for Philip's Macedonian subordinates or Athenian contacts.

Part of Hyperides' interest in the speech, then, is to distinguish between fitting honorands and those who have been improperly honored; to contrast the heroes of the Athenian democracy, men properly recognized by the *polis*, with those stooges of Macedon whose receipt of honors devalues the honors themselves. It is this that encourages Hyperides' interest in the tyrannicides,[68] a pair more extensively celebrated than any others by the Athenian state; so too does the fact that Philippides' *synêgoros*, Democrates of Aphidna, was both a descendent of the valiant tyrannicides and himself one of the suspected Macedonian sympathizers—a contradictory combination that Hyperides could use to good effect in his character assassination of Philippides' supporters. It is thus that Hyperides is prompted to mention the censorship law, in a passage directed against Democrates (whom Hyperides has just described as daily denigrating the *dêmos* in the agora):

> καίτοι ὦ Δημ[όκρα]τες μόνωι σοὶ οὐκ [ἔνι λέγ]ειν περὶ τοῦ δήμου φλα]ῦρον οὐδέν. διὰ τί; [ὅτι πρ]ῶτον μὲν οὐ παρ' ἑτέρου σ' ἔδει μαθεῖν, ὅτι ὁ δῆμος χάριτας ἀποδίδωσιν τοῖς εὐεργέταις, ἀλλὰ παρὰ σαυτοῦ· α[ὐ]τὸς γὰρ ὑπὲρ ὧν ἕτερο[ι] εὐεργέτησαν νῦν τὰς [τ]ιμὰς κομίζει. ἔπε[ι]θ' ὅτι ἐν νόμωι γράψας [ὁ] δῆμος ἀπεῖπεν μήτε [λ]έγειν ἐξεῖναι [μ̣ηδενὶ] κακῶς Ἁρμόδιον καὶ Ἀρ[ιστογείτονα μήτ' ᾆ̣σα[ι ἐπὶ τὰ

> *κακίονα. ἦ κ[αὶ δεινόν ἐστιν, [ε]ἰ το[ὺ]ς μὲν σοὺς προγόνους ὁ] δῆμος οὐδὲ μεθυσθέντ]ι ᾤετο δεῖν ἐξεῖναι κακ]ῶς εἰπεῖν, σὺ δὲ νήφω[ν τ]ὸν δῆμον κακ[ῶς] λέγεις.*
>
> Yet you, Democrates, are the one man who has no right to say anything disparaging about the people. And why? First, because nobody needed to tell you that "the people repay benefactors in kind" when you are now reaping the rewards for services that others have rendered.[69] And second, because the people wrote a prohibition in a law, forbidding anyone either to slander Harmodius and Aristogeiton in a law or to sing rude songs about them. So if the people saw fit to make it impossible even for a drunkard to slander your ancestors, how terrible that you defame the people sober! (*Against Philippides* 2–3)

In framing this attack on Democrates, Hyperides imputes to Democrates the importation of language appropriate to the symposium into the sober and public world of the agora. The jury has just been told that he "makes jokes (*γελωτοποιεῖ*) about the misfortunes of the *polis*" and "reviles you (*λοιδορεῖθ' ὑμῖν*) in the agora" (2.2), and the allusion to Democrates' entitlement to *sitêsis* reinforces the sympotic overtones of Hyperides' language here. This is a device he deploys later in the speech against Philippides himself, who is asked if he thinks he can avoid courtroom justice in his usual method, "by capering and joking" (*κορδακίζων καὶ γελωτοποιῶν*: 2.7). A comic dance glossed repeatedly by the lexicographers as "shameful," the *kordax* was associated too with drunken sympotic foolery.[70]

The kinds of sympotic misbehavior with which Hyperides castigates both Democrates and Philippides is once again politically charged. It is, however, not now simply the case of suspicions of the aristocratic and oligarchic leanings of elite symposiasts, but a more particular strategy of tainting the accused and his *synêgoros* with Macedonian behavior. Philip of Macedon himself was consistently reviled in Athenian forensic and political oratory for his attachment to the symposium, and more especially for what was perceived to be a characteristically Macedonian lack of restraint in that arena. In his second *Olynthiac* Demosthenes had this to say about Philip: "*εἰ δέ τις σώφρων ἢ δίκαιος ἄλλως, τὴν καθ' ἡμέραν ἀκρασίαν τοῦ βίου καὶ μέθην καὶ κορδακισμοὺς οὐ δυνάμενος φέρειν, παρεῶσθαι καὶ ἐν οὐδενὸς εἶναι μέρει τὸν τοιοῦτον*" ("Any fairly decent or honest man, who cannot stomach the licentiousness of [Philip's] daily life, the drinking and the lewd dancing, is pushed aside as of no account": Dem. 2.18). We find very similar accusations leveled elsewhere, both at Philip and at those in Athens suspected of supporting his cause.[71] This nexus in our Athenian orators between pro-Macedonian (and thus antidemocratic) tendencies and sympotic behavior may well conceal a kernel of truth. Philip is known to have cultivated correspondence with one particular Athenian dining club who dubbed themselves "the Sixty" and frequented the sanctuary of Heracles at Cynosarges. The anecdotal tradition bases the connection on a shared fondness for jokes: Philip, himself ever the *gelôtopoios*, wrote to the Athenian group requesting a collection of their witticisms. Jocularity itself could have a subversive undercurrent (one might recall that Homer's Thersites sought to stir up strife [*eris*] against the kings at Troy [*ἐριζέμεναι βασιλεῦσιν*] using whatever he thought would make the Achaeans laugh [*Il.* 2.214–15]),[72] and there are reasons to suspect that the contact may have been more insidious and political. The curious tradition reported only by Clement of Alexandria that at Athens "they passed a law to perform *proskynêsis* at Cynosarges to the Macedonian Philip" (*Protrepticus* 4.54.5–6) could conceivably stem from a perceived political connection between the Sixty and Philip, and some of the Sixty—notable among them the arch antidemocrat Callimedon—would indeed later rise to prominence under the oligarchy imposed on Athens by the Macedonian Antipater in 322 BCE. In the political climate post-Chaeronea, then, the Athenians' renewed interest in the censorship of dangerous speech within the symposium was entirely apposite.

Censoring the Symposium: Some Concluding Observations

We have seen that while *parrhêsia* was quintessentially a feature of Athenian democracy and had its origins as a political concept in the self-defining of the Athenian *dêmos*, the symposium had long practiced a form of *parrhêsia*, and had even come to attract the label to itself. We have seen too, however, that there were inherent tensions between the freedoms of symposium speech and that of the Athenian *dêmos*. Engendered by the social exclusivity of the setting and by the adoption of poetic personae, the frankness of the symposium was a freedom to say anything and to use any type of language, even language deemed shameful. The freedom exalted in the symposium was thus the very type of freedom that occasioned anxiety at the *polis* level, where there were apprehensions that the *dêmos*' *parrhêsia* might manifest as the deployment of the kind of frankness that marked out the speaker as of low status. It was moreover as this very sympotic version of freedom—the licensing of *any* speech—that the *dêmos*' elitist detractors could choose to misrepresent democratic *parrhêsia* (so for example Isoc. 7.20); the latter more properly constituted the freedom fearlessly to speak "the truth without reprisal,"[73] particularly when that truth pertained to the welfare of the city. Sympotic freedom of speech and democratic *parrhêsia* were thus at odds with each other, and yet intertwined. It is perhaps not mere coincidence, then, that the suggested context of the introduction of the law against "saying and singing bad things about the tyrannicides" follows closely upon the emergence, in the 420s, of *parrhêsia* as a slogan of the democracy itself.[74]

In reacting against the denigration of Harmodius and Aristogeiton, the *polis* was responding to a concern, felt also within sympotic circles themselves, for the potential for the symposium's form of free speech to generate conflict and stasis. It is yet another mark of the Athenians' tolerance even for socially disruptive speech (and of their reluctance to resort to legal redress for matters of speech)[75] that so little attempt to regulate sympotic license is attested, and this despite the residual democratic misgivings about the political tendencies of some sympotic groups. Only during the turbulent period leading up to the oligarchies of the late fifth century, and again in the context of the threat to Athenian democratic sovereignty posed by Philip of Macedon, do we seem to find traces of a concern for censorship—whether through the moving of the law curtailing antityrannicide speech and song, or as the context for the recollection of that law.

If these historical contexts have been correctly identified, then these findings cohere neatly with the picture that tends to emerge of Athenian censorship in general, and of comedy in particular. In an extensive analysis of the Athenian slander law, with its prohibition on false accusations of parricide and shield throwing, Wallace has concluded that the framing of those restrictions seems to reflect a concern with protecting the political interests of the city itself.[76] The political interests of the city are similarly fundamental to the rare instances when the Athenians seem to have had some concern with regulating those cultural sites that usually enjoyed a great degree of *parrhêsia*. Thus, although some late traditions make claims for laws curtailing freedom of speech on the Athenian comic stage, it seems that in reality restrictions were only very rarely applied. Indeed the stage may arguably have been exempt from the laws that operated against slander in other forums, given that (for example) the prohibitions against speaking ill of the dead or of alleging the casting away of one's shield are violated in extant comedy.[77] There is only a single credibly attested law regulating comic speech as such, and that decree—the scope of which (*περὶ τοὺ μὴ κωμωιδεῖν*) is very vague—is stated to have been passed in 440/39, only to be repealed in 437/36: so *schol* Ar. *Ach.* 67.[78] The dates are significant, coinciding as they do with the near-disastrous Samian War—a war that comic poets were keen to credit to Pericles' liaison with the Milesian Aspasia, and a war that threatened not only the very substance of Athens's naval empire but also, by extension, the survival of the radical democracy itself. Acute political threat triggers censorship of a license that Athenians were, in less threatening circumstances, willing to tolerate. The pattern in the symposium is not much different. That setting perhaps similarly enjoyed some measure of tacit license through its Dionysian associations, its speech set apart (to borrow from Halliwell's description of stage license) by its "perceived enclosure within a frame of recognizably comic or quasi-comic conduct."[79] That license will have been further encouraged by the private nature of the symposium (at least until it spilled into the streets in rowdy *kômos*), for the freedom to live as one pleased was itself among the principles lauded by the democracy. Thus the *parrhêsia* of the symposium would normally be tolerated to a degree that surpassed that of more public discourse—until a crisis threatened the very fabric of Athenian democracy.

NOTES

1. For *isêgoria* see [Xen.] *Ath. Pol.* 1.2: "Any of the Athenians who wants to can speak." For a quantitative assessment of this *isêgoria* (in terms of the numbers who did speak before the assembly), see Hansen (1984).

2. Cited above, pp. 61–62. Compare Dem. 7.1; 9.3. The Athenians even named one of their state galleys *Parrhêsia*: see *IG* II^2 1624.81.

3. Compare Aesch. 3.6; Din. 2.1; more negatively, Isoc. 7.20. On democracy and free speech, Raaflaub (1980) cf. (2004b) 223–25 and now Saxonhouse (2006) esp. 85–99, are fundamental. See also Raaflaub (2004a), who argues cogently that *parrhêsia* was a concept formulated by the democracy; that is to say, unlike *isonomia* and *isêgoria* (on which, Raaflaub [2004a] 45; [2004b] 94–96), it did not have its roots in aristocratic values.

4. On the law against speaking ill of the dead, see Dem. 20.104; [Dem.] 40.49; Plut. *Sol.* 21.2; *schol.* Ar. *Pax* 648–52; Ael. Arist, *Or.* 3.502; *Lex Cantab.* s.v. *κακηγορίας δίκη*; *Suda* s.v. *ἀποιχόμενα*. On speaking ill of magistrates, see Lys. 9.6, 16; Dem. 21.32–33. On Athenian law restricting speech, see Wallace (1994)

5. On the traditions alleging restrictions of comic speech, Sommerstein (1986); Halliwell (1991a); Wallace (2005).

6. For Hyperides' authorship of the *Against Philippides*, see Whitehead (2000) 27–28.

7. Thus already Halliwell (1991a) 49.

8. Ath. 15.695a-b; Ar. *Vesp.* 1225ff.; van der Valk (1974) 8–9.

9. Thus Halliwell (2004), who differentiates (at 115–16) between legally imposed restrictions on speech and "unwritten law," with the latter encouraging reticence in the indulgence in shameful speech; compare also Halliwell (2008) 219–37. Self-imposed reticence was even more pronounced in the deliberative arena than the forensic one, as Plutarch (*Prae. ger. reip.* 810c–d) observes. See also Konstan (2012) on *parrhêsia* as a freedom to express unpopular opinion without fear of repression, a freedom that carried with it a concomitant risk of speaking shamelessly.

10. Needless to say, of course, the speaker nonetheless goes on gleefully to report the details, but the potential shame that might accrue to him has been deflected by his feigned reticence. Cf. also Dem. 2.19; 6.31–32; 21.79; 18.103; Aesch. 1.55.

11. As has long been noted, there are potential ambiguities in Thersites' status; see Blok (1995) 202n16 for earlier scholarship, and more recently Marks (2005). Marks contends indeed that Thersites is one of the *basileis*, and that the Homeric description of his physical deformity and his abusive behavior is a manifestation of the lowly persona adopted by some aristocratic poets (particularly within the abusive iambic genre). It is true that in other strands of the tradition, Thersites does indeed hold a place among the *basileis* (see p. 51), and that the traditions that informed the epics may thus have had a place for an aristocratic, iambic Thersites. Even if the Thersites of the traditions was a "blame poet" figure, however, the framing of the episode in the *Iliad* problematizes an elite reading of him in that work. The "lowly" personae of an Archilochus and a Hipponax are artifices articulated by the poets themselves as an ironic stance; Thersites' baseness, by contrast, is constructed in the third person by the narrator (cf. Rosen [2007] 74). As such it is qualitatively different from the pose of the iambic poets, and different too from Odysseus's assumption of the *guise* of a beggar in *Od.* 13.430ff. (a passage to which Marks appeals for comparison). Furthermore, elite poets assumed their lowly personae and delivered their abuse within ritual contexts, or within symposia where rivalries were mediated and judged by social peers. (On iambic performance, see now Rotstein [2010]; note also Collins [2004] 66, emphasizing the importance of social exclusivity for the combative and abusive aspects of symposium performance.) Thersites performs instead before the army. Removed in the *Iliad* from the socially or ritually sanctioned performance space of poet, Thersites' lowly stature becomes something fundamentally different: the persona of lowliness is transformed into reality. The Iliadic narrative in fact signals a hierarchical distinction between Thersites and the *basileis* through the beating that the former receives, for while Odysseus sways the *basileis* with soft words (*Il.* 2.189), to the men of the people (*Il.* 2.198) he delivers reproofs and blows. In sum, while the possibility of an elite aspect (or origin) of Thersites arguably still lurks in the *Iliad* episode, the explicitly low rank ascribed to him at Pl. *Gorgias* 525e and the evocation of him in later treatments of lower-status figures such as Cleon (see p. 46) demonstrate that some ancient audiences—and crucially for present purposes, some

classical Athenian audiences—perceived a clear social distinction between Thersites and the *basileis.*

12. So *Il.* 2.212–14, 246. Thersites' failure to adhere to the literary conventions of blame poetry—that is, to conventions that may have made his audience more receptive to his criticisms—is touched upon by Kouklanakis (1999) 40.

13. Proclus *In Platonis Rem Publicam Commentarii* 2.319 (Kroll); Eustathius *Commentarii ad Homeri Iliadem Pertinentes* 1.314 (van der Valk) = 206.10–11; Quint. *Inst. Or.* 11.2.37.

14. The emphasis on Thersites' physical and moral baseness at *Il.* 2.216–19 and the unanimous pleasure that the Achaeans derive from his chastisement at *Il.* 2.270–77 guide the response of the audience.

15. Saxonhouse (2006) 3.

16. Demosthenes claims (9.3) that Athenian *parrhêsia* was so complete that it extended even beyond the ranks of citizens, that is, to slaves and *xenoi*; so similarly (of course with more hostile intent) [Xen.] *Ath. Pol.* 10–12 on *isêgoria.*

17. Carter (2004) 206; Saxonhouse (2006) 88–89.

18. For verbal echoes between Pericles and Cleon, compare Thuc. 2.61.1 and 3.38.1, also 2.63.2 and 3.37.2; for characterization of Cleon's speech as slanderous, see Thuc. 5.16.1. Similarities between Homer's Thersites and Thucydides' Cleon are discussed by Cairns (1982).

19. On the elitist view of poverty and shamefulness more broadly, note the Old Oligarch's contention: "among the best people there is minimal wantonness and injustice but a maximum of scrupulous care for what is good, whereas among the people there is a maximum of disorder and wickedness; for poverty draws them rather to disgraceful actions, and because of a lack of money some men are uneducated and ignorant" (*Ath. Pol.* 1.5).

20. The fragment is frustratingly devoid of context. Jacoby suggested assigning it to book 2 of the *Atthis*, with other material on Dionysus (cf. FF6–7 and FF170–73), but this is purely speculative; cf. Harding (2007) 210.

21. Konstan et al. (1998) 3–4 define Hellenistic *parrhêsia* (of the sort featured in Philodemus's *On Frank Criticism*) as a private virtue exercised among *philoi* rather than a political right of a democratic city. Such Hellenistic *parrhêsia* distinguished the *philoi* of a potentate from his flatterers, or again might be used by a teacher to improve his students within an intellectual milieu. The relevance of the sympotic space both to the interactions of a royal court and to the intellectual circle is obvious.

22. For the symposium as a site for the performance of iambic abuse, see Bowie (2002) 38; Rotstein (2010).

23. On Sparta, see Halliwell (1991b) 291–92; (2008) 44–50.

24. For comparison of the culture of Macedonian symposia with those of the Greek *poleis*, see Carney (2007).

25. Aesch. 1.168. The interest of the Macedonian court in the sympotic performance of praise and blame is evident too at Plut. *Alex.* 53, in which the court historian

Callisthenes is encouraged to deliver a set of speeches, one praising and the other denigrating the Macedonians.

26. Plut. *Alex.* 50–52.4; Arr. 4.8.1–9.9; Curt. 8.1.19–2.13; Justin 12.6.1–18. For discussion of the political background to the episode, see Carney (1981).

27. Rösler (1995) 106–9 on the cultural association of wine and truth, which is given its most detailed exposition at Pl. *Leg.* 649a–650b. It is notable that Athenaeus, to whom we owe the Philochorus fragment cited above (p. 47), quotes the Philochoran material in conjunction with Alcaeus's famous tag "wine and truth" (*οἶνος καὶ ἀλήθεια*).

28. For comic license, see Halliwell (2004). On the resonances between iambic poetry, with its pronounced vituperative element, and comedy, see Arist. *Poet.* 1448b24–1449a5; cf. West (1974) 33–39; Rosen (1988) (challenged by Bowie [2002], but see further Rosen [2013]); Rotstein (2010). The broader relationship perceived between the post-symposium *kômos* and the origins of comedy (a potential relationship hinted at by the association of the term comedy with the verb *kômazein* (revel) in Arist. *Poet.* 1448a20) is beyond the scope of this discussion; Rothwell (2007) 8–15 canvasses briefly some of the fundamental issues. (The revels intended by Aristotle are not, of course, narrowly sympotic: for nuanced discussion of Aristotle's notorious identification of comedy with phallic rites in particular, see Csapo [2013].)

29. Scurrilous insults were a standard component of the Dionysiac and Eleusinian processions (with the latter known as the *gephurismos*), such that the phrases "to parade" (*πομπεύειν*) and "from the carts" (*ἐξ ἁμάξης*—a reference to the carts in which people stood, hurling abuse) became metaphors for slander: Dem. 18.11, 122, 124 with Harpocration s.v. *πομπείας καὶ πομπεύειν*; Photius s.v. *τὰ ἐκ τῶν ἁμαξῶν*; Suda s.v. *ἐξ ἁμάξης*; *schol.* Ar. *Equ.* 546–48. Verbal license played a part in other festivals too, such as the Thesmophoria and Haloa. For a comprehensive survey of evidence for rituals in which ridicule and obscenity (whether visual or verbal) played a part, see now Halliwell (2008) 160–91.

30. Abuse forms part of a broader cultural "dialogue" played out between two reciprocal genres of poetry, which both claimed a space within the symposium: the poetries of blame and of praise. Nagy (1979) 222–25 identifies as poetic convention the antithesis between these two discourses. Compare Pind. *Nem.* 7. 61–63; *Pyth.* 2.52–53.

31. Suggested already for the transgressive license of comedy by Halliwell (1991a) 53. While less obvious than in comedy, an analogous assumption of "character" may be discerned in sympotic discourse and poetry. Worman (2008) 8 suggests as much: "Perhaps because of the tensions that developed around class status in the democratic city-state, the iambic speaker may occupy a complex position in relation to his audience and his own usage. The patent imposture of low-class figures isolates crude talk as derisive quotation, but at the same time it signals to elite listeners the wit and wisdom of the (male) ventriloquist." One could consider here the extent to which the "I" of Archilochus's blame poetry and likewise his target, Lykambes, are constructs through which the speaker plays out a role traditional to the dictates of the poetic genre; Archilochus's claim that his mother was a slave woman called Enipo ("Blame") certainly suggests as much. See further Nagy (1979) 247–48.

32. For Anaxarchus's use of literary quotation to deliver rebukes, see Diod. Laert. 6.90; Plut. *Quaest. Conv.* 737a, Philod. *De vitiis* (*P.Herc* 1675 col.iii 32ff.). Anaxarchus's meaning is analyzed by Bosworth (1996) 142, who shows that the negative connotations of the quotation are realized only if the original context of the line cited from the *Orestes* (l. 271) is remembered. For Cleitus, see Plut. *Alex.* 51.8, with Instinsky (1961) 250–52.

33. Tac. *Ann.* 13.15.3. For an ingenious identification of the song performed by Britannicus as Ennius's *Andromacha*, see Glucker (1978).

34. Collins (2004) 63–83 (see esp. 79–83 on the Cleitus episode) explores the possibility that such violence stems from a recognition that the abuse has hit too close to home for the comfort of the target of the abuse.

35. Thersites' bad relationship with Achilles is present in the *Iliad*; see especially *Il.* 2.220. For analysis of Thersites' attack on Achilles over Penthesilea, see Blok (1995) 195–289; Fantuzzi (2012) 271–79.

36. Rosen (2003), cf. (2007) 67–116, argues for the sympotic context of the *Aethiopis* (and also for a difference of Thersites' function in this work compared to the *Iliad*). The representation of the *Thersitoktonos* on an Apulian red-figure volute crater (Boston MFA 03.804; see *LIMC* 8.1 [Suppl.] s.v. Thersites 3) seems to locate the incident within a banquet.

37. Compare the explicit association of insult and laughter in the symposium in the lines cited above (p. 48) from *IEG* 27.

38. So again Rosen (2003) 123, arguing Thersites' abusiveness in the symposium ought to have been understood (and was by at least some of his audience) as the performance of a "'satirist' rather than a true subversive" and that as a result "he did not deserve [his] sufferings."

39. Note in this context the mockery among *philoi* in the Spartan *syssitia*, above, p. 48 (mockery that would be halted at the request of the target). Much of Archilochus's abuse is directed at his *philoi*; only "Lykambes" seems to be designated as an enemy, or *ekhthros* (cf. Nagy [1979] 243–45). Pertinent too is the fact Cleitus's ire at the singing of verses that denigrated the performance of his fellow generals (above, pp. 50–51) is roused because the audience was not confined to the Macedonian *philoi* of the king, but included "outsiders" such as Persian nobles (so explicitly Plut. *Alex.* 50.9).

40. For the function of sympotic discourse in reinforcing the cohesive identity of the *hetairoi* by encouraging negative attitudes to those outside the *hetaireia*, see Henderson (1999). The power of wine to accentuate violent tendencies may have made the evocation of civil strife within sympotic discourse arguably more potent than in other contexts; the intoxicated violence of the Centaurs at the wedding of Peirithoos (Hom. *Od.* 21.295–304) provided reminder enough of this.

41. On this elegy in general, see Marcovich (1978) 1–16.

42. Or think, too, of the undercurrents of *stasis* in some of Archilochus's verses (esp. *IEG* 105–6). Notable too is the fact that in the *Aethiopis*, according to Proclus's summary (*Chrest.* p. 105.25–26 OCT), Achilles' murder of Thersites produced *stasis* among the Achaeans; for differing views of the scope of that stasis, see Fantuzzi (2012) 273n20.

43. So Nagy (1979) 222–25; cited for the use of strife as the counterpoint of praise are Pind. *Nem.* 4.93; *Nem.* 8.22, 25.

44. The indulgence in such abuse may at times have functioned to help distinguish the sympotic groups from, and socially elevate them above, the *dêmos* at large, by signaling the rejection of democratic norms; such behavior would further foster the cohesiveness of the sympotic group itself. It is thus analogous to other forms of transgressive activity by symposiasts, most famously the profanation of the Mysteries and mutilation of the Hermai. One might also note the behavior of the self-styled *Kakodaimonistai*, who met to dine on days of ill omen in order to display their contempt for the laws of gods and men; or of another group that took delight in stealing and consuming purificatory victims from the shrines of Hecate (Dem. 54.39). See Murray (1990).

45. The repudiation of blame by Pindar in *Pyth.* 2.52–53 is made with reference to Archilochus as "blame poet" par excellence: "I shun the deep bite of slander. For at a far remove I have seen fault-finding Archilochus many times in his helplessness fattening himself on harsh words of hatred."

46. By claiming to report merely what Archilochus himself has revealed in his poetry, Critias could claim to be innocent of abusiveness himself; of course the effect of his paraphrase is to allow Critias to be effectively a blame poet himself. Aelian's introduction of the Critias material with *αἰτιᾶται Κριτίας* attests as much.

47. Aesch. 1.28–32; Dem. 22.30–32.

48. Rotstein (2007) 142–43, cf. 151.

49. Critias criticizes the Athenian symposia of his day (symposia that have become more "democratic" in ideology) through implicit contrast with Spartan *syssitia* (88 B6 DK), and through a rejection of the democratic "new music" styles, on which see Wilson (2003). On the dichotomy between Athenian and Spartan drinking habits forged by philo-Laconian observers such as Critias, see Murray (1991) 87–92; Halliwell (2008) 125–27.

50. Rotstein (2007) 149ff. (esp. 151n71) suggests that non-elite sympotic groups were responsible for the promotion of the poet Archilochus as a "democratic icon." On the emergence of non-elite symposia within Athens, see Fisher (2000).

51. Explicit reference is made to *parrhêsia*: thus Demades employs *parrhêsia* in his rebuke (*χρήσασθαι παρρησίᾳ*), and Philip admires the man who has dared to address him with such frankness (*τὸν δ' ἄνδρα τὸν χρησάμενον τῇ παρρησίᾳ θαυμάσαι*).

52. Contrast the apologia of Just. 9.5.1; Plut. *Amat.* 751c.

53. Plut. *Demos.* 20.3: Philip "sings" in iambics the decree by which Demosthenes had mobilized the Greeks for war (in a manner not dissimilar from that of Ar. *Ach.* 479ff., where Pericles' decrees are rendered as *skolia*).

54. Steiner (2002) for sympotic behaviors among magistrates (notably including parodies of ostracism). On the democratization of symposia, cf. above Note 50.

55. So Humphreys (1978) 101–2.

56. Particularly interesting in this regard are the fragments of Solon's poetry (esp. *IEG* 38–40 and 41, with Noussia [2001]) that deal with sympotic themes such as lists of exotic foods characteristic of sympotic dining. These may have had a political purpose

(perhaps an admonition against extravagant luxuries for those of the elite whose excesses Solon aimed to moderate), although any such interpretation must remain speculative.

57. Cf. Ober (1998) 46 (with bibliography cited in his n. 62).

58. Wilson (2003) 197–99. Similarly Critias seems to criticize the "democratization" of the symposium, identified as the intrusion of "democratic" musical modes into that formerly aristocratic sphere.

59. Rotstein (2007) 151.

60. So Norwood (1930) (but note too the rather different identification of this work postulated by Hornblower [2000]). Treatises on the constitutions of Sparta and Thessaly number among Critias's works (see 88 B31–37 DK). A degree of overlapping interest in the different components of Critias's work is suggested by the fact that a fragment that may belong to the *Well-Balanced Constitutions* unfavorably contrasts Athenian sympotic praxis with that of Sparta (88 B6 DK). As far as the anonymous *Constitution of Athens* goes, one might note that its author's complaint about the mob's disdain for music (and athletics) certainly is congruent with Critias's known interests. Critias engaged with more genres than any other known Greek writer; in addition to his tragedies (the *Peirithoos*, and probably also that *Sisyphus* once commonly ascribed to Euripides), some of his speeches may well have been published: see Usher (1968).

61. I have set out arguments for such a dating in O'Sullivan (2011).

62. In 410/9, in accordance with a decree moved by Demophantus (Andoc. 1.98; Dem. 20.159), the Athenians undertook to show to the descendants of anyone who died attempting to slay a tyrant the very same generosity as shown to Harmodius and Aristogeiton and to their descendants; the privilege at issue was *sitêsis* at the Prytaneum (*IG* I^3 131). In general, the image of the tyrannicides receives great attention across a variety of media in the periods of unrest and of democratic restoration in the late fifth century; note, for example, the use of the tyrannicide statue as a decoration for Athena's shield on a series of Panathenaic vases c. 403 BCE: see Ajootian (1998) 8.

63. The symposium reclaims the aristocratic lovers from the *polis* also in the representation of the tyrannicides on a surviving Attic column *krater* (c. 470 BCE), on which see Neer (2002) 180, with fig. 90; it depicts sympotic revelers borrowing the pose of the tyrannicides from the famous Critius and Nesiotes group in the Agora, with wineskins replacing the tyrannicidal swords. The portrayal within the symposium of Harmodius and Aristogeiton as men motivated by *eros* need not have been hostile in intent. Such portrayal of the tyrannicides might not, however, have been quite so acceptable within the agenda of the democratic *polis*; for argumentation, see O'Sullivan (2011).

64. Thus the *isonomia* that the tyrannicides are alleged to have ushered in could be lauded within aristocratic and democratic circles alike. See also Neer (2002) 181, emphasizing the coincidence of aristocratic and democratic values around the tyrannicides.

65. For the fragmentary *skyphos* (held in the Villa Guilia) and its iconographical resonances, see Neer (2002) 173–80, with fig. 86. Given the existence of such manipulation of the tyrannicides within the visual media of the symposium (and see also above, note 63), it is striking that the Athenians sought only to regulate verbal denigration. The

differentiation between the censorship of words and images is not unparalleled. On trial ostensibly for his literary treatment of Brutus and Cassius, the Roman historian Cremutius Cordus is made to remind the senate (by Tacitus *Ann.* 4.35), that the liberators are still "known by their statues." One tradition on the destruction of images that is almost tantamount to censorship concerns the bronze statue of the grandson of the tyrant Hippias (allegedly recast as a stele bearing his name and that of any future Athenian traitors: so Lyc. *in Leoc.* 117–18), but the historicity of that tradition is suspect (so Rhodes and Osborne [2003] 444–45).

66. Whitehead (2000) 29–30.

67. The tense political climate is most clearly attested by the enactment in 337/36 of a new law against tyranny and the subversion of the democracy (*RO* 79), a law that constitutes an addition to, and a refinement of, a long tradition of "antityranny" legislation at Athens, for which Ostwald (1955) remains fundamental.

68. The tyrannicides may have been rendered particularly topical too by the stigmatization of Philip, and later Alexander, as tyrants in Greek (and especially Athenian) rhetoric: see Dem. 6.25; ps.-Dem. 17.12, 29; Diod. 17.9.5. There is quite an interplay between the Athenians, Alexander, and indeed others around the image of the Athenians' tyrannicides. The Athenians employed a descendant of the tyrannicides as an envoy to Persia to court assistance behind Alexander's back (Curt. 3.13.15); Alexander (according at least to Arr. 3.16) repatriated the stolen tyrannicide statues from Susa, thereby casting himself as benefactor rather than threat to the democratic state; Callisthenes invoked the image of the tyrannicides in a conversation about Alexander's growing despotism (Arr. 4.10).

69. That is, as a lineal descendant of the tyrannicides, Democrates was daily entitled to dinner at state expense in the Prytaneum.

70. *Suda* s.v. *κορδακίζει* cf. *schol.* Ar. *Nub.* 540 on comic origins; associated with drunkenness at Ar. *Nub.* 555. Philippides' offensiveness is magnified by the insinuation that, like Democrates, he indulges in such behavior even when sober; compare Theophr. *Char.* 6.3. Pollux s.v. *εἰς κόλακα* attests to the nexus between aischrology, jesting, and dancing the *kordax*, by labeling them all as pertaining to the flatterer.

71. On the Macedonians themselves, relevant material (largely from Theopompus, and very close in spirit to Dem. 2.18–19) is collected by Athenaeus (6.260). There Philip is *gelôtopoios* (Demetrius Poliorcetes in a later generation will be similarly *philogelôs*: Phylarchus *FGrH* 81 F19) and fond of licentiousness, drinking, and lewd dancing; for further references to lewd dancing at Macedonian symposia, see Carney (2007) 152. In terms of alleged sympathizers of Macedon, note that the rowdy *komasts* deplored by the speaker of Dem. 54. 8–9 (cited above, p. 45) are tainted by Macedonian sympathies. Compare too Dem. 10.75, where the Athenians themselves are depicted as "turning the subject to ridicule and raillery" (*τὸ πρᾶγμ' εἰς γέλωτα καὶ λοιδορίαν ἐμβαλόντες*) whenever they turn their backs on advice given by Philip's Athenian foes and listen instead to the counsel of those in the king's pocket. Hobden (2009), cf. (2013) 129–40, examines Demosthenes' deployment of commensality in his attacks on Aeschines in his speech *On the False Embassy*; again, pro-Macedonian tendencies are insinuated.

72. See Halliwell (2008) 69–77, contrasting the divisiveness of the laughter sought by Thersites with the reconciliatory mirth elicited at the end of *Iliad* 1 by Hephaestus.

73. So Hitz (2005) 599.

74. See Raaflaub (2004b) 224–25 for the evolution of *parrhêsia* as a democratic catchcry.

75. Thus the speaker of Lysias's *Against Theomnestus* can claim that it is a mark of a mean and excessively litigious person to prosecute on the grounds of slander (Lys. 10.2).

76. Wallace (1994).

77. Halliwell (1991a) 51, with reference (among others) to Cleon in Ar. *Pax* 47–48.

78. Halliwell (1991a) 57–59. The other claimed limitation of comic speech that has some claim to plausibility is the so-called decree of Syracosios (*schol.* Ar. *Av.* 1297), which Sommerstein (1986) would locate in the context of political crisis in the wake of the mutilations of the Hermai (but see too Halliwell [1991a] 59–63).

79. See above, pp. 49–50 for the connections between comedy and sympotic abusiveness. A further parallel may be noted in passing, namely an implicitly greater tolerance of abuse both on the comic stage and in the symposium when the audience was constituted of fellow citizens and *philoi*, respectively, compared to the tolerance claimed when "outsiders" were present. For the symposium, see above, Note 39. For the comic stage, see Ar. *Ach.* 502–5, where Dicaeopolis claims to have been prosecuted by Cleon for having criticized the city (τὴν πόλιν κακῶς λέγειν) with foreigners present; note also Hartwig in this volume, pp. 29–33 on the greater freedom of comic speech at the Lenaia (compared to the Dionysia) where the audience was predominantly an Athenian one.

REFERENCES

Ajootian, A. 1998. "A Day at the Races: The Tyrannicides in the Fifth-Century *Agora*." In *Stephanos: Studies in Honor of Brunhilde Sismondo Ridgway*, ed. K. Hartswick and M. Sturgeon, 1–13. Philadelphia: University of Pennsylvania Museum.

Blok, J. 1995. *The Early Amazons: Modern and Ancient Perspectives on a Persistent Myth.* Leiden: Brill.

Bosworth, A. B. 1996. "Alexander, Euripides and Dionysus: The Motivation for Apotheosis." In *Transitions to Empire: Essays in Greco-Roman History, 360–146 B.C., in Honor of E. Badian*, ed. R. W. Wallace and E. M. Harris, 140–66. Norman: University of Oklahoma Press.

Bowie, E. 2002. "Ionic *iambos* and Attic *komoidia*." In *The Language of Greek Comedy*, ed. A. Willi, 33–50. Oxford: Oxford University Press.

Cairns, F. 1982. "Cleon and Pericles: A Suggestion." *Journal of Hellenic Studies* 102: 203–4.

Carney, E. 1981. "The Death of Clitus." *Greek, Roman and Byzantine Studies* 22: 149–60.

———. 2007. "Symposia and the Macedonian Elite: The Unmixed Life." *Syllecta Classica* 18: 129–80.

Carter, D. M. 2004. "Citizen Attribute, Negative Right: A Conceptual Difference Between Ancient and Modern Ideas of Freedom of Speech." In *Free Speech in Classical Antiquity*, ed. I. Sluiter and R. M. Rosen, 197–220. Leiden: Brill.

Collins, D. 2004. *Masters of the Game: Competition and Performance in Greek Poetry*. Washington, DC: Center for Hellenic Studies.

Csapo, E. 2013. "Comedy and the *pompê*. Dionysian Genre-Crossing." In *Greek Comedy and the Discourse of Genres*, ed. E. Bakola et al., 40–80. Cambridge: Cambridge University Press.

Fantuzzi, M. 2012. *Achilles in Love: Intertextual Studies*. Oxford: Oxford University Press.

Fisher, N. 2000. "Symposiasts, Fish-Eaters and Flatterers: Social Mobility and Moral Concerns in Old Comedy." In *The Rivals of Aristophanes: Studies in Athenian Old Comedy*, ed. F. D. Harvey and J. Wilkins, 355–96. London: Duckworth.

Glucker, J. 1978. "Britannicus' Swan-Song." *Pegasus* 2: 9–17.

Halliwell, S. 1991a. "Comic Satire and Freedom of Speech in Classical Athens." *Journal of Hellenic Studies* 111: 48–70.

———. 1991b. "The Uses of Laughter in Greek Culture." *Classical Quarterly* 41: 279–96.

———. 2004. "Aischrology, Shame and Comedy." In *Free Speech in Classical Antiquity*, ed. I. Sluiter and R. M. Rosen, 115–44. Leiden: Brill.

———. 2008. *Greek Laughter: A Study of Cultural Psychology from Homer to Early Christianity*. Cambridge: Cambridge University Press.

Hansen, M. H. 1984. "The Number of *rhetores* in the Athenian *ekklesia*, 355–322." *Greek, Roman and Byzantine Studies* 25: 123–55.

Harding, P. 2007. *The Story of Athens: The Fragments of the Local Chronicles of Attika*. London: Routledge.

Henderson, W. J. 1999. "Men Behaving Badly: Conduct and Identity at Greek Symposia." *Akroterion* 44: 3–13.

Hitz, Z. 2005. "Review of *The Discovery of Freedom in Ancient Greece* by Kurt Raaflaub." *Journal of Philosophy* 102: 594–601.

Hobden, F. 2009. "*Symposion* and the Rhetorics of Commensality in Demosthenes 19, *On the False Embassy*." In *Rollenbilder in der athenischen Demokratie: Medien, Gruppen, Räume im politischen und sozialen System. Beiträge zu einem interdisziplinären Kolloquium in Freiburg i. Br., 24–25 November 2006*, ed. C. Mann et al., 71–87. Wiesbaden: Dr Ludwig Reichert Verlag.

———. 2013. *The Symposion in Ancient Greek Thought and Society*. Cambridge: Cambridge University Press.

Hornblower, S. 2000. "The *Old Oligarch* (Pseudo-Xenophon's *Athenaion Politeia*) and Thucydides: A Fourth-Century Date for the *Old Oligarch*?" In *Polis and Politics: Studies in Ancient Greek History*, ed. P. Flensted-Jensen et al., 363–84. Copenhagen: Museum Tusculanum Press.

Humphreys, S. C. 1978. "Public and Private Interests in Classical Athens." *Classical Journal* 73: 97–104.

Instinsky, H. U. 1961. "Alexander, Pindar, Euripides." *Historia* 10: 248–55.

Konstan, D. 2012. "The Two Faces of *Parrhêsia*: Free Speech and Self-Expression in Ancient Greece." *Antichthon* 46: 1–13.

Konstan, D., D. Clay, and C. E. Glad, tr. and eds. 1998. *Philodemus: On Frank Criticism.* Atlanta, GA: Scholars Press.

Kouklanakis, A. 1999. "Thersites, Odysseus and the Social Order." In *Nine Essays on Homer*, ed. M. Carlisle and O. Levaniouk, 35–53. Lanham, MD: Rowman & Littlefield.

Marcovich, M. 1978. "Xenophanes on Drinking-Parties and Olympic Games." *Illinois Classical Studies* 3: 1–26.

Marks, J. 2005. "The Ongoing Neikos: Thersites, Odysseus, and Achilleus." *American Journal of Philology* 126: 1–31.

Murray, O. 1990. "The Affair of the Mysteries: Democracy and the Drinking Group." In *Sympotica: A Symposium on the Symposion*, ed. O. Murray, 149–61. Oxford: Clarendon.

———. 1991. "War and the Symposium." In *Dining in a Classical Context*, ed. W. J. Slater, 83–103. Ann Arbor: University of Michigan Press.

Nagy, G. 1979. *The Best of the Achaeans: Concepts of the Hero in Archaic Greek Poetry*. Baltimore: Johns Hopkins University Press.

Neer, R. T. 2002. *Style and Politics in Athenian Vase-Painting: The Craft of Democracy, ca. 530–460 BCE.* Cambridge: Cambridge University Press.

Norwood, G. 1930. "The Earliest Prose Work of Athens." *Classical Journal* 25: 373–82.

Noussia, M. 2001. "Solon's Symposium (frs. 32–4 and 36 Gentili-Prato^2 = 38–40 and 41 West^2)." *Classical Quarterly* 51: 353–59.

Ober, J. 1998. *Political Dissent in Democratic Athens: Intellectual Critics of Popular Rule.* Princeton: Princeton University Press.

Ostwald, M. 1955. "The Athenian Legislation Against Tyranny and Subversion." *Transactions of the American Philological Association* 86: 103–28.

O'Sullivan, L. 2011. "Tyrannicides, Symposium and History: A Consideration of the Tyrannicide Law in Hyperides 2.3." In *ASCS 32 Selected Proceedings*, ed. A. Mackay. http://ascs.org.au/news/ascs32/O'Sullivan.pdf.

Raaflaub, K. A. 1980. "Des freien Burgers Recht der freien Rede." In *Studien zur antiken Sozialgeschichte: Festscrift Friedrich Vittinghoff*, ed. H. Wolff et al., 7–57. Cologne: Böhlau.

———. 2004a. "Aristocracy and Freedom of Speech in the Greco-Roman World." In *Free Speech in Classical Antiquity*, ed. I. Sluiter and R. M. Rosen, 41–62. Leiden: Brill.

———. 2004b. *The Discovery of Freedom in Ancient Greece*. Chicago: University of Chicago Press.

Rhodes, P. J. and R. Osborne. 2003. *Greek Historical Inscriptions: 404–323 BC.* Oxford: Oxford University Press = *RO.*

Rosen, R. M. 1988. *Old Comedy and the Iambographic Tradition*. Atlanta, GA: Scholars Press.

———. 2003. "The Death of Thersites and the Sympotic Performance of Iambic Mockery." *Pallas* 61: 121–36.

———. 2007. *Making Mockery: The Poetics of Ancient Satire*. Oxford: Oxford University Press.

———. 2013. "*Iambos*, Comedy and the Question of Generic Affiliation." In *Greek Comedy and the Discourse of Genres*, ed. E. Bakola et al., 81–97. Cambridge: Cambridge University Press.

Rösler, W. 1995. "Wine and Truth in the Greek Symposium." In *In Vino Veritas*, ed. O. Murray and M. Tecuşan, 106–12. London: British School at Rome.

Rothwell, K. S., Jr. 2007. *Nature, Culture and the Origins of Greek Comedy*. Cambridge: Cambridge University Press.

Rotstein, A. 2007. "Critias' Invective Against Archilochus." *Classical Philology* 102: 139–54.

———. 2010. *The Idea of Iambos*. Oxford: Oxford University Press.

Saxonhouse, A. W. 2006. *Free Speech and Democracy in Ancient Athens*. Cambridge: Cambridge University Press.

Sommerstein, A. H. 1986. "The Decree of Syrakosios." *Classical Quarterly* 36: 101–8.

Steiner, A. 2002. "Private and Public: Links Between *symposion* and *syssition* in Fifth-Century Athens." *Classical Antiquity* 21: 347–79.

Usher, S. 1968. "Xenophon, Critias and Theramenes." *Journal of Hellenic Studies* 88: 128–35.

van der Valk, M. 1974. "On the Composition of the Attic Skolia." *Hermes* 102: 1–20.

Wallace, R. W. 1994. "The Athenian Laws Against Slander." In *Symposion 1993: Vorträge zur griechischen und hellenistischen Rechtsgeschichte*, ed. G. Thür, 109–24. Cologne: Böhlau.

———. 2005. "Law, Attic Comedy, and the Regulation of Comic Speech." In *The Cambridge Companion to Ancient Greek Law*, ed. M. Gagarin and D. Cohen, 357–73. Cambridge: Cambridge University Press.

West, M. L. 1974. *Studies in Greek Elegy and Iambus*. Berlin: De Gruyter.

———. 1989. *Iambi et Elegi Graeci Ante Alexandrum Cantati 1 & 2*. Oxford: Oxford University Press = *IEG*.

Whitehead, D. 2000. *Hypereides: The Forensic Speeches*. Oxford: Oxford University Press.

Wilson, P. 2003. "The Sound of Cultural Conflict: Kritias and the Culture of *mousike* in Athens." In *The Cultures Within Ancient Greek Culture: Contact, Conflict, Collaboration*, ed. C. Dougherty and L. Kurke, 181–206. Cambridge: Cambridge University Press.

Worman, N. 2008. *Abusive Mouths in Classical Athens*. Cambridge: Cambridge University Press.

Chapter 4

A Bark Worse Than His Bite? Diogenes the Cynic and the Politics of Tolerance in Athens

Han Baltussen

Every society gets the kind of philosopher it deserves.

Diogenes "the Dog" was a notorious figure in fourth-century Athens.[1] He famously practiced a type of unrestricted *parrhêsia* that led, among other things, to quite antisocial behavior.[2] His subversive ideas blurred and transgressed the boundaries of what was socially acceptable. How, then, was he perceived and tolerated by his contemporaries? Or, to put it in a more provocative form, why did Diogenes, already in antiquity considered a more extreme version of Socrates (on which more later), not suffer the same fate as Socrates? This is a complex question, not only because the sources for Diogenes are late and of variable quality, but also because stories about Diogenes became part of constructions of schematic "histories of philosophy" or traditions, in which stories became changed to fit the patterns and agendas of later authors.[3] It is in addition extremely difficult to find any "facts" about Diogenes in these stories. As Dudley rightly points out, "in analysing the anecdotes about Diogenes, one should expect the illumination rather of character than of fact" (1998: 17). It is tempting to resolve the difference between Diogenes' fate and that of Socrates by simply referring to the changed historical circumstances—a solution that works up to a point—since the transition from fifth-century democracy to the more autocratic regimes of the fourth century had an important role to play in the dynamics of tolerance.[4]

We should, however, at least acknowledge that there is a paradox here that requires a separate explanation: while the mild-mannered Socrates operating under democratic rule was killed, the abrasive Diogenes survived living under more autocratic regimes. And it is clear from the meager historical evidence regarding fourth-century impiety trials that Diogenes was not among the accused, but lived up to a great age.[5] Even if we accept Waterfield's persuasive argument, that Socrates was the victim of personal enmities in the political arena, there is at least room for additional arguments from one other direction. In this chapter I shall redirect attention to Diogenes' philosophical positions and argue that there is reason to consider this evidence as well as the reactions of his contemporaries to establish further insight into the nature of Athenian tolerance with regard to this eccentric thinker. This approach will offer an additional vantage point from which to explain his fate in Athens.

The question of tolerance is pertinent to the topic of censorship: all social groups, small and large, formal and informal, place constraints on the behavior of their members. Among the different possible measures of tolerance, responses to dissenters, mavericks and iconoclasts are useful for finding out about the extent to which ethical boundaries are holding up against challenges. Diogenes may well stand at one extreme end of the scale, where tolerance acquires a kind of disinterested quality. This is the case, I suggest, because Diogenes has crossed a line beyond which punishment is no longer contemplated and his audience sees through his over-the-top manner of presenting his views.[6] One could almost say his case falls outside the standard range of society's interest for evaluative judgment and rejection. Moreover, the simple fact that Socrates had preceded him was *in and of itself* an influential factor in the Athenian attitude toward anyone similar to him. The Athenians soon regretted that they had killed Socrates, as transpires from the reports about the punishment of his accusers. One report speaks of remorse and a backlash against the accusers. In the life of Socrates (D.L. 2.43) the severe countermeasures, intended to make up for Socrates' execution, are described in some detail: "he was taken from among men and not long after the Athenians felt remorse . . . they banished other accusers but put Meletus to death." Next, in the life of Antisthenes (D.L. 6.10), Antisthenes is "held responsible for the exile of Anytus and the execution of Meletus." In support of this Athenian volte-face Paul Zanker has pointed to the statuette of Socrates, dated to the late fourth century and now in the British Museum, which shows him as a respectable citizen.[7] These bits of evidence indicate that Socrates' fate was due to the fickleness of Athenian political and legal processes. They also help to explain why they would kill him after forty years of philosophical activity.[8]

In what follows I explore the question of tolerance by examining the elements internal to Diogenes' thinking and the reactions to some of them by his contemporaries. This approach can offer an additional explanation for why he was not convicted or killed, despite his more extreme behavior. One modern notion will assist in this analysis: we can make use of identity and deviance theory, a perspective from sociology, which clarifies why Diogenes insisted on his eccentric behavior (i.e., he considered his isolation as a badge of honor). Finally, we can take some further support for the acceptance of Diogenes by his contemporaries from the fact that they regarded him as an "embodiment of the ἐγκράτεια which [Xenophon] so emphasizes as Socrates' dominant character."[9] The paradox that Diogenes posed—by trying to *teach* sensible ideas in a distinctly *unpalatable* manner—can thus be resolved. Humor was one major factor in this process of acceptance.[10] In other words, it seems that his contemporaries understood his message despite his antics and abrasive style.

Sources and Evidence

The surviving stories about Diogenes present us with two major issues: it is claimed that he left us no writings (on which more below, note 16) and the sources for his life and thought are mostly late. When viewed together the evidence is not always consistent: as with most Hellenistic philosophers, the fragmentary state of the evidence may stand in the way of a coherent reading of his life and thought. On this point it is important to remember that Diogenes' strategy probably caused this confusion: one of his central aims was to subvert the notion of what philosophy is or does, and to offer an alternative. On this point, he is in line with his teacher Antisthenes, who proclaimed that philosophy is all about *action*, not talk or learning (D.L. 6.11, τὴν τ' ἀρετὴν τῶν ἔργων εἶναι, μήτε λόγων πλείστων δεομένην μήτε μαθημάτων).[11]

Usually dated to around 200 CE, Diogenes Laertius's biographical account is rather late and also highly derivative.[12] This is in itself not always a stumbling block: Diogenes Laertius often mentions the sources he himself used, and for some parts of the work we can check the content against other sources. Moreover, Diogenes Laertius was not the most perceptive of thinkers, and his accounts can be quite misguided or wrong (when he relies on others, simplifies or compresses the doctrines).[13] Nonetheless, his limited understanding of philosophical matters may also work in our advantage, as he may have been less prone to "improve" the ideas (or wording) he was reporting.

The uncertainty surrounding the evidence can be countered, at least to a degree, by the *cumulative* force of the anecdotes: Diogenes Laertius and his sources appear to have had no other option but to record brief vignettes and anecdotes, which illustrates the nature of the tradition, and how the sources reported it; so we may not be too far off if these reflect Diogenes' method: he practiced what he preached.[14] Even if not all are historically accurate in every detail, they present a fairly consistent picture of a man who favored communicating mostly by way of *succinct responses* to situations or queries, and not by long diatribes or systematic philosophical expositions. It has been argued that the extant materials do reflect the historical Diogenes, no doubt with some exaggeration and additions (Bosman 2006). As I shall show, certain elements of the vocabulary in Diogenes Laertius support this.

Diogenes Laertius presents a remarkably long report on Diogenes' life and sayings (D.L. 6.20–81).[15] Its structure can be summed up as follow (sections are mine):

1. Origin and stories about his life (D.L. 6.20–21)
2. Anecdotes about his interactions with contemporaries and the world (not necessarily in this order):
   a. D. commenting on customs, activities, (i.e., things he observes, 6.22, 37, and 45 *θεασάμενος*; 6.52 and 65 *ἰδών*)
   b. D. answering questions (*ἐρωτηθείς . . . ἔφη*)
   c. D. responding to reproach and abuse (*ὀνειδιζόμενος, λοιδορούμενος*)
   d. recurring comments (e.g., 6.38 *εἰώθει δὲ λέγειν*)
3. Summary of views (6.70–79, in which 70–73 may be an excerpt from another source)
4. List of works (6.80)[16]
5. Namesakes (6.81, other individuals called Diogenes)

In outline, many *Lives* in Diogenes Laertius have a pattern broadly similar to this one.[17] But there is one crucial difference here: instead of presenting a long summary of doctrines, Diogenes Laertius resorts to recounting close to

150 brief anecdotes and a relatively short account of doctrine.[18] The distinction I have made here between subsections 2a and 2b–c may seem trivial, but it has a sound basis in the text. The one I focus on is the high frequency of certain verb forms of interactive speech (asking and answering questions etc.) which is much higher in book 6 than elsewhere in Diogenes Laertius.[19] This cannot be a coincidence and invites further investigation: it allows us to draw up a picture of Diogenes as interacting with his fellow citizens and illustrates the peculiar nature of his strategy as "performance artist."[20]

Many stories include a brief dialogue between Diogenes and others: 26 out of some 150 anecdotes contain his answer to the phrase "(when) being asked" followed by "he said" (*ἐρωτηθείς . . . ἔφη*); another significant group of stories describe him as responding to a reproach from a bystander (*ὀνειδιζόμενος*). The first category seems to express the curiosity of bystanders, who are puzzled by his behavior. The second category, however, represents a critical and polemical audience that finds fault with his behavior. It will be worthwhile to focus on these types of anecdotes, with a particular emphasis on those coming under 2b–c to find out what the tradition has handed down as signals of dissatisfaction with Diogenes' philosophical method; in addition, it can assist in achieving some insight into the moral values that lie behind these attacks; if so, they could inform us about the contemporary reception and how all this can be taken seriously. I briefly review his philosophical ideas from this angle to show how he could be regarded as a serious thinker *by his contemporaries*, notwithstanding the obnoxious persona he projected while promoting himself and his ideas.

Dog Tales and Cynic Principles

The most comprehensive characterization of Diogenes put into his mouth by the tradition runs as follows: "Asked what he had done to be called a dog, he said 'I fawn on those who give me something, yelp at those who refuse (*τοὺς δὲ μὴ διδόντας ὑλάκτων*), and set my teeth in rascals (*τοὺς δὲ πονηροὺς δάκνων*)'" (D.L. 6.60). His image of the dog philosopher is here upheld by this metaphor of dog-like behavior in a nicely construed tripartite description. This type of response betrays Diogenes' verbal and rhetorical skills (cf. D.L. 6.74 *εὐστοχώτατος*; 75 *θαυμαστὴ . . . πειθώ*) and reveals that he was not simply a "street bum" or a quarrelsome lunatic. The evidence suggests that he was a literate person, a writer of dialogues (and perhaps tragedies, D.L. 6.80; but see note 16), very much like any well-educated person of good upbringing. His linguistic and rhetorical skills are also clear from another feature in the stories: one in six of the anecdotes about him depends on clever talk, puns, and witty repartee.[21] In other words, he knows his way around in literary and philosophical circles. That he abandoned these pursuits for a more erratic and aggressive style of philosophy is a striking feature of his life. We may perhaps compare this conversion story to that of Plato, who early in his life wrote poetry and aspired to writing dramatic works, an ambition he abandoned after meeting Socrates: according to Diogenes Laertius, Plato burned his own works and converted to the life of the philosopher (D.L. 3.5, cf. Ael. *Var. Hist.* 2.30; 14.33). It would seem that something like this happened to Diogenes—even if we need to take these "conversion stories" with a pinch of salt, since they are a common trope in biographical writing and very convenient ways of "explaining" a person's change of direction after the fact. So while the link with Socrates was obvious even in antiquity, we must imagine him as a darker and less benign version. He was, as Plato apparently commented, "Socrates in deranged mode" (D.L. 6.54, Σωκράτης μαινομένος). This type of verdict does not signify mere decline: Diogenes is Socrates "on acid."

The typical product of the post-Socratic era, in which the urban culture showed all the signs and scars of population growth, political turmoil and the effects of affluence, and, as some would see it, subsequent moral deterioration, Diogenes cast himself as a cure of these ailments.[22] There was in Athens in the late fifth century a striking correlation between the growth of wealth and the perceived downturn in moral values. Socrates had been among the first to challenge Athenians to think harder about the just life and how to do the right thing. His big idea was to say that reason will help us live a just life, claiming that if you know what is just, you will do it. Diogenes is one of the "Socratics" who followed this particular type of lifestyle in practice.

Incidentally, it is worth reminding ourselves that the word "Cynic" (κυνικός) or "cynicism" (κυνισμός) in this context has little in common with its modern counterpart: in ancient Greek the word *kunikos*, "dog-like," was supposed to be a derogatory term to label the shameless behavior of the Cynics.[23] To an average law-abiding Greek, the Cynics exhibited the kind of behavior that they associated with dogs (see the passage quoted above); like dogs they grovel for those who give out food, and they bark at those who don't; in addition, dogs are known for other shameless traits, such as grooming their private parts by licking them, eating whenever and wherever they can, and in general showing very few signs of culture and sophistication.[24] The modern cynic is far more nihilistic: he or she is—as the *Oxford English Dictionary* puts it—"a person that shows a disposition to disbelieve in the sincerity or goodness of human motives and actions and is wont to express this with sneers and sarcasm."

The primary evidence for Diogenes' philosophical principles presents a small set of beliefs that seem to grasp some valuable basic truths about human nature. In reading these we will come to understand that, although there is madness in his method, there is also method in his madness. Four aspects in particular seem to sum up what Diogenes was trying to achieve, and they all mark him as a fiercely independent individual who advocates this position in contradistinction to his community: frugality, his challenge to conventions, his belief in hard work, and frank speech.

His attempt to live a frugal life, that is to say, live without material dependence, can be gathered from several stories. One typical story tells us that when he saw a boy drink water with his hands, he smashed his wooden drinking bowl so that he could be seen to be needing even fewer objects to survive. This kind of behavior is part of a recurrent pattern: Diogenes took the simple life very seriously and railed against the needless luxuries the Athenians had acquired (D.L. 6.50 "love of money he declared the mother of all evils," φιλαργυρίαν εἶπε μητρόπολιν πάντων τῶν κακῶν). The Cynics were convinced that wealth creates only problems and anxiety, and argued that real wealth is not about material possessions, but rather about physical strength and mental independence—self-sufficiency in the true sense (αὐταρκεία). This attitude may well reflect a social and political reality of his day in that the gap between rich and poor had been growing, and Diogenes seemed to realize that it was a soul-destroying exercise to pursue luxuries and possessions. The result was that Cynics cared very little about their appearance and lived as beggars.

Then there is his crusade against conventional wisdom. This characteristic seems to make an important philosophical point. I say "seems to make," because without any of his written works we are forced to reconstruct his ideas to justify such a claim. By attacking conventional wisdom and customs, he aims to make people see their "maddening darkness" or delusion (τύφος). Conventional behavior seems to cover up rather than reveal true human nature: we lie, cheat, and deceive each other all the time. Where is honesty in all this? How can we be true to ourselves? According to Diogenes there *is* goodness in all of us, and it starts with striving for self-sufficiency, by which he means being truly independent in how we live; after all, if we experience needs, we basically have to admit that we are enslaved to them. It follows that the needs of the body should be obeyed only to a strict limit, not to excess. Diogenes regarded the body as the bottom line, as "ungovernable," so control over it was limited to answering its basic needs in a measured way. He was convinced that private acts should also be public acts: a liberating notion, no doubt with some wider appeal, but who has ever been able to live by it?[25]

Diogenes believed in "frankness of speech" (παρρησία). He called it "the most beautiful thing in the world" (D.L. 6.69). But his understanding of the term goes beyond both the ancient and the modern political notion of having the right to express your views in the assembly (its original political meaning) without the risk of being sued or arrested.[26] Diogenes believes in a form of *parrhêsia* that gives him license to say whatever he likes regardless of the consequences. As in action, so in speech. He seems to have taken this approach in the belief that there are too many hypocrites and liars in society, but that he would follow the principle of "frank speech" to the limit and without shame.

All this does not come without effort. A fourth point is Diogenes' strong belief in hard work (πόνος), training (ἄσκησις) of body and soul (D.L. 6.70), and self-control (ἐγκράτεια). These features explain the tendency in the sources to make him look like Socrates.[27] He is said to have practiced self-control by standing in the snow just so that he could learn to resist the cold (as did Socrates, *Symp.* 220d). And his berating of others could be offensive and unpleasant, but he did it with the honorable aim to improve people's lives (cf. Plato, passim). He would lecture people at festivals and other public events. He saw it as his duty to do this by attacking established values. He referred to this—with a nod to his own father, a banker accused of manipulating coins in his hometown—as "defacing the coinage" (χάραττειν τὸ νομίσμα), which supposedly was what the Delphic oracle had instructed him to do (another parallel with Socrates as recounted in Plato's *Apology*). We should of course read this as a metaphor, since it has been recognized long ago that it involves a play on words: νόμος ("convention") versus νομίσμα ("coinage"). This should not necessarily be taken to mean that he *advocated* unacceptable conduct. He sees himself as a questioner and a catalyst, much like Socrates declared himself a gadfly and stingray for the Athenians.

So Diogenes took pride in poverty and lowly social status, while he despised luxuries, ambition, hypocrisy, and intellectual snobbery.[28] Clearly this combination of sobriety and simplicity makes him an opponent of culture (νόμος) and a defender of the return to nature (φύσις). He was, we might say, a kind of Rousseau *avant la lettre*. His ambitious and idealistic program of social reform mounts a battle against the "madness" of society, especially the mindlessness of conventional knowledge and the pursuit of luxury and fame. That he prefers confrontation, shock, and challenge made him a contrarian and controversialist, but he could rely on his great rhetorical skills to face anyone in an altercation (D.L. 6.75 θαυμαστὴ δέ τις ἦν . . . πειθώ).

Civic Anxieties and Degrees of Tolerance

In combination with his use of humor and satire, Diogenes' literary talents and didactic insight would no doubt have encountered respect. There is every indication that the Athenians had a weak spot for him (D.L. 6.43 ἠγαπᾶτο δὲ πρὸς 'Αθηναίων). Is it possible that they saw his earnest aim? For a better understanding of the views underlying his actions, we need to assess how his "message" relates to the concerns of his contemporaries. He is, one might say, a performance artist, with admirable stamina and courage. Yet the question remains: why, when Diogenes' *behavior* was clearly more extreme than Socrates', did he not suffer the same fate as Socrates? As we saw in the previous section, his manner of conveying his "message" through performance leaves considerable room for misinterpretation, either because he was not well understood (one could ask: do these anecdotes add up to a philosophical stance?) or because his proposals were considered a threat to the common way of life. The former may lead to ignoring him as a serious thinker, while the latter may lead to rejecting him out of hand. When the "narrative" (and I use the term loosely) of a philosopher's life and thought is determined by a deliberately nonsystematic approach to philosophy, interpretation is very difficult indeed.

The relatively conventional perspective I used in the previous section regarding the philosophical outlook of Diogenes aimed to show that these *could* have been understood by his audience, if they looked past his antics and performative attitude. I now want to raise some further points from the modern perspective of the social sciences. I will use two notions, one from social psychology and one from sociology, as interpretative tools to clarify further the nature of tolerance as a social phenomenon with special reference to nonconformist and isolating behavior, in other words, an outsider. Crucial to this type of analysis are the notions of "in-group" and of deviance (part of the theory of identity).[29]

What made Diogenes so different? When considering groups and mechanisms of belonging, social psychologists speak of "in-groups" to describe the human tendency to create groups that self-regulate their "membership"; this leads to conformist behavior.[30] Diogenes was categorized as a Socratic philosopher and a student of Antisthenes, who in turn was himself regarded a Socratic (D.L. 6.15).[31] This by itself would have earmarked him as an outsider. But Diogenes goes against normal expectations because he *relishes* his status as outsider. He even declared that he became a philosopher *precisely because* he was cast out from his home village (D.L. 6.49). Obviously this has implications for the effect any external judgment would have on him. While the "in-group" of Athenians could not be expected to be sympathetic to his foreign status (he was from Sinope) and strange behavior, he showed other qualities that *could* be of interest or benefit to the community. It has to be admitted that his views on Sparta did not help—at D.L. 6.59 he describes his return from Sparta as going "from the men's apartment to the women's," and there is clear evidence for the annoyance he caused among the general public (6.57, 58: he often speaks on virtue with regard to young men, e.g., he calls blushing "the hue of virtue," 6.54). At this point the notion of deviance can assist: this technical term in social-scientific parlance is defined as the labeling of behavior *in response to* particular acts.[32] In other words, deviance is regarded as a product of social interaction, not necessarily a predicate of certain acts (let alone an inherent character flaw). I suggest that this applies to Diogenes' case well. Professional colleagues and nameless contemporaries responded to Diogenes in a way that demonstrates that they did not ignore him. The evidence suggests that the negative labeling of his behavior is of a later date, arising mostly in the competitive atmosphere of Hellenistic philosophers.[33]

One source has preserved some of the reactions signaling a moral judgment on his lifestyle, but not outright disapproval. How Diogenes was perceived by his contemporaries transpires in specific words in Diogenes Laertius informing us about audience responses. The "interactive nature" of the Diogenes anecdotes relates to the answering of questions (*ἐρωτήθεις*) and his response to rebuke or reproach (*ὀνειδιζόμενος*).[34] Both verbs are markers for a concern on the part of Diogenes' audience.

The following table tries to represent the frequency in a way that highlights the remarkably high occurrence of these verbs in book 6 (cf. note 15). These terms may go some way in gauging whether rejection and disinterested tolerance was the determining factor in the way Athenians behaved toward Diogenes. What is their specific interest, and do they express a particular concern? First, we may consider the broader occurrence of the terms. At D.L. 6.43–48 we find a selection of his obnoxious comments and at 49–69 we find a series of anecdotes in which Diogenes is subjected to questioning on all kinds of different issues:

Table 4.1. Distribution of ἐρωτηθείς in Diogenes Laertius as an Indicator of Interactive Speech Acts

D.L.	*No.*	*Thinkers*
Book 1	14	Thales [2], Solon [2], Chilon, Pittacus, Periander, Bias [2], Anacharsis [3]
Book 2	11	Anaxagoras, Socrates [2], Aristippus [7], Menedemus
Book 3	1	Plato
Book 4	2	Bion [2]
Book 5	8	Aristotle [8]
Book 6	**31**	**Antisthenes [5], Diogenes of Sinope [26]**
Book 7	4	Zeno [3]
Book 8	0	—
Book 9	2	Pyrrho, Timon
Book 10	0	Epicurus

Note: There may be some significance to the fact that the terms occur in sections on the Socratics and very early philosophers (books 1, 2, 6), who lived in times of oral transmission of the intellectual tradition. The frequencies of terms for the cynics are in bold.

Comments

On an Alexander letter (in verse); on temple officials as thieves (46); intervening with young men's choices (47); on poor performers in music or speech; on superstitious or silly individuals (48)

Questions/reproaches

1. In reply to a reproach for his exile, he says "that, you fool, is why I started to philosophize"
2. Or in response to the reminder that he was sentenced to exile by Sinope, he countered with "I sentence them to staying at home"
3. Asked why he begged for alms, he replied "to get practice in being refused"
4. Asked by a tyrant about the best bronze, he suggested the kind of which Aristogeiton and Harmodius were made [they were tyrannicides, i.e., he is being duplicitous and ironic]

5. How Dionysius (of Syracuse) treated his friends: "like purses—when full he hangs them up, when empty, he discards them" (again, ironic)
6. What is wretched in life (ironic: Diogenes himself?), regarding his status (what kind of hound he was?)
7. Comments on a sign on a door; greed; spend-thrift; good men (images of gods)
8. Interactions with Plato (52–54)
9. Questions on certain specific concepts (see below)

Clearly Diogenes takes pleasure in reversing statements back onto the person formulating the question or reproach. The sequence of questions seems to have no clear organizational principle apart from offering alternating declarative statements. But it is important to see that both types of speech act are depicted as *reactive*: Diogenes is very often responding to someone or something in his environment. Often it is to a question, other times it can be as simple as an object (sign on a door, 6.50) or a person ("a good-looking youth lying in an exposed position," 6.53). It is very much part of his rhetorical style, in the sense that his performance is closely linked to a particular situation.[35] It may well be that some of these stories are apocryphal, but they at least confirm the reputation he had as a conversationalist who preferred concrete brevity over expansive theory (several anecdotes recounting his attacks on Plato seem to make that clear; see note 33).

Perhaps more interesting and informative are the brief encounters in which his implicit or explicit challenge to civic standards and values is expressed. His general dislike of the rich and greedy is a common trait of many stories. He called an ignorant rich man "a sheep with the golden fleece" (6.47). Not everyone would have disagreed. Continually pointing out to people they should not pursue wealth is not the same as blaming them for their greed. He also challenges people's view regarding power (when Alexander visits D.L. 6.38) or social interactions ("when someone said 'most people laugh at you,' his reply was 'and so very likely do the asses at them; but as they don't care for the asses, so neither do I care for them'"; D.L. 6.58), or the real nature of a philosopher ("To a man who said, 'you don't know anything, even though you are a philosopher,' he replied 'Even if I am but a pretender to wisdom [προσποιοῦμαι σοφίαν], that in itself is philosophy'"; D.L. 6.64). Despite all this, "he was still loved by the Athenians. At all events, when a youngster broke up his tub, they gave the boy a flogging, and presented Diogenes with another" (D.L. 6.43).

It would seem, then, that his method is one in which several elements contribute to a curious mix of abrasive social criticism and intriguing provocation. Like Socrates, Diogenes liked to heckle people, even other philosophers, and we have some amusing anecdotes about him engaging with the rather self-important and learned ideas of Plato and Aristotle, turning their ideas against them or ridiculing them (listed above). Diogenes was clearly not fond of theoretical speculation.

Diogenes' efforts to live the simple (Socratic) life, while philosophically motivated, would have been comprehensible to his audience. His tactics can be made coherent to a considerable degree, because he practiced what he preached: his life is the example that strengthens his rhetoric. This has the advantage of not requiring elaborate and tedious argumentation, merely action. And in doing so he came to subvert the conventional ideas of his society in showing by example how to penetrate to the true purpose of human life, namely by reason and virtue. For example, if "poverty" is the conventional name for having few material possessions, Diogenes will argue that those possessions are irrelevant for a rich and rewarding life. He claims that curbing one's needs and defying possessions show true strength and self-control. In addition, he presents us with intriguing paradoxes: for instance, he suggests that he has conquered poverty by adopting it. At the heart of all this lies a deep desire for self-knowledge, a focus on self-reflection, in other words an attitude that wants to deal with our internal reality, our true nature, devoid of luxuries, personal comfort, and honors. Such a life may not amount to much, or we may decide it is too extreme in its goals.

If it is hard work to let go of all comforts, forego the little pleasures that we allow ourselves, Diogenes' metaphorical exile from civilized society (and many other Cynics) succeeded in construing a lifestyle that had at the core a very humane philosophy, but a rather user-unfriendly way of expressing it.[36] His approach is one of self-debasement and self-dramatization and, as Branham puts it, "Diogenes made himself 'an object of experimentation and representation'" (1994: 335, based on Bakhtin). Here powerlessness becomes power, poverty becomes wealth, and action trumps words. In much of what he says and does, we recognize the strand of Socratic ideas and ideals, the virtuous life, the searching for truth, and the sense of humor. Like many Cynics, Diogenes used a subversive method to make us stop and think. In his attack on "common coinage," notions of virtue, wealth, power, even philosophy become restamped by his satirical distortion: "Humor is the 'chisel-stamp' of Cynic discourse" (Branham 1994: 343).

These, then, are four central concepts that lie behind Diogenes' abrasive and confrontational behavior: his radical pursuit of self-sufficiency (*autarkeia*) through sustained effort (*ponos*), shamelessness (*anaideia*), and outspokenness (*parrhêsia*). In social terms, they are the markers of a truly liberated person who has found real freedom and virtue. If you can defy established authorities, ignore the temptations of the good life, and find the courage and strength to focus on the inner faculties of human nature, then you can be satisfied that you have reached a detached sense of freedom. This self-imposed "exile" went further than some earlier radicals such as the Pythagoreans and marks him out as the marginalized figure he chose, and relished, to be.[37]

Conclusion

Most chapters in this volume are concerned with specific texts or figures who have had to deal with the pressures, real or potential, of being criticized or rejected by society. This was to be expected within our general theme of "the art of veiled speech"—a means of avoiding rejection and suppression. This chapter has chosen a distinctly different focus in that it has aimed to explore the *boundaries* of societal tolerance by looking at an extreme case of antiestablishment behavior. The way into the issue consisted of a reexamination of Diogenes the "outsider," who claimed *absolute parrhêsia*. The application of recent insights into social practices of group formation and regulation was combined with a philological approach: by taking the verbal cues of *responses* to Diogenes as the focus of investigation and subjecting these to a careful contextualizing analysis, two unusual findings emerged: (1) we saw that the alienation of Diogenes from society was not as extreme as his abrasive methods would suggest, and (2) we gained an improved understanding of the value placed on his thought by his contemporaries. One further result, I suggest, is that we could clarify the implication of the fact that he wore his "double exile" as a badge of honor, thus defusing the impact of societal labeling (in modern terms, his "deviance").

It is the power of their ideas that made the Cynics a force to be reckoned with. Their satire is the perfect tool for debunking the pomp and arrogance of political leaders and self-important individuals (whether intellectuals or not). The value of this type of approach for the history of Greek thought is that it provides us with an important link between Socratic ideas and the Stoics. And since it is a general human trait to dislike arrogant and self-important behavior, their ideas survived in many different and unexpected places. Freedom, independence, self-sufficiency are still desired items, and it has been remarked by scholars that the satirical stance works best within the democratic framework: the first Cynics appeared in city-states with strong democratic tendencies, and when democracies dwindled, so it seems did the Cynic movement.[38]

While the extent to which a society can tolerate and give a place to satire and criticism is often limited, Diogenes offered an alternative that was forcing his fellow citizens to take some distance from the daily rat race, to reconsider the emphasis we place on material possessions, on our day-to-day pursuits, and to think about what really matters. Diogenes' iconic and unparalleled approach, using rhetoric, humor, and the bite of satire and subversion, stands in the tradition of therapeutic philosophizing, which sees no cure in the soft approach. The insistent and sometimes relentless questioning of Socrates turned into ruthless and almost brutal heckling, Socrates' mild irony morphed into cruel satire, and the sophisticated learning of Platonic philosophy (channeled via Socrates) now became a kind of antiphilosophy in the hands of Diogenes. That he had something worthwhile to offer is suggested by the reports on how the citizenry responded: despite all his annoying and outrageous behavior they found a place in their heart for him (D.L. 6.43 *ἠγαπᾶτο δὲ καὶ πρὸς Ἀθηναίων*). Upon his death they went so far as to mount a statue of a dog in Parian—that is, the best quality—marble (D.L. 6.78 *κίονα καὶ ἐπ' αὐτῷ λίθου Παρίου κύνα*).[39] In other words, his contemporaries understood that his bark was worse than his bite, and instead of becoming a "martyr" for an elite philosophy, Diogenes remained an outlandish eccentric with simple lessons for life.

NOTES

I would like to thank David Konstan, Neil O'Sullivan, David Runia, and Marcus Wilson for their thought-provoking comments and questions as I developed this chapter.

1. The epigraph is my version of J. de Maistre's "Every nation gets the government it deserves" (letter, August 1811) and R. Kennedy's "Every society gets the kind of criminal it deserves" (in *The Pursuit of Justice* 1964).

2. This "unrestricted" *parrhêsia* has been compared to comedy (Kindstrand as quoted in Bosman [2006] 94); this is debatable, given that comic playwrights did get into trouble; cf. Hartwig's chapter in this volume, Halliwell (1991), Sommerstein (2004).

3. Dudley (1998) chap. 2. The most elaborate continuous account of his life and thought is found in book 6 of Diogenes Laertius's *Lives of Eminent Philosophers* (hereafter D.L.). Authors mentioned in book 6 are Eubulides (D.L. 6. 20), Theophrastus *Megarian Dialogue* (22), Favorinus *Miscellaneous History* (25, 73), Sotion (26), Menippus *Sale of Diogenes* (29), Eubulus *Sale of Diogenes* (31), Hecato *Anecdotes* (32), Metrocles (33), Diocles (36), Zoïlus of Perga (38), Dionysius the Stoic (43), Cleomenes *Concerning Pedagogues* (75), Cercidas of Megalopolis (76), Antisthenes *Successions of Philosophers* (77), Demetrius *On Men of the Same Name* (79), Sosicrates *Successions* (80), Satirus *Lives* (80), Athenodorus *Walks* (81); the occasional phrase "some [authors] say" offers alternative attributions for anecdotes (20, 32, 58, 59).

4. A persuasive account as to why Socrates was executed has recently been put forward by Waterfield (2009).

5. O'Sullivan (1997) gives a good account of the trials; see also Wallace (2005). As to his age, D.L. 6.76 states he died at the age of nearly ninety. Although most biographical details are extremely tenuous, as Dudley (1998) 24 points out, we have no other evidence of an early demise.

6. See Coetzee (1996) 4–5, who discusses how tolerance can slip into complacency.

7. Zanker (1996) 58–60 comments (to figure 33 on his p. 59), "Socrates is now no longer depicted as the *outsider*, but rather once again as the model citizen" (my emphasis).

8. Waterfield (2009).

9. Long (1988) 154.

10. I agree with Bosman (2006) 99–103, who argues for the importance of humor for Diogenes on cultural and social grounds (theatrical performances in public). See also below, note 14 (Branham).

11. Branham (1996) 83.

12. Cf. above note 3. The best discussion of the sources of D.L. still is Jørgen Mejer's (1978), on whom my analysis in this section depends to a considerable degree.

13. Mejer (1978) 13–14, following U. von Wilamowitz, *Epistula ad Maassium* 1880.

14. Branham (1994) relates it to the so-called *chreia* tradition, collections of anecdotes, as a favorite style of conveying a message among the Cynics. This may be true, but superimposing a literary tradition does not explain the more fundamental phenomenon of disconnectedness in the narrative of Diogenes' thought.

15. In fact, for a philosopher who may not have left any writings—but see Dudley (1998) 25–27, who suggests that dialogues and plays may be his, and 6.23 mentions letters—and had no school of his own in a formal sense (though there were followers, D.L. 6.31, and influences), the length of the D.L. account (61 sections) compares very favorably to Plato's 108 sections (D.L. 3.1–109), Aristotle's 37 (5.1–37), Theophrastus's 21 (5.36–57), Zeno's 160 (7.1–160), and Chrysippus's 23 (7.179–202), to name some of the more famous philosopher colleagues in D.L.

16. There was some debate already in antiquity over the authenticity of his works; at

D.L. 6.73 the tragedies are reported as spurious after Favorinus, who attributes them to a certain Pasiphon. But against this D.L. 6.30–31 (possibly based on Eubulus's *The Sale of Diogenes*, although it is unclear how much the information offered still goes back to this source) recounts Diogenes' role as a tutor to the sons of Xeniades, whom he let memorize "many passages from poets, historians and the writings of Diogenes himself" (τῶν αὐτοῦ Διογένους). This is not the place to try to evaluate the reliability of these sources (on which see Mejer 1978, 10–16) for a definitive answer to this question, but if we exclude the tragedies we still have fourteen "dialogues" to serve this educational function (D.L. 6.80).

17. This also means that the *Lives* contain repetitions, tropes, and some confusions. On the methodology of D.L., see Mejer (1978); Sollenberger (1985) 1–62.

18. D.L. 6.70–76 contains an attempt at giving the main points of doctrine, but it is sketchy and seems to some extent based on his earlier material, as the backward reference at 6.72 illustrates (λόγους ἐρωτῶν οἵους ἄνω προειρήκαμεν). Yet it also contains materials from other sources.

19. A Thesaurus Linguae Graecae database search for ἐρωτηθείς reveals a remarkably high frequency of the participle in book 6 alone: see Table 4.1.

20. For a more detailed analysis of the performance aspect, see Bosman (2006) and Sluiter (2008).

21. Branham (1996) 87.

22. See Waterfield (2009), Ober (2004).

23. Our use of cynic, cynical, and cynicism as an expression of bleak disbelief in humanity is a twentieth-century innovation; according to Roberts (2006) 7, Boileau uses the term *cynique* apparently already in a narrow sense of *impudique* (1674 *Dictionary*). See Branham (1996).

24. Stories about Diogenes confirm this with special attention for the "dog metaphor": D.L. 6.51 "asked which animal has the worst bite (*kakista daknei*) he said: 'of those that are wild, a sycophant's; of those that are tame, a flatterer's.'"

25. He said that "one should be able to perform the works of Demeter [breakfast] and of Aphrodite [indulging sexual pleasures] in public" (D.L. 6.69).

26. Saxonhouse (2006) 8–9, 106. See also Chapter 1 in the present volume.

27. No doubt with some degree of "backfilling" the biography, see Long (1988), Branham (1996).

28. There is a certain ambivalence toward intellectual pursuits in the sources, given "the remarkable variety of literary activity ascribed to the Cynics" (Branham 1996) 85.

29. I base my analysis on Barclay (1995) (I owe this reference to Dr. Silke Sitzler).

30. Becker (1963). For a neuroscientist's look at the outsider as iconoclast, see Berns (2010).

31. He also mentions that Antisthenes "gave the impulse to the indifference (ἀπαθεία) of Diogenes."

32. Barclay (1995) 115–16.

33. On Plato's response, see, e.g., D.L. 6.40 and 6.54. On Hellenistic polemic to

discredit Socrates (as the spring of different schools including the cynics), see Long (1988) 155–56.

34. Cf. *ὀνειδιζόμενος* D.L. 6.56, 58, 66, 67 (overlap with *ἐρωτηθείς* only in 6.56 and 67); we may compare *λοιδορούμενος* which is not found in book 6 (but see 2.70 Aristippus; 9.29 [twice] Zeno of Elea).

35. See Branham (1996).

36. Kennedy (1999) 50 makes the same argument for Hyparchia, the wife of Crates, but adds an interesting angle to it: "The Cynic operated from a position of exile—sometimes chosen, sometimes forced—and while the causes of exile require specific and responsible address in terms of what cynical stances offer, exile did provide *a rhetorical space* for the Cynic rhetor" (my emphasis), even calling Hyparchia's case a "double exile" (ibid., 51).

37. The notion of marginalization I am using is Bremmer's (1992) 206. He identifies several "symbols of marginalization," which connect the Pythagoreans, Cynics, and Christian monks (clothing, laughter, drinking water, vegetarianism).

38. Desmond (2008) 69.

39. One could argue that this too is a posthumous fabrication like the other biographical elements (above, note 3), but the fact remains that we have no positive evidence for a trial against Diogenes.

REFERENCES

Barclay, J. M. G. 1995. "Deviance and Apostasy: Some Applications of Deviance Theory to First-Century Judaism and Christianity." In *Modelling Early Christianity. Social-Scientific Studies of the New Testament in Its Context*, ed. P. F. Esler, 114–27. London: Routledge.

Becker, H. S. 1963. *Outsiders: Studies in the Sociology of Deviance*. New York: Free Press.

Berns, G. 2010. *Iconoclast: A Neuroscientist Reveals How to Think Differently*. Boston: Harvard Business Review Press.

Bosman, P. 2006. "Selling Cynicism: The Pragmatics of Diogenes' Comic Performances." *Classical Quarterly* 56: 93–104.

Branham, R. Bracht. 1994. "Defacing the Currency: Diogenes' Rhetoric and the Invention of Cynicism." *Arethusa* 27.3: 329–59 [= id. 1996. "Defacing the Currency: Diogenes' Rhetoric and the Invention of Cynicism." In *The Cynics: The Cynic Movement in Antiquity and Its Legacy*, ed. R. Bracht Branham and Marie-Odile Goulet-Cazé, 81–104. Berkeley: University of California Press.]

Bremmer, J. N. 1992. "Symbols of Marginality from Early Pythagoreans to Late Antique Monks." *Greece & Rome* 39: 205–14.

Coetzee, J. M. 1996. *Giving Offense: Essays on Censorship*. Chicago: University of Chicago Press.

Cruces, J. L. L. 2004. "Two Sayings of Diogenes in Greek Comedy (D.L. 6.51)." *Hermes* 132: 248–52.

Desmond, W. 2008. *Cynics*. Stocksfield: Acumen.

Dudley, D. R. 1998. *A History of Cynicism: From Diogenes to the 6th Century AD.* 2nd ed. Bristol: Bristol Classical Press.

Fortenbaugh, W. W., P. M. Huby, and A. A. Long, eds. 1985. *Theophrastus of Eresus: On His Life and Work*. New Brunswick, NJ: Transaction Books.

Griffin, M. 1996. "Cynicism and the Romans: Attraction and Repulsion." In *The Cynics: The Cynic Movement in Antiquity and Its Legacy*, ed. R. Bracht Branham and Marie-Odile Goulet-Cazé, 190–204. Berkeley: University of California Press.

Halliwell, S. 1991. "Comic Satire and Freedom of Speech in Classical Athens." *Journal of Hellenic Studies* 111: 48–70.

Hicks, R. D. 1970. *Diogenes Laertius, Lives of Eminent Philosophers*. 2 vols. Cambridge, MA: Harvard University Press.

Kennedy, K. 1999. "Hipparchia the Cynic: Feminist Rhetoric and the Ethics of Embodiment." *Hypatia* 14: 48–71.

Long, A. A. 1988. "Socrates in Hellenistic Philosophy." *Classical Quarterly* 38: 150–71.

Mejer, J. 1978. *Diogenes Laertius and His Hellenistic Background*. Wiesbaden: Steiner.

O'Sullivan, L. 1997. "Athenian Impiety Trials in the Late Fourth Century BC." *Classical Quarterly* 47: 136–52.

Porter, J. 1996. "The Philosophy of Aristo of Chios." In *The Cynics: The Cynic Movement in Antiquity and Its Legacy*, ed. R. Bracht Branham and Marie-Odile Goulet-Cazé, 156–89. Berkeley: University of California Press.

Roberts, H. 2006. *Dogs' Tales: Representations of Ancient Cynicism in French Renaissance Texts*. Amsterdam: Rodopi.

Saxonhouse, A. W. 2006. *Free Speech and Democracy in Ancient Athens*. Cambridge: Cambridge University Press.

Sluiter, I. 2008. "Communicating Cynicism: Diogenes' Gangsta Rap." In *Learning and Language: Philosophy of Language in the Hellenistic Age*, ed. D. Frede and B. Inwood, 139–63. Cambridge: Cambridge University Press.

Sollenberger, M. G. 1985. "Diogenes Laertius 5.36–57." In *Theophrastus of Eresus: On His Life and Work*, ed. W. W. Fortenbaugh, P. M. Huby, and A. A. Long, 1–62. New Brunswick, NJ: Transaction Books.

Sommerstein, A. H. 2004. "Harassing the Satirist: The Alleged Attempts to Prosecute Aristophanes." In *Free Speech in Classical Antiquity*, ed. I. Sluiter and R. M. Rosen, 145–74. Leiden: Brill.

Steiner, G. 1976. "Diogenes' Mouse and the Royal Dog: Conformity in Non-conformity." *Classical Journal* 72: 36–46.

Wallace, R. W. 1994. "The Athenian Laws Against Slander." In *Symposion 1993: Vorträge zur griechischen und hellenistischen Rechtsgeschichte*, ed. G. Thür, 109–24. Cologne: Böhlau.

———. 2005. "Law, Attic Comedy, and the Regulation of Comic Speech." In *The Cambridge Companion to Ancient Greek Law*, ed. M. Gagarin and D. J. Cohen, 357–73. Cambridge: Cambridge University Press.

Waterfield, R. 2009. *Why Socrates Died: Dispelling the Myths*. London: Faber.

Zanker, P. 1996. *The Mask of Socrates: The Image of the Intellectual in Antiquity*. Tr. Alan Shapiro. Berkeley: University of California Press.

Chapter 5

Censorship for the Roman Stage?

Gesine Manuwald

In the mid-republic, about 240 BCE, the Romans adopted the custom of performing dramas at public festivals. While the institution and the literary genre were taken over from the Greeks (with additional influences from non-Roman peoples in Italy), there were significant differences in running the institution from the start: in classical Athens the performance of dramas was an activity of the entire citizenry, organized by the archon in charge, who had been chosen by lot for the year; his responsibilities included selecting the poets that were given the chance to participate in the dramatic *agon*; the citizenry was involved in the performances since dramatic choruses consisted of citizens; and individual citizens were chosen as *choregoi* to provide the necessary funds. In Rome, by contrast, festivals and dramatic performances were activities financed and organized by magistrates in office, who are likely to have taken account of the political context; magistrates bought the dramas from playwrights (perhaps via impresarios) for performance on stage by professional actors. This structure suggests that there might have been political control of what was presented in the theater, namely, that there was a form of "censorship" that ensured that nothing contentious or potentially explosive was brought on stage.

The existing evidence, however, does not unequivocally confirm such a scenario. Obviously, ancient Rome was the first community to have the office of censor, but the duties of these officials rather covered issues of moral and social behavior of individuals, beyond their original economic function.[1] Hence, as part of their duties, the censors seem to have officially confirmed the status of actors, who were looked down upon in Rome and were denied ordinary citizen rights,[2] but they are not known to have checked literary texts before they were distributed. And there is no record of any other office in ancient Rome that was responsible for monitoring the contents of literary works. At the same time there are a few pieces of evidence in the plays themselves and in references to dramas and performances in rhetorical and historical texts indicating that there was no complete freedom for the content and tone of dramas. This is in line with a general tension and ambivalence that can be observed for drama in Rome, particularly in the republican period: dramatic performances were public events, were organized by magistrates and received public funding; at the same time there was opposition from within the nobility to the erection of permanent buildings (so that Rome got its first permanent stone theater only in 55 BCE), there were restrictions on the citizen rights of actors, and it was regarded as disgraceful for members of higher social classes to appear on stage against payment.[3]

Although precise evidence is scarce and scattered—a situation that may distort the picture (as is the case for many issues connected with Roman drama)—this contribution assembles and discusses the available testimonia and infers, with the appropriate caution, in what way the content and tone of Roman drama might have been restricted by formal or informal means. The material is presented in roughly chronological order, so as to take account of the significant literary, social, and political changes between the republican and the imperial periods. Owing to the nature of the evidence, the focus is on "political censorship," but there are also thoughts on possible moral and literary restrictions. It is hoped that at the end of this overview a tentative suggestion on the existence and character of "censorship" in relation to republican and imperial Roman drama can be made.[4] It goes without saying that in this context "censorship" is not a reference to the Roman office (*OED*, s.v. 1), but is used in the modern transferred sense of "[t]he office or function of a censor . . . ; official supervision. *spec.* control of dramatic production and films" (*OED*, s.v. 2a).[5] Even if this may be an anachronistic use of the term, it provides a useful and appropriate concept for describing the situation in Rome.

In the republican period festivals were the only occasions in Rome on which dramas could be released to a wider audience; because these events were organized by public officials, it was technically the magistrates in charge who made decisions on which (originally newly written) plays were performed. Yet it is unclear how much these magistrates knew about the plays by the time the selection was made or what impact their knowledge of them or potential comments on draft versions may have had on the shape of the plays eventually performed. The prologue to Terence's *Eunuchus* suggests that there could be previews for the aediles running the games (Ter. *Eun.* 20–22). But in this case the preview seems to have taken place after the aediles had bought the play, and it is unknown how they reacted and whether their reactions had any consequences for the eventual format of the play given at the festival. In theory such an arrangement enabled individual politicians to ensure that nothing that might compromise them or their peers was presented on stage.[6]

Because of the organization of the theater business, playwrights in republican times were in close contact with noblemen, and some poets are known to have written plays about a general's victories or to have produced dramas for games on particular occasions. Hence modern scholars have often regarded dramatists of this period as "client poets."[7] The consequence of such a position would not be state censorship in the strict sense; it would rather imply that poets were loyal to their patrons and therefore did not include in their plays anything that might jeopardize them. However, other scholars have challenged the notion of republican playwrights as "client poets."[8] While members of the nobility are likely to have entertained good relationships with some poets and to have commissioned playwrights for special occasions, such connections seem not to have determined the overall status of the respective dramatists and the outlook of their poetry: in the republican period all plays were performed at festivals open to the public, and poets are unlikely to have written dramas exclusively for specific patrons. Therefore it is more plausible that dramatists were not attached to particular families as clients and expected to promote these families, but that they rather moved freely among the nobility and worked for various families. Ennius (239–169 BCE), for instance, is said by Cicero to have praised several noblemen (even after their deaths, which made his eulogy less suspicious) and to have given adornment to the entire Roman people by his presentation of individuals (Cic. *Brut.* 57–59; *Arch.* 22). The portrait of the "good companion" in Ennius's *Annales*, often identified with the poet on the basis of Aelius Stilo's comments (Gell. *NA* 12.4), presents a person who is familiar with a nobleman and is his social inferior, but is not completely dependent on him.

Hence the fact that individual noblemen were in charge of dramatic productions seems not to have restricted the poets' freedom automatically and channeled their dramas into a certain direction. This is not contradicted by what is known about the fate of the poet Naevius (c. 280/60–200 BCE). He is often presented as an outspoken playwright, who ended up in jail and later had to leave Rome. But the evidence, both on a feud with the family of the

Metelli expressed by alternate verses[9] and on the poet's imprisonment because of disparagement of Roman politicians,[10] is dubious: with respect to fragments (lacking any context) that seem to comment on freedom of speech at festivals and in the theater,[11] it has been shown that they can also be understood as utterances of typical comedy slaves, perhaps with a metaliterary dimension.[12] More generally, since Naevius inaugurated the dramatic genre of *fabula praetexta*, that is, serious plays on events from Roman history, was the first in Rome to write an epic on a Roman topic (*Bellum Poenicum*), and inserted allusions to a Roman context into comedies set in Greece, his work obviously engaged with political and social aspects of contemporary Rome; this may have given rise to corresponding biographical anecdotes. Yet the surviving evidence does not support the interpretation that Naevius voiced critical positions so clearly in his literary works that he was punished for that reason.

Still, restraint in making direct political (particularly critical) statements on stage might have been what was expected of Roman dramatists. A key piece of evidence for possible restrictions on what could be presented on the Roman stage is Augustine's summary of a conversation in Cicero's *De re publica*: the speaker Scipio is said to have concluded a part of the discussion by showing "that the early Romans were displeased if a living man was either praised or criticized on the stage."[13] In what precedes Greek Old Comedy seems to have been discussed; it is described as attacking demagogues, rebels, and specific well-known individuals. This procedure is judged to be just about acceptable even though it would be better if these people were pilloried by a censor rather than by a poet, while it is presented as totally unacceptable that Pericles, after all his successes, was insulted on stage. Such a treatment would be as inappropriate as "if our own Plautus or Naevius had wanted to speak ill of Publius or Gnaeus Scipio, or Caecilius to do so of Marcus Cato."[14] As a contrast, the Twelve Tables in Rome are called to mind by one of the interlocutors: "although they established capital punishment for very few offenses, included among them this: if anyone should sing offensively or should compose a poem which brought disgrace or offense to someone else." The speaker notes this arrangement with approval since one's lifestyle should be judged by magistrates and in court in a fair process with both parties having the chance to present their views rather than by the creativity of poets.[15]

Because this passage comes from a fragmentary part of *De re publica* and survives only in Augustine's treatise, the accuracy of the report is in doubt, and the overall context is not completely clear, nor is it evident whether this speaker's opinion was endorsed by the interlocutors or even by the writer Cicero. Irrespective of these difficulties, the fact that such an issue is being presented and discussed must mean that it was a concern at the time and that the view put forward was a possible one that would not seem ridiculous to contemporary recipients. According to what is outlined here, the custom of *nominatim laedere* ("to injure or offend someone by name") of Greek Old Comedy was being frowned upon and regarded as inappropriate in Rome. The reason given for such an attitude is not that political comments of this kind were regarded as dangerous or subversive, but rather that drama is seen as an improper venue for comments on people's conduct and as being an unfair vehicle because of its one-sidedness. Drama is presented as a medium that should not assume the role of censor rather than as subject to censorship itself. Importantly, it is said that open criticism on stage was regarded as inappropriate and displeasing to ancient Romans (of uncertain date); there is no mention of laws explicitly restricting the content and tone of dramas (as the Twelve Tables refer to songs and not to dramas and seem to be introduced mainly as an example demonstrating the traditional disapproval of personal insults in literary works in the broadest sense) or of an institution ensuring that dramas brought on stage did not include such elements.

Nevertheless, in all that survives of Roman republican drama there is no direct critical presentation of contemporary politicians; this may imply that poets respected the attitude suggested by Scipio's comments in Cicero's *De re publica*.[16] Moreover, most Latin plays are set in a Greek mythical environment or in Greek or Roman private surroundings. The only dramatic genre that has the potential to make direct statements on political figures without disrupting the dramatic illusion is *fabula praetexta*. However, although the final comment in this section of the dialogue as reported by Augustine refers to both praise and blame of living individuals, what survives of the discussion in Cicero indicates that ridicule and criticism from the stage were the main issue that presented difficulties to some Romans. In line with this, *fabulae praetextae* in the republican period appear to have been generally supportive of Roman ideology, glorifying Rome's foundation stories or recent victories.[17]

While open criticism of contemporary individuals and events seems to have been avoided, there are, at the same time, numerous passages in all genres of Roman republican drama that may be interpreted as comments on the current situation, as modern scholars have suggested. Indeed, beyond a basic tendency to select and adapt topics of interest and relevance to Roman audiences (e.g., relationship between different generations of a family; place of individuals within the community; behavior in war; role of powerful politicians), Roman dramatists have characters talk about a variety of specific issues such as the Bacchanalia, female luxury, praetors' edicts, or other items that would have been of social or political significance to audiences at the time of the first performances. The full force of such references must have been obvious to the original audiences; at the same time such comments would not be openly problematic since the remarks remain veiled and indirect. They precisely avoided a treatment by name that was singled out in the dialogue in Cicero, and they could always be seen as parts of the mythical or fictitious stories actually presented on stage.

For instance, the play *Barbatus* by the *togata* poet Titinius (fl. c. 200 BCE), which survives only in fragments, seems to have included comments on female luxury (*Tog.* 1; 2; 3 R.[3]), like some of Plautus's comedies (Plaut. *Aul.* 167–69; *Epid.* 219–35); in the works of both poets these remarks may allude to the debate on the Lex Oppia and its eventual repeal in 195 BCE (cf. Liv. 34.1.1–8.3). Two further plays by Titinius named after music girls (*Psaltria siue Ferentinatis*; *Tibicina*) could refer not only to a traditional accomplishment of courtesans, but also more specifically to their admittance to Roman dinner parties in 187 BCE (cf. Liv. 39.6.8; also Plaut. *Mostell.* 959–60; *Stich.* 380–81). The fragments of plays written by Titinius's successor Afranius (fl. c. 160–120 BCE) include probable allusions to the "marriage and children laws" of the censor Q. Caecilius Metellus Macedonicus in 131 BCE (*Tog.* 360–62 R.[3]), which are commented upon also by the contemporary satirist Lucilius (Lucil. 676–86 M. = 636–46 W.). The remarkable appearance of a property manager (*choragus*) in Plautus's *Curculio* consists of a speech in which he critically describes a number of different groups of people associated with various locations around the forum (Plaut. *Curc.* 462–86). This comes close to a direct comment on Roman life, but it remains general and does not single out individuals.

However, such conventions, which could be regarded as the result of a kind of collective and indirect censorship or a kind of self-censorship, do not seem to have applied to all groups of individuals in the same way: talking about and disparaging other theater people apparently was possible to some extent. Terence's prologues are well known to illustrate a kind of literary feud among contemporary poets, where Terence has his prologue speakers criticize his opponents' plays, views and behavior (e.g., Ter. *Haut.* 30–34; *Eun.* 7–19a; *Phorm.* 6–11; see below). Yet, these opponents are never mentioned by name, in contrast to poets of an earlier generation (Naevius, Ennius, Plautus), who are referred to as authoritative precedents (Ter. *Andr.* 18–21). Somewhat similarly, also in the second century BCE, two mime actors attacked the poets Lucilius and Accius from the stage; the victims took these actors to court, though only Accius was successful (*Auct. ad Her.* 1.24; 2.19). The differing results (even if the specific circumstances of each case are unknown) may point to the conclusion that naming someone on stage was not generally accepted, but did not inevitably lead to punishment either. Perhaps, greater leniency operated in the case of theater people than in the case of politicians. At any rate, here the private individuals concerned, rather than official institutions, exercised control of what was said on stage, by means of private legal proceedings (in line with the Roman concept of *iniuria*) after the event.[18]

The most forceful intervention in theater business on the part of the authorities, which actually involved censors, occurred in 115 BCE: according to a notice in Cassiodorus's chronicle, the censors L. Caecilius Metellus (Diadematus) and Cn. Domitius Ahenobarbus banned "the performing arts" (*ars ludicra*) from the city of Rome with the exception of "a Latin piper with a singer" (*Latinus tibicen cum cantore*), and also a performance consisting of music and dance called *ludus talarius*.[19] The censors' motives are being debated, as is the question of what forms of performances were covered by this order.

This move was presumably an attempt at eliminating an institution or elements of an institution seen as causing offense. It is plausible, also against the background of other mentions of *ludus talarius* (Cic. *Att.* 1.16.3; *Off.* 1.150; Quint. *Inst.* 11.3.58; Fronto, *Orat.* 10 [p. 157 v.d.H.]), that officials and intellectuals regarded it as a vulgar, low, and licentious dancing spectacle and that therefore the censors banned it on grounds of morality and impropriety. Other forms of the performing arts too might have been regarded as a threat to social and political stability, as there was a general tendency in this period toward the inclusion of comments on the contemporary political situation in dramas, and the court cases just mentioned would have taken place about the same time. Such a reason for the censors' move, the aim to prevent potentially controversial or insulting statements from being made publicly on stage and to eliminate licentious spectacles, would agree with the moral jurisdiction that was part of the censors' remit. What was allowed to remain seems to have been sober traditional performances of music and song; the lack of dramatic dialogue reduced the potential for criticism. However, the censors' intervention did not have a noticeable effect since no major change in the development of Roman drama is recognizable at around 115 BCE.

On the contrary, for the first century BCE there is evidence that dramas could be used to make clear statements about topical political issues: revival performances of tragedies and comedies as well as mime (and Atellana) performances in the first century BCE are notorious for being exploited in the light of the contemporary political situation. However, there is still almost no direct mention of proper names, while there are indications of attempts to limit the freedom of political interpretations.

According to the testimony in Cicero, who is the main witness for the political exploitation of revival performances of existing and well-known plays in the first century BCE, the plots of these plays and, more frequently, individual scenes or lines could be referred to the present situation by actors and/or audiences when verses that originally had a different meaning in the context of the plays were applied to contemporary circumstances.[20] The prime example of this is Cicero's report in the speech *Pro Sestio* of a dramatic performance just after the senate had decided to recall him from exile in 57 BCE: by means of particular emphasis, gestures, and the addition of suitable verses from other plays or even lines composed by himself, the actor expressed his assessment of Cicero and his fate, and the audience emphatically responded to it (Cic. *Sest.* 116–23). Obviously, Cicero delights in this and does not report objections to this kind of performance.[21] If such a procedure had not been universally recognized, Cicero would presumably not have dwelled on it in a public speech. This practice may lead to both supportive and critical reactions to the contemporary situation in dramas, but such comments would still be indirect as parts of a coherent plot with a different focus.

Nevertheless, it seems that the increasing politicization of dramatic performances in the first century BCE, which extended to audience reactions upon prominent individuals entering the theater (e.g., Cic. *Fam.* 8.2.1; *Att.* 2.19.3), triggered initiatives to limit politically explosive consequences. For the *Ludi Apollinares* after Caesar's assassination in 44 BCE the city praetor M. Iunius Brutus, one of Caesar's assassins, had planned a revival performance of Accius's *praetexta Brutus*, a play dealing with the overthrow of the last king Tarquinius Superbus and the inauguration of the Roman Republic. When Brutus had left the city of Rome and C. Antonius, one of Mark Antony's brothers, had taken over his duties, the drama was changed from Accius's *Brutus* to Accius's *Tereus*, though even the performance of this piece (featuring a mythical tyrant) caused demonstrations from the audience in support of the absent Brutus (Cic. *Att.* 16.2.3; 16.5.1; *Phil.* 1.36). Although this is not an act of censorship in the sense that free speech was restricted, the careful selection of plays is an instance of political interference in the arts in order to influence audience reactions and to avoid politically contentious material being brought on stage.

That the choice of dramas was recognized as important for shaping an event in this period can also be seen from Pompey's behavior slightly earlier: Pompey had Sp. Maecius Tarpa arrange the program for the games at the opening of his theater in 55 BCE (Cic. *Fam.* 7.1). This is the only known instance of a festival organizer employing someone to put together the program, and the fact that Cicero mentions this person and his being in charge of the program might indicate that it was unusual. That this arrangement was noteworthy is further suggested by the fact that Horace twice refers to Sp. Maecius Tarpa as an example of a judge of literary works (Hor. *Sat.* 1.10.37b–39; *Ars P.* 386b–88a). Pompey may have hired Sp. Maecius Tarpa to ensure high-quality entertainment at his event; yet in view of the focus of the spectacle as a whole, it is perhaps more likely that Pompey wanted to present the opening games as a celebration of himself and his victories and therefore wished to make sure that the plays performed could not be read in subversive ways.

The same period saw another remarkable instance of an interesting tension between indirect censorship and freedom of speech on stage, this time with respect to a new play. According to the late antique writer Macrobius (*Sat.* 2.7.1–9), who is the most extensive source for this incident, the mime writer Decimus Laberius, who is introduced as "a Roman equestrian of fiercely free speech," was asked by Caesar to appear as an actor in the mimes he was writing, which would put his equestrian status at risk. Laberius, yielding to the force of power, delivered a so-called prologue that alluded to his loss of status, and later in the play he inserted comments about the Roman people losing their freedom and about the "need for him whom many fear to fear many" (Lab. *Mim.* 98–124; 125; 126 R.[3]). The audience realized that these remarks could be referred to Caesar, and Caesar turned his favor to Laberius's rival Publilius Syrus. Later, after a contest between the two poets, Caesar is said to have awarded Publilius Syrus the victory palm and to have reinstated Laberius as a knight.[22] Although Macrobius seems to be conflating details that belong to two distinct events, it can still be inferred that despite Laberius's veiled criticism and its obvious interpretation by the audience, Caesar did not inflict a long-term punishment on Laberius or prevent him from future dramatic activity. Laberius's extant verses do not mention Caesar's name and the play seems only to have contained occasional jibes at Caesar, but not to have consisted entirely of criticism. While the intended meaning became obvious by the audience reaction, the indirect nature of these comments might have made measures against the poet more difficult.

More generally, the fact that new mimes could be used for political comment on current affairs appears to have been a feature that had to be reckoned with by Cicero's time. For that the engagement of mime with the political situation was not as singular as the circumstances in the above case might suggest is indicated by Cicero's fear for a politically active friend that he might be singled out by Laberius and other mime writers if he acted wrongly (Cic. *Fam.* 7.11.2). Elsewhere Cicero corresponds with Atticus about the audience's reaction to mimes by Publilius Syrus, which apparently included an expression of views on the contemporary political situation (Cic. *Att.* 14.2.1). Cicero even seems to expect "utterances of mime actors" and reactions of the people (Cic. *Att.* 14.3.2). Obviously, the dramatic genre of mime could feature such topical remarks; and if comments about influential people had to be reckoned with, there was obviously no official censorship that prevented such politically charged elements in the first place.

This situation does not seem to have altered significantly at the turn from republic to principate, when the political framework changed. The politicization of drama or of dramatic performances to be observed toward the end of the republic in the first century BCE continued into the early imperial period. Those dramatic genres that were taken up in early imperial times seamlessly pursued developments observable at the end of the republic, even though plays no longer had a necessary connection with full-scale performances in the theater: like revivals or plays of new dramatic genres in late republican times, dramas composed in the early imperial period may be seen as making topical political comments. In this era, however, the political emphasis is rather critical, following trends of the late republican period, while in the early days Roman dramas tended to support Roman ideology in one way or another.[23]

Such a development is most obvious in the area of *praetexta*, the only dramatic genre whose plots directly engage with the political situation: republican *praetextae* were typically celebrations of Rome's foundation myths or of recent military victories; only Accius's *Brutus*, composed toward the end of the republican period, might have had a more nuanced range of meanings. By contrast, the only full-scale *praetexta* surviving from the early imperial period, the pseudo-Senecan *Octavia*, is critical of Nero's rule and seems to advocate a more responsible behavior for a ruler and an alternative form of monarchy. The date of the play and the question of whether it was destined for a full-scale performance in a public theater are still being debated.[24] If it was written as late as the Flavian period, as has recently been suggested, or initially only recited among a limited group of people, there would not have been any issues with potential censorship. In any case, it is clear that a public staging of such a play during Nero's reign would have been difficult.

That a performance or a recitation of a play with a potentially critical dimension, even if it did not feature the emperor himself, might cause trouble for the poet is suggested by the opening of Tacitus's *Dialogus de oratoribus* (Tac. *Dial.* 2–3). It shows the writer Curiatius Maternus being visited by friends concerned for him because he recited his drama *Cato* on the previous day and is said to have caused offense to the "powerful." In contrast to the worries of his friends, Curiatius Maternus is not affected by this: he refuses to follow their advice to eliminate material open to "an odd interpretation" and to make the published version of the play "safer"; instead he is determined to go on to express his genuine views in a tragedy titled *Thyestes*, already conceived in his mind. His tragedies and *praetextae* mentioned in this context (*Medea*, *Thyestes*; *Cato*, *Domitius*) cannot be direct presentations of the emperor; yet, because of their subject matter they offer themselves to being shaped or interpreted as commentaries on the current ruler. The contrasting attitudes of Curiatius Maternus and of his friends show that there does not seem to have been formal censorship (then he would not have been able to issue dramas of this character), but that there was control of literature by "the powerful" (presumably the emperor and his council and officials), who might interfere if they suspected anything subversive in literary works.

The early principate also saw performances of Atellanae (Suet. *Tib.* 45; *Ner.* 39.3; *Galb.* 13), which might have been revivals; at any rate famous parts seem to have been known to audiences, and performances were exploited for critical remarks on the emperor, which might lead to repercussions. For a performance during Nero's reign it is recorded that the actor who had suggested an interpretation referring to the emperor was banished from the city and from Italy. Because of a line with an ambiguous joke a writer of Atellanae was burned alive in the amphitheater under Caligula (Suet. *Calig.* 27.4). Without reference to a particular incident Tacitus reports that the emperor Tiberius was of the view that the lack of restraint on the part of actors in life and on stage, and of Atellana plays in particular, had reached a point that it had to be restricted by a senate decree, whereupon actors were banished from Italy (Tac. *Ann.* 4.14.3). Nero too is said by Tacitus to have banished actors from Italy, but this seems to have been provoked by riots among supporters of actors that were triggered by the games rather than by anything that was said or done on stage (Tac. *Ann.* 13.25.4); Suetonius refers this intervention to pantomime actors (Suet. *Ner.* 16.2; 26.2). Domitian banished actors from the stage, while he allowed them to practice their art in private houses (Suet. *Dom.* 7.1). Obviously, in those days the all-powerful leaders in the Roman state took care to control the activities connected with the theater, including both what was said on stage and what happened during performances. They are, however, not to be regarded as "censors" in the proper sense of the word, exercising control in advance; apparently they reacted to situations as and when they felt that it was necessary, rather than issuing particular rules beforehand.

Further details cannot be established, since the plays referred to in the historical narratives do not survive. What is extant from the early imperial period are, besides the pseudo-Senecan *praetexta Octavia*, Seneca's tragedies, for which the context is uncertain.[25] At the same time it is universally acknowledged that tyrants are ubiquitous in Seneca's dramas and that this must be connected with the poet's experiences as tutor and mentor at the imperial court: depending on the precise dating, that is, under which emperor the plays were written and at what point in their reign, the plays might be seen as either protreptic or critical. It seems that irresponsible behavior, being governed by immoderate passions and unbridled use of power on the part of the monarch, are disapproved of. Since all plays stay firmly within the mythical realm, issues of any form of censorship would not have affected them.

Still, it is noteworthy that Seneca must have deliberately chosen this way of expressing himself since he was more direct in some of the works he produced in other literary genres: his treatise *De clementia* (55/56 CE), written shortly after Nero's accession to the throne, gives advice on how to be a just ruler, presumably with the underlying agenda to encourage Nero to develop into such a monarch and to justify imperial rule;[26] the *Apocolocyntosis* (c. 54 CE) is a biting satire on Claudius, composed somewhat earlier, soon after this emperor's death, presumably initially intended for a limited audience. The *Apocolocyntosis* condemns Claudius, expressing a harsh verdict on the deceased emperor, while there will have been a clear political agenda on the part of Seneca as Nero's political adviser.[27] Seneca and Nero fell out at some point, and Seneca withdrew from the imperial court in 62 CE (Tac. *Ann.* 14.52–56); but there is no indication that this might have had to do with Seneca's literary activity.

In all periods of Roman theater, in addition to the "political" status of drama in the community and possible restrictions triggered thereby, there could be issues concerning other aspects of dramatic performances. As the intervention of the censors in 115 BCE suggests (see above), there might have been moral disapproval of stage events (at least of some forms) and the intention to eliminate morally contentious content on the part of the authorities. Indeed, there seems to have been an awareness among both playwrights and audiences of what was morally acceptable and whether dramatic performances complied with these standards; yet this knowledge apparently did not mean that a drama or action that might be regarded as morally problematic could not be brought on stage.

In the prologue to Plautus's *Captivi* it is stressed that this comedy "is quite unlike other plays" as it does not "contain filthy lines that one must not repeat" and does not feature characters like an "perjured pimp, or unprincipled courtesan, or braggart captain" (Plaut. *Capt.* 55–58). The epilogue confirms that "this play was composed with due regard to the proprieties" and that there were "no vicious intrigues, no love affair, no supposititious child, no getting money on false pretences, no young spark setting a wench free without his father's knowledge"; it therefore claims that this play belongs to the few "which make good men better" (Plaut. *Capt.* 1029–34). Even though these comments cannot be taken at face value and play with the generic conventions of *palliata* comedy, they suggest the conclusion that the plot in comedies may present behavior that can be seen as morally problematic or unacceptable. However, this characteristic obviously did not mean that those plays could not be brought on stage; the remarks clearly refer to other plays that were performed. This contrast is thus used to distinguish Plautus's play favorably from those other dramas.

The relative freedom with respect to morals might have to do with the fact that these plays as well as Plautus's own dramas belonged to the dramatic genre of *palliata* comedy and thus were set in Greece; within such a foreign setting with the appropriate customs greater freedom concerning moral and social issues was apparently possible. In the prologue to *Casina*, for instance, a slave wedding that will be shown on stage later in the play is justified by the fact that "it does happen in Greece and at Carthage, and here in our own country in Apulia," with the contrast to Rome implied (Plaut. *Cas.* 68–78; cf. also *Pers.* 25). The underlying idea of a difference between Greece and Rome apparently enabled plots that included features violating Roman customs. This also agrees with a comment by Terence's late antique commentator

Donatus that in *togatae* (in contrast to *palliatae*) slaves were commonly not allowed to be cleverer than their masters (Donat. on Ter. *Eun.* 57). Such a rule implies that for dramatic genres set in ordinary Roman surroundings observing moral standards was expected, but that it was not required for plots set in other contexts.

That a lack of moral standards was noted and disapproved of by some, but not enforced for all dramatic genres is further suggested by the well-known anecdote about Cato watching a mime in the theater: at *Ludi Florales* in 55 BCE the audience was embarrassed at demanding that the mime actresses should strip naked because of his presence; having been informed of the situation, Cato left the theater amid tremendous applause so that the people could enjoy the accustomed spectacle (cf. Val. Max. 2.10.8; Sen. *Ep.* 97.8; Mart. 1, *praef.*). This story shows that not even a person such as Cato tried to enforce moral censorship at performances.

At the same time the expected attitude to the genre of mime becomes obvious by the fact that, although all actors in Rome were of low social status, and appearing on the stage against payment was looked down upon, mime actors and actresses were held in particularly low regard; and if public personalities associated with them, this could be turned into a major reproach against them, as shown by Cicero's criticism of Mark Antony (Cic. *Phil.* 2.20; 2.58; 2.61–62; 2.67; 2.101; 8.26; 10.22; 11.13; 13.24). The fact that actors were denied political and civic rights of ordinary citizens (cf. Cic. *Rep.* 4.10 [= August. *De civ. D.* 2.13]; Tert. *De spect.* 22.2; see above) shows a low regard for the institution, but it does not reveal details on the attitude to individual dramatic genres or elements of them or to the topics presented.

In late antiquity, the church fathers and other early Christian writers vehemently opposed theater and spectacles, one reason being drama's presentation of gods and the amorality of both the plots and the institution in their view (e.g., Lactant. *Div. inst.* 6.20.32–36; Arn. *Adv. nat.* 7.33; Tert. *De spect.*). They obviously applied criteria different from those valid in republican and early imperial times, but their reaction confirms that plots that could be seen as inviting some restrictions were shown on stage; this again suggests that there was no official censorship preventing such aspects from reaching the stage.

Finally, there seems to have been a kind of "censorship" exerted by the poets themselves. Terence's prologues not only shed light on conventions for naming people in dramas (see above), but also reveal that there was rivalry among poets and that competitors closely watched what other people active in the same dramatic genre were doing. From the comments in Terence it appears that it was regarded as a break of conventions if a Roman playwright reused a Greek comedy and brought it on stage as a new play when the same Greek drama had already been used for a Latin play by another Roman playwright (Ter. *Eun.* 19b–34; *Ad.* 1–14); on one occasion one of Terence's opponents is said to have pointed this out at a preview of Terence's comedy for the aediles. For Greek-style tragedy too poets seem to have avoided presenting exactly the same myth or at any rate exactly the same version again. Hence competition among dramatic poets who were watching each other seems to have resulted in an unofficial system of mutual control in terms of literary shape and background.

This overview of key pieces of evidence to be considered in answering the question of whether there was "censorship" for the Roman stage confirms the impression that there seem not to have been specific laws or a formal office that restricted freedom of speech for playwrights or checked plays in advance, while there were established conventions as well as political interests of people at the top and later, from the late republic and the early principate onward, of individual politicians and emperors that made poets largely avoid direct criticism of contemporary public individuals and of concrete political actions. However, this does not mean that Roman dramas were entirely apolitical or irrelevant; on the contrary, they presented topics pertinent to Roman society and included more or less obvious indirect comments on current affairs. Since drama was one of the earliest literary genres to be established in Rome and, at least in the republican period, was at the heart of the community due to its being performed to diverse audiences, its amount of freedom to express topical concerns is an important indication for the political and social climate in the community. The fact that dramas refrained from direct attacks, but did not abstain from comment, which they tended to make via mythical or fictitious figures often in foreign settings, may be indicative of (unwritten) conventions and of the reverence of one's elders at Rome. Accordingly, dramatic genres set in ordinary Roman surroundings seem to have been subject to tighter rules.

One modern playwright has interpreted the situation at Rome as poets trying to make subversive comments in veiled fashion (also suiting his own agenda): in his 2004 play titled *Flatfoot* the Australian writer David Williamson presents "Plautus" ("Flatfoot") as he is under pressure to produce a play for the upcoming games and develops it on the spot in conversation with the magistrate in charge, who in this case exerts considerable control over the content and tone of the play.[28] The magistrate does not want smart slaves or soldiers on stage since "the warriors who won us an Empire *cannot* be ridiculed" (p. 8). But "Plautus" manages to convince him that all his figures are Greek, ostensibly Greek, yet could still be read as impersonating particular Romans whom he constructs as enemies of this magistrate.

Eventually, Williamson has "Plautus" end with the following assessment: "And they laughed so hard at the conceited General that you'd've thought no Roman soldier would ever be able to hold his head up again. The best comedy, inoffensive as it might appear, is always, always, a weapon of attack. But anyone who thinks theater can totally change society take note. The Roman Empire lasted another six hundred years, and the Roman Soldier went on to slaughter millions more. But on that day when the play was performed it made so many people feel better about their lives. At least for a while. I hope it still did that for you" (p. 49).

Although this presentation of Roman republican theater is fictitious, there is some truth in it, and it is perhaps a more concise and poignant description than any scholar can provide.

NOTES

1. On the office of censor cf., e.g., Kunkel et al. (1995) 391–47. They point out that from the mid-republic onward the duties of the censors included the population census, overseeing the centuries of knights with public horses, looking after the membership of the senate, leasing state property, maintaining public buildings, and regulating the use of public spaces. However, even the Romans themselves saw the economic function of the office as less important, although it was considerable. Instead, the censors were regarded as preservers of ancient Roman tradition in the face of signs of decline in morals or way of life, which was a consequence of increasing wealth and the influx of Greek customs. This agrees with the fact that most sources on the censors focus on measures against "unworthy" citizens, mainly senators and knights; in such contexts censors are associated with activities such as "directing" or "judging morals" ("regimen morum, regere mores; iudicium de moribus").

2. Cf. Aug. *Civ.* 2.13 = Cic. *Rep.* 4.10[22]: "cum artem ludicram scaenamque totam in probro ducerent, genus id hominum non modo honore ciuium reliquorum carere, sed etiam tribu moueri notatione censoria uoluerunt" ("Since they considered acting and the theater as a whole to be disgraceful, they wanted that type of person not only to lack the honors of other citizens but even to be deprived of citizenship through censorial punishment"; tr. J. E. G. Zetzel).

3. On the ambivalence regarding the theater in Rome cf. also Edwards (1993) 98–136.

4. In the interests of readability, presentation of minor details and discussion of scholarly views have been kept to a minimum. For a fuller treatment of many of the issues alluded to here see Manuwald (2011), where, however, the question of censorship is not dealt with explicitly.

5. Cf. also *OED*, s.v. censor 2 b. "*spec.* An official in some countries whose duty it is to inspect all books, journals, dramatic pieces, etc., before publication, to secure that they shall contain nothing immoral, heretical, or offensive to the government. More explicitly *dramatic censor*, *film censor*." For a description of "censorship" in contrast to "censure" cf. also Braund (2004) 409: "Free speech is a concept central in any society that calls itself a democracy. But allowing free speech generates difficulties for democracy too. Most problematic are cases where an individual's exercise of free speech consists of expressing hostile views towards other individuals or groups in society. A democracy has two strategies to deal with this situation: censorship and censure, that is, legal coercion and social coercion. Censorship or legislation can be used to curb or outlaw or punish speech-acts that could incite hatred and violence, though there is a possibility of infringing the right of 'freedom of speech' as enshrined, for example, in the First Amendment to the United States Constitution. An alternative strategy is education in the broadest sense, with the aim of encouraging people into attitudes of humaneness and tolerance and showing society's collective censure and disapproval of anti-social behavior in ways that apply social rather than legal pressure."

6. Since the specific arrangements for aediles acquiring plays from poets are uncertain, it is not quite clear what the implications for the "copyright" and the authors' rights on their pieces were (to use modern terminology). Presumably the poet was remunerated for providing the script, and it then passed into the possession of the aediles and/or the impresario for further use (for some considerations on this issue and further references see Schickert [2005] 92–98, though some of the conclusions there are based on rather limited evidence).

7. Cf., e.g., Martina (1979); Gold (1987) 42–50.

8. Cf. Gruen, esp. (1990) 79–123; Goldberg (1995) 31, 111–34.

9. Cf. Ps.-Asc. on Cic. *Verr.* 1.29 (p. 215 St. = pp. 68–69 *FPL*[4]). These verses are quoted as examples for a particular metrical form in a number of later grammarians (Caesius Bassus *Gramm. Lat.* 6, p. 266.4–9; Atil. Fortunat. *Gramm. Lat.* 6, p. 294.2–4; Ter. Maur. *Gramm. Lat.* 6, p. 400.2515–19; Mar. Plot. *Gramm. Lat.* 6, p. 531.17). The story is developed in Jerome (Hieron. *Ab Abr.* 1816, 201 BCE [p. 135g Helm]). For skeptical discussions of the sources and the narratives constructed on this basis see Jocelyn (1969); Gruen (1990) 92–106, esp. 96–100.

10. Plautus's description of a barbarian poet in jail (Plaut. *Mil.* 211–12), in combination with Festus's testimony that the Latin poet Naevius was called a "barbarian" by Plautus (Paul. Fest. p. 32.14–16 L.), does not prove conclusively that the Plautine passage refers to Naevius, particularly since no reason is given for the imprisonment of the "barbarian poet." The view that Naevius's comedies *Hariolus* and *Leon* were written in jail as compensation (cf. Gell. *NA* 3.3.15) might have arisen from them being more in line with traditional Roman concepts than other works by Naevius.

11. Cf. Naev. *Pall.* 72–74 R.[3] = 69–71 W.: "quae ego in theatro hic meis probaui plausibus, / ea non audere quemquam regem rumpere, / quanto libertatem hanc hic superat seruitus" ("that a belief, which I have tested by the applause I get here in the theater, no Grand Duke in the world dares to shatter—by what a lot does slavery here beat this freedom!"); *Pall.* 113 R.[3] = *Inc.* 27 W.: "libera lingua loquemur ludis Liberalibus" ("At Liber's Games we'll talk with tongues at liberty"; tr. E. H. Warmington).

12. Cf., e.g., Goldberg (1995) 37; for a general call for caution in reading contemporary allusions into isolated lines cf. Gruen (1990) 94–95.

13. Cf. Aug. *Civ.* 2.9 (= Cic. *Rep.* 4.12): "dicit deinde alia et sic concludit hunc locum ut ostendat ueteribus displicuisse Romanis uel laudari quemquam in scaena uiuum hominem uel uituperari" ("He then says some more, and ends this discussion in such a way as to show that the early Romans were displeased if a living man was either praised or criticized on the stage"; tr. J. E. G. Zetzel). For the interpretation of Cicero's text cf. also Büchner (1984) ad loc.

14. Cf. Aug. *Civ.* 2.9 = Cic. *Rep.* 4.11[20b]: "quem illa non attigit, uel potius quem non uexavit, cui pepercit? esto, populares homines improbos, in re publica seditiosos, Cleonem Cleophontem Hyperbolum laesit; patiamur, etsi eiusmodi ciues a censore melius est quam a poeta notari; sed Periclem, cum iam suae ciuitati maxima auctoritate plurimos annos domi et belli praefuisset, uiolari uersibus et eos agi in scaena non plus decuit, quam si Plautus noster uoluisset aut Naeuius Publio et Gnaeo Scipioni aut Caecilius Marco Catoni maledicere" ("Whom did it not taint, or rather whom did it not ravage? Whom did it spare? Granted that it attacked evil popular politicians who caused discord in the commonwealth—Cleon, Cleophon, Hyperbolus. Let us endure that," he says, "even though it is better for such citizens to be rebuked by the censor rather than by a poet. But it was no more proper for Pericles, at a time when he had been in charge of this country in peace and war with the highest authority for many years, to be attacked in poetry performed on the stage, than it would be if our own Plautus or Naevius had wanted to speak ill of Publius or Gnaeus Scipio, or Caecilius to do so of Marcus Cato"; tr. J. E. G. Zetzel).

15. Cf. Aug. *Civ.* 2.9 = Cic. *Rep.* 4.12[20c]: "nostrae contra XII Tabulae, cum perpaucas res capite sanxissent, in his hanc quoque sanciendam putauerunt, si quis occentauisset siue carmen condidisset quod infamiam faceret flagitiumue alteri. praeclare: iudiciis enim magistratuum, disceptationibus legitimis propositam uitam, non poetarum ingeniis habere debemus, nec probrum audire nisi ea lege ut respondere liceat et iudicio defendere" ("Our own Twelve Tables, by contrast, although they established capital punishment for very few offenses, included among them this: if anyone should sing offensively or should compose a poem which brought disgrace or offense to someone else. And they were quite right: we ought to have our lives set out for the judgments of magistrates or formal court proceedings, not for the wits of poets; nor should we hear an insult except under the condition that we can answer and defend ourselves at law"; tr. J. E. G. Zetzel).

16. In the second century BCE the equestrian C. Lucilius, who was the first Roman poet to write satires in the later canonical sense, was known for freely criticizing politicians

in his verses (cf. Hor. *Sat.* 2.1.62–70; Pers. 1.114–15), but no repercussions are attested. This may have been connected with his social status and/or the literary genre.

17. On the relevance of the discussion in Cicero's *De re publica* for *fabulae praetextae*, see also Manuwald (2001) 121–23.

18. On the Roman offense of *iniuria*, which came to include any action that compromised someone else's honor and could lead to legal proceedings (*actio iniuriarum*), see Kaser (1955) 520–22.

19. Cf. Cass. *Chron.* pp. 131–32 *MGH* AA 11.2: "his conss. L. Metellus et Cn. Domitius censores artem ludicram ex urbe remouerunt praeter Latinum tibicinem cum cantore et ludum talarium." In this text *ludum talarium* is an almost certain emendation of the corrupt text in Cassiodorus (cf. the critical apparatus in the quoted edition by Mommsen). The construction of the entire phrase can be interpreted in different ways: the accusative *ludum talarium*, added by *et*, is commonly seen as a continuation of the *praeter*-phrase and hence understood as something that was allowed to remain together with *Latinus tibicen cum cantore*. Yet these words could also be another object of the predicate *remouerunt* and thus be a further element that was banned, along with *ars ludicra*. Since other references to *ludus talarius* suggest that it was seen as something base and licentious, the second interpretation, grammatically possible in a text in the style of Cassiodorus's chronicle, is perhaps the more likely one (cf. Leppin [1992] 186–88).

20. On various aspects of this political dimension of theater and performances cf., e.g., Nicolet (1980) 363–73; Feldherr (1998) 169–78; Parker (1999).

21. Feldherr (1998) 170–71 draws attention to the fact that this political exploitation relished by Cicero happens at the same time at which Cicero has Scipio, in *De re publica*, argue for political restraint of dramas (see above).

22. On these events as well as their historical and literary problems cf. Panayotakis (2010) 43–56 (who distinguishes between Caesar's challenge in 47 BCE and the contest between the two mime writers in 46 BCE).

23. Boyle (2008: esp. xxxiii–xxxiv) suggests that upon the transition from the republican to the imperial period Rome's theater became less political since performances of Atellana, mime, and pantomime dominated the repertoire, while there were still (less frequent) politically charged more discursive dramas. In view of the diverse evidence, such a clear-cut distinction cannot be easily made.

24. On the play cf., e.g., Manuwald (2001) 259–339; Ferri (2003); Boyle (2008). On the question of dating cf., e.g., Ferri (2003) 5–30; Boyle (2008) xiii–xvi (with further references). On the issue of performance cf., e.g., Ferri (2003) 54–69; Kragelund (2005) 86–98; Boyle (2008) xl–xlii.

25. For a discussion and arguments for performance cf., e.g., Boyle (1997) 10–12 (with references); for "recitation" cf. esp. Zwierlein (1966); for "reading" cf. Fantham (1982) 34–49.

26. On the date and character of the work cf., e.g., Braund (2009) 16–23.

27. On the date and character of the work cf., e.g., Adamietz (1986). On the purposes of and possible connections between *De clementia* and *Apocolocyntosis* cf. Leach (1989).

28. Cf. D. Williamson (2004). Page citations are based on this edition.

REFERENCES

Adamietz, J. 1986. "Senecas *Apocolocyntosis*." In *Die römische Satire*, ed. J. Adamietz, 356–82. Darmstadt: Wissenschaftliche Buchgesellschaft.

Boyle, A. J. 1997. *Tragic Seneca: An Essay in the Theatrical Tradition*. London: Routledge.

———. 2008. *Octavia: Attributed to Seneca: Edited with Introduction, Translation, and Commentary*. Oxford: Oxford University Press.

Braund, S. M. 2004. "*Libertas* or *Licentia*? Freedom and Criticism in Roman Satire." In *Free Speech in Classical Antiquity*, ed. I. Sluiter and R. M. Rosen, 409–28. Leiden: Brill.

———. 2009. *Seneca: De Clementia: Edited with Translation and Commentary*. Oxford: Oxford University Press.

Büchner, K. 1984. *M. Tullius Cicero: De re publica: Kommentar*. Heidelberg: C. Winter.

Edwards, C. 1993. *The Politics of Immorality in Ancient Rome*. Cambridge: Cambridge University Press.

Fantham, E. 1982. *Seneca's Troades: A Literary Introduction with Text, Translation, and Commentary*. Princeton: Princeton University Press.

Feldherr, A. 1998. *Spectacle and Society in Livy's History*. Berkeley: University of California Press.

Ferri, R. 2003. *Octavia: A Play Attributed to Seneca: Edited with Introduction and Commentary*. Cambridge: Cambridge University Press.

Gold, B. K. 1987. *Literary Patronage in Greece and Rome*. Chapel Hill: University of North Carolina Press.

Goldberg, S. M. 1995. *Epic in Republican Rome*. New York: Oxford University Press.

Gruen, E. S. 1990. *Studies in Greek Culture and Roman Policy*. Brill: Leiden.

Jocelyn, H. D. 1969. "The Poet Cn. Naevius, P. Cornelius Scipio and Q. Caecilius Metellus." *Antichthon* 3: 32–47.

Kaser, M. 1955. *Das römische Privatrecht: Erster Abschnitt: Das altrömische, das vorklassische und klassische Recht*. Munich: Beck.

Kragelund, P. 2005. "History, Sex And Scenography in the *Octavia*." *Symbolae Osloenses* 80: 68–114.

Kunkel, W. Hartmut Galsterer, Christian Meier, and Roland Wittmann. 1995. *Staatsordnung und Staatspraxis der römischen Republik: Zweiter Abschnitt: Die Magistratur*. Munich: Beck.

Leach, E. W. 1989. "The Implied Reader and the Political Argument in Seneca's *Apocolocyntosis* and *De Clementia*." *Arethusa* 22: 197–230.

Leppin, H. 1992. *Histrionen: Untersuchungen zur sozialen Stellung von Bühnenkünstlern im Westen des Römischen Reiches zur Zeit der Republik und des Principats*. Bonn: R. Habelt.

Manuwald, G. 2001. *Fabulae praetextae: Spuren einer literarischen Gattung der Römer*. Munich: Beck.

———. 2011. *Roman Republican Theatre*. Cambridge: Cambridge University Press.

Martina, M. 1979. "Ennio '*poeta cliens*.'" *Quaderni di Filologia Classica dell'Università di Trieste* 2: 13–74.

Nicolet, C. 1980. *The World of the Citizen in Republican Rome*. Tr. P. S. Falla. Berkeley: University of California Press.

Panayotakis, C. 2010. *Decimus Laberius: The Fragments: Edited with Introduction, Translation, and Commentary*. Cambridge: Cambridge University Press.

Parker, H. N. 1999. "The Observed of all Observers: Spectacle, Applause, and Cultural Poetics in the Roman Theater Audience." In *The Art of Ancient Spectacle*, ed. B. Bergmann and C. Kondoleon, 163–79. New Haven, CT: Yale University Press.

Schickert, K. 2005. *Der Schutz literarischer Urheberschaft im Rom der klassischen Antike*. Tübingen: Mohr Siebeck.

Williamson, D. 2004. *Flatfoot, Incorporating the Comedy The Swaggering Soldier by Titus Maccius Plautus*. Sydney: Currency Press.

Zwierlein, O. 1966. *Die Rezitationsdramen Senecas: Mit einem kritisch-exegetischen Anhang*. Meisenheim am Glan: Hain.

Chapter 6

The Poet as Prince: Author and Authority Under Augustus

Ioannis Ziogas

> What is it with Dictators and Writers, anyway? Since before the infamous Caesar–Ovid war they've had beef. . . . Rushdie claims that tyrants and scribblers are natural antagonists, but I think that's too simple; it lets writers off pretty easy. Dictators, in my opinion, just know competition when they see it. Same with writers. *Like, after all, recognizes like.*
>
> —Junot Diaz, *The Brief Wondrous Life of Oscar Wao*

There has been an increasing awareness in recent scholarship that Augustus's new political regime created space for an unprecedented rivalry between poets and rulers.[1] Hardie (1997b: 182), discussing the last book of the *Metamorphoses*, notes, "Ovid's final triumph is to reverse the expected dependence of poet on *princeps*, as chronicler and panegyrist. In an ineluctable collusion between artist and ruler we finally see the prince of poets foist on his master a poetics of principate." Building on Hardie, Feldherr (2010: 7) states that "the poet not only mobilizes reflection on the imperial regime but creates a new space for the experience of power. Ovid is not just writing about the emperor; he is, in this sense, writing as emperor." Competition (*aemulatio*) is often viewed as the driving force of Latin poetry. While *aemulatio* is mostly approached from a literary perspective, it is remarkable that Augustan poets blend the politics of poetry with the poetics of empire and pit themselves against the *princeps*.

Such a daring pose inevitably creates tension between poetic influence and imperial authority.

For the purposes of this chapter, I focus on Virgil and Ovid, and their attempts to edit, destroy, and self-censor their works. The power of controlling the publication of poetry and banning books belongs, by and large, to the emperor. Augustus was actively involved in rescuing the *Aeneid* from destruction, against Virgil's will, and was presumably responsible for censoring Ovid's poetry. Emperor and poets strive to shape artistic creation, define its meaning, and make it known to the Roman world. A crucial aspect of this dynamic power play revolves around whether the poet or the prince decides what can be published and what must never see the light of day.

Let me start by explaining briefly in what terms Augustan poets present themselves as emperors. An imperial symbol shared by the poets and the prince is the laurel wreath. In *Res Gestae* 34, Augustus reports that by a decree of the senate he was named Augustus and the door posts of his house were publicly clothed with laurels (see Cooley 2009: 262–64). Ovid specifically refers to the laurels adorning Augustus's door posts in the story of Apollo and Daphne (*Met.* 1.562–63). The etiological closure of this story foregrounds Apollo's double identity as the god of poetry and the divine patron of the Roman emperor. Apollo's appropriation of the transformed Daphne further symbolizes Ovid's imperial enterprise of transposing Greek myth to Roman history. The victorious laurels of the Roman Triumph are intertwined with Ovid's poetic triumph of cultural metamorphosis.

Horace, who most likely invented the concept of the laureate poet, drew a clear parallel between poetic and imperial laurels (see Miller 2009: 311). At the end of *Ode* 3.30, the *sphragis* of his first collection of odes, he invites the Muse Melpomene to crown him with a laurel wreath ("lauro cinge uolens Melpomene comam"; "willingly crown my hair with laurel, Melpomene"; 3.30.16), a gesture clearly referring to a victorious general as is obvious in Ovid ("I nunc, magnificos uictor molire triumphos, / cinge comam lauro"; "go now, victor, prepare magnificent triumphs, crown your hair with laurel"; *Am.* 1.7.35–36). The Greek Muses appear as slaves in a Roman Triumph and Horace as a *triumphator*:

<u>princeps</u> Aeolium carmen ad Italos
<u>deduxisse</u> modos.

I was the prince who brought Aeolian song to Italian measures.
(Hor. *Carm.* 3.30.13–14)

Claiming primacy in Latin literature is a recurring motif in Roman poetry (cf. Hinds 1998: 52–63), but Horace does not say that he was *primus*, but *princeps*, a daring term to use under Augustus. In this context, *deduxisse* suggests the technical term for leading captives in triumphal parade (Miller 2009: 311). Overall, the prophecy of the poet's deification by means of his poetry (*Odes* 2.20; 3.30) is set against the anticipation of the prince's apotheosis. Horace's achievement explicitly rivals the sepulchral monuments of the pyramids (*Ode* 3.30.1–2); his poetic tomb, which guarantees his immortality, will outlive any royal memorial.

The image of the poet as a victorious general is already found in Virgil. In the beginning of the second half of his *Georgics*, Virgil envisages his poetic triumph in terms of Ennius's immortality ("uictorque uirum uolitare per ora"; "and victorious I fly through men's lips"; *Georg.* 3.9) (cf. "uolito uiuos per ora uirum"; "I fly alive through men's lips"; *Epigrams*, fr. 18 Vahlen = 46.2 Courtney). Virgil imagines himself leading the Greek Muses as captives for his triumph:

> primus ego in patriam mecum, modo uita supersit,
> Aonio rediens deducam uertice Musas;
>
> I will be the first to return to my native land, provided that I live,
> bringing the Muses from the Aonian summit.
>
> (Virg. *Geor.* 3.10–11)

With his *Georgics*, Virgil conquers (cf. *uictor*) Greek poetry and transfers it to Roman soil—a transference cast as a triumphal procession (cf. *deducam*).[2]

A key term that defines a common ground for poets and the prince is *auctoritas*. The potential of the dynamic tension between imperial and artistic authority created by the crucial word *auctoritas* has not been fully appreciated. Karl Galinsky calls *auctoritas* a principal concept, a notion considered to be at the center of the prince's rule.[3] Augustus and *auctoritas* are etymologically related, and it is no coincidence that in his *Res Gestae* the prince mentions the decree of the senate which named him Augustus right before he adds that he surpassed all in *auctoritas* ("auctoritate omnibus praestiti"; *RG* 34).

The Latin *auctoritas* is hard to translate. Dio Cassius says it is impossible to find a Greek word for it (ἑλληνίσαι γὰρ αὐτὸ καθάπαξ ἀδύνατόν ἐστι; Dio 55.3.5),[4] and it is equally hard to come up with an English equivalent. "Authority," as Pat Southern points out, has connotations of an official appointment or magistracy, while Augustus's *auctoritas* defied legal status (Southern 1998: 104–5). Unlike *potestas*, a power justified by law, *auctoritas* refers to a higher kind of moral leadership and transcends the strict formalities of the republican constitution (cf. Galinsky 1996: 12–13; Cooley 2009: 271–72); it designates influence and power beyond any legal basis (cf. Kienast 1982: 72–73; Crook 1996: 121–23). Augustus presented himself as an *auctor*, an old term attested in the Twelve Tables and denoting a prestigious guarantor or an influential advisor (cf. Galinsky 1996: 12–13; Southern 1998: 230).

Of course, *auctoritas* and *potestas* are not always mutually exclusive. Levick (2010: 12–15) is right to stress that Augustus's authority was generated by immense powers conferred by law (*contra* Galinsky 1996: 4–8, 10–41). Lowrie (2009: 283–84) further argues that since the Romans did not have a written constitution based on law, it is not accurate to say that *potestas* is law-based while *auctoritas* is extralegal. She adds that *potestas* resides in a fixed form, the granting of power for a set period deriving from elected office, while *auctoritas* attaches to the individual rather than the office and is consequently more fluid.[5]

The flexibility in the notion of a term not clearly defined within the prescribed parameters of an elected office makes *auctoritas* open to appropriation. What is more, it creates an intriguing overlap between Augustus, the *auctor* of the new regime, and the Augustan poets, the *auctores* who were writing under the principate. An example that illustrates the tension between the authority of a poet and the prince comes from Donatus's *Life of Virgil* (*vita Verg.* 39–41). Feeling that death is near, Virgil asks for the manuscript of his *Aeneid*, intending to burn his incomplete epic. Even though he asked Varius to destroy the *Aeneid* if anything happened to him, Varius refused to heed the poet's request. Virgil loses control of his work and then the prince takes over:

> ceterum eidem Vario ac simul Tuccae scripta sua sub ea conditione legauit, ne quid ederent, quod non a se editum esse. edidit autem <u>auctore Augusto</u> Varius, sed summatim emendata, ut qui uersus etiam imperfectos, si qui erant, reliquerit.

> Then he left his manuscripts to that same Varius and Tucca on the condition that they should not publish anything that he had not published. But Varius published [the *Aeneid*] under Augustus' influence, but only slightly corrected, so that he left even incomplete lines as they were. (*vita Verg.* 40–41)

It is important to point out that Augustus does not give orders to anyone, but his will prevails by means of his influence. We can actually read the story as a clash between the *auctoritas* of Virgil and that of Augustus. Virgil's inability to exert his influence first upon Varius and then upon many people as he asks for the manuscripts of his own work contrasts sharply with the prince's undisputed authority, which makes Varius ignore Virgil's wish. The author (*auctor*) of the *Aeneid* competes with the author of the principate. Within this context, the phrase *auctore Augusto* is related to the dynamics of the new regime, which supposedly replaces official appointments with a new style of leadership that inspires its followers.

The story from Virgil's life tells us that it is thanks to Augustus that we have the *Aeneid*. By ensuring the survival and publication of Virgil's epic, the prince actively becomes the *auctor* of the *Aeneid*, not only the guarantor or sponsor of the work but, to some extent, its authorizer. Varius only slightly corrects Virgil's unfinished epic, but the prince's intervention inevitably leaves an indelible mark on the work. With his imperial gesture, Augustus himself becomes the first pro-Augustan reader of the *Aeneid*. By saving the manuscript from destruction, he appropriates Virgil's work and authorizes an interpretation according to which the *Aeneid* is an epic politically affiliated with the principate. Needless to say, this interpretation has been influential for centuries.

Augustus's attempt to impose his interpretation on the *Aeneid* is subtly pointed out by Ovid in *Tristia* 2, a letter addressed to the emperor, in which Ovid defends his poetry and argues that it has been grossly and maliciously misinterpreted. Augustus is not only the first pro-Augustan reader of Virgil, but also Ovid's first anti-Augustan reader. In defense of his love poetry, the exiled poet says that even the *Aeneid*, Augustus's favorite poem, includes a famous extramarital love affair between Aeneas and Dido:

> et tamen ille tuae felix Aeneidos auctor
> contulit in Tyrios arma uirumque toros,
> nec legitur pars ulla magis de corpore toto,
> quam non legitimo foedere iunctus amor.

> And yet that fortunate author of your *Aeneid* brought arms and the man to Tyrian beds, and no part from the whole corpus is read more than the love united in an illegitimate pact. (Ov. *Tr.* 2.533–36)

It is a remarkable phrase to say that Virgil is the author of Augustus's *Aeneid*. Virgil is *felix*, "fortunate" but also "productive," a suitable meaning for an adjective modifying *auctor*, a word etymologically related to *augeo* ("to increase"). With *felix* Virgil is contrasted with Ovid, who often describes himself as *infelix* in his exile poetry (*Tr.* 1.2.62; 3.1.6; 3.2.26; *Pont.* 2.3.38; 2.7.48).[6] But *auctor* is also etymologically linked to Augustus and his authoritative influence (*auctoritas*). Jennifer Ingleheart is right to point out that Ovid's *auctor* alludes to Augustus and his connection with the *Aeneid* (Ingleheart 2010: 384). Although Virgil is the author, Augustus's imperial influence appropriates his work;[7] the emphasis shifts from the poet to the authority of the prince whose decision to save the *Aeneid* not only contrasts with Virgil's authorial intention to burn his work but also invests the epic with the prince's authoritative interpretation. The key point is that, unlike the English "author," the Latin *auctor* describes both the creator of a work and the guarantor of its meaning.[8] Writing poetry and controlling its interpretation, influence, and reception are the domain of an *auctor*. Thus, Augustus succeeds Virgil and controls the reception of the *Aeneid*. Virgil's epic belongs to the emperor.

Augustan poets sometimes write as emperors, but it is also significant that the prince was also an author. The interaction between the poetics of the principate and the empire of poetry goes both ways. Suetonius attests that Augustus wrote both poetry and prose (*Div. Aug.* 85). His works include an autobiography (*De vita sua*) in thirteen books, a hexameter poem titled *Sicilia*, and epigrams that he reportedly composed at the time of the bath. Although he started working on a tragedy with great enthusiasm, he never finished it, and when his friends asked him what had happened to it, he said that "his Ajax had fallen on his sponge" ("respondit Aiacem suum in spongiam incubuisse"; *Div. Aug.* 85). In this witty anecdote, we see Augustus destroying his unfinished tragedy because he is not satisfied with it. As an author he has full power to self-censor and erase one of his works. This is an authorial choice that he will not allow Virgil to make.

Macrobius reports that Augustus wrote scurrilous poems attacking Asinius Pollio, who was wise enough not to respond to imperial lampoon (2.4.21): "Pollio, cum fescenninos in eum Augustus scripsisset, ait: at ego taceo. Non est facile in eum scribere qui potest proscribere" ("Pollio, when Augustus wrote fescennine verses against him, said: 'But I am silent. It is not easy to be a scribe against one who can proscribe'"). Pollio's witty pun on *scribere-proscribere* suggests how close writing and the fatal wrath of the emperor can be; besides composing satirical poems, Augustus features as the author of proscriptions. And freedom to write invective is safely granted only when the *auctor* is Augustus. Otherwise, it can be pretty dangerous and thus Augustan writers resort to veiled criticism.[9] This is exactly what Pollio does. Even though he says he will remain silent, he does not. He actually responds to Augustus's attacks, and his witticism can be read either as a recognition of the emperor's political power or as a caustic criticism of Augustus's autocracy in the spirit of fescennine lampoon.

Likewise, the passage from the *Tristia* cited above can be read as Ovid's veiled criticism of Augustan appropriation of the *Aeneid*. What is remarkable in these lines is that Ovid implicitly confronts the Augustan reading of the *Aeneid* with his own interpretation. By challenging Augustus's manipulation of Virgil's epic, Ovid rivals the imperial attempt to claim the *Aeneid* for the principate. Although Virgil is introduced as the author of Augustus's *Aeneid*, the next three lines read the *Aeneid* through the distorting lens of Ovid's elegiac poetics. Of course, tendentiously elegiac readings of epic poems are a marked trope of the elegiac genre. Propertius, for instance, reads the *Iliad* as a love poem (cf. 2.1.49–50; 2.8.29–38), and Ovid follows him by interpreting Homeric poetry in terms of love elegy (*Tristia* 2.371–80). But in *Tristia* 2 this generic appropriation of martial epic by Roman love elegy becomes a direct challenge to Augustus's sponsorship of the *Aeneid*. Imperial and poetic *auctoritas* compete in interpreting Virgil's epic.

Ovid has exploited the elegiac potential of Virgil's Dido in *Heroides* 7.[10] In *Tristia* 2 he embeds the programmatic opening of the *Aeneid* (*arma uirumque*) in "Tyrios . . . toros." The elegiac frame of lovemaking distorts the epic beginning of Virgil's epic. Alessandro Barchiesi notes that *arma* can be interpreted in Latin as a sexual euphemism (Barchiesi 1997: 28). Similarly, Richard Tarrant points out that Ovid turns the opening words of the *Aeneid* into an obscene hendiadys; *arma uirumque* equals *uirum armatum*, an armed, that is, erect, man.[11] Such a lascivious pun may further point to the tradition according to which Virgil was the author of *Priapea*.[12] More to the point, it signifies Ovid's redirection of Virgil's epic language for erotic ends. It should be noted that turning Virgil's epic weapons into sexual metaphors is a distinctly Ovidian trope. In *Metamorphoses* 10, for instance, when Cinyras realizes that his daughter tricked him into an incestuous affair, he readies his sword ("pendenti nitidum uagina deripit ensem"; "he snatched his shining sword from the sheath which hung there"; *Met.* 10.475). *Met.* 10.475 refers to *Aen.* 10.475 ("uaginaque caua fulgentem deripit ensem"; "and he snatched his flashing sword from the hollow sheath"). Given the context of lovemaking in the *Metamorphoses*, Ovid's line adds sexual innuendo to Virgil's arms.[13] Thus, in *Tristia* 2, Virgil's *Aeneid* is taken away from Augustus's authority and transposed to Ovid's poetic universe. In the end, Virgil becomes the author of Ovid's *Aeneid*.

Aeneid 4 is read as an elegiac story of extramarital love,[14] an essentially Ovidian and anti-Augustan interpretation of Virgil's epic. If teaching adultery was one of the reasons for Ovid's exile, then Virgil's poetry is equally culpable. Sergio Casali is right to point out that Ovid's "Aeneid" is a critical reading of Virgil's, but an unsettling one since in the *Aeneid* there were "other voices" than the one we call "Augustan."[15] By characterizing the affair of Aeneas and Dido as illicit, Ovid makes Aeneas, an essentially Augustan hero, liable to Augustus's legal regulations against adultery, and turns Virgil into a poet of illegitimate love. Michèle Lowrie (2009: 361) points out that Virgil is presented as an author (*auctor*) who has offered a well-read exemplum of illegitimate love affair and Augustus also calls himself *auctor* in describing the passage of his marriage legislation (*RG* 8.5).[16]

Augustus saved the *Aeneid*, but Ovid snatches Virgil's epic from the prince. That the phrase "tuae felix Aeneidos auctor" refers to Augustus's involvement in securing the publication of the *Aeneid* is further suggested by Ovid's Virgilian pose in attempting to burn his *Metamorphoses*. Virgil's prosperous career (*felix*) is contrasted with Ovid's unfortunate exile (*infelix*):

> carmina mutatas hominum dicentia formas,
> infelix domini quod fuga rupit opus.
> haec ego discedens, sicut bene multa meorum,
> ipse mea posui maestus in igne manu.
>
> The verses which tell of the changed forms of human beings, an unfortunate work which the exile of its master broke off. These verses, as I was leaving, like so many other things of mine, I myself in sorrow placed with my own hands in the fire. (*Tr.* 1.7.13–16)

It has long been recognized that Ovid reenacts Virgil's dying wish to burn the *Aeneid*.[17] Given that Ovid repeatedly presents his exile as death,[18] the burning of the *Metamorphoses* symbolizes the death and cremation of the poet, who puts his own vitals on the funeral pyre (cf. "imposui rapidis uiscera nostra rogis"; "I put my own vitals upon the consuming pyre"; *Tr.* 1.7.20). The parallel between book burning and cremation completes Ovid's Virgilian death scene. Yet, unlike Virgil, Ovid is able to put his manuscript on fire.

But the drama of self-immolation is quickly deflated. We are told right after the dramatic burning of the *Metamorphoses* that the work survived because several copies had already been made (*Tr.* 1.7.23–24). The whole episode seems tongue-in-cheek, and as Nita Krevans points out, it is repetition and difference with a vengeance: Augustus, the hero of the Virgilian story, is conspicuously absent (Krevans 2010: 207). I would add that Ovid's contrived story casts doubt on the importance of Augustus's *auctoritas* in saving the *Aeneid* since the story presumes that there was a single manuscript of Virgil's epic. But, if there were more copies (which is actually likely), Augustus's imperial gesture would look like an Ovidian conceit; the *Aeneid* would have survived anyway.

By burning his *Metamorphoses*, Ovid stresses that fire is incapable of destroying his work, a point that he emphatically makes in the *sphragis* of his epic ("Iamque opus exegi, quod nec Iouis ira nec ignis . . . poterit . . . abolere"; "I have completed a work now, which neither the wrath of Jupiter nor fire will be able to destroy"; *Met.* 15.871–72). Neither Ovid's nor Jupiter's/Augustus's anger is able to obliterate a poetic work which transcends the powers of physical destruction.[19] Reception of poetry exceeds authorial intentions and imperial authority.[20] Multiple copies, new editions, recitations, discussions, and rereadings constantly liberate poetry from the interpretative tyranny of an *auctor*, whether this author is the poet or the prince. Far from inviting us to fall into the trap of biographical fallacy, the stories of Virgil's dying wish and Ovid's funeral pyre of the *Metamorphoses* present us with an early example of Roland Barthes's "death of the author." Only in Ovid's case, the emperor dies before the poet.

Of course, Augustus is not famous for saving books from the fire. The story from Virgil's life takes on added meaning if we take into account that it contrasts with Augustus's policy of censorship and book burning. Suetonius (*Div. Aug.* 31) reports that Augustus collected and burned more than two thousand Greek and Latin prophetic books ("quidquid librorum fatidicorum Graeci Latinique generis"; "whatever prophetic books of Greek and Latin origin"; *Div. Aug.* 31), and spared only the Sibylline books, though not all of them.[21] The public burning of prophetic books occurs at a time when the Augustan poets were often using the word *uates* ("prophet") instead of the Greek *poeta*.[22] But the poetry of a *uates* risks ending up in Augustus's bonfire. Ovid says in the *sphragis* of his epic that fire cannot destroy his work and adds that, if the prophecies of the *uates* are true, he will live forever in fame ("fama, / siquid habent ueri uatum praesagia, uiuam"; *Met.* 15.878–79). The end of the *Metamorphoses* could be read as a defiant comment on Augustus's attempt to silence the prophets by burning their books. Ovid, a *uates* in his own right (cf. *Met.* 15.876), has access to prophetic forebodings, and, not unlike the *Metamorphoses*, the truth of the seers defies the fires of imperial censorship.

But we can also read Ovid's act of self-censorship from a different angle. Ovid's decision to burn his epic can be seen as an imperial gesture to censor the unauthorized work of a prophet and as a fulfillment of Virgil's unfulfilled dying wish. From that perspective, Ovid appropriates the power of the emperor only to show its limits: the manuscript burns, but the poetry survives. *Tristia* 1.7 mentions the burning of the *Metamorphoses* and concludes with Ovid adding an epigram to the head of the book. In other words, the elegy begins with self-censorship and ends with revision: it moves from destruction to expansion. The last lines of *Tristia* 1.7 will be the first lines of Ovid's transformed work. Instead of destroying his epic, Ovid makes it longer, becoming an *auctor* in the etymological connotations of the word. Let us have a look at this intriguing epigram:

> et ueniam pro laude peto, laudatus abunde,
>   non fastiditus si tibi, lector, ero.
> hos quoque sex uersus, in prima fronte libelli
>   si praeponendos esse putabis, habe:
> "orba parente suo quicumque uolumina tangis,
>   his saltem uestra detur in Vrbe locus.
> quoque magis faueas, non haec sunt edita ab ipso,
>   sed quasi de domini funere rapta sui.
> quicquid in his igitur uitii rude carmen habebit,
>   emendaturus, si licuisset, erat."

> And I ask for a favor instead of praise; I shall be praised profusely, if you do not despise me, reader. Receive these six lines also, if you think they should be placed at the very head of my little book: "You who touch these scrolls bereft of their parent, let a place in your city be given at least to these. And your indulgence may be greater since these were not published by their master but snatched from what might be called his funeral. So whatever flaw this rough poem may have he would have corrected, had it been permitted him." (*Tr.* 1.7.31–40)

Ovid bemoans the unfinished state of his epic, while he is actually revising it, writing a preface, and adding new lines. At the same time, he stresses that a new edition of the *Metamorphoses* is not in his hands. Ovid casts himself as a dead poet sending letters from an exilic underworld. It is up to the reader (*lector*, *Tr.* 1.7.32) to "collect"[23] Ovid's lines and decide whether they deserve to be added to the *Metamorphoses* or not. Ovid seems to have lost authorial control over his work. Now the *lector* is the new *auctor*.[24]

But what was the decision of the anonymous reader whom Ovid invites to become the editor of the *Metamorphoses*? We do not really know, but (to the best of my knowledge) no edition of the *Metamorphoses* begins with the six-line epigram from the *Tristia*. Ovid's suggestion of a new and paradoxically elegiac beginning of his epic has been heeded neither by his readers nor by his editors; the poet's authorial suggestion has been entirely ignored. Stephen Hinds, who offers one of the most perceptive interpretations of *Tristia* 1.7 in modern scholarship, argues that "by re*writing* its opening lines, Ovid will force us to re*read* the entire poem in a slightly different light" (Hinds 2006: 436; emphasis original), but he does not entertain the idea of actually printing an edition of the *Metamorphoses* with the new preface at the head of the book. To be sure, Ovid does not force his readers to start reading his epic with the passage from *Tristia* 1.7. If Hinds has done so, he is certainly an exception.[25] Ovid says it is up to the reader to decide. But the virtual disregard of Ovid's suggestion by the vast majority of his readership shows who the real *auctor* of the *Metamorphoses* is. By printing "In noua fert animus" as the first words of the poem in *his* OCT, Richard Tarrant makes an editorial choice and censors six lines which Ovid himself recommended be placed in front of *his* work.

Ovid's suggestion to add a preface to his *Metamorphoses* is far from absurd. In fact, Ovid refers to Catullus's preface in specific details. Curiously, the epic *Metamorphoses* is described as a *libellus* (*Tr.* 1.7.33), alluding to Catullus's *libellus* (1.1; 1.8).[26] Catullus dedicates his book to Cornelius Nepos, and his dedication appears as the first poem of the collection in standard editions of Catullus. Catullus 1 refers to Cornelius in the second person, resembling a dedication in front of a book sent as a gift. Likewise, Ovid sends a letter to a friend asking him to include a prefatory epigram in the *Metamorphoses*. Ovid describes his epic to his friend in terms of Catullan modesty: "carmina . . . qualiacumque legas" ("read my poems whatever they are"; *Tr.* 1.7.11–12) is a clear reference to Catullus's *qualecumque* (1.9), the poet's little book, whatever it is (cf. Krevans 2010: 207). What is more, if we read Catullus 1 through the lens of Ovid's *Metamorphoses*, we realize that Catullus's preface begins and ends in terms similar to the beginning and the end of Ovid's epic: Catullus's neoteric book (cf. "nouum libellum"; 1.1) corresponds to Ovid's innovative epic (cf. "In noua"; *Met.* 1.1), while the last line of Catullus 1 ("plus uno maneat perenne saeclo"; "let it [i.e., the little book] last longer than a generation"; 1.10) is similar to the closure of the *Metamorphoses* (cf. "perennis"; *Met.* 15.875).[27] The whole program of the *Metamorphoses* is encapsulated in the frame of Catullus 1.

Ovid's allusions to Catullus further pit the *Metamorphoses*' supposedly rough material (cf. "rude carmen"; "rough poem"; *Tr.* 1.7.22; 39) ("defuit et scriptis ultima lima meis"; "my writing lacked the last touch of the file"; *Tr.* 1.7.30) against Catullus's finely polished book ("lepidum nouum libellum / arida modo pumice expolitum"; "a charming little book, just now polished with dry pumice stone"; 1.1–1). But the reason why Catullus's little book is polished, while Ovid's is rough, is in part related to imperial politics. If Catullus could call Caesar a "voracious adulterer" ("uorax adulter"; 57.8) with impunity, this is certainly something Ovid could not do. Not because the new Caesar was not adulterous (he was actually notorious for his adulteries; cf. Suet. *Div. Aug.* 68–70), but because it was dangerous. In the background of the Catullan allusions in *Tristia* 1.7 lies the crucial issue of Augustus's policy of intolerance.[28]

Ovid's statement that his epic is unrefined and incomplete is puzzling since the *Metamorphoses*, as we have it, does not give the impression of being an unrevised work. Of course, we should read this judgment along the lines of Ovid's pose to replicate the Virgilian deathbed scene. An unfinished epic snatched from the funeral pyre of its author and edited by others is what happened to the *Aeneid*, and the line "emendaturus, si licuisset, erat" (*Tr.* 1.7.40) has actually haunted Virgilian scholarship, not Ovid's *Metamorphoses*.[29]

But there is another way in which Ovid's preface refers to the publication of the *Aeneid* and comments on authorial intention and editorial authority. The new beginning of the *Metamorphoses*, curiously befitting Virgil's epic more than Ovid's, recalls not only Catullus 1, but also the preface to the *Aeneid*. Servius (*in Aen. praef.*) tells us that Virgil's literary executors removed from the beginning of the *Aeneid* the first four lines of the epic. According to Servius, Augustus rescues the *Aeneid* and then orders Tucca and Varius to remove the unnecessary bits from their edition but not add anything to Virgil's work. The editors can cut down passages but cannot, for instance, complete Virgil's half lines. Following the emperor's orders, Tucca and Varius start by removing the preface:

> unde et semiplenos eius inuenimus uersiculos, ut "hic cursus fuit" (*Aen.* 1.534), et aliquos detractos, ut in principio; nam ab armis non coepit, sed sic
> Ille ego qui quondam gracili modulatus auena
> carmen, et egressus siluis uicina coegi
> ut quamuis auido parerent arua colono,
> gratum opus agricolis, at nunc horrentia Martis
> arma uirumque cano
>
> Hence we find half lines, such as "this was the course" (*Aen.* 1.534), and other lines removed, for instance in the beginning: "I am he who once composed a song on a slender shepherd's pipe, and after leaving the woods, I made the neighboring plowlands obey the husbandman, even if he was greedy, a work pleasing to the farmers, but now I sing of the dreadful arms of Mars and the man."

Edward Brandt suggested that the lines attested in Servius were placed under Virgil's portrait on the front cover of an edition of the *Aeneid* (Brandt 1927). This is all the more likely if we take into account *Tristia* 1.7. Ovid writes to someone who possesses his portrait and asks his friend to remove the ivy from his image since Bacchus's wreath is a symbol of fortunate poets (*Tr.* 1.7.1–4). The epigram at the end of *Tristia* 1.7 should be placed at the head of the new edition of the *Metamorphoses*, presumably under Ovid's portrait. Thus, *Tristia* 1.7 can be read as Ovid's instructions about the front cover of his epic; the poet himself designs the frontispiece of his *Metamorphoses*. In any case, my point is that the six-line preface in *Tristia* 1.7 replicates the so-called pre-proemium to the *Aeneid*. If we agree that *Tristia* 1.7 is a reenactment of the Virgilian deathbed scene and a comment on the role Augustus played in the afterlife of the *Aeneid*, then Ovid's neglected preface to the *Metamorphoses* parallels the editorial issue of the *Aeneid*'s pre-proemium.

Of course, the authenticity of the *Aeneid*'s preface is disputed. Most critics agree that the passage is spurious,[30] even though Servius and Donatus (*vita Verg.* 42) accepted the verses as authentic. It is no part of my brief to argue that ancient commentators knew better than modern scholars; what matters for my purposes is that it seems that Ovid did know the pre-proemium and alluded to it. This has already been suggested, although not in reference to the epigram in *Tristia* 1.7, but to the opening epigram of the *Amores.* Gian Biagio Conte argues that the four-line proem to the *Amores* is a reworking of the *Aeneid incipit*, and suggests that Ovid must have found the pre-proemium in a contemporary edition of the *Aeneid* (Conte 1986: 84–87). But let us have a look at the *Amores* epigram:

> Qui modo Nasonis fueramus quinque libelli,
> tres sumus; hoc illi praetulit auctor opus.
> ut iam nulla tibi nos sit legisse uoluptas,
> at leuior demptis poena duobus erit.
> Arma graui numero. . . .

> We who were five slim books of Naso are now three; the author preferred this work to the previous one. Even though you may still take no pleasure in reading us, yet with two books taken away the punishment will be lighter.
> Arms in weighty numbers. . . . (*Amores*, *Epigram*, 1.1.1)

Building on Conte, Joseph Farrell argues convincingly that it makes perfect sense to assume that Ovid alludes to the pre-proemium to the *Aeneid* (Farrell 2004: 46–52). Farrell draws attention to specific verbal parallels between the prefaces to the *Amores* and the *Aeneid*: "Qui modo" echoes "qui quondam," "ut iam" recalls "ut quamuis" at the head of the hexameter, "at" is found in both passages, and "opus . . . uoluptas" alludes to "gratum opus." What is more, Ovid's "arma graui numero" (*Am.* 1.1.1) is a playful reference to Virgil's "arma uirumque cano" (see McKeown 1989 ad loc.). Thus, the introductory epigram followed by *arma* reworks the pre-proemium to the *Aeneid*, which is also followed by *arma.* The shift from the epigram to the first line of *Amores* 1.1 rewrites the transition from the pre-proemium to the proem in the *Aeneid.*

The preface to the *Amores* is a comment on the editorial authority of the poet. Ovid, the *auctor* of the *Amores*, has full control over the publication of his work. He decides to cut down two books and effectively executes his editorial plan. The author's revision can be read as an act of self-censorship. Interestingly, the epigram plays with the etymology of *auctor* from *augeo*: the author does not make his poetry "grow," but on the contrary he reduces the number of the books (cf. McKeown 1989 ad loc.). The beginning of the *Amores* invites the readers to compare the revision of Ovid's elegiac collection with the editorial adventures of the epic *Aeneid.* From the perspective of genre, the slender poetics of Ovid's elegiac *libelli* are contrasted with Virgil's *maius opus* (cf. *Aen.* 7.45); the Alexandrian project of the *Amores* confronts Virgil's "big book."[31] Note that the last books of the *Aeneid* grow longer, thus suggesting a problematization of closure in Virgil's unfinished epic.[32] The Iliadic half of the *Aeneid* is *maius* not only stylistically but also literally, in terms of its length. By contrast, Ovid significantly reduced the length of his collection in his revised edition.

My point is that Ovid alludes to the pre-proemium in order to invite us to compare the edition of his *Amores* with that of the *Aeneid.* In this comparison, Augustus is again conspicuously absent from the publication of Ovid's elegiac collection. The first edition of the *Amores* is forever lost to us.[33] Two books of Ovid's elegies are no longer available simply because Ovid decided so. By contrasting the *Amores* with the *Aeneid*, Ovid makes clear that only *he* is in charge of his work, unlike Virgil, who loses control of his epic when Augustus oversees the publication of the *Aeneid* and thus becomes its *auctor*. Ovid's *auctoritas* deletes two books of the *Amores*, while the *Aeneid* survives because Augustus ignored Virgil's dying request. Since Augustus plays no role in the editorial procedures of the *Amores*, Ovid, not the prince, is the absolute *auctor.*

Ovid's *incipit* of his *Amores* can be read as a response to Virgil's career, from the beginning of the *Eclogues* to the afterlife of the *Aeneid.* In *Eclogue* 1, a young god who is to be identified with Augustus (cf. Servius *ad Ecl.* 1.1; Coleman 1977: 73–74, 80), saves Tityrus, Virgil's alter ego, and allows him to indulge in bucolic song at his leisure (cf. *Ecl.* 1.6–10; 42). Interestingly, Tityrus's fortune, guaranteed by the *deus*, is contrasted with Meliboeus's exile (cf. "nos patriam fugimus"; "We are exiled from our fatherland"; *Ecl.* 1.4). Virgil's life comes full circle: Augustus rescues Tityrus/Virgil in the beginning of his poetic career and saves the *Aeneid* after the poet's death.[34] By contrast, Augustus is absent from Ovid's first steps in the poetic arena and actually replaced by another young *deus*, the mischievous Cupid of *Amores* 1.1. In the end, far from supporting his poetry, Augustus bans Ovid's works and banishes the poet, who resembles the exiled Meliboeus. In the Virgilian *rota*, the beginning of Virgil's career curiously resonates with the end of Ovid's.

The absence of Augustus from Ovid's poetry is as important as his presence. The juxtaposition between poet and prince reaches its climax in the last lines of the *Metamorphoses*; Augustus's deification (*Met.* 15.861–70) is followed by Ovid's apotheosis (*Met.* 15.871–79). The last word referring to Augustus is *absens* (*Met.* 15.870), which is sharply contrasted with the last word of the epic ("uiuam"; "I shall live"; *Met.* 15.879). In the context of a prayer (cf. "faueantque precantibus absens"; "and listen to our prayers in your absence"; *Met.* 15.870), it is remarkable that Augustus appears as a "deus absens" instead of a "deus praesens."[35] Joseph Farrell notes that in the end of Ennius's *Annals* there might be an additional element of competition, as Ennius caps his patron Fulvius Nobilior by writing a new ending for his work, in effect concluding with the poet's death instead of his patron's triumph (Farrell 2002: 43). In the *sphragis* of the *Metamorphoses*, in which Ennius is an important presence,[36] the rivalry between poet and prince is pointed. Ovid's imperial poetics compete with the authority of the emperor.[37]

The most striking example of Augustus's marked absence from Ovid's poetry (and one that demands a separate treatment) is found in the six "silent books" of the *Fasti*. By not finishing his elegiac calendar, Ovid might comment on the devastating role that Augustus played in his poetic career, but also manages to turn the tables by including neither the month of Augustus nor the emperor's birthday in his work. In an imperial gesture, Ovid enacts a *damnatio memoriae* of the emperor who condemned his work.

Poets and prince take part in a power game that revolves around the dynamics of censorship, publication, and interpretation. The significant term *auctor* is the critical point where the authorities of the prince and the poets converge and collide. A careful reading of Ovid's various comments on the editorial adventures of his works can give us a new perspective on the range and limits of an *auctor*'s power to create a work, define its meaning, and control its reception. The common claim on *auctoritas* inevitably becomes a source of tension between emperors and poets. In my view, the question of whether Augustan poets support or subvert the principate misses the point. What is particularly intriguing is that Augustus is actively engaged in interpreting and appropriating poetic works, while Virgil, Horace, and Ovid present their poetic careers in terms of imperial conquest. In the end, Ovid may be essentially anti-Augustan not in his opposition to the prince, but in his attempt to be equal to Augustus (the other meaning of the Greek "anti").[38]

NOTES

I happily acknowledge the financial support of the Australian Research Council for my research for this chapter. I would also like to thank the editors of this volume for their support and friendship. G. Rowe, "Reconsidering the *Auctoritas* of Augustus," *Journal of Roman Studies* 103 (2013): 1–15 and F. Martelli, *Ovid's Revisions: The Editor as Author* (Cambridge: Cambridge University Press, 2013) appeared too late for me to take them into account in this chapter.

1. Diaz is quoted in Ingleheart (2011) 17n67.

2. Mynors (1990) ad loc. notes that *deducam* "is used not only of descent from a mountain like *detulit*, but of bringing home from a triumph, as in Hor. *carm.* 1.37.31, Livy 28.32.7." *Deducere* is routinely interpreted as a buzzword for the Alexandrian stylistic ideal of λεπτότης and far less frequently read in the context of Roman imperial discourse.

3. Galinsky (1996) 10–41. A detailed study of *auctoritas* is Magdelain (1947).

4. It is rendered as ἀξίωμα ("honor" or "rank, position") in the Greek translation of the *Res Gestae*.

5. Lowrie (2009) 279–308 discusses *auctoritas* and its relation to representation and performance in Augustan Rome.

6. For further references, see Ingleheart (2010) 62, 384. Interestingly, *infelix* characterizes Dido (*Aen.* 4.68; 450; 529; 596), the unfortunate queen whose love affair did not produce any offspring and was thus "fruitless."

7. Barchiesi (1997) 27 notes, "The *Aeneid*, favored by the prince and appropriated by Augustan discourse (*tuae*), has made the fortune of its author, *felix* in opposition to Ovid, who is forced to write *tristia* on account of the *Ars Amatoria*." See also Thomas (2001) 74–78.

8. The guarantor or sponsor of a work of art (*auctor*) was basically the patron to whom the work was dedicated. See Dupont (2004) 171–74; Pierre (2005) 241–42; Lowrie (2009) 283.

9. On the art of veiled criticism under authoritarian regimes in Greece and Rome, see Ahl (1984).

10. See Barchiesi (2001) 42–47, for *Heroides* 7, Dido's letter to Aeneas, which elaborates the Virgilian text by exposing its elegiac potential. In Ziogas (2010) I argue that Virgil actually engages in an intergeneric dialogue between martial epic and Roman love elegy in the Dido story and elsewhere in the *Aeneid*.

11. Tarrant (2002) 24. For the sexual meaning of *arma*, see Adams (1982) 19–22, 224; Lowrie (2009) 361. Ingleheart (2010) 385 also comments on the obscene double entendre to *arma* in *Tr.* 2.534, and cites *Am.* 1.9.26, for *arma=mentula*. See also the fine discussion in Thomas (2001) 76–77. *Tr.* 2.533–34 alludes to *Aeneid* 4.507–8, but "the epic moved from indecorous and erotic *emphasis* back to epic decorum, while the elegist begins sounding epic but ends revelling in fully established erotic innuendo" (Thomas [2001] 77).

12. Suetonius says that Virgil wrote *Priapea* when he was young (*vita Verg.* 17); cf. Servius, *praef. Aen.*

13. Smith (1997) 71–72 notes, "Yet by alluding to Virgil's line here, Ovid seems also to effect a contrast between the line on the battlefield as it occurs in the *Aeneid* passage and its application, in *Metamorphoses* 10, in a sex scene."

14. Aeneas is called Dido's "Phrygian husband" at *Met.* 14.79–80 ("non bene discidium Phrygii latura mariti / Sidonis"; "The Sidonian woman, who would not endure the departure of the Phrygian husband calmly"). Bömer (1986) ad loc. notes that Juno, in an ironic speech, refers to Aeneas as Phrygian husband (*Aen.* 4.103). The contrast between *Tr.* 2.536, where the affair between Dido and Aeneas is called illegitimate, and *Met.* 14.79, where Aeneas is called Dido's husband, is sharp (and I thank Bob Cowan for raising this point). It is possible that in the *Metamorphoses* we have a case of embedded focalization; the primary narrator adopts Dido's point of view. In the *Aeneid*, the queen refers to her affair with Aeneas, who is about to leave, as *coniugium antiquum* ("old wedlock"; *Aen.* 4.431).

15. Casali (2006) 153–54, in reference to Ovid's "little *Aeneid*" in the *Metamorphoses.* For Ovid's "Aeneid" and Virgil, see Hinds (1998) 104–22; Thomas (2001) 78–84; Papaioannou (2005).

16. Ovid calls Augustus the *auctor* of *leges* in *Met.* 15.833.

17. See, for instance, Wilkinson (1955) 238; Nagle (1980) 29; Krevans (2010) 206–8.

18. Exile as death is a pervasive and significant theme in the *Tristia* and *Ex Ponto*; see Nagle (1980) 21–32.

19. Jupiter is paralleled to Augustus in *Met.* 1.204–5; 15.857–58. The analogy between Jupiter and Augustus features prominently in the exile poetry. Ovid refers specifically to the anger of Jupiter and of Augustus at *Tr.*3.11.61–62; 71–72. (cf. Segal [1969] 291).

20. Gibson (1999) argues that in *Tristia* 2 Ovid shows how reception of a text is not in the hands of the author.

21. For other incidents of burning books on divination, see Livy 39.16.8; cf. Winsbury (2009) 136. Augustus also did not allow the proceedings of the senate to be published (cf. "Auctor et aliarum rerum fuit, in quis: ne acta senatus publicarentur" *Div. Aug.* 36; "he was the initiator of other things too, among them the following: that the proceedings of the senate should not be published"). Augustus wants to control publications, whether the case is the proceedings of the senate or the *Aeneid.* Interestingly, Augustus prevents the publication of the proceedings as an *auctor*. For censorship and book burning under Augustus, see Krevans (2010) 207–8. Ovid's books were banned from the public libraries (cf. *Tr.* 3.1 with Nagle [1980] 85–87).

22. For the concept of *uates* in Augustan poetry, see Newman (1967).

23. The reader also collects Ovid's lines (*lector* from *lego*). Ovid puns on *lego* ("to read" and "to collect") in the penultimate line of the *Metamorphoses* (*ore legar populi*, *Met.* 15.878: "I shall be read on the lips of the people"). Hardie (2002) 94–95 argues that the phrase *ore legar* recalls the popular belief that the soul of a dying person could be caught with his last breath. Thus, *ore legar populi* can be translated as "I shall be caught on the lips of the people."

24. Konstan (2006) argues that readers in antiquity were not passive recipients of texts. For Konstan, in classical antiquity readers expected texts to offer challenges, not just

passive pleasure, and writers fashioned their works for such a public. Kyriakidis (2013) focuses on the importance of the reader in *Tr.* 1.7 and points out that the reader will be Ovid's successor.

25. See also Kyriakidis (2013). Johnson (2008) offers a reading of Ovid's *Metamorphoses* through the lens of the poet's exile.

26. On Ovid and Catullus, see Wray (2009); Ziogas (forthcoming).

27. Farrell (2009) 168n10 argues that Catullus's request is modest in comparison with the boast of Horace that he has created a *monumentum aere perennius* ("a monument more durable than bronze"; *Carmen* 3.30.1) and that of Ovid, who has an eye on Horace in the *sphragis* of the *Metamorphoses.*

28. According to Suetonius (*Iul.* 73), Catullus apologized for his vitriolic invective and Caesar invited him to dinner on the same day. By contrast, Caesar Augustus never accepted Ovid's *apologia.*

29. It is typical to argue that inconsistencies in the *Aeneid* are due to the fact that Virgil's epic lacked the poet's final touch. Fortunately, Virgilian scholarship has moved beyond the practice of explaining away instead of interpreting inconsistencies in the *Aeneid* (see especially O'Hara [2007]).

30. The list of secondary sources on the pre-proemium is quite long. The best discussion is Gamberale (1991).

31. Virgil's *maius opus* (*Aen.* 7.45) alludes to the *μέγα βιβλίον* of Callimachus (fr. 465 Pf.); see Thomas (1986) 63.

32. Book 8 has 731 lines, book 9 has 818, book 10 has 908, book 11 has 915, and book 12 has 952. On closure in the *Aeneid*, see the excellent analysis of Hardie (1997a) 142–51.

33. I assume that the first edition existed.

34. There is an intricate ring composition revolving around the first *Eclogue* and the end of the *Aeneid*; see Putnam (2010) 31–38.

35. By contrast, Ovid apostrophizes Augustus as "per te praesentem . . . deum" ("by you, a present god") at *Tr.* 2.54; cf. Lowrie (2009) 364, 378–79.

36. Cf. the pun on *perennis* (*Met.* 15.875). The last lines "ore legar populi perque omnia saecula fama / . . . uiuam" ("I shall be read on the lips of the people and through all the ages I shall live in fame"; *Met.* 15.878–79) allude to Ennius's epitaph ("uolito uiuos per ora uirum"; "I fly alive through men's lips"; *Epigrams*, fr. 18 Vahlen = 46.2 Courtney).

37. Interestingly, Augustus is described as the *auctor* of laws (cf. *Met.* 15.832–39), in a passage that resembles Augustus's *RG* 8.5 in specific details (cf. Hardie [1997b] 192–93; Lowrie [2009] 379–80).

38. The term anti-Augustan has become increasingly unpopular after Kennedy (1992); see, however, Davis (2006).

REFERENCES

Adams, J. N. 1982. *The Latin Sexual Vocabulary*. Baltimore: Johns Hopkins University Press.

Ahl, F. M. 1984. "The Art of Veiled Criticism in Greece and Rome." *American Journal of Philology* 105: 174–208.

Barchiesi, A. 1997. *The Poet and the Prince*. Berkeley: University of California Press.

———. 2001. *Speaking Volumes: Narrative and Intertext in Ovid and Other Latin Poets*. London: Duckworth.

Bömer, F. 1986. *P. Ovidius Naso: Metamorphosen. Buch XIV–XV*. Heidelberg: Winter.

Brandt, E. 1927. "Zum Aeneisprooemium." *Philologus* 83: 331–35.

Casali, S. 2006. "Other Voices in Ovid's 'Aeneid.'" In *Oxford Readings in Ovid*, ed. P. Knox, 144–65. Oxford: Oxford University Press.

Coleman, R. 1977. *Vergil: Eclogues*. Cambridge: Cambridge University Press.

Conte, G. B. 1986. *The Rhetoric of Imitation: Genre and Poetic Memory in Virgil and Other Latin Poets*. Ithaca, NY: Cornell University Press.

Cooley, A. 2009. *Res Gestae Diui Augusti: Text, Translation, and Commentary*. Cambridge: Cambridge University Press.

Crook, J. 1996. "Augustus, Power, Authority, Achievement." In *Cambridge Ancient History*, vol. 10: *The Augustan Empire, 43 BC–AD 69*, ed. A. K. Bowman, E. Champlin, and A. Lintott, 113–46. Cambridge: Cambridge University Press.

Davis, P. J. 2006. *Ovid and Augustus: A Political Reading of Ovid's Erotic Poems*. London: Duckworth.

Dupont, F. 2004. "Comment devenir à Rome un poète bucolique? Corydon, Tityre, Virgile et Pollion." In *Identités d'auteur dans l'antiquité et la tradition européenne*, ed. C. Calame and R. Chartier, 171–89. Grenoble: Editions Jérôme Millon.

Farrell, J. 2002. "Greek Lives and Roman Careers in the Classical Vita Tradition." In *European Literary Careers: The Author from Antiquity to the Renaissance*, ed. P. Cheney and F. A. de Armas, 24–46. Toronto: University of Toronto Press.

———. 2004. "Ovid's Virgilian Career." *Materiali e Discussioni per l'analisi dei testi classici* 52: 41–55.

———. 2009. "The Impermanent Text in Catullus and Other Roman Poets." In *Ancient Literacies: The Culture of Reading in Greece and Rome*, ed. W. A. Johnson and H. N. Parker, 164–85. New York: Oxford University Press.

Feldherr, A. 2010. *Playing Gods: Ovid's Metamorphoses and the Politics of Fiction*. Princeton: Princeton University Press.

Galinsky, K. 1996. *Augustan Culture: An Interpretive Introduction*. Princeton: Princeton University Press.

Gamberale, L. 1991. "Il cosidetto preproemio dell'*Eneide*." In *Studi di filologia classica in onore di Giusto Monaco*, ed. A. Butteto and M. von Albrecht, 963–80. Palermo: Università di Palermo.

Gibson, B. 1999. "Ovid on Reading: Reading Ovid: Reception in Ovid *Tristia* II." *Journal of Roman Studies* 89: 19–37.

Hardie, P. 1997a. "Closure in Latin Epic." In *Classical Closure: Reading the End in Greek and Latin Literature*, ed. D. H. Roberts et al., 139–62. Princeton: Princeton University Press.

———. 1997b. "Questions of Authority: The Invention of Tradition in Ovid *Metamorphoses* 15." In *The Roman Cultural Revolution*, ed. T. Habinek and A. Schiesaro, 182–98. Cambridge: Cambridge University Press.

———. 2002. *Ovid's Poetics of Illusion*. Cambridge: Cambridge University Press.

Hinds, S. 1998. *Allusion and Intertext: Dynamics of Appropriation in Roman Poetry*. Cambridge: Cambridge University Press.

———. 2006. "Booking the Return Trip: Ovid and *Tristia* 1." In *Oxford Readings in Ovid*, ed. P. Knox, 415–40. Oxford: Oxford University Press.

Ingleheart, J. 2010. *A Commentary on Ovid, Tristia, Book 2*. Oxford: Oxford University Press.

———, ed. 2011. *Two Thousand Years of Solitude: Exile After Ovid*. Oxford: Oxford University Press.

Johnson, P. 2008. *Ovid Before Exile: Art and Punishment in the Metamorphoses*. Madison: University of Wisconsin Press.

Kennedy, D. 1992. "'Augustan' and 'Anti-Augustan': Reflections on Terms of Reference." In *Roman Poetry and Propaganda in the Age of Augustus*, ed. A. Powell, 26–58. London: Bristol Classical Press.

Kienast, D. 1982. *Augustus: Prinzeps und Monarch*. Darmstadt: Wissenschaftliche Buchgesellschaft.

Konstan, D. 2006. "The Active Reader in Classical Antiquity." *Argos* 30: 7–18.

Krevans, N. 2010. "Bookburning and the Poetic Deathbed: The Legacy of Vergil." In *Classical Literary Careers and Their Reception*, ed. P. Hardie and H. Moore, 197–208. Cambridge: Cambridge University Press.

Kyriakidis, S. 2013. "The Poet's Afterlife: Ovid Between Epic and Elegy." In *Generic Interfaces in Latin Literature: Encounters, Interactions and Transformations*, ed. T. Papanghelis, S. Harrison, and S. Frangoulidis, 351–66. Berlin: De Gruyter.

Levick, B. 2010. *Augustus: Image and Substance*. Harlow: Longman.

Lowrie, M. 2009. *Writing, Performance, and Authority in Augustan Rome*. Oxford: Oxford University Press.

Magdelain, A. 1947. *Auctoritas Principis*. Paris: Société d'édition "Les Belles Lettres."

McKeown, J. C. 1989. *Ovid: Amores*, vol. 2: *A Commentary on Book One*. Leeds: Francis Cairns.

Miller, J. 2009. *Apollo, Augustus, and the Poets*. Cambridge: Cambridge University Press.

Mynors, R. A. B. 1990. *Virgil: Georgics*. Oxford: Oxford University Press.

Nagle, B. R. 1980. *The Poetics of Exile: Program and Polemic in the Tristia and Epistulae ex Ponto of Ovid*. Brussels: Latomus.

Newman, J. K. 1967. *The Concept of Vates in Augustan Poetry*. Brussels: Latomus.

O'Hara, J. 2007. *Inconsistency in Roman Epic: Studies in Catullus, Lucretius, Vergil, Ovid and Lucan*. Cambridge: Cambridge University Press.

Papaioannou, S. 2005. *Epic Succession and Dissension: Ovid, Metamorphoses 13.623–14.582 and the Reinvention of the Aeneid*. Berlin: De Gruyter.

Pierre, M. 2005. "Rome dans la balance: La poésie augustéenne imite-t-elle la poésie grecque?" In *Façons de parler grec à Rome*, ed. F. Dupont and E. Valette-Gagnac, 229–54. Paris: Belin.

Putnam, M. C. J. 2010. "Some Virgilian Unities." In *Classical Literary Careers and Their Reception*, ed. P. Hardie and H. Moore, 17–38. Cambridge: Cambridge University Press.

Segal, C. 1969. "Myth and Philosophy in the *Metamorphoses*: Ovid's Augustanism and the Augustan Conclusion to Book XV." *American Journal of Philology* 90: 257–92.

Smith, R. A. 1997. *Poetic Allusion and Poetic Embrace in Ovid and Virgil*. Ann Arbor: University of Michigan Press.

Southern, P. 1998. *Augustus*. London: Routledge.

Tarrant, R. 2002. "Ovid and Ancient Literary History." In *The Cambridge Companion to Ovid*, ed. P. Hardie, 13–33. Cambridge: Cambridge University Press.

Thomas, R. 1986. "From Recusatio to Commitment: The Evolution of the Vergilian Programme." *Papers of the Liverpool Latin Seminar* 5: 61–84.

———. 2001. *Virgil and the Augustan Reception*. Cambridge: Cambridge University Press.

Wilkinson, L. P. 1955. *Ovid Recalled*. Cambridge: Cambridge University Press.

Winsbury, R. 2009. *The Roman Book: Books, Publishing and Performance in Classical Rome*. London: Duckworth.

Wray, D. 2009. "Ovid's Catullus and the Neoteric Moment in Roman Poetry." In *A Companion to Ovid*, ed. P. Knox, 252–64. Chichester: Wiley-Blackwell.

Ziogas, I. 2010. "The Permanence of Cupid's Metamorphosis in the *Aeneid*." *Trends in Classics* 2: 150–74.

———. Forthcoming. "Ovid and Catullus: Evolution and Revolution in Latin Poetry." In *From Middles to New Beginnings*, ed. A. Michalopoulos and S. Papaioannou. Newcastle: Cambridge Scholars Publishing.

Chapter 7

"*Quae quis fugit damnat*": Outspoken Silence in Seneca's *Epistles*

Marcus Wilson

The letters of Cicero are replete with information, opinion, and gossip about events and personalities involved in the political life of the last century BCE. That is his chief preoccupation in both life and consequently in his correspondence. The younger Seneca was arguably even more centrally involved at the heart of political decision making in the time of Nero than Cicero had been during the closing years of the republic.[1] In collaboration with the Praetorian Prefect, Burrus, he effectually ran the Roman Empire between the death of Claudius when the new emperor was still a teenager (54 CE) and the time when Nero began to assert his power and Burrus died in 62, the point from which Tacitus dates the waning of Seneca's influence.[2] According to the historical sources, for twelve years between his return from exile in 49 and his decision to pull out of his involvement with the imperial court in 62, Seneca had an intimate and unrivalled knowledge of the workings of the empire and the dynastic intrigues of the Julio-Claudian family. He had previously published works with strong political themes, like his response to his own banishment in the *Ad Helviam*, his satire on the deification of Claudius, and his policy document on the qualities of a good emperor, the *De Clementia*, addressed to Nero.[3]

Seneca's letters date from the year 62 to 65,[4] that is, between his loss of influence at court and his death; and even allowing for the likelihood that they were no ordinary correspondence but composed for publication and addressed to the author's own alter ego,[5] they are remarkable, among other things, for their silence on recent or current political or imperial events or debates.[6] It is one of the paradoxes of the epistles that they are avowedly a revelation of self, and do contain autobiographical elements, but completely suppress everything Seneca experienced during the height of his public career. There is no mention of the names of Nero, Agrippina, Britannicus, or other major figures of the time: Corbulo, Thrasea Paetus, Tigellinus, Petronius, nor even Lucan, his own nephew. It is only with familiarity that we tend to forget how extraordinary this silence is.[7] Seneca knew them all, was Nero's speechwriter, and was on record, according to Tacitus, as criticizing Nero's artistic and athletic ambitions (*Ann.* 14.14; 14.52). He had successfully defended himself from accusations of political subversion (*Ann.* 14.65), and seen off numerous private insinuations about his wealth and political influence.[8] But if Seneca was concerned at the end of his life to look to his legacy, to the way he would be seen by posterity, it seems, on the surface at least, that he was fixed on defining that legacy wholly in terms of his philosophical rather than his political achievements.[9] He possibly saw little need to put the true facts on record for the benefit of historians, most of whom he held in contempt,[10] but did he feel no urge to defend his decisions and lay claim to his public successes?

Perhaps his real thoughts were being kept for his will, a place where dissident Romans sometimes expressed their true feelings, to be read out after they died,[11] but Tacitus tells us quite explicitly that as soon as the centurion told Seneca his life was forfeit, Seneca asked for writing tablets to revise his will and the centurion (presumably under orders) refused to allow this (*Ann.* 15.62). He did dictate a last work as he bled to death, and this was later published (*Ann.* 15.63). Tacitus assumes all the readers of his *Annals* know this last work of Seneca: "aduocatis scriptoribus pleraque tradidit, quae in uulgus edita eius uerbis inuertere supersedeo" ("he summoned his secretaries and dictated much to them which, as it has been published for all readers in his own words, I forbear to paraphrase"). What a pity! We do not know how long after Seneca's death it was published. In all probability it was kept back until after Nero's overthrow.

Dio (65.25.2) says he entrusted his deathbed writings to people who would keep them out of Nero's clutches. Tacitus invites his readers to bring to mind Seneca's posthumous publication, and our modern inability to do so, since the work is lost, hampers our understanding of Tacitus's view of Seneca no less than our understanding of Seneca himself.[12] To press Tacitus's statement a little further, he implies that if Seneca's last work were not already widely circulated and well known, it would have been the sort of thing he would normally include in his historical narrative, in summary form at least. That suggests it was not purely philosophical in character but carried the kind of political connotations that interest the historian. Presumably Seneca had a reason for keeping his last work from Nero as Dio said he did.

To come back to Seneca's writings that do survive and that we can read, it is worth pointing out that he does not just quietly omit political content from the epistles, but he parades that omission. In the first place he specifically contrasts the political focus of Cicero's correspondence with the personal, philosophical, and apolitical character of his own epistles (*Ep.* 118.2–3):

> Numquam potest deesse, quod scribam, ut omnia illa quae Cicero implent epistulas, transeam: quis candidatus laboret; quis alienis, quis suis uiribus pugnet; quis consulatum fiducia Caesaris, quis Pompei, quis arcae petat; quam durus sit faenerator Caecilius a quo minoris centesimis propinqui nummum mouere non possint.
>
> Sua satius est mala quam aliena tractare.

> I will always have plenty to write about to you, though I pass over in silence all those things with which Cicero fills his letters: who is in trouble in the election; who has gone into debt to fund his campaign; who is competing but spending his own money; whose candidature is backed by Caesar, or by Pompey or by his own bank balance; what a scrooge is Caecilius from whom even his mates can't borrow a cent at less than 12% interest.
>
> It's better to deal with one's own problems than other people's.

So by specific contrast with Cicero, Seneca here disparages everything political as transitory, peripheral, and a distraction.

The second and more persuasive means Seneca used to parade his disregard of public and political issues is his continual reiteration of the theme of withdrawal or retirement from engagement with public office and all unnecessary social and administrative obligations.[13] This is hinted at in the very first words of the first letter: "uindica te tibi" ("reclaim ownership of yourself"). He writes as one who has largely disentangled himself from public affairs and takes, or invents, as his correspondent someone who is actively seeking to do the same, namely Lucilius. The theme runs as an undercurrent throughout the collection (and especially the first half), often mentioned at the beginning of a letter, rising to greater prominence as a major or preeminent theme at frequent intervals, in, for instance, *Epistles* 5, 8, 14, 19, 22, 36, 62, 68, 72, 74, 103, and 118. Disengagement from the world is the first step toward philosophy. Seneca insists on a strict dissociation: there is the inner world of philosophy and the outer world of political, administrative, and business careers and the latter is treated as antithetical to the former. This disjunction is far from being a necessary or logical position for a philosopher. Traditionally philosophy embraced political theory: think of Plato's *Republic*, Cicero's *Republic* and *Laws*, Aristotle's *Politics*, and, in early Stoic tradition, Zeno's *Republic*.[14] The Stoics in particular theoretically approved of involvement in political life and Seneca himself had previously written the Stoic manual of imperial best practice, the *De Clementia*. In the *De Tranquillitate* he had argued against giving up on and abandoning political service (*Tranq.* 3–5), even in difficult political conditions. His embracing of a private contemplative existence in his final years in the course of writing the letters leads him into a position very close to the followers of Epicurus, the rival philosophical school infamous for its rejection of the value of an active life in politics. So Seneca, in advocating withdrawal so forcefully and consistently in the *Epistles*, places himself at odds with Stoicism, his own past life, and his lifelong philosophical project. He takes his Epicurean sympathies beyond this one issue in the early books of epistles: he is reading Epicurus, he quotes Epicurus in preference to Stoic authorities, he praises Epicurus, and he adopts Epicurean arguments about, for instance, the insignificance of death and the mutual benefit of deep personal friendships. Many scholars have found Seneca's apparent inconsistency on the question of political activity disturbing, and they have consumed a lot of ink seeking to reconcile his later statements with his earlier works and life and with Stoic theory.[15] It would not be so problematic if he had merely left politics out of the letters, but he uses the letters to positively repudiate politics on the grounds that it is destructive of philosophical progress. Turning to philosophy becomes, in the epistles, a form of voluntary exile, where philosophy becomes a remote location cut off from Roman political life. To go into voluntary exile, though, is itself a politically loaded gesture.[16] The epistles are so ostentatiously apolitical, they are political.[17]

The context in which this apolitical (or antipolitical) aspect of Seneca's thought is considered makes all the difference to our understanding of the motivations behind the composition of the epistles. Usually it is approached as an issue of compliance or noncompliance with the Stoic doctrine of political engagement.[18] Instead of trying to understand Seneca's apparent inconsistency narrowly in terms of ancient philosophical doctrines, it is, I think, more revealing to view it in the context of the dangers attendant in Seneca's time on appearing to cast aspersions upon the emperor by means of the written word. For Romans of the early empire, the republic was remembered as practically synonymous with the virtue of *libertas*, when freedom to speak one's mind, especially in the senate, was a hallowed institution, at least in the ideology of the early empire if not in historical reality.[19] Tacitus begins his *Annals* with a synopsis of Roman constitutional history: "Urbem Romam a principio reges habuere; libertatem et consulatum L. Brutus instituit" ("Rome at the beginning was ruled by kings. *Libertas* and the consulship were established by Lucius Brutus"). He identifies the republic with twin indicators, freedom of political expression and the splitting of political authority between two magistrates. There had long been a possibility of taking legal action for defamation under the Twelve Tables (*infamia* or *flagitium*, 8.1), but this protected personal and family reputations and seems never to have been used to curb political debate. In the late republic at least, it seems to have been taken for granted that the proper response on being attacked verbally in public was to counterattack in kind, to seek not a legal but an oratorical remedy.[20] Contrary to the use of the title in modern times, it was not the function of the Roman Censor to enforce controls on publications. Nor was book burning in keeping with the *mores maiorum*. One rare episode, the exception that proves the rule, was preserved in the historiographic record. Valerius Antias, in a story repeated by Livy (40.29), told how in 181 BCE the accidental discovery was made by farm workers digging on the Janiculum of a sealed box containing fourteen books written apparently by Numa five hundred years earlier. These were handed over to the city praetor, who read enough of them to decide they contradicted much of what the Romans now considered sacred to their cultural and religious tradition and referred the matter to the senate. After accepting the praetor's word that the books were politically incorrect, the senate ordered that they be burned in public in the *comitium*. This, if it ever happened, seems to have been an isolated incident, in response to very peculiar circumstances. In the early imperial period there is a unanimous view that the criminalization of dissident writing did not begin until the later principate of Augustus, and that the law adapted for this purpose was the law of *maiestas* (conventionally but somewhat misleadingly translated as "treason").[21] Tacitus famously wrote (*Ann.* 1.72), "Primus Augustus cognitionem de famosis libellis specie legis eius tractauit, commotus Cassii Seueri libidine, qua uiros feminasque inlustris procacibus scriptis diffamauerat" ("It was Augustus who first, under the pretext of this law, extended legal inquiry to written libel provoked by the license with which Cassius Severus had defamed respectable men and women with his impertinent writings"). Yet the earliest and almost archetypal case of book burning under the principate seems to have been implemented without recourse to this new application of the *maiestas* law. A minutely detailed account was preserved by Seneca's own father. As he reports, the target was Titus Labienus, the orator and prorepublican historian (Elder Seneca *Contr.* 10. praef. 5). "In hoc primum excogitat est noua poena; effectum est enim per inimicos ut omnes eius libri comburentur: res noua et inuisitata supplicium de studiis sumi" ("It was against him that there was first devised an unprecedented punishment: his enemies saw to it that all his books were cast into the flames. This was a strange and uncustomary thing, that the punishment of execution should be extended to literature"). Labienus's crime was too much *libertas*: "his freedom of speech was such that it exceeded the definition of freedom" ("libertas tanta ut libertatis nomen excederet").[22] The elder Seneca goes on to lament the legalized destruction of literary monuments and thanks the gods that the practice had not been devised in the time when his hero, Cicero, was publishing. A century later, Tacitus, having experienced the oppressive regime of Domitian, made it his business to trace the expanding scope of the *maiestas* law in the first century and especially its use as a tool of political censorship. He makes the trial of Cremutius Cordus the historian in 25 CE into a telltale symptom of escalating repression (*Ann.* 4.34–35). He was driven to suicide and his books were burned.[23] Seneca (the younger) celebrates their republication (Cremutius's daughter had secretly preserved a copy) in his *Ad Marciam*.

The suppression of Labienus's historical works cannot have taken place without Augustus's (at least tacit) approval. It was in this more intolerant cultural atmosphere of the later Augustan period (which also saw the banishment of Ovid in 8 CE), that Tacitus located the beginnings of the redirection of the *maiestas* law to apply to the censorship of writing. It was typical of Augustus to adapt an existing legal provision to suit his current needs, giving an aura of tradition to a wholly unprecedented governmental innovation. Cassius Dio (56.27) dates Augustus's introduction of book burning to 12–13 CE. "When he discovered that scurrilous writings had been composed concerning certain people, he ordered them to be tracked down. Those that were found in the city he ordered to be burned by the aediles, those found elsewhere to be burned by the local officials, and a number of the authors he caused to be punished." Suetonius agrees on this date for the book burning, though he refers to other types of books (*Aug.* 31):

> Postquam uero pontificatum maximum . . . suscepit, quidquid fatidicorum librorum Graeci Latinique generis nullis uel parum idoneis auctoribus uulgo ferebatur, supra duo milia contracta undique cremauit ac solos retinuit Sibyllinos, hos quoque dilectu habito.
>
> After he took on the office of Pontifex Maximus . . . whatever prophetic writings in Greek and Latin were in the public domain anonymously or under the names of less respectable authors were collected and burned on his authority to the number of more than two thousand; only the Sibylline books were exempted, and even of these only a certain number were preserved.

He outlawed the use of a nom de plume (*Aug.* 55), and stopped publication of the proceedings of the senate in the *acta diurna* (*Aug.* 36.1).

The *maiestas* law was broad and ill defined and could potentially be expanded to cover any action that implied criticism or disrespect of the emperor. Other literary victims of the *maiestas* law before Seneca came to write his epistles include Clutorius Priscus (21 CE), Gaius Cominius (24), Sextius Paconianus (35), and Mamercus Scaurus (34).[24] *Delatores* had a huge financial incentive to find new grounds for *maiestas* prosecutions against the wealthy, for if they obtained a conviction they walked away with a quarter of the accused's property,[25] plus whatever additional reward the emperor might grant.[26] The successful prosecutors of Thrasea Paetus, namely Cossutianus Capito and Eprius Marcellus, profited to the tune of five million sesterces each (*Ann.* 16.33). As the prosecution argument, reproduced by Tacitus, in that trial shows, nonparticipation in politics, political silence, could be turned into evidence of criminal dissent, especially if combined with Stoic philosophy.[27] Cossutianus claimed Thrasea had absented himself from the senate for three years, and his austere personal manner, his *uirtus*, was itself an implicit rebuke to the emperor, as if charging him with moral laxity. He failed publicly to congratulate Nero on his successes or commiserate with his disappointments (*Ann.* 16.22). Thrasea has placed himself in relation to Nero as Cato was to Caesar in the civil war that shook the Roman world a century earlier. Eprius Marcellus took this even further (16.28). Thrasea was no less than a traitor and public enemy ("proditorem palam et hostem") in setting himself up in opposition to the institutions and ceremonies of the *maiores* by boycotting senate meetings, religious sacrifices, and the oath of allegiance. His silence was an expression of condemnation ("silentium . . . omnia damnantis"), and his threat of going into exile was a sign of perverted ambition ("ambitionis prauae"). Refusal to participate in the political process as a criticism of those in power had a history at Rome, as witness Marcellus's self-exile in Mytilene after the Battle of Pharsalus as a living reprimand to Julius Caesar (or so Seneca portrays his thinking in the *Ad Heluiam* 9.4–10.1).

While Seneca died before the trial of Thrasea, the writing of his letters coincided with Thrasea's public strategy of noncompliance, and the same considerations certainly entered his mind as to how his withdrawal from political involvement might be interpreted by opportunistic enemies (of whom there were many) and by Nero himself. Tacitus, in the scene he invents of Seneca seeking permission from Nero to surrender his wealth and retire from the court (*Ann.* 14.53–56), has Nero make the point, in replying, that it will seem to reflect badly on himself (*Ann.* 14.56), that abstention from the imperial court, that political silence, is liable to be read as a political act:

> Non tua moderatio, si redderis pecuniam, nec quies, si reliqueris principem, sed mea auaritia, meae crudelitatis metus in ore omnium uersabitur. quod si maxime continentia tua laudetur, non tamen sapienti uiro decorum fuerit, unde amico infamiam paret, inde gloriam sibi recipere.
>
> It's not your moderation, if you return your wealth, not your peaceful life, if you abandon the *princeps*, that will be the subject of everyone's talk, but my greed and the threat of my cruelty. Though your personal restraint will be praised, it is not fitting for a wise man to attract glory to himself by an action that brings disrepute (*infamia*) upon his friend.

Tacitus has, it seems to me, put his finger in this speech he invents for Nero exactly on the "catch-22" that Seneca and other Stoics faced. It was treason to speak their minds and treasonous not to speak at all or to withdraw from public and political life. Should Seneca retire from the court, Nero insinuates, his action will be read as bringing *infamia* upon Nero himself; this is clear grounds for a charge of having damaged the emperor's *maiestas*. Seneca in *Epistle* 4.8 expresses the problem he was up against more directly and succinctly: "quae quis fugit, damnat" ("in avoiding things one condemns them").

A number of curious features of the epistles come together and make sense when examined in the context of the legal and political climate in which Seneca was operating.[28] He was trying to deflect charges against him, either sown in the emperor's mind or marshaled by *delatores* like those who would soon destroy Thrasea. The most significant of these features are, first, his self-censorship, his omission of references to Nero, or the court, or his own public career over the previous dozen years; second, his thematizing of a radical disjunction between philosophy and politics, since to be a philosopher, he now argues, requires as a prerequisite the complete repudiation of public and political involvement; and third, his uncharacteristic enthusiasm for Epicurus in the first three books of the epistles.[29]

To take up the last of these, scholars of the history of philosophy have been frustrated by Seneca's "eclecticism," by his Epicurean stance in the early epistles that seems irreconcilable with his avowed Stoicism.[30] But what makes little sense in the context of the philosophical schools makes perfect sense in the context of the Roman law of treason. Seneca knew perfectly well that on a theoretical level Stoics and Epicureans were diametrically opposed on the issue of political participation. In the *De Otio* (3.2) he had written, "Duae maxime et in hac re dissident sectae, Epicureorum et Stoicorum. . . . Epicurus ait: 'Non accedet ad rem publicam sapiens, nisi si quid interuenerit'; Zenon ait: 'Accedet ad rem publicam, nisi si quid impedierit'" ("The two sects, the Epicureans and the Stoics are wholly at variance on this question. . . . Epicurus says, 'The wise man will not go into politics unless some crisis necessitates it.' Zeno says, 'He will enter politics unless circumstances prevent it'"). Seneca also knew there was some ambivalence, if not hypocrisy, in the Stoic position because the founders of the philosophy, while advocating political activity, stayed out of politics themselves (*Tranq.* 1.10): "Zenona, Cleanthen, Chrysippum, quorum tamen nemo ad rem publicam accessit, et nemo non misit" ("of Zeno, Cleanthes and Chrysippus, none entered political life and none did not encourage others into it"). Not only does Seneca praise Epicurus and quote him in the majority of the letters of the first three books (in contrast to his previous and his later practice), he shows that he is, over the period of their composition, also reading Epicurus's letters. One letter to which he pays particular attention is the letter to Idomeneus (cited in Seneca's *Epistles* 21 and 22), in which the Greek philosopher advised his addressee on how best to extract himself from involvement in government. This reliance on Epicurus rather than on Stoic authorities was an astute move on Seneca's part because it allowed him to bypass the awkward Stoic principle that a philosopher might only withdraw from politics if the political environment was so oppressive or corrupt as to make progress impossible. That doctrine of orthodox Stoicism was a godsend for ambitious prosecutors, since the doctrine itself connected political silence or nonparticipation with a negative judgment of the ruler. Withdrawal from political life amounted to a public denigration of the *princeps* as a tyrant. To withdraw from active participation in public life, in line with Stoic doctrines, was to damn the reigning emperor's character and was therefore "treasonous," as Thrasea would soon learn to his cost.[31] So Seneca transforms himself into a temporary Epicurean for the purpose of retiring without giving offense, forestalling any risk of prosecution under the *maiestas* law; and later in the epistles turns himself back into a Stoic and attacks vigorously a range of other Epicurean ideas. This is a virtuoso performance of philosophical acrobatics concocted to dive under the radar of the Julio-Claudian censorship system.

Scholars have struggled rather unsuccessfully to tie Seneca down to a stable philosophical position, especially on this question of political activity, drawing evidence from across all his many texts, and from different periods of his life, in the expectation of a general consistency and compliance with orthodox Stoicism as we derive it from other sources. But this world was no peaceful scholarly enclave. To express certain thoughts in Nero's Rome was perilous, possibly a capital crime. Seneca's sensational philosophical gymnastics begin to make more sense when viewed against the backdrop of a particularly vicious culture of "censorship." His earlier reflections on political participation in *De Tranquillitate* and *De Otio* were not forged under the pressure of his own immediate need to get clear of Nero's inner circle. He could afford in those earlier writings to try to approximate a Stoic ideal. During the composition of the early epistles the issue is urgent and pragmatic: not whether it is time to leave but how to go about it. As he writes at *Epistle* 14.7, "sapiens numquam potentium iras prouocabit. immo declinabit, non aliter quam in nauigando procellam" ("The wise man will never provoke the anger of those in power. Rather, he will alter his course just as you would in steering a ship away from a storm"). In *Epistle* 14 especially Seneca discloses his full philosophical survival strategy. A safe retirement must be subtle and unobtrusive. There should be no parade of austerity in dress, speech or action, or anything to indicate too extreme an aversion to the customs of society. Later in the collection in letter 73 he returns to the topic of the relation of philosophy to political authority, but this time the argument is restored to a more Stoic perspective.[32] Philosophy itself is to be associated with peacefulness, and is defended from any imputation of political disruption. *Pax et libertas*, says Seneca (*Ep.* 73.8), "peace and freedom of expression": these are the indivisible goods (*indiuidua bona*) loved by philosophers and citizens. Philosophers are uniquely appreciative of good rulers without whom they would not enjoy the necessary undisturbed leisure conducive to thought (*Ep.* 73.10): "Confitebitur ergo multum se debere ei cuius administratione ac prouidentia contingit illi pingue otium et arbitrium sui temporis et inperturbata publicis occupationibus quies" ("A philosopher will therefore recognize that he is indebted to the person whose management of affairs and providence enable him to enjoy a productive leisure, control of his own time and peace undisturbed by public duties"). In addition to reconfiguring his Epicurean and Stoic philosophical allegiances in the course of writing the epistles so as to step around the question of participation in politics, Seneca can also be seen altering his epistolographic practice in other ways when dealing with this sensitive subject.

Take his deployment, for instance, of both literary quotation and historical *exemplum*. What does Seneca do in letter 73, immediately after the passage reproduced above, to cap his argument but to adduce the authority of Virgil? While he has quoted Virgil often in earlier epistles, it is usually from the *Aeneid*. Now for the first time in the epistles Seneca has recourse to the *Eclogues*. *Eclogue* 1, of course:

> O Meliboee, deus nobis haec otia fecit:
> namque erit ille mihi semper deus.
>
> O Meliboeus, a god created this *otium* for me.
> For he will always be a god in my eyes.

Seneca recasts himself as Tityrus, not exactly a dangerous subversive or political threat. And if the use of poetry changes in these letters on withdrawal, so also does the use of history. The hero of Republicans and Stoics alike, Cato the younger, invoked frequently by Seneca throughout his prose corpus for his unflinching confrontation of death,[33] is criticized, just the once, in *Epistle* 14.13. He should have had enough sense as a good Stoic to quit politics, since the state of Rome at the time of Cato's political resistance was beyond remedy. Seneca addresses him directly over the gulf of the intervening years: "Potest aliquis disputare an illo tempore capessanda fuerit sapienti res publica. 'quid tibi uis, Marce Cato? iam non agitur de libertate: olim pessumdata est'" ("One might dispute whether politics at that time ought to have been taken up by a wise man. 'What do you think you're doing Cato? It's not a struggle for freedom of speech. That was killed off long ago'"). It has been the fashion among historians for the last half century to dismiss the notion that there was a "Stoic opposition" under the later Julio-Claudian and Flavian emperors.[34] Nostalgia for the republic, so the argument goes, came from a disgruntled group of senators and had little or nothing to do with philosophy. Their Stoicism was incidental to their political stance, especially since traditionally the earlier Stoics were not hostile to any particular type of constitution.[35] That, I would suggest, is beside the point, and the wider argument is, in the end, untenable. Opposition arose not from any abstract preference for one type of constitution but from a pragmatic moral test that could be applied to any ruling authority whether monarchic, aristocratic, or democratic: was it possible in that political environment to make a difference by participation in public life, or were conditions so inimical as to render participation futile? Seneca writes (*Ep.* 14.7–8),

> Interdum populus est quem timere debeamus; interdum si ea ciuitatis disciplina est, ut plurima per senatum transigantur, gratiosi in eo uiri; interdum singuli, quibus potestas populi et in populum data est. hos omnes amicos habere operosum est, satis est inimicos non habere . . . idem facit sapiens; nocituram potentiam uitat, hoc primum cauens, ne uitare uideatur. pars enim securitatis et in hoc est, non ex professo eam petere . . .

> Sometimes it is the people that we ought to fear; at other times, if the constitution is such that decisions are in the hands of a senate, that is the body that needs to be cultivated; in other cases it is an individual who is endowed with power by the people over the people. It is a laborious task to retain friendly relations with these types; it is enough to avoid having them as enemies. . . . A wise man avoids power that has the potential to injure, taking care first of all not to appear to be avoiding it. A crucial part of safety lies in this, that you do not aspire to it openly.

The test of whether a Stoic should reject political participation is essentially the same test that governs the decision on whether suicide is justified in the individual's particular circumstances, the only difference being that it is applied to political life rather than life itself. Stoic philosophy was, as I have argued, at the heart of the opposition to the emperors in the first century, as Tacitus himself saw perfectly clearly.[36] But Stoicism was not so much proactively anti-imperial as forced into a defensive position by the Roman censorship mechanism. It was a philosophy vulnerable to attack under the legal mechanism that was put in place for controlling silence—no less than for controlling speech—in the form of the wide interpretation of the crime of *maiestas*.

It has similarly been a puzzle in philosophical scholarship that Seneca seems to flaunt his exterritorial dalliance with Epicureanism in the earlier books of the epistles, before returning to his Stoic roots in the latter stages of the correspondence. Seneca's so-called eclecticism has even been taken as evidence for a characteristic intellectual aberration of the times. The argument of this chapter points to a missing piece of the puzzle, specifically a historical censorship regime that necessitated philosophical eclecticism on pain of death. Consistency in Stoic doctrine was liable to be read as political subversion, a contravention of the law of *maiestas*. It gave an open invitation to the enemies of those Romans professing Stoic values to use legal means to harness the real or imagined anxieties of the emperor to their destruction.

To qualify as a victim of the *delatores* a Stoic also had to be rich. You had to be *in* the senate, for instance, for your nonattendance to have any meaning. Treason trials had at least as much to do with money as with politics.[37] In the same way that modern presuppositions about religion and other cultural practices have proven to be obstacles to a sympathetic understanding of Roman institutions, the same goes for modern attitudes to wealth. Not only do centuries of Christianity, in which poverty has been sometimes regarded as a virtue in itself, foster cultural misapprehensions, but modern consumer capitalism superimposes a no less murky cloud of distorting anachronism.[38] Poverty was never a Stoic virtue but was, along with wealth, defined as "indifferent."[39] In modern societies wealth buys security, or is thought to buy security: from homelessness, physical danger, bad or nonexistent medical attention, inadequate education, loss of property, loss of travel opportunities, and loss of access to legal remedies or political or further commercial opportunities. In first century Rome, wealth, especially great wealth, was practically synonymous with insecurity, a trap set by the unreliable goddess *Fortuna*.[40] Little wonder, then, that the most dependable censorship tool possessed by the emperor was enrichment. In this too, it was Augustus who showed the way. As Tacitus says of the Roman nobility who survived the civil wars:

"ceteri nobilium, quanto quis seruitio promptior, opibus et honoribus extollerentur" ("the rest of the upper class, according to each person's servility, were raised up by enrichment and tokens of status"; *Ann.* 1.2). Not only did enrichment lock the emperor's *amici* into a web of obligation, into accepting the duties of reciprocity that came as the unspoken consequence of *beneficia*,[41] but it also painted a very large target on their backs. In modern capitalist systems wealth is earned or possessed rather than conferred, and if we impose this model on ancient Rome we risk missing half the picture, by focusing only on the person in possession of riches while ignoring the interests of the enricher. Wealth was conceptualized not as a purely individual possession but as part of a relationship.

The greater the enrichment, the more exposed a person became. Tacitus shows Seneca, in his interview with Nero,[42] placing much emphasis on his enrichment by the emperor (*Ann.* 14.53), after which he asks for protection (*praesidium*) in the form of permission to give back most of his wealth (*Ann.* 14.54): "cum opes meas ultra sustinere non possim, praesidium peto. iube rem per procuratores tuos administrari, in tuam fortunam recipi" ("Since I cannot any longer sustain my wealth, I ask for protection. Order my property to be administered by your own managers and to be absorbed back into your own estate"). It underestimates Tacitus's political acumen to read this as implying hypocrisy on Seneca's part. That Seneca's request is sincere is a much more telling comment on the principate itself as a system in which the other side of the magnanimity of the emperor is the radical insecurity of the rest of the governing class, an insecurity guaranteed by the *maiestas* laws and lucrative financial incentives for bringing prosecutions. The modern habit of reading Seneca's disparagement of wealth in his philosophical writing as merely hypocritical is, I would suggest, to view his situation narrowly through the lens of modern capitalist ideology and miss the very different function of wealth in Roman imperial society, and especially its function as a mechanism of political control.[43] Seneca was all too aware that his enrichment placed him at the top of the candidate list of profitable *maiestas* prosecutions, should Nero show any hint of withdrawing his personal favor. When the author of the *Octavia* brings Seneca on stage to reveal his innermost thoughts in a soliloquy, those thoughts take their cue from a deep uneasiness attributed to the philosopher over the precariousness of his present position and nostalgia for his exile in the years before Nero came to power.[44] No less than Tacitus (at *Ann.* 14.53–54) the dramatist has captured something of the genuine dilemma Seneca faced in 62 CE:

Quid me, potens Fortuna, fallaci mihi
blandita uultu, sorte contentum mea
alte extulisti, grauius ut ruerem edita
receptus arce totque prospicerem metus?
melius latebam procul ab inuidiae malis
remotus inter Corsici rupes maris
ubi liber animus et sui iuris mihi.

Why, powerful Fortuna, with your seductive and deceptive
looks, have you raised me on high, though I was content in my
former station? So that being placed on a higher peak I can look
out on innumerable threats and crash all the more heavily?
I was better off out of sight from the dangers of envy, exiled
amidst the rocks of the sea around Corsica, where
my soul was free and subject only to its own laws.

As is commonly the case with public health and public order controls, the most effective methods of censorship in imperial Rome were preemptive.

NOTES

1. Seneca himself draws comparisons between his own letters to Lucilius and Cicero's letters to Atticus (*Ep.* 21.4–5; 118.1–2).

2. Tac. *Ann.* 14.52.1: "Mors Burri infregit Senecae potentiam" ("The death of Burrus broke the influence of Seneca").

3. On the date, genre, and purpose of the *De Clementia*, see Braund (2009) 16–67.

4. Griffin (1976) 396, 400.

5. Lucilius, Seneca's correspondent, is characterized as a slightly younger version of himself (addressed as *Iunior* on occasions in the *NQ*). He is in the process of extricating himself from a position of political responsibility, interested in philosophy, a writer of books and letters, and a reader of the same books as Seneca. See Griffin (1976) 416–19 for discussion. Gowers (2011) rightly identifies Lucilius as a fictional creation, but misreads the significance of his name as a recollection of the satirist rather than a play on Seneca's own *praenomen*, Lucius.

6. Edwards (1997) 38n27: "Interestingly, there is no reference to the emperor in Seneca's Letters"; Edwards (2009) 157: "A factor which perhaps gives Seneca's recurrent engagements with the idea of slavery particular bite is an aspect of freedom which he never refers to directly in the letters . . . that is to say freedom in the political sphere"; Gibson (2012) 61: "But the author evidently aims to foster a time-free zone, inasmuch as he largely

avoids reference to contemporary events of the kind that might allow a secure dating for individual letters."

7. Rightly emphasized by Veyne (2003) 162.

8. Tac. *Ann.* 13.42–43; 14.52; 65. See Mayer (2010) for analysis of Suillius's attack on Seneca at Tac. *Ann.* 13.42.

9. As is widely acknowledged, e.g., Newman (2008).

10. E.g., *NQ* 3 pref. 5–6; 4.3.1; 7.16.1–2; *Apoc.* 1. On Seneca's use of history, see Mayer (2008); for Seneca's disparagement of historiography, see Wilson (2007). Gibson (2012) shows that the modern expectation that the publication of a person's collected correspondence should mirror an implicit historical or biographical narrative is misplaced when applied to ancient letter collections. He allows Seneca's epistles as a partial exception in that they are sequential.

11. Cramer (1945) 162–63.

12. Ker (2009a) 69: "However we understand it, the implication is the same: Tacitus presupposes his reader's independent access to Seneca's published words."

13. Griffin (1976) 315–66 provides a survey of the relevant passages and various interpretations. See also Momigliano (1969).

14. Schofield (1991) details the development of political thought specifically among Stoics. Long and Sedley (1987) 1.429–37 present a selection of sources.

15. Griffin (1976) 315–66, esp. 332–34.

16. Williams (2006) has argued persuasively that for Seneca the idea of exile was symbolically empowering. See also Ker (2009b).

17. Veyne (2003) 159: "This is the mystery—lying in plain sight—of the *Letters to Lucilius*; their character as oppositional writing in such circumstances has been insufficiently stressed"; 162: "This is what biographers of Seneca have failed to stress sufficiently: the *Letters* are an oppositional work—doubly so."

18. Griffin (1976) 315 begins her discussion with this observation: "Of all the issues treated in the Greek philosophical schools, none had more appeal for the Romans than the choice between a life of service to the *res publica* and a life of *otium* devoted to philosophy." On *otium* in general and in Seneca, see André (1962).

19. On *libertas*, see also Chapter 1 in the present volume.

20. Cramer (1945) 159.

21. Bauman (1967) and (1974) provides a detailed history and analysis of the development of the law. See also Rutledge (2001).

22. His crime is probably datable to around 6 CE.

23. Edwards (2007) 139–43 explores the implications of this episode.

24. For details of the trials, see Bauman (1967) and (1974).

25. Tac. *Ann.* 4.20.1–3.

26. Rutledge (2001) 35–44 discusses the whole question, though he is excessively cautious in estimating the profits to be made.

27. See Wilson (2003) 538–40 for further argument on this. Veyne (2003) 159:

"Allowing the government to govern was not enough: warm endorsement was required and silence held as disavowal."

28. Griffin (1976) 360 argued (in response to the position of Waltz [1909]) against the idea that the *Epistles* were written by Seneca as a means of self-protection, on the grounds that some features of the letters seem critical, and even potentially provocative of Nero. The examples given, though, are speculative; and she was referring to an extreme version of the argument that posited self-protection as the sole motivation for the entirety of the collection. Two further points might be made: it underestimates Seneca's skill as a writer to imagine that he cannot imply criticism while seeming to say the opposite, to combine subtle attacks with defense; and, in the course of the composition of the *Epistles*, Seneca's own situation changed, not least because the early "Epicurean" letters had successfully marked out a kind of fictional apolitical space that gave him room to take more risks in his subsequent epistolographic practice.

29. Seneca also, of course, finds literary and philosophical advantages to the emphasis on Epicurus in the first three books, to do with the epistolary genre and the protreptic character of the early parts of the correspondence. The external context of political repression serves to explain the sudden and unprecedented prominence of Epicurean doctrine and quotation in the first thirty letters but does not, on its own, exhaust the significance of Epicurus in these texts.

30. Inwood (2005) 23–24; (2007) xix, seeks to reject the "eclecticism" approach and advocate a Seneca always firmly grounded in Stoic tradition. His (2007) selection of letters for commentary, though, begins only in book 6. At (2005) 2–3 he lumps Seneca's references to Epicurean doctrines together with his references to Plato and Aristotle: "Seneca's intellectual engagement with Platonism, Aristotelianism, and even with Epicureanism was shaped by a wide range of substantial philosophical interests and concerns." Yet the number and concentration of references to Epicurus and his school in the first three books of epistles have no parallel in the pattern of references in the Senecan corpus to any other philosophical tradition.

31. Wilson (2003) 538–39. Prosecutors could also draw on a long-standing biographical and rhetorical *topos* of the "philosopher and the tyrant," on which see Chitwood (2004) 10, 132–34.

32. On *Epistle* 73, see the discussions of Rudich (1997) 66–69 and Veyne (2003) 159–62.

33. See Edwards (2007) 114–16 for the political connotations typically read into Cato's death; also Ker (2009a) 78–85.

34. Prominent proponents of this approach are Wirszubski (1950), Brunt (1975), Vogel-Weidemann (1975), Rutledge (2001) 357n23.

35. A key claim in the case put forward by Brunt (1975).

36. Tacitus's analytical insight into the underlying causes of the political conflicts of the early empire is often too glibly dismissed on the grounds of his membership of the educated senatorial minority. His conception of his role as a historian cannot be reduced

to that of a partisan orator along the lines proposed by Rutledge (2001) 181: "And let us not doubt that the *Agricola*, *Historiae*, and *Annales* are just that—prosecutions."

37. *Contra* Rutledge (2001) 37, who attempts to play down the profit motive.

38. Veyne (2003) 10: "the Roman nobility had perfectly bourgeois ideas," among innumerable other examples.

39. Brunt (1975) emphasizes rather the recognition among Stoics that some indifferents were preferable, wealth, for instance, over poverty. This, though, never was allowed to override the principle that both were ultimately classed as neither good nor bad in themselves, as is clearly articulated by Veyne (2003) 163.

40. Seneca particularly represents *Fortuna* as the enemy of the virtuous Roman, on which see Asmis (2009).

41. A relationship of considerable interest to Seneca, examined in detail in his *De Beneficiis* and *Ep*. 81. On the *De Beneficiis*, Inwood (2005) 65–94 draws out the complex interaction between the philosophical tradition and Roman social hierarchy, as negotiated by Seneca. On its political aspect, see Veyne (2003) 167: "He had in *On Benefits*, justified at length the right of the governed to rid themselves of a sovereign who did not respect the social contract."

42. Recent contributions to the interpretation of this much discussed passage of the *Annals* include Ker (2009a): 47–49, 71; Woodman (2010).

43. For discussion generally of the issue of Seneca's wealth, see Griffin (2008) 54–58.

44. Dated by most to within a decade after Nero's death. Boyle (2008) lxvi.

REFERENCES

André, J. M. 1962. *Recherches sur l'otium romain*. Paris: Les Belles Lettres.

Asmis, E. 2009. "Seneca on Fortune and the Kingdom of God." In *Seneca and the Self*, ed. S. Bartsch and D. Wray, 115–38. Cambridge: Cambridge University Press.

Bauman, R. 1967. *The crimen maiestatis in the Roman Republic and the Augustan Principate*. Johannesburg: Witwatersrand University Press.

———. 1974. *Impietas in principem: A Study of Treason Against the Roman Emperor with Special Reference to the First Century AD*. Munich: Beck.

Berry, D. and A. Erskine, eds. 2010. *Form and Function in Roman Oratory*. Cambridge: Cambridge University Press.

Boyle, A. J. 2008. *Octavia: Attributed to Seneca: Edited with Introduction, Translation, and Commentary*. Oxford: Oxford University Press.

Boyle, A. J. and W. Dominik, eds. 2003. *Flavian Rome: Culture, Image, Text*. Leiden: Brill.

Braund, S. M. 2009. *Seneca: De Clementia: Edited with Translation and Commentary*. Oxford: Oxford University Press.

Brunt, P. A. 1975. "Stoicism and the Principate." *Papers of the British School at Rome* 43: 7–35.

Chitwood, A. 2004. *Death by Philosophy: The Biographical Tradition in the Life and Death of the Archaic Philosophers Empedocles, Heraclitus, and Democritus*. Ann Arbor: University of Michigan Press.

Cramer, F. H. 1945. "Bookburning and Censorship in Ancient Rome: A Chapter in the History of Freedom of Speech." *Journal of the History of Ideas* 6: 157–96.

Dominik, W., J. Garthwaite, and P. Roche, eds. 2009. *Writing Politics in Imperial Rome*. Leiden: Brill.

Dominik, W. and J. Hall, eds. 2007. *A Companion to Roman Rhetoric*. Malden, MA: Blackwell.

Edwards, C. 1997. "Self-Scrutiny and Self-Transformation in Seneca's Letters." *Greece and Rome* 44: 23–38.

———. 2007. *Death in Ancient Rome*. New Haven, CT: Yale University Press.

———. 2009. "Free Yourself! Slavery, Freedom and the Self in Seneca's Letters." In *Seneca and the Self*, ed. S. Bartsch and D. Wray, 139–59. Cambridge: Cambridge University Press.

Fitch, J., ed. 2008. *Seneca*. Oxford: Oxford University Press.

Gibson, R. 2012. "On the Nature of Ancient Letter Collections." *Journal of Roman Studies* 102: 56–78.

Gowers, E. 2011. "The Road to Sicily: Lucilius to Seneca." *Ramus* 40: 168–97.

Griffin, M. T. 1976. *Seneca: A Philosopher in Politics*. Oxford: Oxford University Press.

———. 2008. "*Imago Vitae Suae*." In *Seneca*, ed. J. Fitch, 23–58. Oxford: Oxford University Press.

Habinek, T. 2000. "Seneca's Renown." *Classical Antiquity* 19: 264–303.

Henderson, J. 2004. *Morals and Villas in Seneca's Letters: Places to Dwell*. Cambridge: Cambridge University Press.

Inwood, B. 2005. *Reading Seneca: Stoic Philosophy at Rome*. Oxford: Oxford University Press.

———. 2007. *Seneca: Selected Philosophical Letters*. Oxford: Oxford University Press.

Ker, J. 2009a. *The Deaths of Seneca*. Oxford: Oxford University Press.

———. 2009b. "Outside and Inside: Senecan Strategies." In *Writing Politics in Imperial Rome*, ed. W. Dominik, J. Garthwaite, and P. Roche, 249–71. Leiden: Brill.

Long, A. A. and D. Sedley. 1987. *The Hellenistic Philosophers*. Cambridge: Cambridge University Press.

Mayer, R. 2008. "Roman Historical Exempla in Seneca." In *Seneca*, ed. J. Fitch, 299–315. Oxford: Oxford University Press.

———. 2010. "Oratory in Tacitus' *Annals*." In *Form and Function in Roman Oratory*, ed. D. Berry and A. Erskine, 281–93. Cambridge: Cambridge University Press.

Momigliano, A. 1969. "Seneca Between Political and Contemplative Life." In *Quarto contributo alla storia degli studi classici e del mondo antico*, 239–56. Rome: Edizioni di storia e letteratura.

Newman, R. 2008. "*In umbra virtutis*: *Gloria* in the Thought of Seneca the Philosopher." In *Seneca*, ed. J. Fitch, 316–34. Oxford: Oxford University Press.

Rudich, V. 1997. *Dissidence and Literature Under Nero: The Price of Rhetoricisation*. London: Routledge.

Rutledge, S. H. 2001. *Imperial Inquisitions: Prosecutors and Informants from Tiberius to Domitian*. London: Routledge.

Schofield, M. 1991. *The Stoic Idea of the City*. Cambridge: Cambridge University Press.

Veyne, P. 2003. *Seneca: The Life of a Stoic*. Tr. D. Sullivan. New York: Routledge.

Vogel-Weidemann, U. 1979. "The Opposition Under the Early Caesars: Some Remarks on Its Nature and Aims." *Acta Classica* 22: 91–107.

Volk, K. and G. Williams, eds. 2006. *Seeing Seneca Whole: Perspectives on Philosophy, Poetry and Politics*. Leiden: Brill.

Waltz, R. 1909. *La vie politique de Sénèque*. Paris: Perrin.

Williams, G. 2006. "States of Exile, States of Mind: Paradox and Reversal in Seneca's *Consolatio ad Helviam Matrem*." In *Seeing Seneca Whole: Perspectives on Philosophy, Poetry and Politics*, ed. K. Volk and G. Williams, 147–73. Leiden: Brill.

Wilson, M. 2003. "After the Silence: Tacitus, Suetonius, Juvenal." In *Flavian Rome: Culture, Image, Text*, ed. A. J. Boyle and W. Dominik, 523–42. Leiden: Brill.

———. 2007. "Rhetoric and the Younger Seneca." In *A Companion to Roman Rhetoric*, ed. W. Dominik and J. Hall, 425–38. Malden, MA: Blackwell.

Wirszubski, C. 1950. *Libertas as a Political Idea at Rome During the Late Republic and Early Principate*. Cambridge: Cambridge University Press.

Woodman, A. 2010. "*Aliena facundia*: Seneca in Tacitus." In *Form and Function in Roman Oratory*, ed. D. Berry and A. Erskine, 294–308. Cambridge: Cambridge University Press.

Chapter 8

Argo's Flavian Politics: The Workings of Power in Valerius Flaccus

Peter J. Davis

Of the three full-length epic poems of the Flavian period (70–96 CE), it is Valerius Flaccus's *Argonautica* that seems the most apolitical: unlike Silius's *Punica*, it does not implicitly contrast Rome's republican past with its imperial present; and, unlike Statius's *Thebaid*, it does not focus primarily on the sensitive subject of civil war. Indeed, it more resembles the fragmentary *Achilleid* in presenting a piece of remote but familiar mythology. How could the story of Jason and the Argonauts function as political critique? This chapter explores some of the elements of Valerius's political code, the means whereby the poet constructs the poem's relevance to Flavian Rome and its politics.

If the witch Circe is to be believed, the story of Jason's voyage to Colchis was already familiar to the first audience of Homer's *Odyssey*, for she speaks of *Argo* as being "in the minds of all" (Ἀργὼ πᾶσι μέλουσα; 12.70). In the eight or so centuries between Homer and Valerius Flaccus the story of Jason and Medea had been retold countless times in both Greek and Latin, in epic, lyric, and elegiac poetry as well as on the tragic stage. Thus Valerius's Flavian readers might well have been familiar with versions of the myth as told by Eumelus, Pindar, Euripides, Apollonius of Rhodes, Ennius, Pacuvius, Accius, Varro of Atax, and Ovid.[1] By composing an *Argonautica* Valerius positioned himself as heir to a lengthy mythological tradition.

By choosing to write on this portion of Argonautic legend, the story of the voyage itself and of Jason's adventures at Colchis,[2] and by choosing to write a lengthy narrative poem in dactylic hexameters, Valerius also placed himself within the epic tradition, a tradition that stretched via Valerius's Roman predecessors back to Homer himself. At this point it is important to note a clear distinction between the epic traditions of the Greeks and Romans. Insofar as some Greek epics, the *Iliad* for example, concern themselves with the contest for power, they may be called "political" in a broad sense. They cannot be said, however, to engage with the politics of any one Greek city or with the relationships between two or more city-states. For the Romans, by contrast, epic poetry was the preeminent literary medium for reflection upon Roman power and identity.

This concern is most clear in epics which explicitly present Rome's history. While the first Roman epic, Livius Andronicus's adaptation of Homer's *Odyssey*, has no obvious Roman relevance, the second, Naevius's *Bellum Punicum* (*The War with Carthage*) clearly does, for it presents a poetic account of Rome's history from the fall of Troy and the foundation of the city to the end of the First Punic War in 241 BCE. Naevius's innovation proved to be a major turning point, for concern with Rome became the central theme of all subsequent epics. Ennius's *Annales* followed Naevius's example in treating Rome's history from the fall of Troy initially in fifteen books down to 189 BCE and then in three additional books to 171 BCE. For writers of the late republic the *Annales* were a classic: for Lucretius he was "our Ennius," the one who wrote "eternal verses" (1.117, 121), while for Cicero he was "our greatest poet" (*Balb.* 51.15). This tradition continued with the *Civil War* of Lucan (forced by Nero to commit suicide in 65 CE), a savage account of the civil wars that brought the Caesars to power, and the *Punica* of Silius Italicus (d. 102 CE), an account of the war against Rome's greatest foreign enemy, Hannibal.

Virgil and Ovid, however, writing under the autocratic regime of the emperor Augustus, attempted a strategy of complex indirection, for they rejected representation of Rome's actual history in the manner of Naevius and Ennius in favor of mythological narratives.[3] Both, however, underlined the relevance of their work to contemporary politics. Thus in the *Aeneid*, Virgil foreshadows the Augustan future/present at key points in the poem, while Ovid brings his manifold narrative from the creation of the world up to "my own times" (*Met.* 1.4), concluding with Caesar Augustus and the poet himself (*Met.* 15.852–79). For poets writing under increasingly restrictive governments the advantages of such a strategy are obvious, and so it is not surprising that Valerius (like his contemporary Statius) followed the example established by Virgil and Ovid.

How then does Valerius suggest that his poem concerns the Roman present as much as the remote Hellenic past? The first and most obvious way is through the allusions to Rome and Italy that are to be found in every book. In the proem to book 1 Valerius implies that he is one of the "quindecimuiri sacris faciundis" and addresses Vespasian, while also mentioning Domitian's poetic skills and Titus's conquest of Jerusalem. Later in book 1 Jupiter promises that he will soon foster other nations ("gentesque fouebo / mox alias"; 1.555–56), a clear allusion to the Virgilian Jupiter's promise that Juno will join him in fostering the Romans ("mecumque fouebit / Romanos"; *A.* 1.281–82). In book 2 we find reference to Diana's cult at Aricia and Jupiter's at Alba Longa (2.300–305) and to the Latin *fasti* (2.245). In books 3 and 4 Valerius recalls the recent eruption of Vesuvius in similes (3.208–9, 4.507–9). Book 5 gives us an allusion to the Gates of War (5.307).[4] In book 6 we are reminded of Roman military equipment and Roman civil wars (6.55–56, 402–6), while in book 7 we learn that Colchis has a Campus Martius and that Aeetes' astonishment resembles that of a captain whose ship is driven back from Tiber's mouth (7.61–62, 83–86). Valerius even refers to Argo's crew as a "legion" ("horruit Argoae legio ratis"; "the legion of Argo's ship shuddered"; 7.573), an extraordinary term to use in a naval context.[5] In book 8 the adorning of Medea as a bride is compared to the bathing of Cybele's statue in the river Almo (8.239–42), a practice mentioned by Ovid in *Fasti* 4.[6] And the world-historical importance of Argo's voyage enunciated in book 1 is recalled in the poem's final book when the Minyae recall the prophecy of Mopsus that this quarrel would pass to another generation, that another rape would lead to another war (8.397–99), the war, as Valerius's readers know, that would ultimately lead to Rome's foundation.

Equally important is the fact that Valerius uses language that suggests that parallels exist between the ways in which politics operate in mythic Colchis and contemporary Rome. Consider, for example, Valerius's treatment of the situation in Colchis before the arrival of the Greeks. Phrixus's ghost has warned Aeetes of the dangers that lie ahead if the fleece is stolen and if Medea remains in Colchis (5.236–40). In addition, a priest has interpreted omens as signifying that the fleece should be returned to Thessaly (261–62). When Aeetes rejects this advice, his brother Perses leads the opposition to the king:

> tunc ordine regi
> proximus et frater materno sanguine Perses
> increpitare uirum; sequitur duce turba reperto.
> ille furens ira solio se proripit alto

praecipitatque patres ipsumque ut talibus ausis
spem sibi iam rerum uulgi leuitate serentem,
ense petit.

Then Perses, next in rank to the king and a brother of his mother's blood, reproached the man; the crowd, having found a leader, takes his side. Aeetes, raging with anger, rushes from his lofty throne and drives the *patres* headlong and attacks Perses himself with the sword as if by such daring he were sowing hope of power for himself on the basis of the inconstancy of the *uulgus*. (V. Fl. 5.265–71)[7]

One of the most striking elements of this passage is Valerius's use of the word *patres*, highlighted as it is by the alliteration of "p" sounds. Variously translated as "fathers" or "the lot" or "councilors,"[8] *patres* is the precise technical term used to designate members of the Roman senate.[9] As Wijsman notes, "the author provides the Colchians with a senate, just as Rome has one."[10] That this understanding of *patres* is correct, becomes even clearer when Valerius describes a procession of Colchians led by Absyrtus, the king's son. After Aeetes' heir come other members of the royal family, actual and potential, and then the "patres: quos praecipuo Titania tellus / legit honore patres" ("the *patres* whom the Titanian land has chosen for outstanding *honor*"; 5.463–64). Here it is important to note that *legit* ("has chosen") is precisely the correct technical term for appointment to membership of the Roman senate,[11] and that *honor* includes among its meanings "(high) public or political office."[12] And as Rome has a *populus*, so Colchis has a *uulgus*, a term commonly used to designate the Roman people at their most inconstant.[13] Thus Colchis, equipped with senate and people, has an apparently republican constitution. But it also has a *tyrannus* (5.264), a tyrant who actually wields the power, a tyrant who treats the senate with contempt.

We find similar use of language in book 8. When Absyrtus arrives with his fleet, he claims the support of all the Colchians: "quin omnes alii pariter populique patresque / mecum adsunt" ("In fact, all the others, *populi* and *patres* alike, are here with me"; 8.281–82). Because Absyrtus claims popular support as a means of strengthening his claim, the people are no longer the *uulgus*, they are now *populi*.[14] In fact, the language here recalls Virgil's description of Augustus's entry into battle with his fleet "cum patribus populoque" ("with the senators and people"; *A.* 8.679). Like the Virgilian Augustus, Absyrtus invokes the presence of the senators and people as justification for his actions.

But the Colchians are not the only people in the *Argonautica* with quasi-Roman constitutional arrangements. That Iolcus is organized in a similar fashion is made clear early in book 1 when Jason contemplates his response to Aeetes' proposed expedition to retrieve the golden fleece:

> Heu quid agat? populumne leuem ueterique tyranno
> infensum atque olim miserantes Aesona patres
> aduocet?
>
> Ah, what is he to do? Should he summon the people, inconstant
> and hostile to the aged tyrant, and the senators who have long
> since pitied Aeson? (V. Fl. 1.71–73)

Similar thoughts occur to Aeson when he is under pressure, for he too considers "whether he should rouse the senators and the kingdom's fickle mob" ("an patres regnique acuat mutabile uulgus"; 1.761). As in Colchis, the principal elements of Iolcus's constitution are senate, people, and tyrant.

The importance of Valerius's use of this kind of constitutional language becomes even clearer when we consider the political situation which unfolds at the end of book 1, for when Cretheus's ghost counsels Aeson to kill himself in order to avoid Pelias's murderous plans (1.749), both of Jason's parents eagerly commit suicide (1.816–18). Valerius's contemporary readers could hardly avoid recalling the senatorial suicides so characteristic of the sixties and seventies. As McGuire points out, "his narrative mirrors several of the historical suicides in many of its details—the monarch's death sentence itself, the decision of the wife to join her husband in death, the arrival of the palace magistrates or troops at the home of the condemned and the more public and official presence of the ruler's agents."[15]

But there is another element in this situation that McGuire does not discuss, for Aeson and Pelias are brothers. The relationship is made clear from the outset, for we learn at the beginning of book 1 that Pelias fears his brother's son ("fratrisque . . . / progeniem"; 1.26–27), while at the end of the book the king prepares "brotherly weapons" ("fraterna . . . arma"; 1.747) in order to destroy Aeson. But this is not the only toxic relationship between *fratres*, because Jason decides to punish Pelias by snatching away his *frater*, Acastus. The nature of this relationship is underlined by the omen which precedes their encounter: an eagle, a *raptor* (1.160), seizes a lamb and carries it off over the Aegean deep (1.156–60). When they meet, Acastus embraces his brother's breast ("fraternaque pectora iungens"; 1.163).[16] It is of course Jason's seizing of his *frater* that makes Pelias decide to kill his (1.693–99). But as it is on earth, so it is in heaven, for the hostility between siblings that characterizes Iolcus is also to be found on Olympus. Thus it is that Mopsus envisages Juno, Jason's supporter, embracing Neptune, Jason's opponent, not out of affection, but in order to control his rage: "thus hold your brother's breast, Juno, thus, in your embrace" ("sic amplexu, sic pectora fratris, / Iuno, tene"; 1.214–15).

But the most important siblings in book 1 are not these mythological characters, but the two brothers of the prologue, Titus and Domitian. Addressing Vespasian, the poet declares,

> uersam proles tua pandit Idumen,
> sancte pater, Solymo nigrantem puluere fratrem
> spargentemque faces et in omni turre furentem.

> Your son reveals the overthrow of Idume, holy father, his brother black with Jerusalem's dust, scattering torches and raging on every tower. (V. Fl. 1.12–14)

As Feeney observes, Valerius here stresses "harmonious links between Vespasian, Titus and Domitian,"[17] for Vespasian is the ruler, Titus the conqueror, and Domitian the poet, who records his brother's victories. Each has his designated role. We should note, first, that this picture of family concord forms part of a *recusatio*: there is no need for Valerius to sing of Jerusalem's capture when the Flavian family already boasts a great poet; and, second, as Valerius's readers must have known, the truth was wholly otherwise, for Suetonius reports that Domitian was constantly plotting against his brother.[18] Dio confirms the plots and claims that if Domitian did not actually kill his brother, then he was certainly more concerned with securing power than with his tragic loss.[19] As Jones puts it, "No doubt brotherly affection was at a minimum."[20] In Valerius's proem reference to family harmony is a reminder of precisely the opposite.

If we turn to books 5 and 6, we find a situation that strikingly resembles that in the narrative of book 1. Like Pelias, Aeetes is a tyrant, a king who acts against the best interests of his people (5.264). And just as Pelias decides through fear of prophesies to dispatch Jason to fetch the golden fleece (1.26–30), so Aeetes, terrified by the warnings of Phrixus's ghost (5.233–40), rejects divine demands that he hand over that same fleece. Jason, in fact, makes the connection between Pelias and Aeetes: "alium hic Pelian, alia aequora cerno" ("Here I see another Pelias, another sea"; 7.92). But if the tyrants take similar decisions, their subjects respond very differently, for where both Jason and Aeson reject the possibility of using the "inconstant people" against the tyrant ("populumne leuem"; 1.71–73) (cf. "mutabile uulgus"; 1.761), Perses takes the opposite course and exploits the "mob's inconstancy" ("uulgi leuitate"; 5.270). As in Iolcus there is rivalry between brothers, but in Colchis the result is civil war.

That rivalry between brothers is both a cause and an emblem of civil war is a recurring trope in Roman literature. Thus Horace, writing during the civil wars of the forties and thirties BCE, had argued that the fratricide involved in Rome's foundation had determined the city's destiny:

> sic est: acerba fata Romanos agunt
> scelusque fraternae necis,
> ut inmerentis fluxit in terram Remi
> sacer nepotibus cruor.

> Yes, that's how it is: bitter fate drives the Romans on and the crime
> of a brother's killing, ever since the blood of innocent Remus
> flowed onto the land, a curse for his descendants. (*Epod.* 7.17–20)

Lucan invokes the same causal scheme in book 1: "fraterno primi maduerunt sanguine muri" ("Our first walls were drenched with a brother's blood"; 1.95), and it is fratricide that particularly characterizes *Civil War*'s climactic battle (7.453, 465, 550, 626, 763, 775). That Horace and Lucan should view the origin of Rome's propensity to self-destruction a matter of urgency is not surprising: Horace writes as civil war rages, while Lucan reflects on the struggle between Caesar and Pompey as a precondition of Julio-Claudian rule.

For Valerius, writing in the immediate aftermath of the events of 69 CE,[21] civil war was a recent and living memory, and his readers are reminded of that fact in his account of the conflict between Perses and Aeetes. Thus Colaxes leads a legion (*legio*, 6.48) whose men bear shields adorned with a Roman emblem, the triple thunderbolt (6.55–56), an emblem borne by the *Legio XII Fulminata*, a legion led by Titus himself during the Jerusalem campaign.[22] More striking still is a simile in which Ariasmenus's slaughter of his own men is likened to combat between two Roman armies:

Romanas ueluti saeuissima cum legiones
Tisiphone regesque mouet, quorum agmina pilis,
quorum aquilis utrimque micant eademque parentes
rura colunt, idem lectos ex omnibus agris
miserat infelix non haec ad proelia Thybris.

As when Tisiphone most savage stirs Roman legions and aspiring kings, whose columns gleam with javelins, with eagles on either side, and their parents cultivate the same countryside, the same unhappy Tiber had sent these men chosen from every region, but not for wars like this. (V. Fl. 6.402–6)

Commentators rightly see allusion here to the proem to *Civil War*, with both Lucan and Valerius stressing kingship and the presence of eagles and javelins (*pila*) on either side. It does not follow, however, as Wijsman claims, that Valerius intends the reader to think only of "the strife between Caesar and Pompey,"[23] for the image is generic, with the present tenses (*mouet*, *micant*) emphasizing that these actions are not unique, but recurrent in Rome's history.[24] And so too is civil war in Colchis. It is noteworthy that at the end of book 6 Minerva, even though she supports Jason and Aeetes, intervenes to rescue Perses from certain death (6.739–51), not because her allegiances have changed, but in order to carry out Jupiter's will, for he has determined that the struggle between Aeetes and Perses must continue for decades, with Perses driving out Aeetes and being driven out in turn by a child of Medea (5.680–88).

But civil war in the *Argonautica* is not limited to Rome and Colchis. Valerius introduces the Lemnos episode in book 2 with reference to civil war on Olympus, to the rebellion of the gods led by Jupiter's wife against her husband (2.82–91). Reference to civil war on the divine plane is then followed by description of the rebellion of Lemnos's wives against their husbands. For our purposes it is important to notice two things. First, as Dominik has pointed out,[25] where Valerius's model, Apollonius of Rhodes, devotes only 24 lines to the massacre, Valerius devotes 233. Indeed Valerius devotes twice as many lines to the massacre (233) as he does to the visit of the Argonauts (117). Clearly the Latin poet is more interested in the massacre than the actual visit. Second, Valerius represents the violent events on Lemnos as an example of civil war.

One of the most striking aspects of Valerius's account of the Lemnian massacre is its use of allusion to Virgil's account of the Greek capture and destruction of Troy in *Aeneid* 2. The Flavian poet highlights the connection with a question, an exclamation, and a prayer:

> unde ego tot scelerum facies, tot fata iacentum
> exsequar? heu uatem monstris quibus intulit ordo,
> quae se aperit series! o qui me uera canentem
> sistat et hac nostras exsoluat imagine noctes.

> But how shall I enumerate so many scenes of crime, so many deaths of the fallen? Ah, to what monstrosities has his narrative brought the poet, what a sequence is revealed! If only someone would stop me from singing the truth and release my nights from such visions. (V. Fl. 2.216–19)

This elaborates upon Aeneas's anguished question:

> quis cladem illius noctis, quis funera fando
> explicet aut possit lacrimis aequare labores?

> Who could unfold in speech that night's destruction, who unfold its deaths or match its suffering to tears? (Virg. *A.* 2.361–62)

And the connection is confirmed by details. In the prelude to the massacre Valerius describes the women in terms which recall the plight of Troy's women in *Aeneid* 2. Just as Virgil's Trojans "cling to the doors and plant kisses" ("amplexaeque tenent postis atque oscula figunt"; 2.490), so Valerius's Lemnians "redouble kisses on their beds and very doorposts" ("oscula iamque toris atque oscula postibus ipsis / ingeminant"; 2.168–69). And as the Trojan women mass together ("condensae"; 2.517) "beneath heaven's naked arch" ("nudoque sub aetheris axe"; 2.512), so Lemnos's women gather "massed together beneath the naked stars" ("sese nudisque sub astris / condensae"; 2.171–72).

But if the Lemnian women resemble the women of Troy at the beginning of Valerius's narrative, they soon come to resemble Virgil's Greeks. As the Greeks attack "a city buried in wine and sleep" ("urbem somno uinoque sepultam"; 2.265), so the women attack men "sleepy with food and wine" ("dapibus uinoque soporos"; 2.221). And like Virgil's Greeks, the women of

Lemnos hurl torches at their city's roofs (2.235–36; cf. *A.* 2.478) and burst into their city's homes ("inruerant"; V. Fl. 2.747, *A.* 2.757). In this section of the narrative it is only Hypsipyle who resembles a Trojan, for Valerius employs allusion to suggest that her rescue of Thoas resembles Aeneas saving of Anchises and Hecuba's attempts to protect Priam (e.g., V. Fl. 2.257–58; cf. *A.* 2.525).[26]

Thus Valerius employs reference to *Aeneid* 2 in order to highlight the differences between Troy and Lemnos. Where Troy is invaded by a foreign army, Lemnos is attacked not by outsiders but by the island's own women, women who act with all the treachery and violence of Virgil's Greeks. Hypsipyle, moreover, underlines the civil nature of this conflict when she declares to Thoas: "nostrum hoc facinus" ("this crime is ours"; 2.251).

But if in book 2 the Argonauts encounter a city recovering from recent civil war, in book 3 they actually experience a quasi–civil war themselves. At the end of book 2 Valerius emphasizes the warmth of feeling that Cyzicus feels for Jason. While in Apollonius Cyzicus and his men approach the Argonauts in friendship (*φιλότητι*; 1.961) and offer a warm welcome (*ἐυξείνως ἀρέσαντο*; 1.963), the Valerian Cyzicus rushes down to greet the Argonauts, clasps Jason's hand, embraces him, and makes a speech of welcome. As Manuwald points out, the Roman Cyzicus is more enthusiastic than his Greek equivalent.[27] Equally important is the fact that Cyzicus emphasizes the shared values of the two peoples:

> uestra fides ritus<que> pares et mitia cultu
> his etiam mihi corda locis.

> Your good faith and religious rituals are the same as ours and in
> this place are hearts made gentle by civilization. (V. Fl. 2.646–47)

Hence it is not surprising that the concept of guest friendship is invoked by both Jason and the narrator (*hospita*, 2.650, 661; *hospitiis*, 3.18). More striking is the fact that the narrator speaks of the two men as uniting their families by joining hands: "manibusque datis iunxere penates" (3.14).[28]

If we turn to the battle itself, we find narrative elements typical of internal, not external conflicts. Hercules, for example, kills Admon, promising the dying warrior the gift of dying at the hands of a mighty hero. The narrator comments, "horruit ille cadens nomenque agnouit amicum" ("he shuddered as he fell and recognized a friendly name"; 3.171). Friend kills friend. And even though Argo's crew and the Cyzicans are not actually related, Valerius contrives a near-fratricide, for Castor almost strikes Pollux (3.186–89). Brother comes close to killing brother. And the battle's aftermath sees both Jason and the narrator invoking such concepts as guest friendship, friendship, treaty, and alliance.[29] Although the war on Cyzicus is actually fought by different peoples, it has the properties we expect in civil war. We might also add that Valerius gives the episode a Roman coloring through reference to Bellona (3.60) and the gates of war (3.253).[30]

I now turn to a broader political and social issue reflected in the *Argonautica*: the problem that the principate posed for the display of aristocratic *uirtus*.[31] I proceed by considering Valerius's treatment of the problem in *Argonautica* in the light of a nearly contemporary text in which this is a central issue, Tacitus's *Agricola*. I begin where Tacitus ends, with the afterlife of Agricola:

> Si quis piorum manibus locus, si, ut sapientibus placet, non cum corpore extinguuntur magnae animae, placide quiescas, nosque domum tuam ab infirmo desiderio et muliebribus lamentis ad contemplationem uirtutum tuarum uoces, quas neque lugeri neque plangi fas est. admiratione te potius et immortalibus laudibus et, si natura suppeditet, aemulatu colamus: is uerus honos, ea coniunctissimi cuiusque pietas.[32]

> If there is any place for the ghosts of pious men, if, as wise men hold, great souls are not extinguished with the body, may you rest in peace, and may you summon us, your family, from feeble longings and womanish laments to reflection on your virtues (*uirtutum*), which we must not mourn or bewail. We should show our devotion rather by veneration and immortal praise and, if our nature should be up to the task, by rivalry: this is true respect, this is every kinsman's duty. (Tac. *Ag*. 46.1–2)

There are three key points here. First, Tacitus holds out the possibility that the souls of the pious dead survive in some form of afterlife. Second, the best way to respect the dead is to contemplate their virtues and to seek to rival them. Third, there is an intimate connection between *uirtus* and the members of one's family.

If we turn to the *Argonautica*, we find that Valerius holds a very similar conception to that outlined by Tacitus. First, Valerius links the achievement of *uirtus* in this life with its celebration in the afterlife. He does this at the end of book 1 and early in book 5. Thus the souls of Aeson and Alcimede are escorted to a place reminiscent of Virgil's home of the blessed (1.827–51; cf. *A.* 6.637–88). Unlike Virgil, however, Valerius specifies in the last three words of the book that this is the dwelling place of those who deserve "the rewards of life-giving virtue" ("almae uirtutis honores"; 1.851). The point is reinforced in the first book of the poem's second half when the Argonauts complete their passage through the Cyanean rocks, for Fama takes the message of their achievement down to the ghosts below, the ghosts who are stirred by "virtue" ("uirtus"; 5.86).

This brings us to Tacitus's second point, the importance of rivalry. That Valerius views virtue as essentially competitive is clear from the fact that book 5's underworld ghosts are stirred not just by "uirtus," but by "aemula uirtus" ("rivalrous virtue"). In book 5 the phrase suggests a competition between the living and the dead, but elsewhere in the *Argonautica* the contest takes place not only between different generations, but also between the ruler and the prominent individual. Thus we are told at the very outset of the poem that Pelias's fear arises from his hatred of Jason's virtue: "super ipsius ingens / instat fama uiri uirtusque haud laeta tyranno" ("above all the hero's great reputation and virtue, never pleasing to a tyrant"; 1.29–30).

The idea that "uirtus" is essentially competitive is not confined to Valerius and Tacitus. The phrase "aemula uirtus" first occurs in Horace (*Epod.* 16.5) where it is used of defeated Capua, and in Lucan (1.120), where it characterizes the relationship between Caesar and Pompey.[33] And Silius Italicus's Hannibal represents his aspiration to compete with Hercules as "aemula uirtus" (1.510). While the competition for virtue in these cases is either destructive or futile, it can also be presented as positive. Cicero, for example, argues as follows: "aemulatio autem dupliciter illa quidem dicitur, ut et in laude et in uitio nomen hoc sit; nam et imitatio uirtutis aemulatio dicitur . . . est enim laudis" ("Rivalry, however, is used in two different ways, so that it can be both praiseworthy and vicious; for rivalry is used of the imitation of virtue . . . in this sense it merits praise"; Cic. *Tusc.* 4.17.7). For republican Cicero the competition for virtue is the only acceptable form of rivalry.

Rulers like Pelias and Domitian, however, see things differently. I have already noted the Valerian narrator's observation that *uirtus* is never pleasing to tyrants (1.30). And it is precisely this fear of Jason's *uirtus* that prompts Aeetes to dispatch Jason to Colchis. While I cannot claim that Domitian dispatches Agricola to Britain for the same reason, Tacitus makes it clear that the emperor fears Agricola's *uirtutes* despite his quiet return: "causa periculi non crimen ullum aut querela laesi cuiusquam, sed infensus uirtutibus princeps" ("the cause of danger was not any crime or complaint of causing harm, but a *princeps* hostile to virtue"; 41.1).[34] Pelias and Domitian are rulers who feel threatened by the existence of outstanding individuals, men who might prove victorious in the contest for *uirtus* and fame.

For outstanding individuals like Jason and Agricola, however, the opportunity to display *uirtus* is of prime importance. Tacitus is explicit on the point when he praises Petilius Cerealis, governor of Britain, for allowing Agricola room to display his virtues ("habuerunt uirtutes spatium exemplorum"; 8.2). That the expedition to Colchis gives Jason the same opportunity is clear from the fact that his *uirtus* is recognized by Jupiter, his enemies, his men, and of course Medea.[35] Equally telling is the desire of the youthful prince Acastus to join the Argonauts precisely because he craves the chance to display his *uirtus*: "si primos duce te uirtutis honores / carpere, fraternae si des adcrescere famae" ("if under your leadership you give me the rewards of virtue and let me grow to match a brother's fame"; 1.177–78). Indeed Valerius's narrator claims that until Pelias commands the expedition the Greeks in general have lacked the opportunity for great achievement ("necdum data copia rerum"; 1.100–102).

I would like now to take up Tacitus's third point: the connection between *uirtus* and the family. For Tacitus rivalry in virtue is a familial obligation: we owe it to our ancestors to model ourselves upon them and to try to surpass their excellence. In *Argonautica* 5 the same point is made, but in reverse, for we see the underworld heroes inspired by their sons' glory ("natorum laudibus"; 5.83). Indeed their admiration is prompted by fatherly devotion, by "pietas," as well as "aemula uirtus" (5.86). And we see the same phenomenon when the ghost of Cretheus appears and speaks admiringly of his grandson's imminent achievements (1.741–46). Note too that it is Cretheus who inspires his son Aeson to join the company of the blessed through suicide and so receive virtue's rewards (1.750–51, 851).

The similarities between the accounts of virtue that we find in the *Argonautica* and *Agricola* suggest that Valerius and Tacitus are concerned with a common cultural and political problem: the monarch's monopolization of the means of acquiring *uirtus* and his resentment of its acquisition by others. Whereas for Cicero competition between aristocrats for *uirtus* is unproblematic, for imperial writers such competition is risky, being viewed by the ruler as a danger to his own position.

Even more important than the poem's depiction of societies with political structures analogous to those of the Romans, its concern with those societies' propensity to fraternal strife and civil war and the problem of *uirtus*, is the fact that the poem places Rome and its history within a wider historical framework. Consider, for example, the address to Vespasian in the proem:

> tuque, o pelagi cui maior aperti
> fama, Caledonius postquam tua carbasa uexit
> Oceanus Phrygios prius indignatus Iulos,
> eripe me populis et habenti nubila terrae
> —namque potes—ueterumque faue, uenerande canenti
> facta uirum.
>
> And you, Oh greater is your glory for opening the sea, after the Caledonian Ocean carried your sails (it previously resented those Julians from Phrygia), rescue me from the masses and the cloud-covered earth (for you can) and support me, venerable lord, as I sing the deeds of ancient heroes. (V. Fl. 1.7–11)

That these lines are overtly eulogistic is clear. Nevertheless, the details merit close examination. Galli points out that the structure of the opening phrase recalls Virgil's address to Neptune in the proem to the *Georgics*:[36]

> tuque, o cui prima frementem
> fudit equum magno tellus percussa tridenti,
> Neptune.
>
> And you, Oh for whom the earth, first struck by the great trident, poured forth the neighing horse, Neptune. (Virg. *G.* 1.12–14)

Why should Valerius allude to these lines from the *Georgics* in the proem to *Argonautica*? First, and most generally, it situates *Argonautica* within a tradition of poetry that reflects upon the origins and development of human societies. Second, these lines from Virgil's proem are concerned with primacy (in this case the creation of the first horse), a concept that is paramount in *Argonautica*'s proem (the poem's first word is *prima*). Third, Valerius presents the invention of riding, like the invention of sailing, as one of human history's key technological advances.[37] Allusion to the *Georgics* is thus an effective way of linking Rome's current emperor with the poem's thematic concerns.

So too is reference to Vespasian's participation in the Claudian invasion of Britain. To claim that Vespasian was responsible for "opening the sea" is obvious hyperbole. More important, however, is the fact that the poet's hyperbole sets up an analogy between the emperor and the poem's hero, because what the poet claims for Vespasian ("pelagi . . . aperti"), Jason claims for himself ("pelagus . . . aperimus"; 1.169). Jason's claim is entirely optimistic, for he foresees a vast expansion of human knowledge:

> o quantum terrae, quantum cognoscere caeli
> permissum est, pelagus quantos aperimus in usus!
>
> Oh how much of the earth, how much of the sky is granted to us to know. To what great purposes we are opening the sea! (V. Fl. 1.168–69)

Jason's words, however, are sinister in their import, for they form part of his attempt to seduce his cousin Acastus into participation in Argo's voyage. And, as Pollini points out,[38] these lines clearly allude to the proem to Lucan's *Civil War*:

> heu, quantum terrae potuit pelagique parari
> hoc quem ciuiles hauserunt sanguine dextrae.
>
> Ah, how much of the sea and land could have been won with this blood shed by the hands of citizens. (Luc. 1.13–14)

Allusion to Lucan at this point, as Zissos observes,[39] foreshadows the Argonauts' involvement in the struggle between Perses and Aeetes in book 6. In other words, participation in civil war is one of the great purposes for which the Argonauts are opening the sea. And if we think back to Vespasian's opening of the sea in the proem, we might well reflect that he too was a civil warrior.

But what has all this to do with censorship? If we accept the current consensus that most of *Argonautica* was composed during the reign of Vespasian, then Valerius was writing under a relatively benign emperor. Suetonius and Dio both praise his leniency.[40] And modern historians concur. Levick puts it like this: "It was to Vespasian's credit that there was no gratuitous violence, only what was seen to be required for the dynasty's security."[41] Even so,

Dio reports that Vespasian expelled philosophers from Rome in the earliest years of his rule and that he so objected to Helvidius Priscus's exercise of freedom of speech (παρρησίαν) that he had him executed.[42] It should also be pointed out that writers like Lucan and Seneca were Valerius's contemporaries and that they had died only five years before Vespasian's accession. And so it is not surprising that Flavian epic poets preferred to avoid dangerous myths like that of Thyestes and troublesome historical figures like Cato:[43] it was far safer to resort to foreign mythology or to the victory over Carthage. Indirection was the safest way of avoiding censorship.

NOTES

1. Epic poetry: Eumelus's *Corinthiaca* (c. 730 BCE), Apollonius's *Argonautica* (third century BCE), Varro's *Argonautae* (first century BCE), Ovid's *Metamorphoses* (first century CE); lyric poetry: Pindar's fourth *Pythian* (fifth century BCE); elegiac poetry: Ovid's *Heroides* 6 and 12 (first century BCE); tragic stage: Euripides' *Peliades*, *Medea*, and *Aegeus* (fifth century BCE), Ennius's *Medea Exul* (third/second century BCE), Pacuvius's *Medus* (third/second century BCE), Accius's *Medea siue Argonautae* (second century BCE), Ovid's *Medea* (first century BCE).

2. In the literature of which we have knowledge, this part of the story of Jason and Medea is related only by epic poets: Apollonius, Varro, and Valerius Flaccus.

3. I pass over the *Argonautica* of Varro of Atax, written perhaps in the 40s BCE. For a text of the poem's fragments and discussion of its form and content, see Hollis (2007). Braund (1993) argues that this poem reflected "Roman imperialist ideology" and "Caesar's claims to world-empire." Given the state of the poem, such a claim has to remain speculative.

4. Cf. Enn. *Ann.* 7.226 (Skutsch), Virg. *A.* 1.294, 7.607.

5. *OLD*, after defining *legio* as §1 "the largest unit of the Roman army," offers §2 "any large military force mainly of infantry." In other words, *legio* is used of land forces.

6. Ov. *Fasti* 4.337–40.

7. All quotations from Valerius Flaccus come from Liberman (1997, 2002).

8. "Fathers": Mozley (1936); "the lot": Slavitt (1999); "councilors": Barich (2009).

9. Liberman (2002) translates *patres* as "les grands." Spaltenstein (2004) 458 says that "*Patres* désigne les notables."

10. Wijsman (1996) 143. See also Zissos (2008) 123–24 (on 1.72). Galli (2007) 84 does not explicitly identify the *patres* of 1.72 as senators, but she does cite as parallel Cipus's summoning of the "venerable senate and people" at Ov. *Met.* 15.590–91: "extemplo populumque grauemque senatum/conuocat."

11. *OLD* s.v. 6 §b, c. This is pointed out by Wijsman (1996) 222. Spaltenstein (2004) 509 disagrees, claiming that "ce sont seulement des 'grands.'"

12. *OLD* s.v. §5.

13. E.g., Cic. *Muren.* 35–36; Hor. *Epist.* 2.1.8; Liv. 2.7.51, 24.31.14, Tac. *Hist.* 1.69.7, 1.80.12.

14. For the use of the plural (*populique*) for the singular see the examples cited in *OLD* s.v. 3 (including Ov. *Met.* 7.101 of the Colchians).

15. McGuire (1997) 192–93.

16. Cf. 1.178 where Acastus aspires (depending on punctuation) to a brother's *uirtus* or *fama*. *Frater* is used of course of both a brother and a cousin (*OLD* s.v. *frater* §1, §2).

17. Feeney (1991) 335.

18. Suet. *Tit.* 9.3, *Dom.* 2.3.

19. Dio 66.26.

20. Jones (1992) 20.

21. For a persuasive statement of the case that Valerius was writing under Vespasian, see Stover (2012) chap. 1. This seems to be the current consensus. Liberman (1997) xviii–xxiv disagrees.

22. Fucecchi (2006) 110, citing Jos. *BJ* 5.1.6 (= 5.41–42), Tac. *Hist.* 5.1.10.

23. Wijsman (2000) 161.

24. Spaltenstein (2005) 120 argues that "en effet, c'est un tableau général, une évocation de la guerre civile en soi." Fucecchi (2006) 348 agrees.

25. Dominik (1997). See also Poortvliet (1991) 66.

26. See Hershkowitz (1998) 137–38.

27. Manuwald (1999) 29–30.

28. Modern editions print *penates* for V's *nepotes*. The point would stand with either reading.

29. Guest friendship: *hospite* 288, *hospitio* 293, *hospita tellus* 304; friendship: *amicos* 289; treaty: *foedera* 291; alliance: *socios* 312.

30. For a fuller discussion of this episode as civil war, see Stover (2012) chap. 4.

31. The issue is raised by Zissos (2009). Zissos 355 points out that "one of the central conflicts within elite Roman culture at this time was the incompatibility between aristocratic ambition and desire for public distinction on the one hand and the new limitations imposed by the political configurations of the principate on the other" and argues that "this tension surfaces almost immediately in Valerius' narrative."

32. I adopt Heinsius's emendation *aemulatu* in this final sentence. Others prefer *similitudine*. For discussion of the textual problems at this point, see Ogilvie and Richmond (1967) 314. They favor the paleographically plausible *similitudine*. *OLD* defines *similitudo* as "the fact or condition of being like something else." But the sense requires an activity ("striving to resemble"), not a condition ("resemblance"). The argument of Ogilvie and Richmond that "we can all strive to emulate a great man but actually to resemble him presupposes that we are granted the power to do so" does not persuade.

33. Cf. V. Max. 4.1.12.11 where rivalry in virtue ("ab aemulatione uirtutis") leads to enmity between Scipio Africanus and Metellus Macedonicus.

34. See also the remark of Calgacus that rulers dislike *uirtus* in their subjects: "uirtus

porro ac ferocia subiectorum ingrata imperantibus" (31.4). Tacitus also notes that Agricola's father earned Caligula's displeasure because of his virtues ("iisque ipsis uirtutibus iram Gai Caesaris meritus"; 4.1).

35. V. Fl. 5.682; 6.590, 735; 7.439; 8.341, 391.

36. Galli (2007) 40.

37. For this, see Davis (2010) 5–7.

38. Pollini (1984) 52n6.

39. Zissos (2004) 21–38, 24–25.

40. Suet. *Vesp.* 12–15; Dio 66.11.1.

41. Levick (1999) 94.

42. Dio 66.13.1 (expulsion of philosophers); 66.12.1 (freedom of speech).

43. For the risks inherent in writing about Thyestes and Cato, see Tac. *Dial.* 3.1–4.

REFERENCES

Barich, Michael, tr. 2009. *Valerius Flaccus, Argonautica.* Gambier, OH: XOXOX Press.

Braund, David. 1993. "Writing a Roman Argonautica: The Historical Dynamic." *Hermathena* 154: 11–17.

Davis, P. J. 2010. "Jason at Colchis: Technology and Human Progress in Valerius Flaccus." *Ramus* 39: 1–13.

Dominik, William J. 1997. "*Ratio et Dei*: Psychology and the Supernatural in the Lemnian Episode." In *Studies in Latin Literature and Roman History*, vol. 8, ed. Carl Deroux, 29–50. Brussels: Latomus.

Feeney, Denis C. 1991. *The Gods in Epic: Poets and Critics of the Classical Tradition.* Oxford: Oxford University Press.

Fucecchi, Marco. 2006. *Una Guerra in Colchide: Valerio Flacco, Argonautiche 6, 1–426.* Pisa: ETS.

Galli, Daniela. 2007. *Valerii Flacci Argonautica I: Commento.* Berlin: De Gruyter.

Hershkowitz, Debra. 1998. *Valerius Flaccus' Argonautica: Abbreviated Voyages in Silver Latin Epic.* Oxford: Oxford University Press.

Hollis, Adrian S. 2007. *Fragments of Roman Poetry C.60 BC–AD 20.* Oxford: Oxford University Press.

Jones, Brian W. 1992. *The Emperor Domitian.* London: Routledge.

Levick, Barbara. 1999. *Vespasian.* London: Routledge.

Liberman, Gauthier, ed. 1997, 2002. *Gaius Valerius Flaccus, Argonautiques.* 2 vols. Paris: Les Belles Lettres.

Manuwald, Gesine. 1999. *Die Cyzicus-Episode und ihre Funktion in den Argonautica des Valerius Flaccus.* Göttingen: Vandenhoeck & Ruprecht.

McGuire, Donald T. 1997. *Acts of Silence: Civil War, Tyranny, and Suicide in the Flavian Epics.* Hildesheim: Olms-Weidmann.

Mozley, J. H., ed. and tr. 1936. *Valerius Flaccus.* London: William Heinemann.

Ogilvie, R. M. and Ian Richmond. 1967. *Cornelii Taciti De Vita Agricolae*. Oxford: Oxford University Press.

Pollini, E. 1984. "Il motivo della visendi cupido nel Giasone di Valerio Flacco." *Maia* 36: 51–61.

Poortvliet, H. M. C. 1991. *Valerius Flaccus Argonautica Book II: A Commentary*. Amsterdam: VU University Press.

Slavitt, David R., tr. 1999. *The Voyage of the Argo: The Argonautica of Valerius Flaccus*. Baltimore: Johns Hopkins University Press.

Spaltenstein, François. 2004. *Commentaire des Argonautica de Valérius Flaccus (Livres 3, 4 et 5)*. Brussels: Collection Latomus.

———. 2005. *Commentaire des Argonautica de Valérius Flaccus (Livres 6, 7 et 8)*. Brussels: Collection Latomus.

Stover, Tim, 2012. *Epic and Empire in Vespasianic Rome: A New Reading of Valerius Flaccus' Argonautica*. Oxford: Oxford University Press.

Wijsman, H. J. W. 1996. *Valerius Flaccus Argonautica, Book V. A Commentary*. Leiden: Brill.

———. 2000. *Valerius Flaccus Argonautica, Book VI. A Commentary*. Leiden: Brill.

Zissos, Andrew. 2004. "L'ironia allusiva: Lucan's *Bellum Ciuile* and the *Argonautica* of Valerius Flaccus." In *Lucano e la tradizione dell'epica latina*, ed. Paolo Esposito and Enrico M. Ariemma, 21–38. Naples: Alfredo Guida Editore.

———. 2008. *Valerius Flaccus' Argonautica, Book 1: A Commentary*. Oxford: Oxford University Press.

———. 2009. "Navigating Power: Valerius Flaccus' *Argonautica*." In *Writing Politics in Imperial Rome*, ed. W. Dominik, J. Garthwaite, and P. Roche, 351–66. Leiden: Brill.

Chapter 9

Compulsory Freedom: Literature in Trajan's Rome

John Penwill

> te uero securi et alacres quo uocas sequimur. iubes esse liberos: erimus; iubes quae sentimus promere in medium: proferemus.
>
> Stress-free and eager, we follow where you summon us. You order us to be free: free we shall be. You order us to express what we believe openly: express it we shall.
>
> —Pliny, *Panegyricus* 66.4

> insidias et campus habet.
>
> Even level ground has its pitfalls.
>
> —Martial, *Epigrams* 12.14.5

Since the establishment and effective institutionalization of the principate after Actium the rules for writers radically changed. While a Catullus could savagely lampoon the leading political figures of his day, or a Lucretius could present a radical critique of prevailing political ideology, those writing in the time of Augustus and his successors had to practice what Fred Ahl aptly called the art of safe criticism.[1] It was the age of the subtext, or what the leading theoretician of the Flavian era, Quintilian, termed *emphasis*.[2] Much work has been done over the past half century on what remains of literature produced in the period from Augustus to Domitian to tease out (in Quintilian's phrase) the *aliud latens*, the "something hidden," lurking within these works, and to appreciate the subtle and nuanced nature of the games being played. Being too obvious was of course a dangerous procedure, as the fates for example of Ovid, Lucan, and the younger Helvidius made only too plain. On the other hand the production of safe, politically impeccable, and essentially meaningless works for recitation at poetry readings held little appeal for those who aspired to make their mark as writers of importance.[3] These wrote for the *cognoscenti* who were aware of the rules of the game, relying on the fact that the asses' ears of the majority would not only not get the point but not realize that there was a point to be got.[4]

But suppose the rules are suddenly changed? With the assassination of Domitian and the accession of Nerva, this would appear to have been the case. Or so it was constructed. The ideology of the new reign as manifested in inscriptions and on the coinage was *libertas restituta* and *salus publica*.[5] Writers at the time celebrate the new era and contrast it with the old. So Tacitus at *Agricola* 2–3:

> (2.3) dedimus profecto grande patientiae documentum; et sicut uetus aetas uidit quid ultimum in libertate esset, ita nos quid in seruitute, adempto per inquisitiones etiam loquendi audiendique commercio. memoriam quoque ipsam cum uoce perdidissemus, si tam in nostra potestate esset obliuisci quam tacere. (3.1) nunc demum redit animus; et quamquam primo statim beatissimi saeculi ortu Nerua Caesar res olim dissociabiles miscuerit, principatum ac libertatem, augeatque cotidie felicitatem temporum Nerua Traianus, nec spem modo ac uotum securitas publica, sed ipsius uoti fiduciam ac robur adsumpserit, natura tamen infirmitatis humanae tardiora sunt remedia quam mala; et ut corpora nostra lente augescunt, cito extinguuntur, sic ingenia studiaque oppresseris facilius quam reuocaueris: subit quippe etiam ipsius inertiae dulcedo, et inuisa primo desidia postremo amatur. (3.2) quid, si per quindecim annos, grande mortalis aeui spatium, multi fortuitis casibus, promptissimus quisque saeuitia principis interciderunt, pauci et, ut i<ta> dixerim, non modo aliorum sed etiam nostri superstites sumus, exemptis e media uita tot annis, quibus iuuenes ad senectutem, senes prope ad ipsos exactae aetatis terminos per silentium uenimus? (3.3) non tamen pigebit uel incondita ac rudi uoce memoriam

> prioris seruitutis ac testimonium praesentium bonorum composuisse. hic interim liber honori Agricolae soceri mei destinatus, professione pietatis aut laudatus erit aut excusatus.
>
> Without doubt we have provided a prime example of submissiveness; and just as time past saw the ultimate of what liberty meant, so we saw the ultimate of slavery, with even the normal exchange of conversation denied to us because of the prosecutions. We would have lost our memory along with our voices if there were in us the same faculty for forgetfulness as for silence. But now at last our spirit is returning; and while right at the outset of this most blessed age Nerva Caesar has brought together things formerly incompatible, the principate and liberty, and Nerva Trajan is daily augmenting the happiness of our times, and also public confidence has now passed beyond hoping and praying into a firm expectation that prayers will be fulfilled, nevertheless such is the nature of human infirmity that effecting a cure takes longer than the disease; and just as our bodies are slow to develop but quick to perish, so you will quash talent and enthusiasm more easily than restore it—for the sweetness of actually doing nothing creeps up on us, and inertia, despised at first, in the end comes to be loved. Bear in mind that for fifteen years, a massive period of our mortal existence, many have perished, some through chance occurrences but the most energetic through an emperor's savagery, while the few of us who remain are, if I may so put it, survivors not only of others but also of ourselves, given that so many years were torn away from the middle of our lives in which those of us who were young became old and those already old came to the very threshold of life's end—and all in silence. Nonetheless I shall find it in no way irksome to have put on record, albeit in a crude and unrefined style, our former slavery and bear witness to our present happiness. Meanwhile this book, the purpose of which is to honor my father-in-law Agricola, will be praised or at least excused through its avowal of *pietas*.

This theme is revisited later in the biography at 41–45, where the focus is more particularly on the alleged horrors of Domitian's reign. The implication of the opening chapters is that in this new and blessed age it is possible to write politically charged biography without suffering the fates of Arulenus Rusticus for his biography of Thrasea or Herennius Senecio for his of the elder Helvidius (*Ag.* 2.1). But that is itself a political statement. In fact the very act of writing the *Agricola* becomes a vehicle for endorsing the professed ideology of this new regime; the biography is not allowed simply to speak for itself but comes prefaced with observations about the fact that under Nerva and Trajan we now have *libertas* that enables such a work to be written. The rhetorical image of repressed writers crawling out of the woodwork like prisoners released from fifteen years solitary confinement, their skills in composition and expression all but lost due to being unable to communicate with anyone in all that time, an image manifestly at variance with the literary sophistication displayed in the writing of both this introduction and the work as a whole,[6] advertises itself as another example of the flattery that had become an integral part of literary composition under the principate, from book 1 of the *Georgics* on. The same can be said for the gratuitous reference to Trajan at 44.5.[7]

Let us delve a bit deeper here. The polarity constructed in 2.3 is not in fact between the reign of Domitian and those of Nerva and Trajan, but between the extreme of *libertas* that was characteristic of what Tacitus calls the *uetus aetas* and the extreme of *seruitus* from which he has just emerged.[8] By *uetus aetas* Tacitus presumably means the last century of the republic, a theme he will return to in the *Dialogus de Oratoribus*.[9] Here the allusion is more Aristotelean; Nerva and Trajan, introduced as a third element with *nunc demum redit animus* at the start of 3.1, become the mean between the two extremes: of *libertas* under the republic, of *seruitus* under Domitian.[10] *Libertas* under Nerva is not that of the republic but one that can coexist with *principatus*, that is, one significantly qualified. And here we may start to see the traces of a subtext. This *beatissimum saeculum* (the phrase is repeated at 44.5) is not the product of political (r)evolution (as was the establishment of the Augustan principate) but a matter of pure chance; and for it we are dependent on the whim of the *princeps*.[11] It could easily have been so different. And as far as *libertas* is concerned, it may well be nothing but the dream of a sick, frail old man,[12] quickly snuffed out by the intervention of the Praetorians in 97, which led to the adoption of Trajan.[13] *Libertas* disappeared from the coinage with the death of Nerva;[14] it disappears also from Tacitus's carefully crafted introduction, being replaced by *felicitas*, a word whose semantic range encompasses both "happiness" and "good luck."

The freedom of the new age is also the subject of several poems by

Martial. At the beginning of *Epigrams* book 11, published for the Saturnalia of 96, just over three months after Domitian's assassination, there is a series of six poems (11.2–7) either directly or indirectly celebrating Nerva's accession, preceded by an introductory address to Parthenius (11.1). The overt tone is Saturnalian and playful, with the exception of 11.4:

sacra laresque Phrygum, quos Troiae maluit heres
  quam rapere arsuras Laomedontis opes,
scriptus et aeterno nunc primum Iuppiter auro
  et soror et summi filia tota patris,
et qui purpureis iam tertia nomina fastis,
  Iane, refers Neruae, uos precor ore pio:
hunc omnes seruate ducem, seruate senatum;
  moribus hic uiuat principis, ille suis.

Hallows and home-gods of the Phrygians, whom Troy's inheritor
  saw fit to seize ahead of Laomedon's riches doomed to fire,
and Jupiter, now for the first time rendered in everlasting gold,
  and sister and daughter absolute of the highest father,
and you, Janus, now a third time bringing to purple *fasti*
  the name of Nerva, all of you I beseech with dutiful voice:
this man preserve as our Leader, all of you, preserve the Senate;
  may it live according to its *princeps*' principles, and he by his own.

Here amid the frivolity we have what appears to be a heartfelt prayer, whose tone recalls that of Virgil's prayer for the preservation of Octavian at *Georgics* 1.498ff.; and we are again reminded that this new age we are celebrating hangs by a thread, dependent on the *mores principis*. And yet there is irony here, both internal and contextual. The association of Jupiter with gold in line 3 cannot fail to evoke Domitian's extravagant restoration of his Capitoline temple;[15] likewise the invocation of the Capitoline Triad brings to mind Domitian's claim of a special relationship with its third member, Minerva.[16] And Janus, who is now propelling Nerva into his third consulship, was presumably also propelling him into his second as Domitian's colleague in 90. Ghosts from the past still lurk. The use of *aeterno* ("everlasting") to qualify the gold of Jupiter's image also has its irony, since in the lifetime of many of his readers (and of Martial himself, in Rome for both) the Temple of Jupiter had been destroyed by fire not once but twice, in 69 and 80.[17]

And the context. *Epigram* 11.1 imagines the book, decked out in its Saturnalian best (*cultus Sidone non cotidiana*; "dolled up in no ordinary Sidonian purple") off to the palace to see Parthenius as an avenue to reaching the emperor. The conceit is in fact recycled from book 5, where the same Parthenius is presented with the book, again in purple garb, for relaying to Domitian (5.6).[18] *Plus ça change. Epigram* 11.2 introduces the Saturnalia theme explicitly:

triste supercilium durique seuera Catonis
 frons et aratoris filia Fabricia
et personati fastus et regula morum
 quidquid et in tenebris non sumus, ite foras.
clamant ecce mei "io Saturnalia" uersus:
 et licet et sub te praeside, Nerua, libet.
lectores tetrici salebrosum ediscite Santram
 nil mihi uobiscum est: iste liber meus est.

Grim looks and stern brows of unbending Cato,
 and you, Fabricia, ploughman's daughter,
and rule of pride's mask and *mos maiorum*,
 and all that in darkness we aren't anyway, get out!
See, my verses cry out "Hurrah for the Saturnalia!"—
 it is allowed, and with you as ruler, Nerva, it's a pleasure, too.
Censorious readers, go off and learn Santra's irregular verbs;
 I've got nothing for you: *this* is the book you'll get from me.

The first half of the poem is largely a conventional dismissal of traditional, conservative Roman moralism, a precursor to ringing in the Saturnalia in the second half. This is the silly season, where normal codes of behavior are turned on their head. And it is in this context that Nerva makes his first appearance. The phrasing of line 6 (*et licet et sub te praeside, Nerua, libet*) in fact suggests that Nerva is playing the role of *Saturnalicius princeps*, the Lord of Misrule, who gives orders to members of the household to do various tasks that are designed to embarrass; a well-known previous holder of this position was Nero on that celebrated occasion when he ordered Britannicus to get up and sing (Tac. *Ann.* 13.15). The two aspects of the Saturnalia that this poem evokes are, first, that it is only temporary, that come the end of the festival everything reverts to normal and the Catos and their ilk return to play their customary roles as moral paradigms; and secondly, that the position of *princeps* at this festival is allocated by lot. The subtext then would be that we might as well enjoy this new regime that promises an overturning of what we had in the old, censorious one (Domitian's assumption of the title *censor perpetuus* in 85 is relevant here) because it is likely to be just as temporary as the Saturnalia; and secondly, that Nerva's principate is again, as we saw hinted at in the *Agricola*, a matter of luck. *That* sets the tone; and *that* is the backdrop against which we need to read or reread 11.4.

Consider too what follows a few epigrams later (11.15.1–4):

sunt chartae mihi quas Catonis uxor
et quas horribiles legant Sabinae:
hic totus uolo rideat libellus
et sit nequior omnibus libellis . . .

I have pages which Cato's wife could read
and those repulsive Sabine women:
but I want *this* book to be a complete laugh
and exceed all other books in depravity . . .

Once again prudish tradition is herded off elsewhere (with an echo of Ovid's *immundae Sabinae* who aren't up with the modern lifestyle).[19] Fearnley suggests that the high proportion of obscenity that characterizes book 11 and that this poem foreshadows is Martial's way of celebrating the new *libertas*.[20] I would see it slightly differently. First it needs to be seen as inviting comparison with books 5 and 8, which the first two lines clearly evoke. There Martial professed to defer to Domitian's allegiance to the virgin goddess Minerva by eliminating his customary in-your-face obscenity:[21] not a *mentula*, a *cunnus*, or a *futuo* in either of them. For Nerva on the other hand we go the other way: our new *Saturnalicius princeps* has *libertas* as his catchcry, so *libertas* is what we'll give him—not celebration so much as verse which, as with Domitian, reflects the perceived attitudes of the *princeps*. The game goes on. The other thing to note about 11.15 as programmatic statement is line 3. It's all just a laugh, really—and everyone thought I was being so serious back in 11.4. Go back and read it more closely.

I turn now to a very different poem (10.72):

frustra, Blanditiae, uenitis ad me
attritis miserabiles labellis:
dicturus dominum deumque non sum.
iam non est locus hac in urbe uobis;
ad Parthos procul ite pilleatos
et turpes humilesque supplicesque
pictorum sola basiate regum.
non est hic dominus sed imperator,
sed iustissimus omnium senator,
per quem de Stygia domo reducta est
siccis rustica Veritas capillis.
hoc sub principe, si sapis, caueto
uerbis, Roma, prioribus loquaris.

In vain, Flatteries, you come to me,
with worn-out lips, all pathetic:
I'm not going to use the phrase "master and god."
There's no longer room for you in this city:
so off with you to the faraway cap-wearing Parthians
and as shameful, self-abasing suppliants
kiss the feet of their painted kings.
Here there is no "master" but a commander,
yes, and the most just senator of all,
through whom from her Stygian dwelling
rustic, dry-haired Truth has been brought back.
Under this *princeps*, Rome, if you are wise,
beware of speaking in those former terms.

This comes from the second edition of book 10, published probably in 98, the first year of Trajan's principate. Book 10's programmatic statement (10.2) declares that while there is some revised old material here which the reader will recognize, the majority is new (*pars noua maior erit*; 10.4). This creates anticipation of a political interpretation, with poems flattering Domitian replaced by ones extolling Trajan. But while those in the former category have certainly been excised, those in the latter, as Fearnley observes,[22] are extremely thin on the ground: four in a book of 104 epigrams. In fact, 10.2, with its clear allusion to Horace *Odes* 3.30, is much more about survival. The final couplet (*at chartis nec furta nocent et saecula prosunt / solaque non norunt haec monumenta mori*; "but writings thefts do not injure and the passage of time benefits; these are the only monuments that do not experience death"; 10.2.11–12) is a grim reminder that this is in fact not true, as demonstrated by the recent experience of public book burnings (*Agricola* 2.1). If writers and their works are to survive, the implication is, they must not only please the reader (the addressee of 10.2) but also operate within limitations that are all too familiar. *Libertas* belonged (if it ever belonged at all) to the heady days of late 96 and early 97; as far as Martial is concerned, the party is now over. The ultimate irony of that final couplet is that Martial has himself engaged, and successfully engaged, in his own book burning. The first edition of book 10 will form no part of the "collected works."

It is with these considerations in mind that we approach 10.72, buried about three-quarters of the way through the book.[23] The overall tone of this poem is much sterner (despite the hendecasyllabic meter) than the Saturnalia poems with which book 11 opened. Indeed the Saturnalian freedom cap is now banished along with the *blanditiae* to the Parthians; there is no room for either in this city. The message is "get your terms right": NO DOMINVS (that belonged to the previous regime)—the correct term is IMPERATOR (just check the coins in your pocket if you don't believe it).[24] And by the way, SENATOR too[25]—this is SPQR, remember, and just so you do remember, a nice rhyming couplet to reinforce the point. The final couplet issues a somber warning: if you are wise, make sure the words you use are the politically correct ones for the times. *Veritas*, old style plain, rustic, straight-haired truth, is back from the dead; this too is part of the current political correctness. Now we tell it how it is—because that is what we have been told to do. This of course was lampooned in 11.7 where with the change of *princeps* Paula found herself unable to use the old Domitianic lies to her husband about where she was going when she was off to see her lover; now that Truth had become all the rage, well, that's what she told him—and off she went again. But in 10.72 we are back in the regulated world of the Catos and the daughters of Fabricius. And while one set of *blanditiae* has been sent packing to the Parthian court, another has taken its place; this poem, just as much as the Domitianic ones, addresses the *princeps* in the manner of the *princeps*' own choosing. What else can you do when freedom is compulsory?

In fact this is not, nor is it intended as, the language of genuine *libertas*. And Martial's ostentatious announcement of a second edition, addressing a *lector* who was obviously familiar with the first, shows a poet both engaging in and exposing the hollowness of *damnatio memoriae*, excising the Domitianic poems just as SPQR had trashed Domitian's golden statues—or rather recycled them *in usum hominum ac uoluptates*, "for the use and pleasure of humanity" (Plin. *Pan.* 52.5). The attentive reader will note the same has happened here: *nota leges quaedam sed lima rasa recenti / pars noua maior erit*, "you will read some stuff you already know, but rubbed out by recent filing; / you'll find much more new stuff, though" (10.2.3–4). Those who have read the first edition will know what has been erased and what added; and the instruction *lector, utrique faue* ("reader, be responsive to both"; 10.2.5) is telling. The trashed first edition becomes key text for the second; and that is what enables us to discern the subtext of 10.72. The Praetorian revolt and the consequent executions of Parthenius and others implicated in the assassination of Domitian, together with the adoption of Trajan, showed that the early days of Nerva were indeed just a Saturnalian episode, and that Rome and its empire were still under the control of a military dictatorship.[26] The final two epigrams of the revised book 10 foreshadow Martial's departure for Spain after thirty-four years in Rome. The "Rome spring," like the "Prague spring" of 1967 and the "Arab spring" of 2011, has failed to live up to its promise. It is time to go.[27] The allusions to *Tristia* 1.1 in 10.104 and 12.3 (the latter written in Spain) show that Martial is drawing a parallel between himself and the exiled Ovid;[28] setting up this parallel itself constitutes a forceful comment on the political situation in Rome. *Libertas* may be what Trajan has required of the senate and magistrates, but for the poet the old rules and the old dangers still apply. The *iudiciorum subtilitas* of Martial's Roman readers,[29] the absence of which in Bilbilis he laments in the preface to book 12,[30] is still required if the full import is to be discerned.

Some examples from book 12 may serve to illustrate this. First 12.5 (12.4 SB):

longior undecimi nobis decimique libelli
  artatus labor est et breue rasit opus.
plura legant uacui, quibus otia tuta dedisti:
  haec lege tu, Caesar; forsan et illa leges.

The over-long labor of our eleventh and tenth books
  has been pruned, and erasure has produced a short work.
Let the idle classes, whose secure leisure comes as your gift, read
    the longer version;
  you, Caesar, read these; perhaps you will then read those, too.

We have already seen Martial advertising a second edition of book 10, where the image of erasure was also employed; now we are told that an even further pared down version of books 11 and 10 is available—an executive summary that even Caesar will have time to read.[31] Martial is of course playing games here. As the third line makes clear, Caesar is the figure who provides leisure for everyone else and is obviously too busy to read epigrams; the poem is intended for the experienced Martial reader, one who has read both the original and revised versions of book 10 and observed their relationship with book 11.[32] Caesar of course is not such a reader, but is provocatively (and conventionally) invited to become one. The summary comprises 12.5 (with obvious allusions both to 10.1 and to the preface to Ovid's *Amores*,[33] from which it takes over the theme of abbreviation resulting in less effort to read) plus the twelve epigrams that follow. First 12.6:[34]

contigit Ausoniae procerum mitissimus aulae
  Nerua: licet tuto nunc Helicone frui.
recta fides, hilaris clementia, cauta potestas
  iam redeunt; longi terga dedere metus.
hoc populi gentesque tuae, pia Roma, precantur:
  dux tibi sit semper talis, et iste diu.

The gentlest of leaders has lighted upon the Ausonian palace—
  Nerva: now it is allowed to enjoy Helicon in safety.
Upright integrity, cheerful tolerance, judicious power
  now return; our long time of fear is in full retreat.
This do your peoples and communities pray for, dutiful Rome:
  that your Leader remain always thus, and himself live long.

The poem addresses Nerva as *procerum mitissimus* and in an ironic echo of 11.4 prays that he have long life—ironic because he is now well and truly dead and succeeded. The *recta fides*, *hilaris clementia*, and *cauta potestas* of line 3 (the echo in line 4's *iam redeunt* of Virgilian golden age prophecy in *Eclogue* 4 renders the irony all the more poignant) are not celebration of present felicity but rather recall the promise and failure of Nerva's brief flirtation with *libertas*.[35] *Epigram* 12.8 is the ideological and iconographical equivalent of Trajan's column, highlighting the supremacy of Rome and imaging Trajan as her soldier and military leader; as itself a hendecasyllabic poem it virtually demands comparison with 10.72 as an exercise in *blanditiae* (as does 12.15, dealing with Trajan's donation of the private imperial treasures to Jupiter). Most telling is 12.11:

> Parthenio dic, Musa, tuo nostroque salutem:
> nam quis ab Aonio largius amne bibit?
> cuius Pimpleo lyra clarior exit ab antro?
> quem plus Pierio de grege Phoebus amat?
> et si forte (sed hoc uix est sperare) uacabit,
> tradat ut ipse duci carmina nostra roga,
> quattuor et tantum timidumque breuemque libellum
> commendet uerbis "hunc tua Roma legit."

> Give greeting, Muse, to your and our dear Parthenius:
> for who drinks more deeply from Aonian waters?
> whose lyre sounds more gloriously from Pimplean cave?
> whom does Phoebus love more of his Pierian flock?
> And if by chance (though scarcely to be hoped) you find him at leisure,
> beg that he personally hand our songs to the Leader,
> and that he commend this shy and brief little book
> with four words only: "This your Rome reads."

Ostensibly all we are doing here is revisiting the conceit of 5.6 and 11.1, where as we have seen Parthenius is the avenue to the emperor. The motif of Parthenius's "busyness" is carried over from 11.1, where it was said that the book had no chance because Parthenius has no time to read *libri* but only *libelli* (*libros non legit ille sed libellos*; "books he does not read, only briefs"; 11.1.5).[36] Well, here we have a *libellus*, only a few poems long, short enough for any secretary or emperor to read. The allusion to 5.6, though, is more significant. There too the addressee of the poem is the Muse (in fact the whole company of them, *Musae*, 5.6.2), and the instructions they are to give their Parthenius are just to hold the *libellus* and pretend that it is not for the emperor at all; he, as patron of the Muses, will ask for it without prompting (5.6.16–19).[37] That was Domitian; in the case of Trajan it needs to be personally handed over with words of commendation: if you want to know how your subjects are thinking, read this book. *Epigram* 12.11 is also remarkable for the prominence given to Parthenius's status as poet (acknowledged but nowhere near so highlighted in the other poems that mention him), set out in traditional terms in the first four lines, the first half of this carefully constructed epigram. It establishes Parthenius's credibility as judge of poetic excellence and so his qualification as go-between on behalf of his fellow poet; but there is at the same time a wonderful banality in this enormous talent being forced to express itself in those four basic, prosaic words: *hunc tua Roma legit.*[38] Poetic language and modes of expression are clearly not Trajan's forte. And finally—as readers would be only too well aware—the brute fact of the matter is that even as this executive summary is being compiled Parthenius is dead, a victim of the Praetorian uprising in 97 that put an end to the "Rome spring." Martial could of course pretend (and would if any imperial eyebrows were raised) that his presence here is simply part of a compilation of previously written epigrams that constitute this condensation of books 11 and 10. After all, Nerva, addressee of 12.6, is dead, too. The epistolary introduction to Priscus lays stress on the haste with which this book was put together,[39] suggesting that Martial is raiding the filing cabinet for previously unpublished work. But this is surely disingenuous. This mini version of 11 and 10 is not a recycling of already existing work but a set of poems composed precisely for the purpose of reiterating in summary form the issues raised by those books. In the case of 12.11 we know that Parthenius is dead and why. There is thus bitter irony in the present tenses of the first four lines; irony too in the instruction *dic salutem* of line 1, which morphs from a conventional greeting formula into a lament for the loss of the *salus publica*, one of the hopes for the "Rome spring" that featured on Nerva's coinage. This is a mission from beyond the grave.

We can see from this that where relations with the emperor are concerned Martial is up to his old tricks, and that (no matter what the reality) his perception was that the need for *emphasis* did not die with Domitian. We can also discern use of sequencing of poems to deflate or expose, a technique that John Garthwaite has perceptively analyzed in books 6 and 9.[40] For example, between 12.6 and 12.8 comes a couplet focusing in a facetious way on the theme of calculating years,[41] exactly what the majestic Roma is doing for Trajan in the poem immediately following; that they are both hendecasyllables reinforces the link. Then there is 12.14, the key *sententia* from which forms the second epigraph to this chapter. The poem is a warning to Priscus, dedicatee of book 12, currently his house guest and hailed in 12.4 (12.3 SB) as his Maecenas, to be careful as he goes chasing after hares; riders have been fatally thrown even on apparently level ground. Far better to watch others take the risks and the consequent falls (12.14.7–8).[42] Given the context it is hard not to read this as political metaphor: the aura of "gentleness" that

Martial allows Trajan to inherit from Nerva (*mitissimus*, 12.6.1, of Nerva; *mitissime*, 12.9.1, of Trajan)[43] may offer the promise of a continuing *libertas* and forbearance, but the reality may not match the ideology. In this, juxtaposition again offers a subtext: the *mitissime* of 12.9.1 does not sit easily with the military strongman image promulgated in 12.8. Better to lie low, particularly when the governor we are dutifully celebrating in 12.9, A. Cornelius Palma, is clearly very much in favor with the new emperor.[44] The final line of 12.9, *misisti mores in loca nostra tuos* ("you have sent your character into our land," 12.9.4), can be read in more ways than one.

This revisiting of books 11 and 10 is immediately followed by a hendecasyllabic poem addressed to Juvenal (12.18).[45] Here Martial represents Juvenal as living the kind of life that he, Martial, used to live in Rome; haunting the Subura and the Aventine and wearing out his toga making all those early morning calls. But Martial has said goodbye to all that; on the surface the poem seeks to paint the rosiest possible picture of the life he has chosen to live (the discrepancy with his negative remarks about Bilbilis in the preface is pointed and intentional), but echoes of the *Tristia* persistently intrude to continue the theme of Ovidian exile adumbrated in 10.114 and 12.3,[46] and there is a strong sense of boredom and frustration with this life of self-imposed *otium*. The final line—*sic me uiuere, sic iuuat perire* ("so it pleases me to live, so it pleases me to die")—sums it up neatly: this is living death. To live is to continue playing the *emphatic* game exemplified in the nostalgic revisiting of themes from books 11 and 10 that immediately precede. Juvenal is thus being challenged: if the friendship that had been going since at least the early nineties (see Martial 7.24) is to bear fruit, now is the time.[47] The conversations between Martial and Juvenal will undoubtedly have covered not only the frustrations and dangers of being an active poet and social commentator in Rome but also issues relating to the art of safe criticism and techniques of *emphasis*. Subtlety is the key.

And yet at first sight there would appear to be nothing at all subtle about Juvenal. In his first satire he represents himself as so outraged by the state to which Rome has fallen that he cannot confine himself to the relatively gentle genre of epigram: it *has* to be satire. What is hard is *not* to write it (*difficile est saturam non scribere*; 1.30)[48]—to express himself in what Quintilian, advocate of *emphasis*, identified as the quintessentially Roman genre (*satura quidem tota nostra est*; *Inst.* 10.1.93). I have argued elsewhere (though not in the same terms)[49] that the (almost) juxtaposition of this remark on satire to the oleaginously fulsome praise of Domitian's *De Bello Capitolino* is Quintilian's own subtle way of expressing what Juvenal would later write of the same emperor once safely supplanted (*nihil est quod credere de se / non possit cum laudatur dis aequa potestas*; "there is nothing that power equal to the gods is incapable of believing about itself when it is being praised"; Juv. 4.70–71).[50] Such is the state of Rome that satire breeds there like maggots in a rotting corpse; Juvenal's first satire is heavy with the rhetoric of moral decline, finally declaring that we have reached the end of the progression so neatly expressed by Horace in the closing stanza of *Odes* 3.6. For us it is no longer possible for our generation to produce a worse one, because we are now at the bottom: *nil erit ulterius quod nostris moribus addat / posteritas* ("there is nothing further that posterity can add to our morals"; *Sat.* 1.147–8). And in he bursts with that tirade against the irrelevance of poetry (the poetry of idle relaxation as practiced by Pliny and his circle after the day's real work is done)[51] and declares that *he* is going to follow the lead of Lucilius (*Sat.* 1.19–21):

cur tamen hoc potius libeat decurrere campo
per quem magnus equos Auruncae flexit alumnus,
si uacat ac placidi rationem admittitis, edam.

But why it pleases me rather to charge across this plain
over which Aurunca's great *alumnus* steered his horses,
if you have a moment and are calmly receptive to reason, I'll tell you.

The tirade goes for 150 lines, at which point the satirist (as is characteristic of the genre) introduces an interlocutor (*Sat.* 1.150–71):[52]

dices hic forsitan "unde
ingenium par materiae? unde illa priorum
scribendi quodcumque animo flagrante liberet
simplicitas?" cuius non audeo dicere nomen?
quid refert dictis ignoscat Mucius an non?
"pone Tigellinum, taeda lucebis in illa
qua stantes ardent qui fixo gutture fumant,
ut latum media sulcum deducis harena."
qui dedit ergo tribus patruis aconita, uehatur
pensilibus plumis atque illinc despiciat nos?
"cum ueniet contra, digito compesce labellum:

accusator erit qui uerbum dixerit 'hic est.'
securus licet Aenean Rutulumque ferocem
committas, nulli grauis est percussus Achilles
aut multum quaesitus Hylas urnamque secutus:
ense uelut stricto quotiens Lucilius ardens
infremuit, rubet auditor cui frigida mens est
criminibus, tacita sudant praecordia culpa.
inde ira et lacrimae. tecum prius ergo uoluta
haec animo ante tubas: galeatum sero duelli
paenitet." experiar quid concedatur in illos
quorum Flaminia tegitur cinis atque Latina.

Perhaps at this point you'll be saying
"Where will you get skill equal to the material? Where will you get
that freedom to write whatever they liked with burning passion
that your predecessors enjoyed?" Whose name dare I not speak?
Who cares if Mucius forgives what's said about him or not?
"Just mention Tigellinus and you'll become a beacon of blazing pitch
there where they stand burning and smoldering with throat transfixed,
as you draw out a broad furrow across the middle of the arena."
So this guy who gave aconite to three uncles, he's just to be carried along
up there on his feathered cushions and look down on us with contempt?
"Yes, and when he's opposite you, seal your lip with your finger.
Just saying the words 'There he is' is to be marked as an informer.
No problem about putting Aeneas in the ring with the fierce Rutulian,
that's quite safe; love-struck Achilles is a threat to no one;
the long search for Hylas lost in his quest for water, fine.
But each time burning Lucilius drew his (poetic) sword
and raged, the hearer flushed red, his mind went numb under
the accusations, his inmost self sweated silently in guilt.
Thence arise anger and tears. So turn these things over with yourself
in your mind first, before the trumpets: once helmeted, it's too late

to regret declaring war." OK, I'll see what may be allowed me
against those whose ashes are housed along the Flaminian and
Latin Ways.

The plural of the first passage (*admittitis*, 1.21) is reduced to a singular (*dices*, 1.150), the grand address to the world at large whittled down to a tap on the shoulder by a concerned friend. Like his counterpart in Persius *Satire* 1 the interlocutor is unnamed, but it is tempting to see Martial lurking behind this mask of anonymity; we might say that Juvenal has given us a clue toward this identification by appropriating the conceit of riding too recklessly over the plain from *Epigram* 12.14[53] to designate the literary activity of Lucilius that he proposes to emulate.[54] When at the end of the first satire this figure is finally given the opportunity to speak, he sounds a caution: we do not in our day have the *scribendi simplicitas*, which really amounts to freedom to write what we like, that was available to poets under the republic. Under the principate, under *this* principate, optimal though it may be, things are different (despite what you might read in Pliny's *Panegyricus*). The specific example he cites in his warning is that of Tigellinus; if you were to attack him the way Lucilius attacked Q. Mucius Scaevola you would suffer the same fate as Tacitus records being meted out to the Christians as punishment for incendiarism in the Great Fire of 64 (*Annals* 15.44). This has struck commentators as a bit odd,[55] but if we take the hint that this is Martial talking it makes a good deal more sense. Martial first came to Rome around the time of the great fire; the events of that year, the bloodbath of the Pisonian conspiracy (which severely impacted on a number of his fellow Spaniards) and the power wielded by Tigellinus, would have made a lasting impression and made him very well aware of the need for discretion and subtlety when he embarked on his own career as a poet. So the message is learn when to keep your mouth firmly shut, no matter what the provocation. And those epics you express such contempt for may have more in them than you think if you read between the lines. The three examples the interlocutor cites at lines 162–64 suggest the *Aeneid*, Statius's *Achilleid* and Valerius Flaccus's *Argonautica*;[56] each is at least ambivalent toward the regime under which it was composed, and each has its own subtle ways of expressing that ambivalence.[57] Charging in like Lucilius, declaring war on powerful individuals, carries a real risk of reprisal. Whether or not the interlocutor's role in this satire reflects conversations Martial and Juvenal had with each other, the satirist persona at the end is suitably deflated: *experiar quid concedatur* ("I'll try out what may be allowed").

"What may be allowed," of course, is to jump on the bandwagon of political correctness. The whole burden of the interlocutor's advice is to steer the satirist away from dangerous confrontation back into excoriating the previous regime. That is certainly allowed, and very much part of the zeitgeist of Trajan's Rome. (See—who else?—Pliny.)[58] But when measured against the satiric tradition (such as we have it), the backdown is in fact remarkable. When Horace represents himself as receiving similar advice from Trebatius at Hor. *Sat.* 2.1.60–62, he responds by appealing to the precedent of Lucilius and talking his interlocutor around: truth will be sufficient protection. Juvenal's enthusiastic appropriation of the Lucilius role earlier in *Sat.* 1 is on the other hand quickly dropped. Likewise when Persius's interlocutor gives his warning at *Sat.* 1.107–10, he does not desist from his exposé of the fact that in Rome everyone (which must include the emperor) has ass's ears.[59] Juvenal seemingly abandons his grand plan to include every vice and foible in his *farrago*. Intertextual allusion highlights the capitulation and invites the reader to subject it to greater scrutiny.[60] What game is Juvenal playing here?

On one level, what Juvenal is doing is the same as Martial had done. Satire more than any other is a genre that requires freedom of speech to flourish, the *scribendi simplicitas* of which Juvenal has his interlocutor speak. That it is not safe to write as Lucilius had done implies that all this talk of *libertas* is essentially a sham, that the imperial system is just as it had always been, that nothing has changed.[61] This as we saw was the *aliud latens* of Martial's post-Domitianic output. But there is more to it than that. If we actually *say* that our satiric *modus operandi* is to dredge up and ridicule figures from the past, the implication is that the past becomes cipher for the present; and so by observing political correctness and excoriating the individuals and practices that characterized the previous regime, we are in fact satirizing the imperial system itself—in its current as well as its past instantiation.[62] To say that it is too dangerous to attack Tigellinus is on the face of it ludicrous after both he and his emperor are long dead; but if Tigellinus is symptomatic of a weakness inherent in the imperial system itself, then of course it *does* make sense. Consider *Satire* 4. From the evidence of the scholiast it would appear that the turbot council is a lampoon on Domitian's military council as represented in Statius's *De Bello Germanico*.[63] But if Domitian is to be seen as a cipher for the current administration, the poem takes on a whole new dimension, becoming a lampoon on any artistic representation of imperial councils of war. And by the time *Satire* 4 was written such representations were looming large over Rome's center, as Trajan's column displayed its numerous ideologically impeccable and consistently flattering representations of Trajan surrounded by his staff.[64] Domitian was not the only emperor to style himself Augustus Germanicus Dacicus. So while on the one hand writing satire would appear to be index of a new era of Lucilian *libertas*, the ending of the programmatic *Satire* 1 draws attention to the self-censorship necessary for survival. There had been satirists under Domitian, too (Turnus and the unnamed *clari* of Quintilian *Inst.* 10.1.94 *fin.*), whose need for circumspection was obvious; that Juvenal presents himself as similarly circumscribed makes a telling point.[65]

But the meek acceptance of *Satire* 1's interlocutor's advice is not merely a smokescreen. Rome is indeed facing the deepest moral crisis of its history, and cries out for a Lucilius to make its citizens aware of the fact. Of course that too is a satiric commonplace, as both Horace and Persius had identified Lucilius as their literary ancestor. But for them Lucilius was a precedent that they could follow and to which they could appeal; Juvenal on the other hand, after flamboyantly adopting the same pose, presents himself as being warned off. The essence of the moral crisis lies not in the activities of social upstarts, extortionate governors, and women perpetually on heat, but in the fact that the satirist can no longer proceed beyond generalized images of vice to naming individual perpetrators, to fill in the blanks, to be a Lucilius in a world desperately in need of one, to see the victims of his satiric barbs squirming and sweating—and that the reason for this is lack of a powerful *patronus* to protect him. At the beginning of *Satire* 7 Juvenal was to write *et spes et ratio studiorum in Caesare tantum* ("literature's hopes and way of doing things reside wholly with Caesar"), but when it comes to defending the satirist against the *ira* of powerful individuals as Scipio Aemilianus defended Lucilius, Caesar is definitely not to be relied on. The *patronus-cliens* relationship, once one of the cornerstones of Roman social cohesion, has degenerated into a system of handouts and humiliation; and this was in Juvenal's view its ultimate failing.[66] The principate does not protect but dictates; we writers who want to expose the system's shortcomings must appear to operate within the bounds of *quod conceditur*, and determine at our own risk (*experiar*) how they can be circumvented safely.[67] Caesar is responsible not only for what literature is but also for what it is not. The poets who receive financial support in *Satire* 7 are those who write the kind of stuff that Juvenal began *Satire* 1 by castigating. There are no satirists among them.

Seeking exempla from the past is also the *modus operandi* of Tacitus, not only in his historical writing (particularly the *Annals*) but also in the *Dialogus de Oratoribus*, a work published probably (as Syme argues)[68] in 107, the tenth year of Trajan's reign. It is set in 75 CE, the middle year of Vespasian, and through the character of Maternus explores the conflicting demands of personal safety and artistic integrity for a writer under the principate.[69] The introductory dedication to Fabius Justus suggests that the work is a response to a question he "often" asks, namely, why oratory has declined. But as Bartsch and others have pointed out, this is not an accurate description of what the work actually contains.[70] If it were just that it would be perfectly bland and perfectly safe; oratory has "declined" because the principate has removed the need for it, and thus this phenomenon reflects the fact that we live in politically more settled times (*Dial.* 41.3–4). The more dangerous topic, on which the blurb is silent, is that of literature in general and how it may be employed to express political dissent. That is why it is set in the past, relegating the implied restrictions on *libertas* and the risks involved in producing literature (in Maternus's case plays for private recitation) that could be read as subversive to the previous dynasty. But the choice of Vespasian rather than Domitian is interesting, on two counts. First, Vespasian largely enjoyed a good reputation for tolerance (see esp. Suet. *Vesp.* 15), an image that Trajan (if we can rely on Pliny's *Panegyricus*) was also concerned to cultivate; thus it is suggested that even in reigns that allegedly support *libertas*, some circumspection is necessary. Secondly, it enables Tacitus to represent himself as a young man (if Syme is right in fixing his birth date in 56 or 57 he would not yet be twenty)[71] on the threshold of his career, a Scipionic moment of choice between Pleasure and Virtue:[72] to go with the flow and enjoy the kind of life depicted in Pliny's *Letters*, or to follow the lead of Maternus and give vent to his *saeua indignatio* through the medium of literature. That he chose to write the *Annals* rather than embark on that promised history of Nerva and Trajan shows that he adopted the latter course;[73] that he follows the precedent set by Virgil's failure to produce the celebration of Octavian's military achievements promised at *Georgics* 3.46–48 and writing the *Aeneid* instead, underscores the point. Far from celebrating the felicity of the new age, it is a work that remorselessly details the consequences of the loss of *libertas* and the willing acceptance by Romans, particularly upper-class Romans, of one-man rule.[74] And written into the promise itself we find a telling distinction between Nerva and Trajan: Nerva's rule is termed *principatus* whereas Trajan's is *imperium*.[75] As for Martial, so for Tacitus, the adoption and succession of Trajan meant resumption of military dictatorship.

For Pliny, freedom of speech is what distinguishes the new era of Nerva and Trajan from the old of Domitian. What this means in effect is not that one is free to openly criticize the structure or the conduct of imperial government, but rather that fulsome praise of the *princeps* is now taken as an expression of genuine regard as opposed to forced sycophancy. See, for example, *Ep.* 3.18, where Pliny records the fact that he gave a *recitatio* of the expanded version of the *Panegyricus* to an enthusiastic group of friends over three days; that they were so enthusiastic he regards as a consequence of this new "freedom." Writers wishing to probe the inconsistencies and hypocrisies of the age found that just as before they had to resort to a form of coded discourse. Juvenal represents himself in *Satire* 1 as setting out to exploit the opportunities offered by the proposition that you are free to say what you think, only to be firmly warned off, thus exposing the fault lines in the marriage of *principatus* and *libertas*. Martial continues to employ his techniques of arrangement and allusion to signal to seasoned Martial readers that the realities of Rome's political life and the position of the artist within it have not changed. Tacitus adopts the persona of his character Maternus, using his literary talent to represent the past in such a way that it forces attention on the essential nature of the principate, one that remains firmly in place no matter who is currently in power.[76] *optimus est post malum principem dies primus* ("the first day after a bad emperor is the best"; *Hist.* 4.42); and it all slides back downhill from there.

NOTES

1. Ahl (1984a).

2. See esp. Quint. *Inst.* 9.65. For discussion see, e.g., Ahl (1984a) 187–97; Ahl (1984b) 82–85; Bartsch (1994) 67–71, 93–96; Winkler (1995) 65–67; Nauta (2002) 416–19; Fearnley (2003) 615–16; Pagán (2004) 381–82; McHugh (2004) 392.

3. For which see Juvenal *Sat.* 1.1–13 with Henderson (1995), plus numerous references in Martial (see Shackleton Bailey's index under "Recitation" [1993: iii.333]) and above all Pliny, addicted to recitation both of his own work and that of others (see Sherwin-White [1966: 116 *ad* Plin. *Ep.* 1.13.5]—"It is his passion"). The nadir of meaninglessness comes with the so-called "Old Comedy" recitation of Virgilius Romanus described at Plin. *Ep.* 6.21, which was *so* nice to Pliny (*circa me tantum benignitate nimia modum excessit*)—was Aristophanes ever accused of an excess of *benignitas*?

4. The Great Question that daringly frames Persius's critique of Neronian literary effusion and audience response to it, an *aliud latens* for the reader to pull back out of the hole in which the poet has buried it: *Romae quis non . . . auriculas asini quis non habet?* ("at Rome, who hasn't . . . who hasn't got asses' ears?"; Pers. *Sat.* 1.8 and 121). See Reckford (2009 [1962]) 22–26, 50–51; Sullivan (1991) 78; Freudenburg (2001) 151–83.

5. On the numismatic evidence and its significance, see Grainger (2003) 46–47, and in more detail Shotter (1983).

6. Haynes (2006) 153 remarks, "We are not supposed to believe that we are about to read something poorly written, but something poorly and painfully remembered." In fact the discrepancy between content and style, between what is said and the way it is said, is telling, deliberate, and there for the discriminating reader to pick up.

7. On this passage cf. Wilson (2003) 526–27. Wilson criticizes the position of Ramage (1989) 641, according to which all comparisons between the old regime and the new are to be construed as an expression of support for the latter. On the surface they can be read in no other way, with Pliny's *Panegyricus* being the prime example; such are the perceived constraints within which writers under the principate operate. Freudenburg (2001) 215–34 sees in this an expression of a wider zeitgeist manifested by the literature of the Trajanic period, which is characterized by what he calls "martyr tales" and stories of brutal tyranny that cover not just the reign of Domitian but the whole of the first century from Tiberius onward. A distinction needs to be drawn, however, between those who use these tales in order to show what wonderful times they are now living in (Pliny is the obvious example here) and those who encode within them signs that point to the possibility of an alternative reading.

8. Haynes (2006) 154.

9. See pp. 194–95 below.

10. On moral virtue as a mean between two extremes, one of excess and one of defect, see esp. Arist. *EN* book 2. The philosophical allusion points up another contrast between the new regime and the old, under which philosophers were expelled (*expulsis insuper sapientiae professoribus*; 2.2), while at the same time injecting a cautionary note into the general air of celebration.

11. For Tacitus it is ever thus; to understand the nature of an age, insight into the character of the ruler, whether the ruler be the people, the senate or, as now, a single individual, is essential (*Ann.* 4.33).

12. For Nerva's ill health, see Dio Cassius 78.1.3.

13. On these events and their significance, see, e.g., Syme (1958) 10–17; Eck (2002) 211–12; Grainger (2003) 94–100.

14. Cf. Waters (1969) 394.

15. For the extravagant use of gold in this structure, cf. Plu. *Publ.* 15.4, Sil. *Pun.* 3.623–24, Mart. 9.3.7–8 (implying that not even Jupiter himself could pay for it), with Jones (1996) 51.

16. On which see Jones (1996) 46 with further bibliography there cited. Suetonius (*Dom.* 4.6) records that when Domitian presided at the Capitoline Games he wore a crown on which the Capitoline Triad was depicted.

17. Shackleton Bailey (1993) iii.6 n. c claims that *aeterno* here means "never again to be destroyed by fire." That is to miss the irony completely.

18. The fact that Parthenius was a major player in the assassination of Domitian of course adds an extra *frisson* to this allusion.

19. Ov. *Am.* 1.8.39.

20. Fearnley (2003) 623–25. On the link between sexual and political *libertas* in book 11, see also Hinds (1998) 129–35 and Hinds (2007) 123.

21. See esp. 5.2, 8 *praef.* and 8.1.

22. Fearnley (2003) 619. See also Citroni (1988) 31.

23. For an alternative analysis of this poem, see Fearnley (2003) 626.

24. Pliny's first letter to Trajan congratulating him on his success uses the term twice, just to be sure: *imperator sanctissime* at the beginning and *imperator optime* at the end: *Ep.* 10.1 (cf. also 10.4 and 10.14). On the other hand, Pliny seems not to have got the message about *dominus*; *domine* is his standard way of addressing Trajan from 98 onward. See Roche (2003) 441 with n. 52.

25. Cf. Roche (2003) 431–32.

26. Artistic representations of Trajan show that military strongman was one of the principal images that Trajan was concerned to project. See, e.g., Ny Carlson Glyptotek Cat. 543 (reproduced at Grainger [2003: xii]), the so-called Dezennalientypus portrait busts (Fell [1992: 95]), and of course the column with its fifty-nine Trajans (Beard and Henderson [2001: 180–81]) together with other triumphal representations in the Trajan's Forum/Basilica Ulpia complex (on which see Sear [1998: 157–62]). On Trajan as strengthening rather than diminishing the autocracy of the principate see Waters (1969) 386–87; Rutledge (1998) 145.

27. In his letter noting the death of Martial (*Ep.* 3.21), Pliny records that he paid the poet's travel expenses (*prosecutus eram uiatico secedentem*, 3.21.2) in acknowledgment of his "friendship" (*amicitiae*) and "some verses" he wrote about him (*uersiculis quos de me composuit*). The verses are *Epigrams* 10.19 (10.20 SB), in which Thalia is instructed to take a *libellus* to Pliny's house on the Esquiline; she must not turn up early (presumably so as not to be taken for a client) but only in the evening when the wine is flowing and everyone is relaxed. Here in the revised edition of book 10 Martial is clearly directing a barb at Pliny's attitude to poetry: serious work is done during the day (*totos dat tetricae dies Mineruae*; "he gives all the daytime to stern Minerva"; 10.19.14), whereas poetry is something you do for light relief at night (cf. p. 190 below). Such is Pliny's lack of discernment that he takes this as a compliment, misreading Martial's instructions to Thalia as an order to approach his house "with respect" (*reuerenter*, 3.21.5). For Martial it must have seemed peculiarly appropriate for Pliny to pay his fare; Pliny belongs among the Catos (10.19.21)—for which read Trajan idolizers—and should therefore be happy to facilitate this self-imposed exile. See further Henderson (2001); interpretations such as Garthwaite (1998) 163–65 fail to pick up Pliny's failure to pick up Martial's irony.

28. Fearnley (2003) 632–64 with nn. 49, 50, and 52. Both poems follow *Tristia* 1.1 in employing the conceit of the book of which they are a part being dispatched by the author with a commission. Book 10 is instructed in its final poem to prepare a place for Martial in his Spanish homeland; the last word of this "Trajanic" revision has the poet imposing upon himself what Augustus imposed upon Ovid. Despite the seemingly new ideology, the end result is, as it must be, the same; 12.3 (12.2 SB) is thus enabled to play the same part as *Tristia* 1.1, sent from Bilbilis to Rome as a *peregrinus* ("foreigner," 12.3.2 - *Tr.* 1.59),

bidden to greet its "brothers" (*fratres* 12.3.6 ~ *Tr.* 1.107 = books composed by the author in Rome), and wander through the poet's old haunts where its authorship will be instantly recognized despite the lack of a title (12.3.17–18 ~ *Tr.* 1.61–62). See Pitcher (1998) 62–64 and 71–72 with n. 35; Hinds (2007) 133–34.

29. Cf. Boyle (1995) 95, who in the context of a discussion of the significance of intertextuality—particularly *Ovidian* intertextuality—in Martial draws attention to the fact that Martial right at the beginning (1.1.4) addresses his reader as *studiose* ("expert," "diligent," "scholarly," "engaged").

30. "Illam iudiciorum subtilitatem, illud materiarum ingenium, bibliotecas, theatra, conuictus, in quibus studere se uoluptates non sentiunt, ad summam omnia illa quae delicati reliquimus desideramus quasi destituti" ("that acuity of judgment, that ingenuity of subject-matter, the libraries, the theaters, the gatherings in which serious thought engulfs pleasures without their realizing it—in fact all those things I fastidiously left behind—I now crave like one deserted"). Note how *iudiciorum subtilitas* comes first in this list, and how closely it is aligned to *materiarum ingenium*, the city-located subject matter upon which the poet yearns to (continue to) exercise his talent.

31. Kay (1985) 53 identifies this Caesar as Nerva, as do Citroni (1988) 30 with n. 50, Merli (1993) 253, and Shackleton Bailey (1993) iii.95 n. c, but given that it is the introduction to a subset of book 12 of which one poem (12.8) conspicuously has Trajan as its subject, Trajan would seem the obvious candidate.

32. As Fowler (1995) 41 rightly observes, the implied reader of this epigram and the epigrams it introduces is not in fact Caesar but the *uacui*, the leisured classes who have time to read and read with understanding. Fowler also rightly observes that "what needs to be appreciated . . . is the role of this epigram *within Book 12*" (ibid., emphasis original). For the association of *otia* and the *uacui* again referring to the leisured classes, see 11.3.2 with Kay (1985) 63 ad loc.

33. Note in particular the identical positioning of *libelli* at the end of line 1 and *opus* at the end of line 2.

34. Preserving the traditional numbering of the epigram. Adding the couplet traditionally numbered 12.2 as the first two lines of this one (so Shackleton Bailey) seriously weakens it (1) by creating a logically disjointed poem—a poem to be read by Nerva is not going to be traveling to him after his death—and more seriously (2) by diminishing the focus on Nerva, which is artistically required for the first poem of the collection.

35. It is generally assumed (cf., e.g., Kay [1985: 53]; Citroni [1988: 30]; Sullivan [1991: 55]; Howell [1998: 183]) that 12.5 was written during Nerva's reign, before Parthenius's death at the hands of the praetorians. Sullivan's claim that it was one of the poems excised from the revised edition of book 10 would have some plausibility *if* we assume that book 12 is at least in part a hastily compiled anthology (as of course is suggested by the preface; see below). To my mind however, this poem is too carefully crafted both in itself and in its positioning to be written off in this way; it would certainly suit Martial to draw a veil of randomness over this mini-collection (hence the preface), but he is also aware that his regular readers are quite capable of seeing through this.

36. The double meaning of *libellus* ("little book"/"petition"—*OLD* s.v. 1 and 3) is impossible to translate. The collection is not just a "little book" but also a petition (see esp. the final line of 12.5) requesting that it be read.

37. That 12.11 is alluding to 5.6 is reinforced by the reuse of *timidumque breuemque*, "shy and brief," to describe the book (12.11.7 ~ 5.6.7).

38. This is a clear indication that the *dux* Martial has in mind is Trajan rather than Nerva. Nerva was after all himself a poet and is addressed in a style similar to that which Martial employs for his other poet acquaintances at 8.70 and 9.26. Such a flat and prosaic message as this would not be appropriate for him.

39. . . . *et studui paucissimis diebus ut familiarissimas mihi aures tuas exciperem aduentoria sua* (". . . and I have been hard at work over a very few days in order to present those ears so familiar to me with their gift of welcome"). Cf. Citroni (1988) 6.

40. Garthwaite (1990); Garthwaite (1993).

41. 12.7: *toto uertice quot gerit capillos / annos si tot habet Ligeia, trima est* ("Only three is Ligeia, if she has as many years as she carries hairs on her entire head"); cf. 12.8.1–4: *terrarum dea gentiumque Roma, / cui par est nihil et nihil secundum, / Traiani modo laeta cum futuros / tot per saecula computaret annos* . . . ("Rome, goddess of earth and its peoples, to whom there is no equal and no second, when lately she was joyfully counting up Trajan's future years through so many centuries . . ."). Note too how the last line of 12.6 (*dux tibi sit semper talis, et iste diu*; "may your Leader remain always thus, and himself live long") adumbrates the theme of longevity that 12.7 takes up.

42. The reference in the next couplet to "lying in ambush for Tuscan boars" as a safer sport than hunting hares (*Tuscis . . . insidiemur apris*) leads Howell (1998) 175 and 179n17 to conclude that the poem was composed in Italy rather than Spain and so another "filing cabinet" job. This seems unnecessary. In the context of what I am arguing is political metaphor, the key word is *insidiemur*, which suggests that it is far safer to keep one's head down and hunt while not seeming to be hunting; *Tuscis* is simply a generic term, as it is in Juv. *Sat.* 1.22.

43. As an address, *mitissime Caesar* is taken from Ov. *Tr.* 2.27, where it is used for Augustus. The epithets express no more than a hope. For Ovid the hope was dashed; in Martial what might have been factual with respect to Nerva is in Trajan's case again a hope. The Ovidian intertext does not inspire confidence.

44. Palma and Q. Sosius Senecio were Trajan's first appointments as *consules ordinarii*, taking office in 99 CE. See Syme (1958) 53; Grainger (2003) 120.

45. That this is Juvenal the future satirist is now generally accepted. See Watson and Watson (2003) 145 ad 12.18.2; Armstrong (2012) 59–60.

46. Notably in the fact that this is another poem that must make the journey from Bilbilis to a Rome and a friend still vividly recalled, and in the effect that exile has on the poet's mental state (*rusticumque fecit* = "it has robbed me of my city sophistication"; 12.18.8). Here there is nothing to do but sleep (*ingenti fruor improboque somno*, "I enjoy a huge and indecent amount of sleep," 12.18.13, where *improbo* [*pace* Watson and Watson (2003) 147 ad loc.] does retain its "pejorative force") and pursue a life of aimless

self-indulgence, pathetically clinging to a vestige of *urbanitas* in eyeing off his good-looking *uenator* and *uilicus* (12.18.22–25). As in Ovid, there is a strong sense of nostalgia for a *temps perdu*. To read 12.18 as an unequivocal expression of contentment, as, e.g., Armstrong (2012) 60 does, is in my view a serious misreading.

47. Uden (2011) 270–78 argues that there may be a closer connection between 12.18 and the first book of Juvenal's *Satires* than hitherto realized. Noting that Martial "places Juvenal in an epigrammatic condensing of the satirist's own scenes of city life" (273), Uden suggests that this indicates a knowledge on Martial's part of the whole of *Satires* book 1, which points to a publication date of around 101. If this is true, then of course this is a challenge issued ex post facto. I think however that this goes too far. I am quite happy with the proposition that Martial had a good idea of where Juvenal was heading on the basis of conversations or even drafts, but it seems highly unlikely that he would not have acknowledged the existence of work published or in progress as he does, e.g., with Silius Italicus at 4.14 and 7.63. In fact the aspects of Juvenal's life that Martial alludes to in 12.18 can all be related to the *patronus-cliens* relationship, which I shall argue (pp. 193–94 below) is central to Juvenal's sense of the moral crisis facing Rome and will certainly have formed the subject matter of many conversations. Thus I see no need to reject Braund's (1996) 16 view that book 1 of the *Satires* was "written in the second decade of the second century" rather than the first—although I would suggest "published" rather than "written."

48. The pose adopted by Juvenal as Freudenburg (2001) 209–15 points out is that of someone finally bursting out after years of enforced silence, someone who has had to endure the difficulty of not being able to write satire in spite of all the provocations to it that he goes on to detail at length. The question then has to be asked (and surely the author demands that we ask it): given the fact that under Trajan freedom became compulsory, why keep it bottled up for another twelve years? Or even twenty? Cf. Waters (1970) 77.

49. Penwill (2000) 72–75.

50. Both Courtney (1980) 215 and Braund (1996) 251 ad loc. cite as a parallel to this passage Plin. *Pan.* 4.4: *principem quem aequata dis immortalibus potestas deceret* ("a *princeps* in whom power equal to the immortal gods is so becoming"). Do we detect an implied equation here?—Domitian : fisherman :: Trajan : Pliny? Pliny, who all but confers on his *dominus* the Jovian titles of *Optimus Maximus* (*Pan.* 88.8)? Pliny, who follows Martial (10.72) in ostentatiously disavowing the *dominus et deus* title as one of his flatteries of Trajan (*Pan.* 2.3) only to effectively divinize the same emperor later in the speech and address him as *domine* in all his correspondence from Bithynia? Is Juvenal deliberately alluding to Pliny and so enabling this to be read as applying to all those with power equal to the gods and those who flatter them? Winkler (1995) 67–70 argues, rightly, that Quintilianic *emphasis* pervades the fisherman's address to Domitian at *Sat.* 4.65–69; it would be nice to think that the same might be true of Pliny's *Panegyricus*. Of this I am somewhat doubtful, and my doubts are reinforced not only by what Pliny himself says about the task of praising the *princeps* at *Ep.* 3.13, 3.18, and 6.27 but also by Shadi Bartsch's excellent analysis of the work: Bartsch (1994) 148–87. Cf. also Uden (2011) 119–20. On the *optimus maximus* title,

it is interesting to note that this was in fact conferred on Trajan not only by his fellow Spaniards in dedicatory inscriptions (*CIL* II.2010 and 2054—the latter also assigning to him the Jovian title *conseruator generis humani*) but also on the *Tabula Alimentaria* from Veleia (*CIL* XI.1147, dated 102 CE). See Fell (1992) 53–54, 56–57, 67; and cf. Roche (2003) 444–46.

51. See, e.g., Plin. *Ep.* 4.14, 27; 5.3, 15; 7.4, 9.9–14; 8.19; 9.25. Cf. Hershkowitz (1995).

52. The function of this interlocutorial intervention and the satirist's response to it has occasioned much critical comment. See works cited in notes 55–67 below. The most recent discussion is that of Matthew Roller: see Roller (2012) 293–97. Roller's view is that the satirist "is presenting and performing a strategy for speaking truth to power 'safely'" (297). But surely it is more a case of speaking *about* power—particularly a power that declares freedom to be compulsory.

53. See p. 188 above.

54. The close literary relationship between Martial and Juvenal which would make such an identification yet more plausible is strongly argued by Mason (1963 [1962]), in support of his contention (1963) 96 that "the key to Juvenal's art lies in the study of Martial." See also Anderson (1982 [1970]).

55. Various explanations for the introduction of Tigellinus have been attempted. Freudenburg (2001) 244–45 points out that with his low birth and vile character he is the antithesis of Lucilius's target Scaevola, being the sort of villain that the imperial age produces. The threatened vengeance is thus suitably grotesque and extreme. Uden (2011) 34–35 highlights the danger of taking on the role of *delator* against a figure of such power and influence, and links the punishment to the public humiliation of *delatores* under Titus (Suet. *Tit.* 8.5), where again the location is the arena. For Uden whoever sets out to imitate *ardens Lucilius* in this political climate risks burning in the literal sense.

56. Cf. in general terms Courtney (1980) 117 *ad* 162; Braund (1996) 109 *ad* 162–64; Schmitz (2000) 35–36. That *specific* examples of such epic subject matter are being alluded to here is a not unreasonable assumption in the case of the first and third. In the case of the second, it would involve taking *percussus* as equivalent to *percussus amore* for which cf. Hor. *Epod.* 11.2–3; the normal interpretation is that it refers to Achilles' death (so Braund ad loc., citing Epict. 3.23.35 for this as a recitation theme; cf. Wehrle [1992: 32–33]). The interlocutor is drawing the would-be satirist's attention to the fact that there are more subtle ways of voicing dissent than charging in like Lucilius, and so suggesting a rethink of the strident rejection of epic with which *Satire* 1 commences. Cf. Henderson (1995) 127.

57. Few now dispute that there is at least ambivalence in the *Aeneid*; for the *Achilleid*, see Benker (1987) with Penwill (2000) 69–72; for the *Argonautica*, see Penwill (2013) 30–37 and Davis, Chapter 8 in this volume. The interlocutor does not of course *say* this—that has to be kept secret—but it is something that the discerning reader is invited to infer. Schmitz (2000) 35 is correct in observing that the interlocutor is made to say that writing epic is less dangerous ("gefahrlose") than writing Lucilian satire, but the reason for that is that epic allows for the exercise of *emphasis* in the way that it presents its apparently worn out ("abgenutzten," 34) themes.

58. Cf. note 7 above.

59. Cf. note 4 above.

60. For a fuller analysis of the "pattern of apology" in the programmatic satires of all three poets, see Braund (2004) 418–21. She does not however go on to examine the way in which Juvenal exploits the intertextual reference he has set up. Better is Plaza (2006) 37–52, who talks instead of "programmatic jokes" common to all four satirists. In this instance in response to the interlocutor's intervention and warning, "instead of a knight ablaze with just indignation ['Juvenal'] turns out to be a coward after all. . . . The grand picture of a warrior and the elevated archaism of *duelli* [1.169] are smashed down against the bleak tomb-rows of familiar streets. . . . He is a hysterical and rather inadequately equipped desecrator of graves. . . . The scene is . . . set for the derision of the persona" (47). Cf. Rimell (2005) 81: "Juvenal digs up a century of pent up angst, yet only to hurl it at corpses who cannot answer back." That there is humor in this image is undoubtedly true, but this should not obscure the serious point that is being made.

61. Rimell (2005) 91–92: "The deflating punchline of satire 1 . . . is that freedom of speech is more curtailed than ever, and that therefore he will only dare to slander ghosts."

62. Kenney (2012) 130–31 suggests that Juvenal is simply following the practice of historians and orators in using *exempla* from the past as moral paradigms, citing Livy's preface. Cf. Braund (2009 [1997]) 460: "Juvenal's satires are teeming with negative *exempla*." But in fact Juvenal does not highlight Domitian because Domitian is an example to avoid (à la Pliny) but because Domitians are what the imperial system throws up. And even a set of five (apparently) "good" emperors will eventually produce a Commodus once the dynastic principle reasserts itself.

63. Braund (1996) 251–52; Connors (2005) 142–43.

64. Sear (1998) 159 dates the construction of the column to the seven-year period 107–113, which coincides with the period during which it is likely book 1 of the *Satires* was also being constructed.

65. Waters (1970) 63; cf. Wehrle (1992) 34, 36–38, 117. However, the issue is not so much whether Trajan's regime was in fact totalitarian and repressive as one of perception. Or not even that, but rather one of pitting one set of perceptions (the panegyrist's) against another (the satirist's). For one, we have *libertas restituta* (Plin. *Pan.* 78.3, 93.1–2 and passim) and we live in appreciation and enjoyment of that fact; that is the perception to which the satirist, both in what he writes and when he chooses to publish, applies his Lucilian fire. Not only is this not the best of all possible worlds; rather, it is the polar opposite. As their writings show, for Pliny it is a world to be celebrated, for Juvenal it is one to be torn apart.

66. Cf. Braund (1996) 31: "Book 1 [of the *Satires*] when read as a continuous whole presents a progressively harsher and starker view of the dysfunction and perversion of the patron-client relationship." See also Bellandi (2009 [1974]) and specifically with respect to *Satire* 1 Plaza (2006) 120–24.

67. Pagán (2004) 382: "[T]he unequal relations of power [*sc.* between *princeps* and writer] strained language and caused poets to find new and ever more creative ways of expressing their responses to the new political order."

68. Syme (1958) 670–73. Mayer (2001) 25 is less definite: "some time early in the first decade of the second century."

69. For a fuller analysis of how this exploration plays out in the work, see Penwill (2003). What follows is by way of a few notes. For a more recent discussion, see Uden (2011) 51–60.

70. Bartsch (1994) 98–101.

71. Syme (1958) 63.

72. Sil. *Pun.* 15.18–128, where Scipio is termed *iuuenis* at both beginning and end (18, 129).

73. "Quod si uita suppeditet, principatum diui Neruae et imperium Traiani, uberiorem securioremque materiam, senectuti seposui, rara temporum felicitate ubi sentire quae uelis et quae sentias dicere licet" ("So if life is granted me, I have set aside for my old age as richer and safer subject matter the principate of the deified Nerva and the imperial command of Trajan, given this rare and felicitous time where it is permitted to believe what you wish and express what you believe"; *Hist.* 1.1).

74. On the *Annals* as Tacitus's last word on imperial Rome, see above all Henderson (1989); also Rutledge (1998).

75. Cf. Henderson (1989) 173 "A veiling of the terms used for the 'interruptions' to the Republic [at *Ann.* 1.1] . . . is achieved by the word *princeps*, its power to mean *rex* while barely even saying *principium*." Since this is the age of truth, let's tell it how it is: *principatus* died with Nerva. What we have is an exercise of *imperium*. In fact that's how it's been all along: *qui* [sc. Augustus] *cuncta discordiis ciuilibus fessa nomine principis sub imperium accepit* ("who when the world was worn out by civil war took it all under his command, with the title of *princeps*"; *Ann.* 1.1). And now we find the old *blanditiae* augmented; the *imperator* who succeeded in staving off a rerun of the disastrous civil war that brought the previous dynasty to power is not merely *princeps* but *optimus princeps*, overshadowing and outdoing Augustus and his successors. And as we saw, for Pliny *optimus princeps* has already morphed into *imperator optime* even before the title becomes official (*Ep.* 10.1).

76. On Tacitus's use of figured speech (for which I have been using the term *emphasis*) in the *Annals*, with particular reference to his account of the trial of Cremutius Cordus and the "digression" on his own difficulties with the writing of history that precedes and so informs it, see McHugh (2004). The *aliud latens* here is its commentary on the present. Cf. Roller (2012) 297–98.

REFERENCES

Ahl, F. M. 1984a. "The Art of Safe Criticism in Greece and Rome." *American Journal of Philology* 105: 174–208.

———. 1984b. "The Rider and the Horse: Politics and Power in Roman Poetry from Horace to Statius." *Aufstieg und Niedergang der Römischen Welt* II.32.1: 40–110.

Anderson, W. S. 1970. "*Lascivia* vs *ira*: Martial and Juvenal." *California Studies in Classical*

Antiquity 3: 1–34. Reprint in *Essays on Roman Satire*, 362–95. Princeton: Princeton University Press, 1982.

Armstrong, D. 2012. "*Juvenalis Eques*: A Dissident Voice from the Lower Tier of the Roman Elite." In *A Companion to Persius and Juvenal*, ed. S. M. Braund and J. Osgood, 59–78. Oxford: Blackwell.

Bartsch, S. 1994. *Actors in the Audience: Theatricality and Doublespeak from Nero to Hadrian*. Cambridge, MA: Harvard University Press.

Beard, M. and J. Henderson. 2001. *Classical Art: From Greece to Rome*. Oxford: Oxford University Press.

Bellandi, F. 2009 [1974]. "Naevolus *cliens*." In *Persius and Juvenal*, ed. M. Plaza, 469–505. Oxford: Oxford University Press.

Benker, M. 1987. *Achill und Domitian: Herrscherkritik in der Achilleis der Statius*. Erlangen-Nürnberg: Diss. Friedrich-Alexander-Universität.

Bennett, J. 1997. *Trajan Optimus Princeps: A Life and Times*. Bloomington: Indiana University Press.

Boyle, A. J. 1995. "*Martialis rediuiuus*: Evaluating the Unexpected Classic." *Ramus* 24: 82–101.

Boyle, A. J. and W. Dominik, eds. 2003. *Flavian Rome: Culture, Image, Text*. Leiden: Brill.

Braund, S. M., ed. 1996. *Juvenal: Satires, Book 1*. Cambridge: Cambridge University Press.

———. 2004. "*Libertas* or *licentia*? Freedom and Criticism in Roman Satire." In *Free Speech in Classical Antiquity*, ed. I. Sluiter and R. M. Rosen, 409–28. Leiden: Brill.

———. 2009 [1997]. "Declamation and Contestation in Satire." In *Persius and Juvenal*, ed. M. Plaza, 450–68. Oxford: Oxford University Press.

Braund, S. M. and J. Osgood, eds. 2012. *A Companion to Persius and Juvenal*. Oxford: Blackwell.

Citroni, M. 1988. "Pubblicazione e dediche dei libri in Marziale." *Maia* 40: 3–39.

Clark, G. and T. Rajak, eds. 2002. *Philosophy and Power in the Graeco-Roman World: Essays in Honour of Miriam Griffin*. Oxford: Oxford University Press.

Connors, C. 2005. "Epic Allusion in Roman Satire." In *The Cambridge Companion to Roman Satire*, ed. K. Freudenburg, 123–45. Cambridge: Cambridge University Press.

Courtney, E. 1980. *A Commentary on the Satires of Juvenal*. London: Athlone.

Deroux, C., ed. 2003. *Studies in Latin Literature and Roman History*. Vol. 11. Brussels: Latomus.

Eck, W. 2002. "An Emperor Is Made: Senatorial Politics and Trajan's Adoption by Nerva in 97." In *Philosophy and Power in the Graeco-Roman World: Essays in Honour of Miriam Griffin*, ed. G. Clark and T. Rajak, 211–26. Oxford: Oxford University Press.

Fearnley, H. 2003. "Reading the Imperial Revolution: Martial, *Epigrams* 10." In *Flavian Rome: Culture, Image, Text*, ed. A. J. Boyle and W. Dominik, 613–35. Leiden: Brill.

Fell, M. 1992. *Optimus Princeps? Anspruch und Wirklichkeit der imperialen Programmatik Kaiser Traians*. Munich: Tuduv.

Fowler, D. P. 1995. "Martial and the Book." *Ramus* 24: 31–58.

Freudenburg, K. 2001. *Satires of Rome: Threatening Poses from Lucilius to Juvenal*. Cambridge: Cambridge University Press.

———, ed. 2005. *The Cambridge Companion to Roman Satire*. Cambridge: Cambridge University Press.

Garthwaite, J. 1990. "Martial Book 6 on Domitian's Moral Censorship." *Prudentia* 22: 13–22.

———. 1993. "The Panegyrics of Domitian in Martial Book 9." *Ramus* 22: 78–102.

———. 1998. "Patronage and Poetic Immortality in Martial, Book 9." *Mnemosyne* 51: 161–75.

Grainger, J. D. 2003. *Nerva and the Roman Succession Crisis of AD 96–99*. London: Routledge.

Grewing, F., ed. 1998. *Toto notus in orbe: Perspektiven der Martial-Interpretation*. Stuttgart: Steiner.

Haynes, H. 2006. "Survival and Memory in the *Agricola*." *Arethusa* 39: 149–70.

Henderson, J. 1989. "Tacitus/The World in Pieces." *Ramus* 18: 167–210.

———. 1995. "Pump Up the Volume: Juvenal, *Satires* 1.1–21." *Proceedings of the Cambridge Philological Society* 41: 101–37.

———. 2001. "On Pliny on Martial on Pliny on Anon . . . (*Epistles* 3.21/*Epigrams* 10.19)." *Ramus* 30: 56–87.

Hershkowitz, D. 1995. "Pliny the Poet." *Greece and Rome* 42: 161–81.

Hinds, S. 1998. *Allusion and Intertext: Dynamics of Appropriation in Roman Poetry*. Cambridge: Cambridge University Press.

———. 2007. "Martial's Ovid/Ovid's Martial." *Journal of Roman Studies* 97: 113–54.

Howell, P. 1998. "Martial's Return to Spain." In *Toto notus in orbe: Perspektiven der Martial-Interpretation*, ed. F. Grewing, 173–86. Stuttgart: Steiner.

Jones, B. W., ed. and comm. 1996. *Suetonius: Domitian*. London: Bristol Classical Press.

Kay, N. M. 1985. *Martial Book XI: A Commentary*. London: Duckworth.

Kenney, E. J. 2012. "Satiric Textures: Style, Meter, and Rhetoric." In *A Companion to Persius and Juvenal*, ed. S. M. Braund and J. Osgood, 113–36. Oxford: Blackwell.

Mason, H. A. 1962. "Is Juvenal a Classic?" *Arion* 1 ser. 1.1: 8–44 and 1.2: 39–79. Reprint in *Critical Essays on Roman Literature: Satire*, ed. J. P. Sullivan, 93–176. London: Routledge & Kegan Paul, 1963.

Mayer, R., ed. 2001. *Tacitus: Dialogus de Oratoribus*. Cambridge: Cambridge University Press.

McHugh, M. R. 2004. "Historiography and Freedom of Speech: The Case of Cremutius Cordus." In *Free Speech in Classical Antiquity*, ed. I. Sluiter and R. M. Rosen, 391–408. Leiden: Brill.

Merli, E. 1993. "Ordinamento degli epigrammi e strategie cortigiane negli esordi dei libri I-XII de Marziale." *Maia* 45: 229–56.

Nauta, R. R. 2002. *Poetry for Patrons: Literary Communication in the Age of Domitian*. Leiden: Brill.

Pagán, V. 2004. "Speaking Before Superiors: Orpheus in Vergil and Ovid." In *Free Speech in Classical Antiquity*, ed. I. Sluiter and R. M. Rosen, 369–89. Leiden: Brill.

Penwill, J. L. 2000. "Quintilian, Statius and the Lost Epic of Domitian." *Ramus* 29: 60–83.

———. 2003. "'What's Hecuba to Him . . . ?': Reflections on Poetry and Politics in Tacitus' *Dialogue on Orators*." *Ramus* 32: 122–47.

———. 2013. "Imperial Encomia in Flavian Epic." In *Flavian Epic Interactions*, ed. G. Manuwald and A. Voigt, 29–54. Berlin: De Gruyter.

Pitcher, R. A. 1998. "Martial's Debt to Ovid." In *Toto notus in orbe: Perspektiven der Martial-Interpretation*, ed. F. Grewing, 59–76. Stuttgart: Steiner.

Plaza, M. 2006. *The Function of Humour in Roman Verse Satire*. Oxford: Oxford University Press.

———, ed. 2009. *Persius and Juvenal*. Oxford: Oxford University Press.

Ramage, E. S. 1989. "Juvenal and the Establishment: Denigration of Predecessors in the *Satires*." *Aufstieg und Niedergang Römischen Welt* 2.33.1: 640–707.

Reckford, K. 2009 [1962]. "Studies in Persius." In *Persius and Juvenal*, ed. M. Plaza, 17–56. Oxford: Oxford University Press.

Rimell, V. 2005. "The Poor Man's Feast: Juvenal." In *The Cambridge Companion to Roman Satire*, ed. K. Freudenburg, 81–94. Cambridge: Cambridge University Press.

Roche, P. A. 2003. "Mixed Messages: Trajan and the Propaganda of Personal Status." In *Studies in Latin Literature and Roman History*, vol. 11, ed. C. Deroux, 428–46. Brussels: Latomus.

Roller, M. 2012. "Politics and Invective in Persius and Juvenal." In *A Companion to Persius and Juvenal*, ed. S. M. Braund and J. Osgood, 283–311. Oxford: Blackwell.

Rutledge, S. 1998. "Trajan and Tacitus' Audience: Reader Reception of *Annals* 1–2." *Ramus* 27: 141–59.

Schmitz, C. 2000. *Das Satirische in Juvenals Satiren*. Berlin: De Gruyter.

Sear, F. 1998. *Roman Architecture*. 2nd ed. London: Routledge.

Shackleton Bailey, D. R., ed. and tr. 1993. *Martial Epigrams*. Cambridge, MA: Harvard University Press.

Sherwin-White, A. N. 1966. *The Letters of Pliny: A Historical and Social Commentary*. Oxford: Oxford University Press.

Shotter, D. C. A. 1983. "The Principate of Nerva: Some Observations on the Coin Evidence." *Historia* 32: 215–26.

Sluiter, I. and R. M. Rosen, eds. 2004. *Free Speech in Classical Antiquity*. Leiden: Brill.

Sullivan, J. P. 1978. "Ass's Ears and *Attises*: Persius and Nero." *American Journal of Philology* 99: 159–70.

———. 1991. *Martial: The Unexpected Classic*. Cambridge: Cambridge University Press.

Syme, R. 1958. *Tacitus*. Oxford: Oxford University Press.

Uden, J. 2011. "The Invisibility of Juvenal." PhD dissertation, Columbia University.

Waters, K. H. 1969. "Traianus Domitiani Continuator." *American Journal of Philology* 90: 385–405.

———. 1970. "Juvenal and the Reign of Trajan." *Antichthon* 4: 62–77.

Watson, L. and P. Watson, eds. and comm. 2003. *Martial: Select Epigrams*. Cambridge: Cambridge University Press.

Wehrle, W. 1992. *The Satiric Voice: Program, Form and Meaning in Persius and Juvenal.* Hildesheim: Olms-Weidmann.

Wilson, M. 2003. "After the Silence: Tacitus, Suetonius, Juvenal." In *Flavian Rome: Culture, Image, Text*, ed. A. J. Boyle and W. Dominik, 523–42. Leiden: Brill.

Winkler, M. M. 1995. "*Alogia* and *Emphasis* in Juvenal's Fourth *Satire*." *Ramus* 24: 59–81.

Wirszubski, C. 1950. *Libertas as a Political Idea at Rome During the Late Republic and Early Principate.* Cambridge: Cambridge University Press.

Chapter 10

Christian Correspondences: The Secrets of Letter-Writers and Letter-Bearers

Pauline Allen

There are so few who can carry a letter of any substance without lightening the weight by perusal.

—Cicero, *Letter to Atticus*

The importance and extent of letter-writing in late antiquity,[1] a period that for the purposes of this chapter encompasses the fourth, fifth, and sixth centuries, has been emphasized in recent scholarship.[2] This epistolary activity is all the more surprising given that in the classical period only eminent and politically active people like Cicero, Seneca, and Pliny the Younger could afford a private postal service.[3] Yet there is no general book on the subject of letter-writing in Christian antiquity, although a great deal of attention has recently been paid to travel and information transfer,[4] and to the role of the bishop in this period—not, however, as a letter-writer.[5] For the carriage of literary letters we still rely largely on the 1925 work of Denys Gorce.[6] It stands to reason that if epistolary practice flourished in late antiquity, there must have been a corresponding increase in the role of letter-bearers, and indeed they are mentioned prolifically in surviving episcopal letters, often by name.[7] The best example here is Paulinus of Nola (355–431), about two-thirds of whose letters contain references to the bearer.[8] Although bearers were the purveyors not only of the letter but often also of friendship (*philia/amicitia*) between writer and recipient, both the letter-writer *and* the letter-bearer could have secrets. Moreover, both parties were susceptible to various kinds of censorship because of political, ecclesiastical, or personal exigencies. In the following I examine the nature of the correspondences among Christians that raise issues of secrecy and self-censorship through veiled speech as strategies for circumventing or ensuring these, concentrating for the most part on the evidence provided by bishops' letters.[9] I deal in turn with the status of the bearer, the public/private and semiprivate nature of letters, verbal communication by the bearer, censorship and self-censorship in political, ecclesiastical, and personal contexts, and strategies for *parrhêsia* and avoidance of censorship.

Status of the Episcopal Letter-Carrier

Since the status of the letter-bearer could play a crucial role in the transfer of information as well as in furthering *philia/amicitia* between the letter-writer and the recipient, choosing the right person as carrier was a paramount consideration.[10] Ignatius of Antioch, who was martyred probably in the reign of Trajan (98–117 CE), writes to the community of Philadelphia that they should send a deacon on an embassy to the church of Antioch. This has been interpreted as normative for letter-carrying by deacons,[11] but Ignatius continues with the observation that other churches have sent bishops, and still others presbyters and deacons on the same mission.[12] In the correspondence of Bishop Cyprian of Carthage (249–58) we find subdeacons and acolytes as letter-carriers in exceptional circumstances and an insistence that church correspondence be conveyed by clerics.[13] From the fourth century onward there is an increasing number of deacons as bearers, which may be attributed to the development of the diaconate.[14] With regard to lay letter-bearers, some people were not allowed to carry certain types of letters. For example, Canon 11 of the Council of Chalcedon (451 CE) stipulated, "subject to examination, all paupers and needy persons are to travel with ecclesiastical letters or letters of peace only, and not of commendation, since it befits only reputable persons to be provided with letters of commendation."[15] This alerts us to the fact that there was a definite pecking order when a bishop chose letter-bearers, higher status and trustworthiness being generally preferred above availability. Mathilde Caltobiano suggests that a bishop first tried to recruit a bearer from the ranks of his clergy and only if that was unsuccessful did he look to other possibilities.[16] She also observes that, generally speaking, when the name of the bearer is given it is accompanied by a description of his or her rank or qualifications for the task.[17] Among the ranks of the clergy we find predominantly priests and deacons carrying letters, but there is also evidence of acolytes.[18] Readers and subdeacons, on the other hand, are just about nonexistent as letter-bearers.[19] There are many mentions of monks carrying letters: as just one example we could cite the unnamed monk who carried his own letter of recommendation from Severus, patriarch of Antioch 512–18, to Simeon, bishop of Chalcis.[20] In fact the letters of Paulinus of Nola and his friend Sulpicius Severus of Bordeaux (born c. 360) inform us that there were dedicated monk-couriers.[21] Paulinus's repeat bearer, the monk Victor, stayed with him in Nola for months at a time, performing various services from cooking, giving a haircut and a massage, to nursing Paulinus back to health.[22] There is also evidence of laypeople, including women, bearing letters.[23] Occasionally the letter-writer was obliged to use somebody of lowly status as the carrier of his own private letter of recommendation, as the following extract from a letter of Sidonius Apollinaris (born c. 431), bishop of Clermont-Ferrand, to his kinsman Simplicius illustrates:

> The bearer of this letter [*gerulus*] earnestly begs me to let him take a note from me to you. . . . I picture to myself how novel everything will be to this fellow, who is scarcely an enviable paragon of gentility, when you bid the stranger welcome in your home, the nervous messenger to a talk with you, the bumpkin to your gaiety, the poor man to your table. . . . And after all, although persons of that sort are generally insignificant creatures, yet in the matter of paying regard to our friends by letters affection loses much if it is deterred from indulging in more frequent correspondence by the lowliness of the bearers.[24]

Public/Private and Semiprivate Nature of Letters

Cicero's remark that few can carry a letter without lightening the weight by reading it,[25] or the assertion of the pagan Libanius (b. 314) that "any letter you get is immediately known to people here,"[26] holds true for late antiquity too[27]—which is why Margaret Mullett speaks of the "public intimacy" of the Byzantine letter.[28]

A passage in a letter of Gregory, bishop of Nyssa c. 372 to after 394, to Libanius illustrates the public role of the so-called private letter:

> For it so happened that on that day, as I was visiting the metropolis of the Cappadocians, I met one of my acquaintances who handed me this gift, your letter, as a feast-day present. I was overjoyed at this good fortune and threw open my gain to all who were present. All shared in it, each eagerly acquiring the whole of it, while I was none the worse off. For the letter, as it passed through the hands of all became the private wealth of each, some by memorizing the words through repeated reading, others by taking a copy of them upon tablets. So it returned to my hands.[29]

In one letter Synesius (born c. 370–75), bishop of Cyrene in North Africa, writing to his friend Pylamenes, explains that he has hired a theater to have a public reading of Pylamenes' letter,[30] and refers to letters being read out in the Panhellenion in Constantinople.[31] In another letter, written to his brother in Alexandria, Synesius assumes that his work will be read aloud before the patriarch of that city and his staff.[32] Small wonder, then, that Synesius says he cannot believe it is a good thing to confide secrets to paper, because the function of a letter is to speak to the first comer, not to keep quiet.[33] To another one of his friends, Diogenes, Synesius writes that the addressee has the gift of not only communicating daily affairs by letter but also of having his letters known and admired.[34] The wide dissemination of letters could also act as a guarantee of *parrhêsia*, as Severus of Antioch points out: "How can it not be right that we should also proclaim openly in words the things that we in actual practice think and do?"[35] The near hopelessness of keeping correspondence private is mentioned by Augustine, bishop of Hippo 396–428, as he laments that his writings cannot be kept from those whose minds are not too trained or sharp, who therefore could misconstrue them.[36] If we are to believe Libanius, there were even those (like himself) who took advantage of the public nature of letters: "Well, even if you do not write to me, I feast on your letters, for whenever I find out that anyone has received one, I present myself forthwith, and either by persuasion or by overpowering his reluctance I get to read it."[37] Indeed it was difficult to distinguish between private and official letters.[38] Given that the service of the bearers was at a premium, they would carry both official and personal post at the same time; moreover, it was not uncommon for letters to be copied along the way, thus rendering the distinction between public and private null and void, as the cause célèbre in the correspondence between Augustine and Jerome demonstrates (see in more detail below). Underlying this blurring of the private and public sphere is the absence of any idea of copyright in classical and Christian antiquity, as pointed out by Tornau.[39]

Verbal Communication by the Bearer: Evidence

In a letter to his friend Firminus, Ennodius, bishop of Pavia (b. 474), writes, "I count among the heavenly benefits the good news about you that I have learned from the mouth of the bearer,"[40] a comment that highlights the significance of the parallel line of communication to the written word. Against the backdrop of the public/private or semiprivate nature of antique letters, the need for unwritten information becomes evident. Gillett points to the "oratorical nature of diplomatic missions" in classical Greece and Rome, where envoys were given something written to deliver, but also gave an oral report, for the function of the envoy was negotiation and advocacy, a practice that extended into official episcopal correspondence in late antiquity and beyond.[41] Synesius's comment that a long letter speaks against the familiarity of the bearer with the letter-writer,[42] and Augustine's description of his bearer as "perfidelissimus" even if he carried no letter suggest that the carriage of oral information was the norm rather than the exception.[43] This would particularly be the case when the bearer stayed with the recipient in a situation of *philia/amicitia* for some days before returning with an answer or leaving for other destinations.

In one of his letters Bishop Basil of Caesarea (born c. 330, d. 379) begs off going into details lest the letter become too long (a topos of the epistolographical genre); instead the trustworthy bearer, who has been handpicked, will supplement the information verbally, adding what Basil has forgotten as well.[44] That entrusting verbal information to a bearer could, however, have an infelicitous outcome is illustrated by another of Basil's letters, where it is revealed that the bearer was too upset to convey clearly the distressing news that he was to communicate *viva voce*.[45] In a letter of recommendation by Gregory of Nyssa carried by the recommendee, the author states that the bearer will tell the recipient everything himself, because that is more suitable than going into details in a letter.[46] In fact this is a common technique in letters of recommendation, the topos being that the bearer/recommendee is in a better position to give his personal details than is the letter-writer. So Sidonius Apollinaris: "The present note recommends to you a Jew. . . . It is best that he should tell you with his own lips in a personal interview the whole story of his trouble; for it is unwise to swell with discursive talk the trim compactness proper to the epistolary style."[47] Elsewhere Sidonius expresses the belief that "the most effective recommendation of a person comes from one who has disclosed the precise reasons that justify his recommendation."[48]

Writing to Patriarch Theophilus of Alexandria, Synesius of Cyrene explains that the bearer is being dispatched to carry out business that Synesius cannot specify,[49] and in another communication to Theophilus he comments that the disastrous situation in Pentapolis cannot be described in a letter and will be conveyed by the bearer.[50] The correspondence of Ruricius, who became bishop of Limoges in 485, contains at least two mentions of bearers setting out with only verbal messages. In one case he mentions a messenger who delivered a communication to him orally rather than bringing a letter; and in a second case he receives a bearer who conveys information orally.[51] In the first case Ruricius writes, "Our brother and fellow-priest Capillutus, although he did not deliver your words to me relegated to a written letter, nevertheless exhibited them instead written in his heart, whence no thief can steal them nor brigand snatch them nor tempest eradicate them nor old age erase them."[52] For his part Ennodius of Pavia explains prettily that rather than burden his noble bearer, Pamfronius, with packets of written material, he could have him fulfill the function of the letter by reporting verbally, the more so since Pamfronius is better acquainted with Ennodius's feelings than with his words.[53] This letter was, however, written nonetheless.

Censorship and Self-Censorship in Political Contexts

Sometimes the oral information conveyed by the bearer was the product of either caution or familiarity; on other occasions it was a shortcut on the part of the letter-writer, particularly, as we have seen, in letters of recommendation carried by the person recommended. However, even the carriage of unwritten information was not without its dangers to the bearer, as Sidonius Apollinaris reports. He is referring in the following extract to the procedures of a "thought-police," particularly in Visigothic-occupied Gaul:

> A courier [*tabellarius*] can by no means pass the guards of the public highroads without a strict scrutiny; he may indeed incur no

> danger, being free from guilt, but he usually experiences a great deal of difficulty, as the watchful searcher pries into every secret of the letter-carriers [*gerulorum*], and if their answers to their questions should happen to show the least nervousness [see also Chapter 12 in the present volume], they are believed to carry verbally in their heads the messages not committed to writing; thus the man sent often suffers ill-treatment and the sender acquires an ill name, more particularly in these days when the established treaties of kingdoms long jealous of one another are made unstable by fresh conditions tending to produce discord.[54]

Mathisen's article on prudence shows Sidonius's self-censorship, both in his letters and in his poems, on the topic of the emperor Avitus.[55] Bishop Avitus of Vienne (c. 490–518) writes to his brother Apollinaris an intentionally imprecise letter referring to Ostrogoths under Alaric II marauding in the Rhone valley, and their impending defeat by Clovis. Avitus also hints at a more open letter to follow.[56] Like Bishop Ruricius of Limoges (elected 485), who is generally reticent about the current state of affairs in his jurisdiction where Visigoths were in the ascendant,[57] Avitus is vague (probably deliberately) about political circumstances. Schanzer and Wood speak of his "maddeningly and deliberately vague allusions to circumambient troubles,"[58] and Zelzer reminds us that in such times writers were inclined to disperse various historical allusions throughout their letters, rather than run the risk of writing a proper history.[59] Indeed the biography that Bishop Ennodius of Pavia wrote of his predecessor, Bishop Epiphanius, has much to tell us about the shifting frontiers in the West during the reigns of Germanic kings, a situation often exacerbated by Arian-catholic animosity or distrust.[60]

Censorship and Self-Censorship in Ecclesiastical Contexts

The episcopal letter was one of the chief means of dealing with ecclesiastical situations. In the hands of Cyril, patriarch of Alexandria 412–44, it was a tool for suppressing the views of his enemies, particularly those associated with the see of Antioch. Writing to Bishop John of Antioch and a synod assembled in that city, Cyril says, "We, however, urge you, as brothers and fellow teachers, to command the clerics not to say anything else especially in the churches except true and approved doctrines and those which are judged to be good and to follow rather the confessions of the true faith, and especially not to run after discussions concerning these subjects."[61] Elsewhere in a letter to clerics Cyril recounts that he has written to Bishop John of Antioch with the message that nobody should preach in church the teachings of Theodore of Mopsuestia,[62] while Bishop Rabbula of Edessa, writing to Cyril, accused Theodore of placing an *anathema* at the beginning of his works so that his readers would not divulge the (heretical) contents to others.[63]

The role of episcopal envoys was crucial in resolving or protracting ecclesiastical debates, especially in times of schism. In tricky matters of ecclesiastical politics Bishop Leo I of Rome (440–61), for example, entrusted confidential information to his bearers that they were to convey verbally.[64] In a letter written to Patriarch Flavian of Constantinople, Leo explains that the Roman envoys had left before Leo received Flavian's letter through the Roman deacon, Basil. Flavian's letter had clearly skated over important issues that Basil was able to inform Leo about verbally.[65] In another letter to Flavian Leo writes, "The bearer of this note will surely be able to give you an accurate report of the goal toward which we are striving."[66] On March 21, 458, Leo's legates were sent to Emperor Leo to act as his representatives and explain all points of faith.[67] Verbal reports by envoys are in fact taken for granted, as we see in three letters that Leo sent on the same day (June 13, 449) to different recipients in Constantinople: his envoys are to take his place in conducting unspecified business.[68]

The number of envoys between Rome and Constantinople must have increased substantially during the schism (484–518) around Acacius, the patriarch of Constantinople deposed by Pope Felix. Pope Hormisdas sent at least two missions to the East, the first in July 515 and the second in August 519. On each occasion the letter sent with the envoys was accompanied by an *indiculus*, a list of detailed instructions concerning the conduct of the envoys before their reception by the emperor and the pursuit of their case during their audience with him.[69] These remarkable documents give us precious insights into the conduct of high-ranking late antique diplomatic missions and the triumph of secrecy, self-censorship, and veiled speech over *parrhêsia*. The envoys are instructed minutely to communicate with the eastern bishops in the welcoming party and to accept lodging and travel, but to decline with "smooth excuses" ("blanda excusatione") any invitations to meals or parties.[70] They are to keep the purpose of their mission secret until the official audience with the emperor, and even when he enquires about the contents of the letter they are carrying, they must demur until he has opened the sealed letter and read it. Hormisdas then gives details of possible conversational scenarios, along the lines of "should the emperor say this, you are to make this reply." How realistic these marching orders were, however, is uncertain: Gillett suggests that "Hormisdas' instructions may have been intended more as an exhortation to his envoys than a practical guide to what could be expected at the eastern imperial court."[71]

In other difficult ecclesiastical circumstances there is often no explicit reference to the dramatis personae, as we see, for example, in the correspondence of Theodoret, bishop of Cyrrhus in Syria (423–49), where, while clerics may have accused each other, they have not done so by name.[72] Again, while Ennodius, deacon in Milan before becoming bishop of Pavia, was deeply involved in the schism around Laurentius, bishop of Milan, he makes no explicit mention in his letters about schism. There are only veiled references to the unhappiness of the times or the evils inflicted by enemies, and at one point where Ennodius relates the illness of his bishop, Laurentius, this malady is meant to be understood figuratively as the threat of the schismatics.[73] We know too of the activities of the major-domos (managers of private households) as confidential letter-bearers during the same schism.[74]

The type of letter that is indiscriminately called "festal," namely those letters that particularly in Gaul, Syria, and Cappadocia were sent on important feast days like Epiphany and Easter and were often accompanied by gifts emphasizing the friendship, real or aspirational, between sender and recipient, tend to be written from bishop to bishop and to be vague, clichéd, and short. As Adam Schor observes, while these pieces are like greeting cards, communicating "the safest sentiments," they had a definite social purpose, evoking as they did "the consensus of faith."[75] Despite their veiled terms, they included the recipient in the liturgical life of the church at important times during the year. The Alexandrian festal letter was a different type altogether, being sent by the Alexandrian patriarchs throughout Egypt and often abroad to announce authoritatively and well in advance the dates of the following Lent, Easter, and Pentecost and to deal with disciplinary or doctrinal issues.[76] These compositions were mass media events.[77] Here we find little that is obfuscatory or vague, but on the contrary often a brutal and totalitarian exercise of episcopal power, hence the attempts allegedly made by the Arians to suppress the dissemination of the eleventh festal letter of the exiled patriarch, Athanasius of Alexandria (295–373).[78]

Censorship and Self-Censorship Related to Personal Contexts

Self-censorship, obfuscation, and even suppression of the facts were common particularly in personal situations in classical and Christian late antiquity. We know, for example, how in his letters the pagan Libanius deliberately avoided damaging details that might have involved him in accusations of treason that had befallen other eminent Antiochenes of his time.[79] Exile imposed its own form of censorship, as can be seen from the case of John Chrysostom, whose 237 surviving letters derive solely from his period of banishment in Armenia (404–7).[80] Initially, in his letters to a wide circle of friends, colleagues, and spiritual advisees, John is ostensibly optimistic about returning to Constantinople, but as his isolation wears on, attempts at his rehabilitation are thwarted, and his circle of correspondents contracts, he confines himself in the few letters written toward the end of his life to banal details of his health—a mild case of self-censorship.[81]

A more serious case of exile is that of Severus, anti-Chalcedonian patriarch of Antioch (512–18), who fled into exile in Egypt after the Chalcedonian restoration of Emperor Justin I in 518.[82] Several of Severus's letters give graphic details of the life he led in his twenty-year exile, living in hiding and being moved from place to place. He was, however, able to maintain his epistolary network during this time and even composed a major theological tractate, although he reveals in his correspondence that he had to backdate this work and pretend that it had been written while he was still in patriarchal office (and thus still a legally recognized citizen of the Roman Empire). Severus's writings received the ultimate form of censorship in 536 when his person was condemned by synodical decree and imperial edict and his works were ordered to be burned. Thanks to his followers, however, the major part of them was translated into Syriac and survives to us in this form, as a kind of underground literature. The negative consequences of banishment or relegation on *parrhêsia* can also be seen by the fact that Bishop Gregory I of Rome (590–604), sending a synodical letter to his friend, the deposed patriarch of Antioch, Anastasius, gave the bearer other information to convey secretly, lest Gregory cause further trouble for the bishop, who had been banished because of imperial displeasure.[83]

Strategies for *Parrhêsia* and the Avoidance of Censorship

Apart from entrusting the bearer with verbal information, there were other strategies that letter-writers could employ to ensure the safety and authenticity of the contents of their letters. Although most bishops had a number of stenographers to whom they dictated their letters, the author's handwriting was prized as a guarantee of authenticity in an age where forgery and tampering were rife. Thus Basil of Caesarea writes to his correspondent that the autograph greeting in the letter he received was worth more than many letters.[84]

Augustine of Hippo denounces one letter he has received as a forgery,[85] and tells us of a synodical letter from a group of bishops, who, in order to bolster their numbers on paper, inserted the name of a dead bishop in the list of signatories.[86] Because of the labor-intensive nature of writing letters by longhand (and bishops often complained about their workloads), it sometimes happened that the writer inserted a message in his own hand in the body of the letter or at the end. After all, this was good classical practice, for Cicero began dictating one of his letters to Atticus, then went on to say: "But here I go back on my own hand, for what follows is confidential."[87] By way of exaggeration Bishop Ambrose of Milan (d. 397) replies to Emperor Gratian that in the letter he has received, written entirely in the emperor's hand, the very punctuation marks indicate the writer's faith and conviction,[88] and to Emperor Theodosius Ambrose writes at the end, "Lastly I am writing with my own hand what you alone are to read."[89]

After the letter that Augustine wrote to Jerome in 394/395 was delivered some nine years later,[90] having done the rounds and become public property in Italy and other places—a case of extreme *parrhêsia* to the wrong audience—the bishop of Hippo was forced into damage-control. In the meantime Jerome learnt with great displeasure that Augustine had attacked him in a book. In 398 Augustine wrote again to Jerome,[91] and again the letter did not arrive. Instead it was found the following year on an island in the Adriatic, where it was copied and sent on to its intended recipient. In the epistolary altercation that ensued between the two men, Jerome complained that Augustine's letters arrived without signature.[92] The bishop of Hippo was forced to take further measures: "But whatever opportunity next comes along for me, I will take care, with the help of the Lord, to send copies of all the same letters signed by my hand to Your Fraternity. I order that you may know and write back to me not only whether they were all delivered to you but whether they arrived whole and without error."[93] During his protracted debates with the schismatic Donatists Augustine sent a letter to Theodore, a deacon in Carthage, written in his own hand and explaining his policy with regard to the reception of the Donatists into the church. The deacon was to show this authentic letter to anyone who asked.[94] On another occasion, at the end of a letter to the Arian count Pascentius as part of an ongoing theological debate in which Pascentius was accused of falsifying the written record, Augustine adds carefully: "Augustine has signed this document, which I dictated and reread."[95] Avitus of Vienne speaks of kissing the signature rather than the hand of his absent correspondent.[96] The importance of authentic signatures, together with straight language, in times of ecclesiastical turbulence is also illustrated by a letter of Leo of Rome, who was trying to regulate the reception of heretics into the church: "Let them announce in complete and frank statements, signed by their own hands, that they also completely agree with those decrees. Let nothing obscure be found in their language, nothing ambiguous. For we know that they are clever in this way: they think that none of their views is in jeopardy when they have kept distinct from the main body of the heresy some particular point of teaching that should be condemned."[97] The seal ring was another mechanism for ensuring that a letter was not tampered with, but the recipient needed to be sure that the seal too was authentic. Thus Augustine instructs, "I have sent this letter sealed with the seal that imprints the face of a man looking sideways,"[98] and Avitus of Vienne writes to his brother Apollinaris, bishop of Valence, with instructions for the crafting of his seal ring, which will have a swivel, bear Avitus's monogram written in a circle, and depict the tails of two dolphins at its bezel.[99] If the recipient was in doubt about the authenticity of what he received, he could seek clarification from the purported author of the letter, as did Synesius, for example, who, on encountering a letter seemingly with the signature of his friend Olympius, was suspicious because the document was old, eaten by worms, and almost unreadable.[100]

Despite such precautions, however, hijacking of letters or other documentation was not unheard of. In a letter to his friend Faustus, Sidonius Apollinaris describes the visit of Faustus's messenger to his house with gifts in his baggage. It was only after the messenger left that Sidonius was told of other more valuable literary gifts in the man's baggage that he had not handed over. Sidonius overtook him on horseback, undid his baggage, found the book he wanted, and gleefully proceeded to make extracts from it.[101] Avitus relates how one of his own works was "snatched away from the very hand of the scribe, as yet unproofread and unfinished by me, so that you cannot easily tell whether to be angry at the faults of the author or those of the copyist."[102]

While both these episodes reflect the avidity with which literary works in late antiquity were sought out and read, rather than sinister motives, they illustrate once again that very little of what was written was safe.

Concluding Observations

One of the most important aspects of antique Christian letter-writing that emerges is its relationship to *philia/amicitia*.[103] As Ennodius expresses it, "conversation by letter is the handmaid of a relationship."[104] Although Synesius's statement cited above, to the effect that a long letter speaks against the familiarity of the bearer with the letter-writer, may be tongue-in-cheek,[105] this sentiment sums up a great deal of late antique letter-writing. The preferred scenario, as we have seen, is a bearer who is deliberately chosen, trusted, and familiar to the letter-writer and possibly also to the recipient;[106] otherwise it is simply someone who is around and available at the right time. In the first case the bearer is the purveyor of *philia/amicitia*; in the second case, the product of a hit-and-miss process that could go wrong. (We need think of only the correspondence of Augustine and Jerome.) One way of bolstering *philia/amicitia* and ensuring *parrhêsia* was the sending of gifts with the bearer; another was the provision of hospitality at the bearer's destination.[107] All of this encouraged verbal communication of controversial, important or personal news, a strategic process in which the interception or censorship of the written message was circumvented. Trusted bearers, verbal information, veiled speech, signet rings, autographed and signed letters, and, in the case of papal envoys, elaborate diplomatic processes went some way to ensure free speech in ancient Christian correspondences,[108] but even letters that were preserved intact were not immune from further censorship, albeit often of an involuntary or unwitting kind. For example, the letters of Firmus of Caesarea, a Cappadocian bishop who attended the Council of Ephesus in 431, date from a period of only a few months and owe their survival to being included in a later collection that showcased pearls of Byzantine literature.[109] In the case of the sophist Dionysius, active in Antioch at the end of the fifth century, a later scribe truncated his letters, reducing them to enigmatic notes.[110] And Severus of Antioch suffered a double kind of posthumous censorship, his huge body of condemned letters being translated into Syriac and reduced to about one-fifteenth of their size by a compiler who was interested mainly in matters of canonical discipline.[111]

NOTES

1. Epigraph: Cicero, *Ep.* 13.1 (I.13) to Atticus: "Quotus enim quisque est qui epistularum paulo graviorem ferre possit nisi eam perlectione relevarit?"; ed. and tr. Shackleton Bailey (1990/1999), 1:60–61.

2. Gillett (2012); Ebbeler (2009) 271. Mullett (1997) 11n3 notes that if fourth- and fifth-century Greek letters were excluded from the tally of Byzantine letters, the total number would drop sharply.

3. See Mratschek (2002) 286.

4. See, e.g., Casson (1994); Mratschek (1996) 165–72; Paola (1999); Kolb (2000); Ellis and Kidner (2004); Leyerle (2009) 110–23; Sotinel (2004) 63–71; Sotinel (2009) 125–26.

5. See, for example, Lizzi (1987); Rebillard and Sotinel (1998); Sterk (2004); Rapp (2005); Lizzi (2009) 525–38.

6. Gorce (1925) 191–247.

7. The majority of these, mostly excepting the clergy, are picked up in Martindale (2006a) and (2006b).

8. See Perrin (1992) 1026–27.

9. See Allen (2010b) 130–42.

10. See in more detail Allen (2013).

11. E.g., Davies (1963) 7, followed by Clarke (1984) 1:205.

12. See *Ad Phil.* 10, ed. Holmes (2007) 244–45.

13. See further Clarke (1984) 1:205, 225.

14. This is suggested by Gorce (1925) 211–12. Disappointingly there is nothing on clerics as letter-bearers in Patsavos (2007).

15. Tanner (1990) 1:92.

16. Caltobiano (2001a) 114.

17. Caltobiano (2001a) 116.

18. Augustine, *Epp.* 191, 193, and 194, writes of the Roman acolyte, Albinus, as a repeat bearer. Cf. Gorce (1925) 211 and Paoli-Lafaye (2002) 242–43 on repeat bearers (the latter on Augustine's carriers Innocentius and Firmus). Mathisen (1979) 174 notes that Ruricius's priest-friend Capillutus was "a one-man postal service," carrying *Epp.* 2.21, 31, 33, and 40.

19. As observed by Gorce (1925) 211.

20. *Ep.* 1.37; ed. Brooks (1902/1969) 1:117–19 [text]; (1903/1969) 2:104–6 [tr.].

21. See further Perrin (1992) 1030, 1032, 1034, and 1036.

22. *Ep.* 23.6–9 (cooking), 5 (massage), 10 (haircut); *Ep.* 28.3 (nursing); ed. CSEL 29, 162–67, 161–62, 167–68, 263–64.

23. See further Allen (2013).

24. *Ep.* 4.7.1–3; ed. and tr. Anderson (1997) 2:89. Cf. *Ep.* 6.10 on a deacon-bearer of low status.

25. *Ep.* 13.1 to Atticus. See note 1 above.

26. *Ep.* 16; ed. and tr. Norman (1969) 401.

27. It is often difficult to distinguish between the public and private spheres, as pointed out by Paoli-Lafaye (2002) 235. On papal envoys in general, see Gillett (2003) 227–58.

28. Mullett (1997) 17.

29. Gregory of Nyssa, *Ep.* 14.3–4 to Libanius; ed. Maraval (1990) 202.15–204.25; tr. Silvas (2007) 157.

30. *Ep.* 101; ed. Garzya and Roques (2000) 2:224.

31. *Ep.* 101; ed. Garzya and Roques (2000) 2:227.

32. *Ep.* 105; ed. Garzya and Roques (2000) 2:238.

33. *Ep.* 137 to Herculian; ed. Garzya and Roques (2000) 2:277. Cf. Tornau (2006) 35 on the absence of copyright or confidentiality in late antiquity. On the public reading of letters, see too Constable (1976) 11–12; Trapp (2003) 17.

34. *Ep.* 23; ed. Garzya and Roques (2000) 1:30.

35. *Ep.* 1.55; tr. Brooks (1903/1969) 2:166–67. *Ep.* 29 of the emperor Julian contains similar sentiments.

36. *Ep.* 162.1; NBA 22, 670; tr. Teske (2004) 3:56.

37. *Ep.* 86; ed. and tr. Norman (1969) 2:109.

38. See Paoli-Lafaye (2002) 235.

39. Tornau (2006) 35.

40. Ennodius, *Ep.* 2.7.5; ed. Gioanni (2006) 1:59.

41. Gillett (2003) 11–26. For the later period, see Mullett (1997) 36–37. See below on ecclesiastical contexts.

42. *Ep.* 55; ed. Garzya and Roques (2000) 1:73. Same idea in *Ep.* 84, *verbatim*.

43. *Ep.* 186.1; NBA 23, 78–80; tr. Teske (2004) 3:209. See Mratschek (2011) 109–22. Cf. Basil, *Ep.* 240; ed. Deferrari (1930) 3:449, whose bearer, he says, would have been able to give an accurate report of the situation even without a letter.

44. *Ep.* 203; ed. Deferrari (1930) 3:153.

45. *Ep.* 5; ed. Deferrari (1926) 1:33.

46. *Ep.* 8.5; ed. Maraval (1990) 176.25–27; tr. Silvas (2007) 145.

47. *Ep.* 6.11; ed. and tr. Anderson (1997) 2:277. Note again the topos regarding the length of the letter.

48. *Ep.* 8.13; ed. and tr. Anderson (1997) 2:483–84.

49. *Ep.* 68; ed. Garzya and Roques (2000) 2:189.

50. *Ep.* 69; ed. Garzya and Roques (2000) 2:190.

51. *Epp.* 2.40 and 2.64; MGH AA 8, 341, and 350, respectively.

52. *Ep.* 40; MGH AA 8, 341.5–7; tr. Mathisen (1999) 211. See below on the occupational hazards of letter-bearing.

53. *Ep.* 2.16.1; ed. Gioanni (2006) 1:70.

54. *Ep.* 9.3.2; ed. and tr. Anderson (1997) 2:509–10.

55. Mathisen (1979) 165–71.

56. *Ep.* 87 in the numbering of Schanzer and Wood (2002) 251–57.

57. See Neri (2009) 12.

58. Schanzer and Wood (2002) 79.

59. Zelzer (1994) 548–49.

60. *Vita Epiphanii*; ed. MGH AA 7: 84–109; tr. Deferrari (1952) 301–51. On this *vita* and the caveats to be kept in mind while using it, see Gillett (2003) 148–71, 169.

61. *Ep.* 67; ed. Schwartz, ACO 1/1.4: 37–39; tr. McEnerney (1987) 65.

62. *Ep.* 70; ed. Schwartz (1927) 16–17; tr. McEnerney (1987) 68–69.

63. *Ep.* 73; ed. Schwartz, ACO 4/1: 89 (text extant only in Latin); tr. McEnerney (1987) 76.

64. E.g., *Epp.* 67 and 85. *Ep.* 67; ed. Silva-Tarouca (1935) 20:157–88; *Ep.* 85; ed. Silva-Tarouca (1934) 15:71.

65. *Ep.* 38; ed. Silva-Tarouca (1934) 15:24–25; tr. Hunt (1957) 118.

66. *Ep.* 49; ed. Schwartz, ACO 2/4, 23; tr. Hunt (1957) 128.

67. *Ep.* 164; ed. Silva-Tarouca (1935) 20:165–68, and Schwartz, ACO 2/4, 105–7; tr. Hunt (1957) 252–56.

68. *Epp.* 28, 29, and 30; ed. Schwartz, ACO 2/2: 24–33, Silva-Tarouca (1934) 15:4–5, and Silva-Tarouca (1934) 15:19–21 = Schwartz, ACO 2/4: 15, respectively.

69. *Ep.* 6 with *Ep.* 7 (*seu indiculus*) and *Ep.* 48 with *Ep.* 49 (*seu indiculus*); ed. Thiel (2004) 747–55, 837–40. On the function of the two *indiculi*, see Gillett (2003) 227–30, with further literature at 227n21.

70. *Ep.* 7.1; ed. Thiel (2004) 748.

71. Gillett (2003) 230.

72. Schor (2011) 35.

73. *Ep.* 1.3.14; ed. Gioanni (2006) 1:30. See also the editor's remarks in his introduction, 1, LXXXVII–LXXXVIII, on Ennodius's obfuscatory techniques: "Il faut donc chercher des indices discrets ou des allusions sibyllines."

74. Barnwell (1992) 141–42.

75. Schor (2011) 34. Cf. Mullett's evaluation of the Byzantine letter (1997) 23–31; Hatlie (1996) 221 on deliberate obscurity.

76. See Külzer (1998) 379–90; Allen (2010a) 195–210; Allen (2014). The two types of festal letters are not distinguished by the following scholars: Brok (1951) 101–10; Calvet-Sebasti (2009) 67–81. Schor (2011) 33–34 recognizes the difference. Wagner (1948) 133 mistakenly asserts that the custom of sending festal letters was local to the area of Cyrrhus.

77. This is the term used by Banev (2007) xii–xiii.

78. For details see Allen (2014).

79. See Liebeschuetz (1972) 18–22.

80. See Delmaire (1991) 71–180; idem (2009) 283–91.

81. See Delmaire (1991) 290.

82. On the life and work of Severus, see Allen and Hayward (2004); Alpi (2009); idem (2010) 333–48.

83. *Ep.* 1.25; ed. CCSL 140, 33–34 at 33.32–34; tr. Martyn (2004) 1:148.

84. *Ep.* 146; ed. and tr. Deferrari (1928) 2:353.

85. *Ep.* 22*.11; NBA 23A Supp., 202.

86. *Ep.* 141.1; NBA 22, 308–10. See further Speyer (1971) 171–295.

87. *Ep.* 234 (XI.24.2); ed. and tr. Shackleton Bailey (1990) 1:57.3–5: "Sed ad manum meam redeo; erunt enim haec occultius agenda."

88. *Ep.* 12.3 *extra collectionem*; ed. CSEL 82, 219–21 at 220.26–28; tr. Liebeschuetz and Hill (2010) 275.

89. *Ep.* 11.14 *extra collectionem*; ed. CSEL 82, 212–18 at 217.126; tr. Liebeschuetz and Hill (2010) 268.

90. *Ep.* 28; NBA 21/1, 172–81.

91. *Ep.* 40; NBA 21/1, 302–13.

92. *Ep.* 72.1; NBA 21/2, 572–73. On the whole episode, see Allen (2006) 120–21 with lit.

93. *Ep.* 19*.4; NBA 23A, 158; tr. Teske (2005) 4:298.

94. *Ep.* 61.1; NBA 21/1, 518–19; tr. Teske (2001) 1:245.

95. *Ep.* 238.29; NBA 23, 800–801; tr. Teske (2005) 4:155: "Huic scripturae a me dictatae et relectae ego Augustinus subscripsi."

96. *Ep.* 92 (numbering of Schanzer and Wood 2002); MGH AA 6/2, 99.30–31; tr. Schanzer and Wood (2002) 241.

97. *Ep.* 1; PL 54, 594B; tr. Hunt (1957) 20.

98. *Ep.* 59.2; NBA 21/1, 512; tr. Teske (2001) 1:242.

99. *Ep.* 87 9 (in the numbering of Schanzer and Wood 2002); MGA AA 6/2, 96–97; tr. and comm. Schanzer and Wood (2002) 251–57.

100. *Ep.* 133; ed. Garzya and Roques (2000) 2:270.

101. *Ep.* 9.9.6–9; ed. and tr. Anderson (1997) 2:535–39.

102. *Ep.* 51 (numbering in Schanzer and Wood 2002); ed. MGH AA 6/2, 80.28–32; tr. Schanzer and Wood (2002) 345.

103. On the topos of epistolary friendship, see Thraede (1970) 125–46; White (1992); Pizzolato (1993) (mostly classical); Konstan (1996); Konstan (1997); Fitzgerald (1997). I deal with the nexus between letter-writing and *philia/amicitia* at greater length in Allen (2013).

104. Ennodius, *Ep.* 2.26.1; ed. Gioanni (2006) 1:80: "ministra affectionis est epistolaris confabulatio."

105. *Ep.* 55; ed. Garzya and Roques (2000) 1:73. Same idea in *Ep.* 84; ed. Garzya and Roques (2000) 1:209.

106. See Caltobiano (2001a) 140–42 on Augustine's choices of bearers.

107. Gorce (1991) 191–247 is still important on these aspects. Cf. also Allen (2013).

108. Konstan (1997) 15–17, 22, 112, 150–53, 155–56, speaks about the necessity in

classical correspondence for *parrhêsia*, which he also terms "self-disclosure." This seems to be at odds with the sometimes obfuscatory or terse letters of Christian antiquity and the tension between the private/public or semiprivate aspects of correspondence.

109. See Calvet-Sebasti and Gatier (1989) 10–13, 19–26, for the details.

110. See Gatier (2009) 115–23.

111. See further Allen (1999) 388–90.

REFERENCES

Primary Sources and Translations

Ambrose of Milan. *Letters*. Ed. Michaela Zelzer. *Sancti Ambrosi Opera pars X. Epistulae et acta* (CSEL 82). Vienna: Hoelder-Pichler-Tempsky, 1954/82. Tr. J. H. W. G. Liebeschuetz with Carole Hill, *Ambrose of Milan: Political Letters and Speeches*. Translated Texts for Historians 43. Liverpool: Liverpool University Press, 2010.

Augustine of Hippo. *Letters*. *Opere di San Agostino. Le Lettere*. Nuova Biblioteca Agostiniana 21/1, 21/2, 22, 23, 23A. Rome: Città Nuova Editrice, 1969–92.

———. *Letters*. *The Works of Saint Augustine. A Translation for the 21st Century*. Hyde Park NY: New City Press, 2001–2005. Tr. R. Teske. *Letters* 1–99, vol. II/1, 2001; *Letters* 156–210, vol. II/3, 2004; *Letters* 211–270, 1*–29*, vol. II/4, 2005.

Avitus of Vienne. Ed. Rudolphus Peiper, *Alcimi Ecdicii Aviti Viennensis episcopi opera quae supersunt*. MGH AA 6/2. Berlin: Weidmann, 1883/1961. Tr. and intro. Danuta Schanzer and Ian Wood, *Avitus of Vienne: Letters and Selected Prose*. Liverpool: Liverpool University Press, 2002.

Basil of Caesarea. Ed. and tr. Roy J. Deferrari, *Saint Basil: The Letters*, 4 vols. LCL. London: William Heinemann, 1926–34.

Cicero. *Letters to Atticus*. Ed. and tr. David R. Shackleton Bailey. LCL 7, 8, 97. Cambridge, MA: Harvard University Press, 1990, 1999.

Cyprian of Carthage. Tr. Graeme W. Clarke, *The Letters of St. Cyprian of Carthage I. Letters 1–27*. Ancient Christian Writers 43. New York: Newman Press, 1984.

Cyril of Alexandria. *Letters*. Ed. Eduard Schwartz. *Acta Conciliorum Oecumenicorum* (ACO). *Concilium Universale Ephesinum*, 1/1. Acta graeca. Collectio Vaticana 120–39. Berlin: De Gruyter, 1960; and 1/4, 1965. Collectio Casinensis sive synodici a Rustico diacono compositi pars altera (Berlin: De Gruyter); also idem, *Codex Vaticanus gr. 1431 eine antichalkedonische Sammlung aus der Zeit Kaiser Zenos*. Munich: Verlag der Bayerischen Akademie der Wissenschaften, 1927. Tr. John I. McEnerney, *St. Cyril of Alexandria. Letters 51–110*. Washington, DC: Catholic University of America Press, 1987.

Decrees of the Ecumenical Councils. Ed. and tr. Norman P. Tanner, *Decrees of the Ecumenical Councils*. Vol. 1. *Nicaea to Lateran V*. London: Sheed & Ward, 1990.

Ennodius of Pavia. *Letters*. Ed. Fridericus Vogel. *Magni Felicis Ennodi Opera* (MGH AA

7). Berlin: Weidmann, 1885. Reprint, Munich: Monumenta Germaniae Historica, 1981. Stéphane Gioanni, *Ennode de Pavie. Lettres.* 2 vols. Paris: Les Belles Lettres, 2006, 2010.

Firmus of Caesarea. *Firmus de Césarée. Lettres.* Ed. and tr. Marie-Ange Calvet-Sebasti and Pierre-Louis Gatier. Sources chrétiennes 350. Paris: Cerf, 1989.

Gregory of Nyssa. *Letters.* Ed. Pierre Maraval. *Grégoire de Nysse. Lettres.* Paris: Cerf, 1990. Tr. Anna M. Silvas, *Gregory of Nyssa: The Letters: Introduction, Translation and Commentary.* Leiden: Brill, 2007.

Gregory of Rome. *S. Gregorii Magni Registrum epistularum libri I–VII.* Ed. Dag Norberg. CCSL 140. Turnhout: Brepols, 1982. Intro., tr., and notes by John R. C. Martyn, *The Letters of Gregory the Great.* 3 vols. Toronto: Pontifical Institute of Medieval Studies, 2004.

Hormisdas of Rome. Ed. Andreas Thiel. *Epistolae Romanorum Pontificum genuinae et quae ad eos scriptae sunt a S. Hilaro usque ad Pelagium II.* Reprint, Hildesheim: Georg Olms Verlag, 2004: 739–1006.

Ignatius of Antioch. Ed. and tr. Michael W. Holmes. *The Apostolic Fathers: Greek Texts and English Translations.* 3rd ed. After the earlier work of J. B. Lightfoot and J. R. Harmer. Grand Rapids, MI: BakerAcademic, 2007.

Leo of Rome. PL 54, 593–1218. Also ed. Carolus Silva-Tarouca, *Epistulae contra Eutychis haeresim S. Leonis Magni.* Textus et documenta. Rome: Apud Aedes Pontificiae Universitatis Gregorianae, 1934, 1935. Eduard Schwartz, *Acta Conciliorum Oecumenicorum. Concilium Universale Chalcedonense,* 2/2, *Versiones particulares. Rerum Chalcedonensium collection Vaticana. Canones et Symbolum.* Berlin: De Gruyter, 1936. Idem, 2/4, *Leonis Papae I. epistularum collectiones.* Berlin: De Gruyter, 1932, 2001. Tr. Edmund Hunt, *Letters: St Leo the Great.* New York: Fathers of the Church, 1957.

Libanius. *Selected Works.* Text and tr. A. F. Norman. LCL. Cambridge, MA: Harvard University Press, 1969.

Paulinus of Nola. *Sancti Ponti Meropii Paulini Nolani epistulae.* Ed. Guilelmus de Hartel. 2nd ed. by Margrit Kamptner. CSEL 29. Vienna: Verlag der Österreischen Akademie der Wissenschaften, 1999.

Ruricius of Limoges. Ed. Christianus Luetjohann, *Gai Solii Apollinaris Sidonii epistulae et carmina: Accedunt Fausti aliorumque epistulae ad Ruricium aliosque Ruricii epistulae.* Berlin: Weidmann, 1897: 299–350. Marino Neri, ed. and tr., *Ruricio di Limoges: Lettere.* Pisa: Edizioni ETS, 2009. Ralph W. Mathisen, intro., tr., and comm., *Ruricius of Limoges and Friends: A Collection of Letters from Visigothic Gaul: Letters of Ruricius of Limoges,* et al. Liverpool: Liverpool University Press, 1999.

Severus of Antioch. *The Sixth Book of the Select Letters of Severus Patriarch of Antioch in the Syriac Version of Athanasius of Nisibis.* Ed. and tr. Ernest W. Brooks. Vol. 1, London: Willians & Norgate. Reprint, Farnborough: Gregg International, 1902/1969. Vol. 2, London: Williams & Norgate. Reprint, Farnsborough: Gregg International, 1903/1969.

Sidonius Apollinaris. *Sidone Apollinaire. Tome II. Lettres (Livres I–V)* and *Tome III. Lettres*

(Livres VI–IX). Ed. and tr. André Loyen. Paris: Les Belles Lettres, 1970. W. B. Anderson, *Sidonius. Letters III–IX.* LCL 420. Cambridge, MA: Harvard University Press, 1997.

Synesius of Cyrene. *Synésios de Cyrène. Correspondance. Lettres I–LXIII. Tome II*, and *Lettres LXIV–CLVI. Tome III.* Ed. and tr. Antonio Garzya and Denis Roques. Paris: Les Belles Lettres, 2000.

Teske, R. 2001–5. *The Works of Saint Augustine: A Translation for the 21st Century*. Hyde Park, NY: New City Press. (Letters 1–99, II/1, 2001; Letters 156–210/ Epistulae, II/3, 2004; Letters 211–270, 1*-29* /Epistulae, II/4, 2005).

Theodoret of Cyrrhus. *Théodoret de Cyr. Correspondance.* 3 vols. Ed. and tr. Yvan Azéma. Sources chrétiennes 40, 98, 111. Paris: Cerf, 1964, 1965/1982.

Vita Epiphanii. Ed. Fridericus Vogel. MGH AA 7 (1885–1981), 84–109. Tr. Roy J. Deferrari, *Early Christian Biographies*. Washington, DC: Catholic University of America Press, 1952: 301–51.

Secondary Sources

Allen, P. 1999. "Severus of Antioch and Pastoral Care." In *Prayer and Spirituality in the Early Church*, vol. 2, ed. Pauline Allen, Wendy Mayer, and Lawrence Cross, 387–400. Brisbane: Centre for Early Christian Studies.

———. 2006. "It's in the Post: Techniques and Difficulties of Letter-Writing in Antiquity with Regard to Augustine of Hippo." In *Proceedings of the Australian Academy of the Humanities* 30: 111–29 [= Trendall Lecture 2005]. Canberra: Australian Academy of the Humanities.

———. 2010a. "Cyril of Alexandria's Festal Letters: The Politics of Religion." In *Studies of Religion and Politics in the Early Christian Centuries*, ed. David Luckensmeyer and Pauline Allen, 195–210. Strathfield: St Pauls.

———. 2010b. "How to Study Episcopal Letter-Writing in Late Antiquity: An Overview of Published Work on the Fifth and Sixth Centuries." In *Scrinium: Revue de patrologie, d'hagiographie critique et d'histoire ecclésiastique*, vol. 6, ed. Vladimir Baranov, Basil Lourié, and Kazuhiko Demura, 130–42. Piscataway, NJ: Gorgias.

———. 2013. "Prolegomena to a Study of the Letter-Bearer in Christian Antiquity." *Studia Patristica* 62.10: 481–91.

———. 2014. "The Festal Letters of the Patriarchs of Alexandria: Evidence for Social History in the Fourth and Fifth Centuries CE." *Phronema* 29.1: 1–19.

Allen, P. and C. T. Hayward. 2004. *Severus of Antioch.* The Early Church Fathers. London: Routledge.

Alpi, Frédéric. 2009. "La correspondance du patriarche Sévère d'Antioche (512–518): Un témoignage sur les institutions et la discipline ecclésiastique en Orient protobyzantin." In *Correspondances: Documents pour l'histoire de l'antiquité tardive*, ed. Roland

Delmaire, Janine Desmulliez, and Pierre-Louis Gatier, 333–48. Lyon: Maison de l'Orient et de la Méditerranée.

———. 2010. *La Route royale: Sévère d'Antioche et les Églises d'Orient (512–518)*. 2 vols. Bibliothèque archéologique et historique 188. Beirut: Presses de l'Ifpo.

Andreau, Jean and Catherine Virlouvet, eds. 2002. *L'Information et la mer dans le monde antique*. Collection de l'École française de Rome 297. Rome: École française de Rome.

Banev, Krastu. 2007. "Pastoral Polemics: A Rhetorical Analysis of Theophilus of Alexandria's Letters in the First Origenist Controversy." PhD dissertation, University of Cambridge.

Barnwell, P. S. 1992. *Emperor, Prefects and Kings: The Roman West 395–565*. Chapel Hill: University of North Carolina Press.

Brok, M. F. A. 1951. "À propos des lettres festales." *Vigiliae Christianae* 41: 101–10.

Caltobiano, Mathilde. 2001a. "I latori della corrispondenza di Agostino: Tra idealizzazione e realtà." *Augustinianum* 41: 113–48.

———. 2001b. "'Perlator fidelissimus'; i latori nelle epistole di Sant'Agostino (edizione Divjak)." *Acme: Annali della Facoltà di lettere e filosofia dell'Università degli studi di Milano* 54: 11–32.

Calvet-Sebasti, Marie-Ange. 2009. "Le rituel de l'échange des lettres à l'occasion des fêtes religieuses." In *Correspondances: Documents pour l'histoire de l'antiquité tardive*, ed. Roland Delmaire, Janine Desmulliez, and Pierre-Louis Gatier, 67–81. Lyon: Maison de l'Orient et de la Méditerranée.

Casson, Lionel. 1994. *Travel in the Ancient World*. 2nd ed. Baltimore: Johns Hopkins University Press.

Constable, Giles. 1976. *Letters and Letter-Collections*. Typologie des sources du moyen âge occidental 17. Turnhout: Brepols.

Davies, J. G. 1963. "Deacons, Deaconesses and the Minor Orders in the Patristic Period." *Journal of Ecclesiastical History* 14: 1–15.

Delmaire, R. 1991. "Les 'lettres d'exil' de Jean Chrysostome. Etudes de chronologie et de prosopographie." *Recherches Augustiniennes* 25: 71–180.

Delmaire, Roland. 2009. "Les lettres de Jean Chrysostome: Espérances et désillusions d'un évêque en exil." In *Correspondances: Documents pour l'histoire de l'antiquité tardive*, ed. Roland Delmaire, Janine Desmulliez, and Pierre-Louis Gatier, 283–91. Lyon: Maison de l'Orient et de la Méditerranée.

Delmaire, Roland, Janine Desmulliez, and Pierre-Louis Gatier, eds. 2009. *Correspondances: Documents pour l'histoire de l'antiquité tardive*. Lyon: Maison de l'Orient et de la Méditerranée.

Ebbeler, Jennifer. 2009. "Tradition, Innovation, and Epistolary *Mores*." In *A Companion to Late Antiquity*, ed. Philip Rousseau, 270–84. Chichester: Wiley-Blackwell.

Ellis, Linda and Frank L. Kidner, eds. 2004. *Travel, Communication and Geography in Late Antiquity: Sacred and Profane*. Aldershot: Ashgate.

Fitzgerald, John T. 1997. *Graeco-Roman Perspectives on Friendship*. Resources for Biblical Studies 34. Atlanta, GA: Scholars Press.

Gatier, Pierre-Louis. 2009. "Hiérarchie et politesse dans les correspondances grecques de l'antiquité tardive: Les exemples de Firmus de Césarée et de Denys d'Antioche." In *Correspondances: Documents pour l'histoire de l'antiquité tardive*, ed. Roland Delmaire, Janine Desmulliez, and Pierre-Louis Gatier, 115–23. Lyon: Maison de l'Orient et de la Méditerranée.

Gillett, Andrew. 2003. *Envoys and Political Communication in the Late Antique West, 411–533*. Cambridge: Cambridge University Press.

———. 2012. "Communication in Late Antiquity: Use and Reuse." In *The Oxford Handbook of Late Antiquity*, ed. Scott F. Johnson, 815–46. Oxford: Oxford University Press.

Gorce, Denys. 1925. *Les voyages, l'hospitalité et le port des lettres dans le monde chrétien des IVe et Ve siècles*. Wépion-sur-Meuse: Monastère du Mont-Vierge.

Hatlie, Peter. 1996. "Redeeming Byzantine Epistolography." *Byzantine and Modern Greek Studies* 20: 213–48.

Head, Peter M. 2009. "Named Letter-Carriers Among the Oxyrhynchus Papyri." *Journal for the Study of the New Testament* 31: 279–99.

Kolb, Anne. 2000. *Transport und Nachrichtentransfer im Römischen Reich*. Klio. Beiträge zur Alten Geschichte, Beihefte, NF Bd. 2. Berlin: Akademie Verlag.

Konstan, David. 1996. "Problems in the History of Christian Friendship." *JECS* 4: 87–113.

———. 1997. *Friendship in the Classical World*. Cambridge: Cambridge University Press.

Külzer, Andreas. 1998. "Die 'Festbriefe' (*Epistolai heortastikai*)—Eine wenig beachtete Untergattung der byzantinischen Briefliteratur." *Byzantinische Zeitschrift* 91: 379–90.

Leyerle, Blake. 2009. "Mobility and the Traces of Empire." In *A Companion to Late Antiquity*, ed. Philip Rousseau, 110–23. Chichester: Wiley-Blackwell.

Liebeschuetz, J. H. W. G. 1972. *Antioch: City and Imperial Administration in the Later Roman Empire*. Oxford: Clarendon.

Lizzi, Rita. 1987. *Il potere episcopale nell'Oriente romano: Rappresentazione ideologica e realtà politica (IVe-V secolo d.C.)*. Rome: Edizioni dell'Ateneo.

———. 2009. "The Late Antique Bishop: Image and Reality." In *A Companion to Late Antiquity*, ed. Philip Rousseau, 525–38. Chichester: Wiley-Blackwell.

Martindale, John R. 2006a. *The Prosopography of the Later Roman Empire*, vol. 2: *AD 395–527*. Cambridge: Cambridge University Press.

———. 2006b. *The Prosopography of the Later Roman Empire*, vols. 3A and 3B: *AD 527–641*. Cambridge: Cambridge University Press.

Mathisen, R. W. 1979. "Sidonius on the Reign of Avitus: A Study in Political Prudence." *Transactions of the American Philological Association* 109: 165–71.

McGuire, Martin R. P. 1960. "Letters and Letter Carriers in Christian Antiquity." *Classical World* 53.5: 148–53, 184–85, 199–200.

Mratschek, Sigrid. 1996. "Einblicke in einen Postsack: Zur Struktur und Edition der 'Natalicia' des Paulinus von Nola." *Zeitschrift für Papyrologie und Epigraphik* 114: 165–72.

———. 2002. *Der Briefwechsel des Paulinus von Nola: Kommunikation und soziale Kontakte zwischen christlichen Intellektuellen.* Hypomnemata 134. Göttingen: Vandenhoeck & Rupprecht.

———. 2011. "Die ungeschriebenen Briefe des Augustinus von Hippo." In *"In Search of Truth": Augustine, Manichaeism and Other Gnosticism: Studies for Johannes van Oort at Sixty*, ed. Jacob Albert van den Berg, Annemaré Kotzé, Tobias Niklas, and Madeleine Scopello, 109–22. Leiden: Brill.

Mullett, Margaret. 1997. *Theophylact of Ochrid: Reading the Letters of a Byzantine Bishop.* Birmingham Byzantine and Ottoman Monographs 2. Aldershot: Ashgate.

Neri, Marino, ed. and tr. 2009. *Ruricio di Limoges: Lettere.* Pubblicazioni della Facoltà di Lettere e Filosofia della Università di Pavia 122. Pisa: Edizioni ETS.

Paola, Lucietta Di. 1999. *Viaggi, trasporti e istituzioni: Studi sul cursus publicus.* Pelorias 5. Messina: Dipartimento di Scienze dell Antichità dell'Università degli Studi di Messina.

Paoli-Lafaye, Élisabeth. 2002. "Messagers et messages: La diffusion des nouvelles de l'Afrique d'Augustin vers les régions d'au-delà des mers." In *L'Information et la mer dans le monde antique*, ed. Jean Andreau and Catherine Virlouvet, 233–59. Collection de l'École française de Rome 297. Rome: École française de Rome.

Patsavos, Lewis J. 2007. *A Noble Task: Entry into the Clergy in the First Five Centuries.* Tr. Norman Russell. Foreword by Kallistos Ware. Brookline, MA: Holy Cross Orthodox Press.

Perrin, Michel-Yves. 1992. "*Ad implendum caritatis ministerium:* La place des courriers dans la correspondance de Paulin de Nole." *Mélanges de l'École française de Rome. Antiquité* 104.2: 1025–68.

Pizzolato, Luigi F. 1993. *L'idea di amicizia nel mondo antico classico e cristiano.* Turin: G. Einaudi.

Rapp, Claudia. 2005. *Holy Bishops in Late Antiquity: The Nature of Christian Leadership in an Age of Transition.* Berkeley: University of California Press.

Rebillard, Éric and Claire Sotinel, eds. 1998. *L'Évêque dans la cité du IVe au Ve siècle: Image et authorité.* Rome: École française de Rome.

Rousseau, Philip, ed. 2009. *A Companion to Late Antiquity.* Chichester: Wiley-Blackwell.

Salvo, Lucietta De. 2002. "Mare, commercio e informazione privata nella tarda antichità." In *L'Information et la mer dans le monde antique*, ed. Jean Andreau and Catherine Virlouvet, 299–319. Rome: École française de Rome.

Schor, Adam M. 2011. *Theodoret's People: Social Networks and Religious Conflict in Late Roman Syria.* Berkeley: University of California Press.

Sotinel, Claire. 2004. "How Were Bishops Informed? Information Transmission Across the Adriatic Sea in Late Antiquity." In *Travel, Communication and Geography in Late Antiquity: Sacred and Profane*, ed. Linda Ellis and Frank L. Kidner, 63–71. Aldershot: Ashgate.

———. 2009. "Information and Political Power." In *A Companion to Late Antiquity*, ed. Philip Rousseau, 125–38. Chichester: Wiley-Blackwell.

Speyer, Wolfgang. 1971. *Die literarische Fälschung im heidnischen und christlichen Altertum.* Munich: C. H. Beck.

Sterk, Andrea. 2004. *Renouncing the World yet Leading the Church: The Monk-Bishop in Late Antiquity.* Cambridge, MA: Harvard University Press.

Thraede, Klaus. 1970. *Grundzüge griechisch-römischer Brieftopik.* Zetemata. Monographien zur Klassischen Altertunswissenschaft 48. Munich: C. H. Beck.

Tornau, Christian. 2006. *Zwischen Rhetorik und Philosophie: Augustins Argumentationstechnik in De Civitate Dei und ihr bildungsgeschichtlicher Hintergrund.* Berlin: De Gruyter.

Trapp, Michael B. 2003. *Greek and Latin Letters: An Anthology, with Translation.* Cambridge Greek and Latin Classics. Cambridge: Cambridge University Press.

Wagner, Monica. 1948. "A Chapter in Byzantine Epistolography: The Letters of Theodoret of Cyrus." *Dumbarton Oaks Papers* 4: 119–81.

White, Carolinne. 1992. *Christian Friendship in the Fourth Century.* Cambridge: Cambridge University Press.

Zelzer, Michaela. 1994. "Der Brief in der Spätantike: Überlegungen zu einem literarischen Genos am Beispiel der Briefsammlung des Sidonius Apollinaris." *Wiener Studien* 107–8.2: 541–51.

Chapter 11

"Silence Is Also Annulment": Veiled and Unveiled Speech in Seventh-Century Martyr Commemorations

Bronwen Neil

> There is no speech, nor are there words, whose sounds are not heard.
>
> —Psalm 18:4

Blasphemy and its censorship have long been sources of conflict between religious groups, with a recent case on the world stage of an anti-Muslim depiction of Muhammad in a film directed by an American Coptic Christian and broadcast on the Internet in September 2012. This "disrespect for the prophet" sparked violent riots around the world. Such cases of religious blasphemy and its censorship are by no means new, since blasphemy is inherently a contested concept. In the seventh century blasphemy occupied a liminal space between civic crime and religious sin. In a study of blasphemy in the Christian world from the 1500s up to the present day, Nash highlights the continuing relevance of blasphemy as an index of social change, asserting, "Blasphemy in its historical context illuminates changing views of the sacred and how far these have regulated societies and behavior within them."[1] Leveleux cites the judgment of the late antique bishop, Augustine of Hippo: "blasphemy is worse than perjury, for he who perjures adduces God as the witness of a falsehood, but he who blasphemes speaks falsehoods of God."[2] Augustine here limits blasphemy to a linguistic infringement. In fact, as Leveleux notes, blasphemy was interpreted quite widely from the Old Testament usage to include deviant utterances, profaning the Sabbath, idolatry, neglect of circumcision, and sacrilege and treason.[3]

In the mid-seventh century, Maximus the Confessor (c. 590–662) and Pope Martin I (649–54) died in exile along with several lesser known figures under charges of blasphemy and treason. Their real crimes were their vocal opposition to imperial doctrinal statements, which they perceived as heretical, and their refusal to be silenced by an imperial injunction, known as the *Typos*, issued in 647/48. I examine how imperial censors acted to convict them of blasphemy and conspiracy in order to quell political dissent. The martyrs, or more accurately confessors, since they died in exile—namely, Maximus, Anastasius the Monk, Anastasius the Apocrisiarius, and Martin—and those who sought to commemorate them were forced to self-censor their dissident texts. A brief introduction to the monothelite controversy will demonstrate the reasons why any critique of the imperial and church authorities had to be heavily veiled. It will be seen how easily charges could be fabricated when the emperor saw his own authority as threatened, and how difficult they were to refute, with the onus of proof on the accused. I then consider the strategies of self-censorship adopted in the literary productions of Martin, Maximus, and their circle.[4] Since their lack of early self-censorship is what led to their punishments, they quickly developed the skill to continue their criticisms but in a more subtle way. I examine the classical and scriptural antecedents of the dyothelite productions from exile, and finally contrast them with some rare examples of unveiled speech, in which imperial authority is attacked openly.

Background to the Monothelite Controversy

Monothelitism, the theory of one will in Jesus Christ, arose as the natural corollary of an earlier heresy sponsored by Emperors Heraclius and Constans II, that of monoenergism.[5] In the 630s, under the advice of his patriarch Sergius, Heraclius had introduced the doctrine of a single "energy" or operating activity in Christ, in the hope of achieving a reunion with the so-called monophysite elements of the Alexandrian church. As a political maneuver, monoenergism was largely unsuccessful. Heraclius had not anticipated a theological backlash from Sophronius, bishop of Jerusalem (634–38), and Maximus the Confessor.[6] In 638 the patriarch of Constantinople with imperial support issued a document censoring discussion of either one or two energies in Christ.[7] Monothelitism was the logical corollary of monoenergism—the doctrine of one will in Christ that was promulgated by Sergius of Constantinople and the patriarchs who succeeded him, with the support of Emperor Constans II.[8] It was enshrined in the *Ekthesis*, a document composed by Sergius and signed by Heraclius in 638. The refusal of Sophronius, Maximus, and Popes John IV and Theodore I to accept this document led to Patriarch Paul's promulgation—in the name of Constans II—of the *Typos*, which was posted in 647 or 648 at the main entry to Hagia Sofia and banned any mention of either one or two activities or wills in Jesus Christ.[9] This attempt to undo the past was doomed to failure.

The victims of imperial persecution in this controversy wrote several letters from exile pertaining to their cause, and were commemorated in various texts in Greek and Latin, including the *Narrationes de exilio sancti papae Martini*, *Disputatio Bizyae*, and the *Hypomnesticon*. These letters and testimonies circulated widely in the seventh and eighth centuries and were probably instrumental in the condemnation of monothelitism by the Sixth Ecumenical Council of Constantinople in 681. The difficulties that Maximus and his supporters posed for Emperor Constans II were not inconsiderable. In the *Dispute at Bizya*, the patrician Epiphanius adduces a letter of command from the emperor to Maximus:[10] "Since all the West and those in the East who are causing subversion look to you, and they all stir up strife because of you, refusing to be reconciled with us in the cause of faith, may God compel you to enter into communion with us on the terms of the *Typos* which was published by us." In return for compliance on the matter of the number of wills in Christ, Emperor Constans was apparently prepared to welcome Maximus at the city gate, lay hands upon him and accompany him into the Great Church of Constantinople, where he would concelebrate communion and proclaim him as his father. "For we know with certainty that, when you are in communion with the holy see here, all those who were separated from our communion on account of you and your teaching will be united with us."[11] Even before he became bishop of Rome, Martin was a vocal opponent of the doctrines of monoenergism and monothelitism. As a papal legate (*apocrisiarius*) for Pope Theodore I (642–49), resident in Constantinople, he was charged with opposing the imperial will on this issue. This probably coincided with the issuing of the imperial *Typos* in 647 or 648. His resistance seems to have resulted in his expulsion from the capital c. 648. Upon his appointment as Theodore's successor, Martin took up the cause in the West, convening in

649 the Lateran Synod, which condemned the emperors and their patriarchs in no uncertain terms.[12] This resulted in his arrest in Rome and trial in Constantinople in 653/54.[13] Martin was subsequently exiled to Cherson, on the Black Sea, where he died in September 655. His status as a martyr was not incontestable, since he, like Maximus, died in exile; his supporters usually refer to him and to Maximus as "confessors and martyrs for the truth."

Accusations of Treason and Blasphemy Against Maximus

In his trial at the imperial court in Constantinople in 655, Maximus was first arraigned on charges of conspiracy. His first accuser, the *sacellarius*, charged him with handing over "Egypt, Alexandria, Tripolis, Pentapolis, and Africa" to the Saracens. A witness named John, the former *sacellarius* of Peter, general of Numidia, claimed that Maximus had advised Peter not to follow Heraclius's command to lead an army against the Saracens in Egypt in 633. Maximus is said to have written to the general, telling him that God had no wish to help the reign of Heraclius "and his kin." The damning correspondence between Peter and Maximus could not be produced, but his accuser maintained that "everyone in the camp at that time was speaking of these matters."[14] Camp gossip was apparently sufficient grounds for a charge of treason.

Maximus was then accused of conspiring in the rebellion of Gregory, exarch of North Africa c. 646. The same accuser maintained that Pope Theodore had encouraged Gregory in his revolt, because Maximus had related to the pope a dream in which he had seen Gregory triumph over Emperor Constantine, the West defeating the East.[15] Imperial censorship apparently reached into the oneirosphere.[16]

The final charge brought against Maximus and his disciple Anastasius the Monk at this trial was that of blasphemy. Blasphemy, as we have seen, is a contested concept and even its proper definition is largely contextual. Nash defines blasphemy across time as "the attacking, wounding, and damaging of religious belief."[17] Casey provides an alternative definition of blasphemy in the context of contemporary art as "the transgression of the boundary between sacred and profane."[18] This seems to me to fit better with the charges of blasphemy in the two trials of Maximus and Anastasius the Monk.

In the first trial, that of 655, the imperial censors alleged that Anastasius had refused to recognize the emperor's right to define doctrine, by questioning his status as a priest. Emperors Heraclius and Constans II had claimed this right as inherent in their role as head of the Byzantine church. Maximus defended his disciple, saying he had said no such thing, and recounting a conversation where he argued that every emperor was not a priest, and demonstrated from the liturgy that the emperor belonged to the laity, not the priesthood.[19] The accuser, a certain Gregory, had held this private conversation with Maximus and Anastasius in his cell in Rome some five years earlier. Maximus's spirited defense of his disciple caused the finance minister to call for the death sentence.[20]

Some three years later, Maximus was slandered by a soldier at the camp of Bizya as "the one who blasphemes against the *Theotokos*" ("mother of God").[21] When asked whether the accusation was true, he vigorously denied it with anathemas on any who would believe such a thing. This seems to have been another trumped-up charge of blasphemy, amounting to a charge of Nestorianism. No other evidence survives for Maximus holding irregular views on the Blessed Virgin. If the *Life of the Virgin* preserved in Old Georgian is rightly attributed to Maximus, as many scholars believe, quite the opposite was true.[22] Interestingly this last charge of blasphemy was not adduced in the private context of Maximus's trial in Constantinople, but was leveled publicly, and aimed at offending popular belief among the soldiery.[23]

Four more accusations of blasphemy are leveled at Maximus, Anastasius the Monk, and Anastasius the Apocrisiarius in *The Third Judgment*, a record of the sentence passed on the three dissidents after their second and final trial in Constantinople in 662. Anastasius the Apocrisiarius and Maximus were to be punished by flogging and the amputation of their tongues ("the organ of your licentiousness . . . that is your blaspheming tongue") and their right hands ("which ministered to your blasphemous argument").[24] This last attempt to silence them physically also failed: Anastasius the Apocrisiarius managed to keep writing with two reeds tied to the stump of his right hand, "just as he also spoke with a truly divine and invisible tongue completely without hindrance and restraint, although it had been cut off from the very root."[25] It is interesting to note that these were their punishments, although the prescribed penalty for blasphemy was death.

Maximus's Response: Kaiserkritik

After accusing Anastasius the Monk of refusing to recognize the emperor's sacral status and right to define doctrine, the censors then demanded what objection Maximus could possibly have to remaining silent on the number of wills and operations in Christ, as enjoined by imperial edict in the *Typos*.[26] Maximus boldly likens this strategy of forced silence to the Arians' proposal to Constantine the Great that the contentious theological terms "consubstantial" and "not consubstantial" be removed from all discussion and written documents, for the sake of unity among the churches.[27] As Maximus puts it, "According to divine Scripture, silence is also annulment." He supported this statement with a citation of Psalm 1:4: "There is no speech, nor are there words, whose sounds are not heard."[28] Maximus and Anastasius, like Martin in 648, refused to be silenced by the imperial censors. In a later letter to the monks of Cagliari, Anastasius the Monk also described the emperor and his agents as Arians, begging the monks for their prayers that he might hold fast against "the Arians who are united here."[29] Identifying one's opponent with heretics of previous times was standard practice in attacks on heresy. The admission of heresy was equated with blasphemy in the seventh-century tract *Questions and Answers* by Anastasius of Sinai, who advises that it is better to submit to martyrdom and torture than to give way to blasphemy and admit heresy.[30] Maximus and his supporters were never charged with heresy, perhaps an indication that the imperial administration knew that it was on shaky ground, in doctrinal terms.

Criticism of the emperor was standard practice in Byzantine literature, as Mischa Meier has shown in his study of *Kaiserkritik* during the reign of Justinian (527–65), in response to perceived imperial mismanagement of wars and other catastrophes. Popular dissatisfaction with the high incidence of famines, plagues, and earthquakes, as well as with Justinian's extended military campaigns in the West, often found expression in "folk religion," for instance in ritual processions, worship of holy images, and increased devotion to the cult of the Virgin Mary.[31] Some criticized Empress Theodora's support for the so-called *miaphysites*, or supporters of one-nature Christology against the Council of Chalcedon (451), and others Justinian's adoption of heresy.[32] In a similar way, Byzantine losses against the Arabs from the 640s were blamed on the imperial adoption of monoenergism and monothelitism by our dyothelite authors, as well as later chroniclers such as Theophanes the Confessor in the early ninth century.

In a debate with an imperial envoy while Maximus was being held at Bizya in 658, Maximus explicitly equated the monothelites with "false apostles, false prophets, and false teachers,"[33] arguing that, just as the one who receives true apostles, prophets, and teachers accepts God, so the one who receives false apostles, prophets, and teachers accepts the Devil. He concluded, "The one, then, who has cast out the saints together with the foul and impure heretics . . . has obviously condemned God together with the Devil."[34] The accusation implicit in his last statement, that heretics are as bad as the Devil himself, was probably understood by his audience, who were "frozen by what had been said, [they] bowed their heads and remained silent for a considerable time."[35] Far from silencing Maximus, his opponents were the ones who were silenced, at least according to the dyothelite author of *Disputatio Bizyae*. From Maximus's response, it seems that the best answer to a charge of blasphemy was that the accuser was an impious heretic. In the next section we compare Martin's reaction to charges of conspiracy.

The Trial of Pope Martin

In the trial of Pope Martin, staged by the senate in Constantinople in 653, the charges did not include blasphemy. Martin was accused of supplying money to the Saracen army, and of sending letters in a conspiracy against Constans (*Narr.* 3).[36] After the Arab incursions in Palestine, Cyprus, Egypt, and North Africa,[37] issues of security were paramount for imperial concerns. Physical evidence of the letters was not adduced at any time during Martin's trial; hearsay was enough to convict an enemy of the emperor. Martin was also charged with conspiring with the exarch of Ravenna, Olympius, against Constans II, and with priming the soldiers to take an oath of allegiance to the usurper.[38] This made him "an enemy and murderer of the emperor and of the Roman way of life," in the words of his accuser Dorotheus, patrician of Sicily.[39]

Those present at the trial called for the death sentence, as in the earlier cases of the imperial pretender George, *magister* of Constantinople in 651 or 652, and the usurper Valentinus before him.[40] The *sacellarius* ordered the executioners to cut up the stole (*pallium*) Martin wore as a symbol of his episcopal authority, and the laces of his papal boots, and to cut him up "limb by limb."[41] Thus deprived of his papal insignia, he was paraded through the city in chains, up to the praetorian prefect's headquarters, with a sword carried in front of him. Two days after his trial concluded, the death sentence was commuted and Martin was sent into exile at Cherson. During his imprisonment for 178 days before the trial, and in the first two years of his exile, he wrote four letters: the first two to a certain Theodore,[42] and two more to an anonymous supporter, the second one being written very shortly before his death. These show significantly more evidence of self-censorship than Maximus's railings against the emperor.

Self-Censorship in Martin's Letters and Its Classical Antecedents

Martin's letters have been compared elsewhere with the works that the classical poet Ovid wrote from exile, especially the *Epistulae ex Ponto* and *Tristia.*[43] In 8 CE Ovid was exiled to Tomis near the Black Sea—not far from Martin's final destination of Cherson, more than six centuries later—where he died nine years later. Even while hoping for a reprieve, Ovid indulged in veiled criticism of the emperor who sentenced him, as in his comments on the art of playing dice, one of Augustus's favorite pastimes, but considered immoral by his Republican predecessors.[44] Ovid was actively seeking an amelioration of his punishment, even if only to be moved to a safer place of exile.[45] For this reason Ovid had to balance his criticisms with servile flattery of the emperor who had the power to release him.[46]

There is in Martin's letters no flattery of imperial rulers such as we find in Ovid's *Tristia.* However, the deposed bishop refrained from speaking out directly against Constans II, the emperor who had condemned both him and his predecessor Pope Theodore I. This is clearly an instance of self-censorship, in the interests of allowing his letters to pass by prison guards without confiscation or censorship. Emperor Constans had yet to judge him at the time of the two letters written in Constantinople.[47] Thus his criticisms of the imperial regime are heavily veiled. Martin was keen to stress that his sufferings were for the orthodox faith and the true church, against the "heretics" who remain unnamed.[48] In *Ep.* 1, Martin calls those who witnessed at his trial perjurers: "Wicked men have witnessed falsely against me, or rather against their own souls."[49] In *Ep.* 2, he interprets his treatment as a sign of the imminent end of the age: "And believe me, my most beloved son, that time is not to be seen as any other than a clear sign of the beginning of sorrows, just as the Lord foretold concerning the coming of the Antichrist."[50] Similarly, Maximus voiced fears that apostasy would usher in the Antichrist.[51]

In his two letters from exile (*Epp.* 3 and 4), Martin is similarly restrained and does not mention his persecutors or his addressee by name. His concern to preserve the identity of his correspondents is probably indicative of the level of danger attached to being in communication with an exile. The mode of conveyance for his letters from Cherson is revealed in *Ep.* 3, where Martin recalls that a carrier came by boat from Constantinople.[52] No letter-carrier, especially a Greek-speaking Byzantine, could be relied upon to transmit letters that were critical of the regime. Martin saves his fiercest criticism for his former supporters in Rome, who had so far failed to send him supplies of bread, wine, and oil, without which he fears he will die.[53] Only at the end of *Ep.* 4 does he let down his guard and pray that God will strengthen his supporters against "every heretic and every party in opposition to our church."[54] Again, these opponents are anonymous.

Pope Martin's four letters about his trial and exile, which were clearly intended for publication, were later incorporated in a narrative titled *Narrationes de exilio sancti papae Martini* (BHL 5592). This narrative was composed for his supporters in Italy and North Africa by an unknown person not long after Martin's death in 655, and incorporated a fifth Greek text, the *Commemoration* (*Hypomnesticon*), written in or after 668 by an anonymous supporter of Maximus and Martin, who has been identified as Theodore Spoudaeus.[55] It is instructive to compare the criticism of imperial authority in the two texts, the *Narrationes* and the *Hypomnesticon*, for what they can tell us about the use of self-regulated speech in texts meant to garner support for the martyrs of the dyothelite cause. In particular, we will see how imperial authority is openly challenged in the latter text.

Unveiled Speech Against the Emperor

Open accusations of impiety against religious and imperial leaders are a striking feature of the *Hypomnesticon*, written in or after 668. The *Hypomnesticon* was circulated together with Anastasius the Apocrisiarius's letter to Theodosius of Gangra and Theodore Spoudaeus, which had been penned in Lazica, Anastasius's final resting place in 668. The dating is important: absent from the Latin version of the text, a prologue to the original Greek version of the *Hypomnesticon* refers to the death of Constans II in the same year. The emperor was killed in Sicily in September 668, on his way to Rome.[56] The author of the *Hypomnesticon* attributed this murder to Constans's ratification of monothelitism in the *Typos* of 647/48.[57] The *Hypomnesticon* referred to the outpouring of Maximus's and Martin's blood after their final trial in 661 as an act of sedition and "the most atrocious evil."[58] The charges of conspiracy brought against Martin are here met with accusations of sedition, and the charges of blasphemy brought against Maximus are met with accusations of profanity: the imperial *Typos* of 648 was described as "absolutely profane and godless."[59] After bemoaning the amputations of Maximus's tongue and right hand, and the hand of Anastasius the Apocrisiarius, and how they were beaten and tortured and dragged in a shameful procession through the streets of Constantinople, the author lashes out, likening the monothelites to the Jews, who failed to receive the word of God: "But those most profane and wretched apostates of the truth did all this to them for no other reason than out of envy alone, truly most wicked, which the old enemy the Devil sowed in them as in the Jews whom they resemble, since they could not to the slightest degree resist the wisdom which had been given to them deservedly by God on behalf of the truth, and only because they [sc. the confessors] did not want to be in communion with them in their so public and godless impiety."[60] Heraclius's descendants are said to have "received the empire and held sway over it in succession like a gangrenous sore,"[61] the last phrase being an echo of 2 Timothy 2:7. Such explicit accusations against the Heraclian dynasty are absent from Martin's letters, and may be explained by the recent occurrence of Emperor Constans's murder.

An extreme example of unveiled speech is afforded by the brief anonymous tract *Against the People of Constantinople.* Written after the death of Maximus in 662 but before the council of 680/81, this piece of invective is "long on rhetoric and short on facts."[62] Its author's chief concern is to confirm the status of the "confessors, who are no less than martyrs."[63] Maximus's opponents are addressed as follows: "You *seeds of wickedness*, incomplete abortions, birds that travel by night, intestines of the earth, idle bellies, giants of the table, and hunters of women."[64] Here again, scripture is used as a vehicle for insults, in the citation of Isaiah 1:4. Constans II, not identified by name, is called "the most irrational, most unintelligent, and most silly emperor."[65] The names of imperial agents are made the subject of mocking puns: the patrician Epiphanius (whose name means "shining forth") is called Apophanius "the unshining"; he is an arsonist (*purikaon*), not a patrician (*patrikion*). Bishop Theodosius is not an overseer (*episkopon*) but an "underseer" (*hyposkopon*).[66] By contrast, the letters of Martin appear a model of propriety. Although the exact date of the text has not previously been narrowed down within the eighteen-year period mentioned above, its vitriolic content against the emperor is again strongly suggestive of a *terminus post quem* of September 668, the death of Constans.

Conclusion

In 681 the Council of Constantinople condemned the doctrines of monoenergism and monothelitism, and their exponents, and exonerated Martin, Maximus, and their followers. The texts under investigation here may well have been instrumental in changing imperial opinion, or at least in giving political impetus to the opponents of monothelitism, who by this time included Pope Agatho (678–81).

Just as blasphemy itself is a blurring of the boundaries between the sacred and the profane, the treatment of blasphemy in the seventh century crossed the boundaries between religious and secular law. Criticism of the emperor, who claimed to be the head of the church, could constitute blasphemy. Denial of the God-bearing status of the Virgin Mary was likewise blasphemous. Accusations of treason were more straightforward, even if the evidence relied on dreams and hearsay. We have seen how the dyothelites, especially Martin, met accusations of treason and blasphemy by veiled speech—allusions to their own "martyrdom" in scripture, by assimilating monothelitism with other, more ancient heresies, and even by interpreting adverse events as signs of the coming of the Antichrist. More open criticism of the emperor, who was charged with heresy, profanity, and impiety, was found in Maximus's reported speeches at his first trial and in a prison camp in Bizya, and in later, anonymous documents. The need for the sensible (and self-preserving) practice of self-censorship was obviated when the culprits had met their demise. These seventh-century texts show that contemporary, twenty-first-century debates on the need to balance freedom of speech (especially in the press and on the Internet) with appropriate respect for religious groups—whether they are majorities or minorities—are not particular to our era or to our new technologies, nor were they solved any less violently in late antiquity.

NOTES

1. Nash (2007) 1.
2. Augustine, *Contra mendacium* 19.39: "Ideo autem pejus est blasphemare quam

peierare, quoniam pejerando falsae rei adhibetur testis Deus, blasphemando autem de ipso falsa dicuntur Deo" (my translation), cited by Leveleux (2001) 110 and n. 67. While Leveleux mostly concentrates on the late medieval period, she devotes a small section to the brief and scattered late antique and early medieval sources at 35–70. She distinguishes between blasphemy as a sign of sin and a mark of heresy at 52–57.

3. Leveleux (2001) 27.

4. A summary of Maximian works can be found in Sherwood (1952). An updated date list will be provided by Marek Jankoviak and Philip Booth (forthcoming).

5. A spate of recent scholarship has appeared on the monoenergist-monothelite controversy: e.g., Winkelmann (2002); Hovorun (2008); Larison (2009); Price (2010) 221–32; Booth (2013). See also my introduction in Allen and Neil (2002) 8–29.

6. On Sophronius, see Allen (2009) 23–34.

7. The *Ekthesis* was drafted by Patriarch Sergius and signed by Emperor Heraclius. See Bronwen Neil's introduction to Allen and Neil (2002) 14–18.

8. On the role of the patriarchs of Constantinople in the mononergist and monothelite controversies, see Jan Louis van Dieten (1972). Constans II "Pogonatas" (641–68) was also known as "Constantine." He is not to be confused with his father, Heraclius Constantine or Constantine III, who ruled briefly after the death of Heraclius, from February to April/May 641. See R. Scott Moore, *Online Directory of Roman Emperors*, s.v. "Heraclonas and Constantine III," http://www.roman-emperors.org/heraclon.htm (accessed February 10, 2012).

9. "Introduction," Allen and Neil (2002) 14–15, 18.

10. *Disputatio Bizyae* 10, ed. Allen and Neil (2002) 108–9.

11. Ibid., modified translation.

12. The Acts of the Lateran Council have been edited by Riedinger (1984).

13. On Martin's trial, see Brandes (1998) 141–212.

14. *Relatio Motionis* 1, ed. Allen and Neil (2002) 50–51.

15. *Rel. Mot.* 2, ed. Allen and Neil (2002) 50–51. The attempted usurpation came to nothing when Gregory was killed in Arab incursions in North Africa in 647. Constans II was succeeded by his son Constantine IV (668–85). See R. Scott Moore, *Online Directory of Roman Emperors*, s.v. "Constans II," http://www.roman-emperors.org/constan2.htm (accessed December 1, 2012).

16. A term coined by Knapp (1979) 5 for that region of the mind in which the personal and collective unconscious converge and "in which dreams and images become discernible to the individual."

17. Nash (2007) 1.

18. Casey (2000–2001) 19–34.

19. *Rel. Mot.* 4, ed. Allen and Neil (2002) 54–55.

20. Ibid., 58–59: "And turning round, the finance minister shouted to the exarch's people: 'Say to the exarch: "Should you have allowed a person like this to live where you rule?"'"

21. *Disputatio Bizyae* 14, ed. Allen and Neil (2002) 114–16.

22. For a summary of the arguments for and against Maximian authorship, see Shoemaker (2006) 307–28. The Old Georgian text is translated by Shoemaker (2012).

23. Cf. Shoemaker (2006) 311 where he recounts Georgian scholar Korneli Kekelidze's theory that the *Life of the Virgin* may have been attributed to Maximus to refute "charges brought forth by soldiers at his trial that he had somehow slandered the Virgin Mary." Shoemaker himself rightly reports (ibid., 311) that "the incident in question is described by a source written very close to the events of Maximus' trial."

24. *The Third Sentence Against Them*, ed. Allen and Neil (2002) 118–19.

25. *Hypom.* 4, ed. Allen and Neil (2002) 152–53: *καθὰ καὶ γλώσσῃ ἀληθῶς θείᾳ τε καὶ ἀοράτῳ ἀνεμποδίστως πάντῃ καὶ ἀκολούτως φθεγγομένου, καίτοι ἀπὸ ἔσω ἐξ αὐτοῦ τοῦ πυθμένος τμηθείσης αὐτῆς*. Cf. Prologue to the Letter of Anastasius the Apocrisiarius to Theodosius of Gangra (*latine*), ed. Allen and Neil (2002) 132. Maximus seems to have kept the cause alive in the few months that remained to him in exile in Lazica, before his death in August 662, which he predicted to the day.

26. *Rel. Mot.* 4, ed. Allen and Neil (2002) 56–57.

27. *Homoousion* and *heteroousion* were disputed terms in the Niceno-Constantinopolitan creed, with the former usually translated in English as "consubstantial" or "of one being": "We believe in one God . . . and his Son Jesus Christ our Lord, *of one being* with the Father."

28. Ibid., 54–55.

29. *Ep. ad monachos Calaritanos* 5, ed. Allen and Neil (2002) 130–31, *Maximus*: "quem et nos habere aduersos Arrianos, qui continuantur hic, supplicate Deo. . . ."

30. Anastasius of Sinai, *Questiones et responsiones*; the new edition of M. Richards is being continued by J. Munitiz; *De blasphemia* 1, ed. A. Papadopoulos-Kerameus (1891) 401.

31. Meier (2003) 45–64. One of the most famous examples of *Kaiserkritik* in this period comes from Procopius, *Anecdota* 18, 36–37 (ed. and tr. H. B. Dewing [2000] 222–25): "Such, then, were the calamities which fell upon all mankind during the reign of the demon who had become incarnate in Justinian, while he himself, as having become Emperor, provided the causes of them. And I shall show, further, how many evils he did to men by means of a hidden power and of a demoniacal nature. For while this man was administering the nation's affairs, many other calamities chanced to befall, which some insisted came about through the aforementioned presence of this evil demon and through his contriving, while others said that the Deity, detesting his works, turned away from the Roman Empire and gave place to the abominable demons for the bringing of these things to pass in this fashion."

32. Justinian seems to have accepted the nonorthodox doctrine of *aphthartodocetism*, the teaching of Julian of Halicarnassus that Christ's suffering in the body during his crucifixion was not real but only apparent.

33. Cf. 1 Cor. 12:28: "God placed in the church first apostles, second prophets, third teachers."

34. *Disp. Biz.* 3, ed. Allen and Neil (2002) 86–87: Ὁ *τοίνυν συνεκβαλλὼν τοὺς ἁγίους τοῖς ἐναγέσι καὶ ἀκαθάρτοις αἱρετικοῖς . . . , τῷ διαβόλῳ τὸν Θεὸν προφανῶς συγκατέκρινεν.*

35. *Disp. Biz.* 4, ed. Allen and Neil (2002) 88–89: *ἀποπαγέντες ἐπὶ τοῖς λαληθεῖσι, κάτω βαλόντες τὰς κεφαλὰς ἐσίγησαν ἐπὶ ἱκανὴν ὥραν.*

36. I would assume that these letters are the *Tome* that is mentioned in the same chapter of *Narrationes*. After the usage adopted for Leo's *Ep.* 28 to Flavian of Constantinople (c. 449), any lengthy letter could be called a tome (*tomus*).

37. Jerusalem was captured in 636; Alexandria in 642 and again in 646; raids on Cyprus began c. 647.

38. *Narr.* 17, ed. and tr. Neil (2006) 194–95. All references to this text come from Neil's edition.

39. *Narr.* 16: 294.

40. Arguments for this identity of the usurper George are given by Neil (2006) 77–82.

41. *Narr.* 20: 202. In the tenth-century Greek *Vita Martini* (chap. 8, ed. Peeters [1933] 225–62, at 258), the emperor is said to have delivered the command to cut off the sack (*psathion*, not *psachnion*) from Martin's head and the laces of his shoes. See Neil (2006) 112–14.

42. There are several candidates for the identity of this figure, including Theodore (brother of Euprepius and, like him, an imperial chief baker) and Theodore Spoudaeus, associate of Theodosius of Gangra and connected to the church of St. Sophia in Constantinople or Jerusalem. The evidence is reviewed in Neil (2006) 95.

43. Neil in Leemans (2010) 179–94. See also McGowan (2009) 48: "It was only under Augustus that *dicta*, or what was said, came to be cause (and perhaps only for Ovid) for criminal prosecution." See also Chapter 6 in this volume. Other important studies are those of Gareth Williams (1994) for the exile poetry generally and Alessandro Barchiesi (2001) 79–104 for *Tristia* 2 specifically.

44. Ov. *Tr.* 2.471–72.

45. Ibid., 2.575–79.

46. As commented by Barsby (1991) 43, "The repeated references to Augustus' clemency, if not openly casting doubt on the emperor's possession of that virtue, at least emphasize his unreasonableness in not extending it to Ovid."

47. His sentence was transmuted from death to exile, thus depriving him of a more straightforward martyrdom, and delaying his passage to heaven, which he claims to regret (*Narr.* 23: 208).

48. *Ep.* 1 (= *Narr.* 3: 168) line 17: *heretici.*

49. (*Narr.* 3: 170) lines 10–11: "falsum contra me, immo contra suas ipsorum animas iniqui uiri testificati sunt."

50. (*Narr.* 5: 172) lines 13–16: "Et crede mihi, desiderantissime fili mi, non uidendum tempus aliud nisi manifeste hoc in quo sint initia dolorum quemadmodum Dominus praedixit aduentum antichristi."

51. "[B]eware lest under the guise of peace we are found to be sick with apostasy, and preaching it, which the divine apostle said would come before the advent of the Antichrist" (*Disp. Biz.* 3, ed. Allen and Neil [2002] 86–87).

52. (*Narr.* 29: 222) lines 7–9.

53. *Ep.* 3 (= *Narr.* 29: 222–24); *Ep.* 4 (*Narr.* 30: 224–28). See also Allen's chapter in this volume (ch. 10).

54. *Ep.* 4 = (*Narr.* 31: 228) lines 11–12: "et confirmet contra omnem hereticum et aduersariam ecclesiae nostrae personam."

55. Ed. and tr. Neil (2006) 166–233. Martin's letters were presumably written in Latin before being translated into Greek by the author of the *Narrationes*—they survive only in the Latin retroversion by Anastasius Bibliothecarius, the ninth-century papal librarian. Theodore Spoudaeus is identified as being "of St. Sophia" (*Sanctae Sophiae*) in the preface to the *Narrationes*, which may indicate a link with the Church of St. Sophia in Constantinople or Jerusalem: see Neil (2006) 129.

56. *Hypom.* (*graece*) 2, ed. Allen and Neil (2002) 150–51.

57. *Hypom.* (*latine*) 1, ed. Neil (2006) 234.

58. *Hypom.* 9, ed. Neil (2006) 262, lines 6–8: "et finis seditionis fiat, et terminus huiusmodi atrocissimi mali pretiosum scilicet illorum sanguinem effundentium." These penalties for the "trespasses and blasphemies" of Maximus and the two Anastasii are prescribed in the *Third Sentence Against Them*, appended to the end of *Disp. Biz.*, 17, ed. Allen and Neil (2002) 118–19.

59. *Hypom.* 4, ed. Neil (2006) 242, lines 12–13: "in profano et penitus sine Deo imperatorio Typo."

60. *Hypom.* 2, ed. Neil (2006) 236, lines 10–18: "haec autem omnia ob nihil aliud in eos gesserunt uere profanissimi et miserrrimi apostatae ueritatis, nisi propter pessimam ueraciter et solam inuidiam quam antiquus hostis daemon in eis seminauit saltem ad modicum quid resistere sapientiae quae illis merito fuerat a Deo donata pro uera scilicet ueritate, et solum pro eo quod noluissent illi communicare cum his in tam publica et sine Deo impietate ipsorum."

61. *Hypom.* 2 (*graece*), ed. Allen and Neil (2002) 148–51: *κατὰ διαδοχὰς γὰρ ἅτε γάγγραινα νομὴν λαβόντες οἱ αὐτοῦ ἀπόγονοι ἐκράτησαν τῆς βασιλείας.*

62. Ed. Allen and Neil (1999) xxiii.

63. *Contra Const.* 4, ed. Allen and Neil (2002) 174–75: *τοὺς δὲ ὁμολογητὰς καὶ οὐκ ἔλαττον μάρτυρας.*

64. *Contra Const.* 2, ed. Allen and Neil (2002) 172–73: *Σπέρματα πονηρά, ἀμβλωθρίδια ἀτέλεστα, πτηνὰ νυκτοπορινά, γῆς ἔντερα, κοιλίαι ἀργαί, τραπεζογίγαντες καὶ γυναικοιέρακες.*

65. *Contra Const.* 1, ed. Allen and Neil (2002) 172–73: *ὁ ἀλογώτατος καὶ ἀσυνετώτατος καὶ εὐηθέστατος βασιλεύς.*

66. *Contra Const.* 1, ed. Allen and Neil (2002) 172–73.

REFERENCES

Primary Sources

Acta Conciliorum oecumenicorum: Concilium lateranense a. 649 celebratum. Ed. Rudolf Riedinger. Acta Conciliorum Oecumenicorum, series 2, vol. 1. Berlin: De Gruyter, 1984.

Allen, Pauline. 2009. *Sophronius of Jerusalem and Seventh-Century Heresy: The Synodical Letter and Other Documents.* Oxford Early Christian Texts. Oxford: Oxford University Press.

Anastasius the Apocrisiarius. *Ep. ad Theodosium Gangrensem.* See *Scripta saeculi VII vitam Maximi Confessoris illustrantia.*

Anastasius of Sinai. *Questiones et responsiones: De blasphemia.* Ed. Athanasios Papadopoulos-Kerameus. Analecta Hierosolymitikês stachyologias 1. Petropolis: V. Kirsvaoum, 1891: 400–404.

Augustine of Hippo. *Contra mendacium.* Corpus Scriptorum Ecclesiasticorum Latinorum 41. Vienna: Tempksy, 1900.

Disputatio Bizyae. See *Scripta saeculi VII vitam Maximi Confessoris illustrantia.*

Martin, bishop of Rome. *Epistulae.* Ed. and tr. Bronwen Neil. *Seventh-Century Popes and Martyrs: The Political Hagiography of Anastasius Bibliothecarius.* Studia Antiqua Australiensia 2. Turnhout: Brepols, 2006: 166–232.

Maximus the Confessor (?). *Vita beatae Virginis.* Tr. Stephen Shoemaker. New Haven, CT: Yale University Press, 2012.

Narrationes de exilio sancti papae Martini. Ed. and tr. in Neil, *Seventh-Century Popes and Martyrs,* 166–232.

Ovid. *Tristia.* Ed. and tr. A. L. Wheeler, *Ovid,* vol. 6: *Tristia. Ex Ponto,* rev. ed. by G. P. Goold. Cambridge, MA: Harvard University Press, 1988.

Procopius. *Anecdota.* Ed. and tr. H. B. Dewing, *Procopius,* vol. 6. Cambridge, MA: Harvard University Press, 2000.

Relatio Motionis. See *Scripta saeculi VII vitam Maximi Confessoris illustrantia.*

Scripta saeculi VII vitam Maximi Confessoris illustrantia. Ed. Pauline Allen and Bronwen Neil. Corpus Christianorum Series Graeca 39. Turnhout: Brepols, 1999. Ed. and tr. Pauline Allen and Bronwen Neil, *Maximus the Confessor and His Companions: Documents from Exile.* Oxford Early Christian Texts. Oxford: Oxford University Press, 2002.

Sophronius of Jerusalem. *Synodica.* Ed. and tr. Pauline Allen, *Sophronius of Jerusalem and Seventh-Century Heresy. The* Synodical Letter *and Other Documents.* Oxford: Oxford University Press, 2009.

Theodore Spoudaeus. *Commemoratio (latine).* Ed. and tr. in Neil, *Seventh-Century Popes and Martyrs,* 182–221.

Theodore Spoudaeus (?). *Hypomnesticon (latine).* Ed. and tr. in Neil, *Seventh-Century Popes and Martyrs,* 234–65. *(graece).* Ed. and tr. in Pauline Allen and Bronwen Neil, *Maximus the Confessor,* 148–71.

Vita sancti papae Martini. "Une vie grecque du pape s. Martin I." *Analecta Bollandiana* 51 (1933): 225–62.

Secondary Sources

Allen, Pauline and Bronwen Neil, eds. Forthcoming. *The Oxford Handbook to Maximus the Confessor.* Oxford: Oxford University Press.

———, eds. and tr. 2002. *Maximus the Confessor and His Companions: Documents from Exile.* Oxford: Oxford University Press.

Barchiesi, Alessandro. 2001. *Speaking Volumes: Narrative and Intertext in Ovid and Other Latin Poets.* London: Duckworth.

Barsby, John. 1991. *Ovid.* Oxford: Clarendon.

Booth, P. 2013. *Crisis of Empire: Doctrine and Dissent at the End of Late Antiquity.* Berkeley: University of California Press.

Brandes, Wolfram. 1998. "'Juristiche' Krisenbewältigung im 7. Jahrhundert? Die Prozesse gegen Papst Martin I. und Maximos Homologetes." In *Forschungen zur byzantinischen Rechtsgeschichte* (Fontes Minores 10), ed. Ludwig Burgmann, 141–212. Frankfurt: Löwenklau Gesellschaft.

Casey, Damien. 2000–2001. "*Piss Christ,* Sacrifice and Liberal Excess." *Law, Text, Culture* 5: 19–34.

Hovorun, Cyril. 2008. *Will, Action and Freedom: Christological Controversies in the Seventh Century.* Leiden: Brill.

Jankoviak, Marek and Philip Booth. Forthcoming. "An Updated Date-List of Maximus the Confessor's Works." In *The Oxford Handbook to Maximus the Confessor,* ed. Pauline Allen and Bronwen Neil. Oxford: Oxford University Press.

Knapp, Bettina Leibowitz. 1979. *Dream and Image.* New York: Whitston.

Larison, Daniel. 2009. "Return to Authority: The Monothelete Controversy and the Role of Text, Emperor and Council in the Sixth Ecumenical Council." 2 vols. PhD dissertation, University of Chicago.

Leveleux, Corinne. 2001. *La parole interdite: Le blasphème dans la France médiévale (XIIIe–XVIe siècles): Du péché au crime.* Paris: De Boccard.

McGowan, Matthew M. 2009. *Ovid in Exile: Power and Poetic Redress in the Tristia and Epistulae ex ponto.* Leiden: Brill.

Meier, Mischa. 2003. "Zur Wahrnehmung und Deutung von Naturkatastrophen im 6. Jahrhundert n. Chr." In *Naturkatastrophen. Beiträge zu ihrer Deutung, Wahrnehmung und Darstellung in Text und Bild von der Antike bis ins 20. Jahrhundert,* ed. D. Groh, M. Kempe, and F. Mauelshagen, 45–64. Tübingen, Gunter Narr.

Moore, R. Scott. *Online Directory of Roman Emperors.* S.v. "Constans II." http://www.roman-emperors.org/constan2.htm.

———. *Online Directory of Roman Emperors.* S.v. "Heraclonas and Constantine III." http://www.roman-emperors.org/heraclon.htm.

Nash, David. 2007. *Blasphemy in the Christian World: A History*. Oxford: Oxford University Press.

Neil, Bronwen. 2006. "Commemorating Pope Martin I: His Trial in Constantinople." *Studia Patristica* 39: 77–82.

———. 2010. "From *Tristia* to *Gaudia*: The Exile and Martyrdom of Pope Martin I." In *Martyrdom and Persecution in Late Antique Christianity*, ed. J. Leemans, 179–94. Leuven: Peeters.

Peeters, Paul. 1933. "Une vie grecque du pape s. Martin I." *Analecta Bollandiana* 51: 225–62.

Price, Richard. 2010. "Monothelitism: A Heresy or a Form of Words?" *Studia Patristica* 48: 221–32.

Sherwood, Polycarp. 1952. *An Annotated Date-List of Works of Maximus the Confessor*. Rome: Studia Anselmiana.

Shoemaker, Stephen. 2006. "The Georgian *Life of the Virgin* Attributed to Maximus the Confessor: Its Authenticity (?) and Importance." In *Mémorial R.P. Michel van Esbroeck, S.J.*, ed. Alexey Muraviev and Basil Lourié, 307–28. Scrinium 2. St. Petersburg: Byzantinorussica.

van Dieten, Jan Louis. 1972. *Geschichte der Patriarchen von Sergius I. bis Johannes VI (610–715)*. Enzyklopädie der Byzantinistik 24. Geschichte der griechischen Patriarchen von Konstantinopel, Teil 4. Amsterdam: A.M. Hakkert.

Williams, Gareth D. 1994. *Banished Voices: Readings in Ovid's Exile Poetry*. Cambridge: Cambridge University Press.

Winkelmann, Friedhelm. 2002. *Der monenergetisch-monotheletische Streit*. Berliner byzantinische Studien 6. Frankfurt: Lang.

Chapter 12

"*Dixit quod nunquam vidit hereticos*": Dissimulation and Self-Censorship in Thirteenth-Century Inquisitorial Testimonies

Megan Cassidy-Welch

Studies of medieval censorship have mostly concluded that the formalization and institutionalization of censorship was a product of the fifteenth- and sixteenth-century Inquisitions. Through the Congregation for the Index of Prohibited Books and the Holy Office, censorship became both a means of prohibiting the dissemination of heterodox ideas in print and a means of monopolizing the circulation of orthodoxies. Indeed, it is often understood that the development of the Inquisition and the development of censorship itself ran parallel. Recent studies have nuanced this relationship, especially in relation to the intellectual transformations of the twelfth and thirteenth centuries, where it has been argued that censorship was an earlier development.[1] Some scholars have traced the links between the medieval universities and censorship, both in terms of the censorship of certain schoolmen's ideas and in terms of the new universities acting as agents of censorship themselves.[2] Yet the historiography on medieval censorship still mostly presents censorship as a "top-down" phenomenon with essentially repressive qualities, and embodied in the work of the later Inquisitions. Furthermore, despite the significant role that the later Inquisitions certainly played in the development of censorship, there has been little work done that links the activities and characteristics of the earlier thirteenth- and fourteenth-century inquisitions to broader issues around the use and meaning of censorship.

In this chapter I suggest that a study of early inquisitorial practices and documentation can add significant historical depth to a broader discussion of censorship. In particular, evidence from thirteenth-century inquisitorial texts reveals both a desire on the part of the inquisitors to censor or eradicate heterodox ideas and an awareness on the part of suspected heretics that their own responses to inquisitorial questioning could be filtered through modes of dissimulation. The interplay of self-censorship and inquisitorial questioning thus raises a range of interesting questions about what we might understand censorship to mean for medieval people on both sides of the inquisitorial process. What were people leaving out or representing in particular ways? What were the narrative strategies at work in the texts that show resistance, refusal, and negotiation? What can we claim for these things as indicators of censorship?

In considering these questions, this essay draws on and extends a longer historiography on what we know about heresy, and particularly "Catharism" from the inquisitorial record. Over the past two decades, the debate among historians of the thirteenth-century inquisitions has focused on the question of whether Catharism existed as a consciously coherent set of religious practices, or whether it was the invention of later historiography, particularly from the nineteenth century, but also within the inquisitorial record itself.[3] Close readings of inquisitorial records have long focused on the construction of these texts as representations of what inquisitors wanted to find, while also seeking some agency on the part of the deponents whose words were documented in what were often circumstances of fear and intimidation. This chapter is less concerned with whether Catharism existed than with how inquisitorial records can be read as representations of religiosity. It is one of the arguments of this essay that the analytical categories of dissimulation and self-censorship can draw our attention to how *both* inquisitor and deponent articulated heterodox ideas in these records. This is important in not only illuminating how self-censorship might have operated in this particular medieval context, but also attending to the historical specificity of heterodox ideas during the thirteenth century. This may be seen first in the historical background of the inquisitorial process during the thirteenth century, and the sources that testify to those processes.

Context

Inquisitorial activity began under the pontificate of Pope Gregory IX, who, in 1231, had authorized the prior of the Dominican convent at Regensburg to act as a papal judge delegate and to appoint other members of the Dominican order of monks to root out heretical activity in Germany and France.[4] In doing this, Pope Gregory IX was building on a foundation of papal legislation condemning and punishing heretics that stretched back to the twelfth century.[5] But Pope Gregory was also doing something new in that he was creating a new system of dealing with the problem of heresy. The first novelty was to use the old Roman law process of *inquisitio* as the appropriate legal means of prosecuting heresy. This meant that no accusation had to be brought against specific acts of heresy in order for investigations of heresy to begin. It was enough that a suspicion of heretical activity be detected for the papal delegates to start their enquiries. Second, Pope Gregory instructed that those in charge of these *inquisitiones* against heresy were specially trained members of the mendicant orders, who answered to him alone. This meant that those who were investigating heresy were the only ones who could now legitimately undertake that work. At this point, in the mid-thirteenth century, there was no sense of "The Inquisition," as Edward Peters and others have long noted. Rather, these were independent investigative tribunals, acting on papal authority, which dealt with outbreaks of heresy where they believed them to be occurring. The institutional inquisitions of Rome and Venice were yet to be developed.[6] Indeed, it is important to remember that in the mid-thirteenth century "inquisition" was a procedure, not an institution.

Inquisitions were particularly active in the south of France in the region now known as the Languedoc from 1233, when Pope Gregory IX issued bulls authorizing the creation of inquisitorial tribunals in the region.[7] This was principally due to the embedded presence there of the heretical groups known as "Cathars" and "Waldensians," both of whom had been the targets of military action during the so-called Albigensian crusade from 1209 to 1229. After the 1229 Treaty of Paris had formally ended the military campaigns of the crusade, it was deemed appropriate to continue the eradication of the last vestiges (or what was hoped to be the last vestiges) of heresy from this region. Thus, a number of inquisitorial tribunals visited the Languedoc throughout the thirteenth and fourteenth centuries. We know of their activities from the vast swathes of documents they produced during their investigations. In fact, for historians, one of the most enduringly interesting features of inquisitorial activity is its meticulous and bureaucratic record keeping. As James Given has described, even the earliest inquisitors of the thirteenth century kept detailed registers that recorded the testimonies of those questioned about heresy, while by the fourteenth century, these registers were supplemented by inquisitors' handbooks or guides for questioning and extracting information from sometimes recalcitrant witnesses.

The central purpose of the inquisitorial process was the production of truth. This was achieved coercively and discursively. By both the application of external pressure (such as lengthy spells in prison, atmospheres of intimidation, and sometimes physical violence) and by the production of written records of confession, inquisitors were able to document and verify the truth. This was not so much the "truth" of ideological *belief* per se, but the truth of an individual's knowledge and participation in heresy more loosely.[8] As John Arnold has outlined, in their written depositions of suspected heretics, inquisitors produced truth through the construction of confessing and autonomous subjects. That is, by recording the process and outcome of confession and by requiring (as they did) deponents to verify their own depositions, inquisitors were able to create what they considered to be the truth of heretical activity and the truth of individual participation in such activity. Thus, written records in which confession and autonomy were central shored up the legal requirements of *inquisitio*: a confession needed to be extracted for sentencing to take place, while a deponent needed to authenticate the process. As Arnold has also recognized, confession and autonomy also reflected a deeper shift toward medieval recognition of the value of interiority in spiritual and religious discourse. After the *Utriusque omnis sexus* decree of the Fourth Lateran Council (1215) required all Christians to confess at least once a year, confessional practice had become more and more central to inclusion in the Christian community, and this was reflected in inquisitorial texts.[9]

Before turning to explore some of individual depositions, it is worth noting that the words we read on the inquisitorial page are several steps removed from their first utterance. Once called before the inquisitors, a suspect was interviewed and his or her words were taken down by the notary in the vernacular. This was then read back to the suspect for verification. The text was then translated into Latin for inclusion in the register. A number of modern scholars have described this process carefully: Caterina Bruschi, for instance, has written of the "filters" through which we read these records, while James Given has argued that written records were extremely useful archives for the inquisitors themselves, who were able to cross reference interrogations in order to establish patterns of communication and heretical networks.[10] A long and complex historiography exists on the ways in which historians can read through the written records, some of which I will outline below. In any case, it is initially important to understand that deponents themselves had some input into the production of inquisitorial texts, although the words we read were penned by inquisitorial agents.

In the south of France, the documentation for the thirteenth century is especially rich, despite the loss of a significant amount of material over time. In one inquisition alone during the 1240s, two inquisitors, Bernart de Caux and Jean de St Pierre, investigated over five thousand individuals, and the surviving testimonies of some of them (two volumes of an original ten are extant) may be found in a single manuscript (Toulouse, BN MS 609). Other inquisitorial records of this time are to be mostly found in the Bibliothèque nationale de France, Paris, among the 258-volume "Collection Doat." This is a seventeenth-century collection of copies of manuscripts from various archives and libraries of southern France made by a team of copyists under the direction of Jean de Doat from 1665 to 1670. Of these 258 volumes, 6 pertain to the thirteenth-century inquisitions in the region. The material therein ranges from copies of papal legislation to copies of depositions given by those brought for questioning to various inquisitors; from sentences for heresy to administrative items; from heretical writings to directions for the building and maintenance of inquisitorial prisons. Much of this material does not survive in any other form, therefore the Doat volumes pertaining to thirteenth-century France are especially important for the history of the region and its encounters with the earliest inquisitors.

For the purposes of this chapter, I focus on a set of inquisitorial testimonies from the 1270s, now located in volumes 25 and 26 of the Collection Doat. These testimonies are the copied records of interrogations of around a hundred men and women who were questioned in Toulouse from 1273 to 1282. These individuals were interrogated by Dominican inquisitors, and some had been interrogated previously. These particular volumes have recently been fully transcribed and edited.[11] For this chapter I have consulted the original items (in the Bibliothèque nationale de France and on microfilm), but for ease of reference below, I cite the Latin and English transcriptions using the printed edition. The 1270s saw something of a revival of the activities of inquisitors in the Languedoc after some twenty years of less regular investigation. This was due to the finalization of Capetian claims to the former lands of the Counts of Toulouse, formal royal protection of the Dominican inquisitors in 1271, renewed military activity by Philip III in 1272 (against the count of Foix) and direct papal support for Philip's activities against heresy.[12] By the later thirteenth century, the inquisitors of southern France were Dominicans, often with legal training and often locals. They were also very concerned to find evidence of long-term association with heretical activities and (as outlined below) many of the deponents were asked to recall events from years before. The Doat volumes that contain the testimonies of interrogations for this period are thus significant sources for the perceived increase in heresy in the region. The testimonies are also rich repositories of information about the ways in which individuals negotiated inquisitorial questioning. It is in this latter context that self-censorship may be explored.

Self-Censorship and Dissimulation in the Testimonies

The men and women who testified before the inquisitors of the 1270s had been detained, sometimes for quite some time, before they gave their depositions. The inquisitorial prison was a feature of the southern French landscape by this time and in Doat 25–26 the Chateau Narbonnais is frequently mentioned as the place where deponents were housed while waiting for interrogation.[13] Sometimes inquisitorial prisons were specially constructed buildings, and sometimes they were sites that had been requisitioned for use as a prison. Imprisonment was used for detentive and punitive purposes. Those suspected of heresy or knowledge of heresy could be detained for some time before being called to testify, while others who had already been sentenced could find imprisonment a part of their sentence, or even their entire sentence. At worst, people could be sentenced to suffer "strict imprisonment," where they were incarcerated for life and fed on the "bread of tribulation and the water of sadness." Miserable as we would assume inquisitorial prisons to be, they were also sites of possibility for those detained in them, and there is significant evidence of networks of communication and information sharing within them. Places like the Chateau Narbonnais were not buildings full of windowless cells where inmates could not talk to each other. They were rather like large shared accommodations, where people could meet, where people could overhear conversations, where information could be disseminated. These physical conditions have some implications for the subsequent presentation of information to the inquisitors, as there was certainly a possibility that answers to questions could be prepared in advance, that people could collaborate to get their stories straight, that the results of interrogations could be shared.[14] There are a number of examples of people who had changed their stories after having been held in prison for some time. One deponent, Bernard Rival, was asked to remember events that took place twenty-five years earlier and found that after his long spell in prison his memory became sharper: he was said to have "corrected himself after being held in prison a long time." Gaubert of Aula "was brought out from prison after denying the truth and keeping silent about it" and was then persuaded to answer further questions.[15]

Modes of negotiating inquisitorial questioning were various but tended to be phrased in terms of negatives. One very frequent response to both general and specific questions was for a deponent to claim that he or she simply could not remember. The records are full of the phrase *dixit quod non recordatur* ("he said that he could not recall"), recorded by a perhaps weary notary. Some deponents claimed that the events to which the inquisitors referred took place such a long time ago that they simply cannot remember them either because the passage of time had dimmed their memories (in one case expressed as "propter oblivionem"),[16] or because they were children when the events took place. One man was asked whether he had ever said that "when he was young he had frequently crossed himself and nothing good ever happened to him, but when he had grown up he left off crossing himself and many good things happened to him." He responded that he did not remember whether he had ever said such things.[17] The refusal to produce informative replies to inquisitorial questions may be interpreted in a number of ways. As James Given has suggested, we could read silence as an act of resistance on the part of the deponents, or an assertion of agency in a process where the balance of power was very unequal.[18] Mark Pegg has also drawn attention to the delicately constructed relationship between inquisitorial questions and deponents' answers. "Questions," writes Pegg, "are very cultural specific predictions about knowledge . . . [a]nswers justify a set of questions because they complete their sense."[19] Questions without answers, then, are not quite nonsensical in this context, but they are incomplete and directionless. Refusal to answer a question could be seen as a course of dialogic evasive action on the part of deponents, a sometimes deliberate mode of dissimulation that had the potential to frustrate the process of producing inquisitorial truths.

Very often, deponents state bluntly that they had never seen heretics or heard heretics. This denial of knowledge was a common initial statement in the register. One typical example is Fabrissa, the wife of Peter Vital, joiner, who was sworn in on February 7, 1273. Fabrissa immediately stated that "she never saw any heretics, to recognize them as such, nor did she adore them, nor did she hear their preachings, nor did she give or send them anything, nor did she have any hope or faith in them, nor does she know anything about the matter of heresy."[20] The questions to which Fabrissa responded were the same for other deponents. These were formulaic questions designed to expose both individual heretical leanings and possible networks of heretical association and activity. Deponents knew this, and some later revealed that they had denied knowledge of heresy during their initial questioning in order to protect other people from the inquisitors. Denial of knowledge of heretics and heresy was sometimes modified during a long set of interrogations. One woman, Petronilla of Villefranche, said "she never saw any heretics" but then admitted that long ago "when she was a little girl," she had indeed seen heretics living openly. Later in her deposition, Petronilla abandoned her claims and ultimately confessed to seeing heretics in her husband's house and eating and drinking with them.[21]

Some deponents were asked to revisit conversations in which they had been involved, and to verify words and comments they had uttered, sometimes long ago. When confronted with evidence of heretical statements or knowledge of heretical activity, some suspects attempted to explain their heretical words by claiming that they were joking, that the words that the inquisitors considered to be dangerous had been made humorously. Durand of Rouffiac agreed that he had indeed said that the soul is nothing else in the body other than blood, but that this was simply "by way of a joke" or playfully (*ludendo*).[22] Gaubert of Aula explained his crude words about creation by admitting that it was true that "he had often spoken to many men and women asking if they believed in that God who makes wind and rain and on their replying that they did, he would conclude 'therefore you believe in an arse and a cunt,'" but that his words were not intended as an insult to God. They were meant as a joke—*sed ratione solatii*.[23] Attempts to defuse the questions resulted in barely concealed disrespect on some occasions, too. The same deponent, Gaubert of Aura, was questioned about his tendency to urinate against the wall of the church and in the cemetery. He responded that no one had ever reproached him for this and that he did not know that he was not supposed to relieve himself on sacred ground. Pressed further, Gaubert announced that he urinated regularly in the church and cemetery—even against a glass window on Easter day—because he had an infirmity and was not capable of holding his urine.[24] More direct insults against the inquisitors themselves were reported in the depositions as well. In the testimony given by William Fournier, it was recorded that his acquaintance, Bernard Demier, had shown William "images of the saints who had suffered for Christ and the said Bernard said to the said witness that it was the same today as formerly: good men were persecuted by bad." Asked for more information, William remembered that Bernard also said to William that the mendicants were "false prophets" who "persecuted good men."[25] The claim that these sorts of words were not serious was one way in which the power of those words was diminished, for the suspect as much as for the inquisitor.

Attempts to moderate words and actions retrospectively may also be found in the testimonies in which suspects declare that once they realized that they were in the presence of a heretic, they removed themselves immediately. One example may be found in the testimony of Bartholomew Iordan of Rabastens, who said that when he was in a house where heretics were present "he did nothing else there except sit and he went away immediately when he heard from the same heretics that no man ought to cross himself."[26] Although this was a singular occasion, he could not remember the names of anyone else who was there, despite acknowledging that there had indeed been many bystanders. Other deponents were keen to distance themselves from knowledge of heresy by reporting to the inquisitors that they had not seen or heard heretics themselves, but they had heard from others that heretics were preaching in the area or that heretics had been seen. John of Torrena informed the inquisitors that although he knew nothing about heretics himself, he had been told by the local priest that the priest had seen heretics at night. The priest told John that he had seen one William Matfred who was "carrying a stick in his hand and taking his dogs with him [. . . William] came out of the wood . . . pretending that he was hunting and went toward Lempaut, and there followed him at a distance two men dressed in . . . black cloth." The priest told the deponent that he "strongly suspected . . . that they were heretics."[27] This sort of information was twice removed from John himself, who had already testified before previous inquisitors and who added to the detail of his statement three more times before he was abjured.

Other attempts to distance a suspect from knowledge of or participation in heretical activity were vicarious. Some who were brought to testify before the inquisitors were concerned to protect children, and did so by making sure that their ages were included in the written record. Bernard Rival, mentioned above, was one witness who was careful to state that twenty-five years ago when he had seen heretics, "Bernarda, his daughter, then a girl of eleven years or thereabouts, and Pons, his son, then a boy of eight years or thereabouts, were in the aforesaid house," but that he "does not remember seeing them together with the heretics" and "believes that the same children did not know what sort of people the aforesaid heretics were."[28] Raymond Hugh told the inquisitors that when he was in a house in the presence of heretics, he did not see them because "he was with the children in the solar."[29] And Bernard Molinier noted that a boy who was in the presence of two heretics in the house of Bernardin Bordas was only "eight years old."[30] Including the young ages of children in the written depositions was a way of removing them from suspicion of heretical association. In the middle of the thirteenth century, the minimum age at which a boy could appear before the inquisitors was fourteen and girls, twelve. This mirrored the current thinking on the age of consent. Boys and girls over these minimum ages were required to testify and were subject to the same sorts of punishments as anyone else. Removing children from the net cast by inquisitors by stating their ages may have been a deliberate and protective strategy.

Occasionally, suspected heretics seem to be defended by deponents who state that they are good people. Stephen Roger of Roumens said that the heretics were "good men and truthful and that they had good faith,"[31] as did Fabrissa of Limoux, who was asked "if she believed that the said heretics were good men, and truthful, and friends of God, and that they had a good faith, and that it was possible to be saved through them if one died in their sect." Her response was "yes."[32] These declarations are often made in the context of "corrected" confessions; that is, they are added to original confessions after sometimes lengthy periods in detention. In Fabrissa of Limoux's case, the notary had already registered that Fabrissa had been "denying the truth and keeping silent about it before us" in her previous testimony. By the time she revealed that she did believe that the heretics were "good men," Fabrissa had already corrected and added to her testimony twice. Sometimes, deponents simply admitted to the charges outright. Raymond Hugh is one who said directly that he had adored heretics, heard them himself, and had seen and heard others adoring them within the last month. He also furnished the inquisitors with the names of those who he accused. Indeed, he said fulsomely that he "received many times and so many times he does not remember the number, the aforementioned heretics."[33]

Other deponents admitted to omitting information and concealing the truth of their knowledge of and association with heresy. Again, Fabrissa of

Limoux provides a good example. It is recorded in her deposition that Fabrissa "acknowledged that she had done wrong because in her other confession she knowingly concealed all these things, contrary to her own oath, as the same witness said for the sake of confession."[34] Another man told his questioners that he had appeared before inquisitors on another earlier occasion and that he had "denied the truth to them, contrary to his own oath, concerning all these things which he had done or committed in heresy and he abjured all heresy before them." The notary recorded that he "acknowledged that he did wrong because afterwards he saw heretics and committed acts of heresy."[35] This sort of open admission was sometimes the product of extended periods of incarceration and questioning. But it was also sometimes the product of other factors. There are a number of interesting moments when deponents are asked directly why they have concealed information or lied outright but are now confessing: "why," reads one deposition, "[did] the witness recently conceal information contrary to his own oath?" Some suspects replied that they were trying to protect their friends.[36] Other deponents state quite clearly that fear motivated their answers. John of Torrena said that he had failed to mention certain information to the inquisitors the first time he was questioned because he was frightened of one of the men he had named in his deposition.[37]

Self-censorship could also occur outside the inquisitorial tribunal, and sometimes involved the overt destruction of written texts. As is well known, the inquisitors of thirteenth-century Languedoc were occasionally greeted by violent protest and refusal to engage with their activities. One of the most notorious moments involved the murder of the inquisitor Guillaume Arnaud and his servants at Avignonet in 1242.[38] But other acts were aimed specifically at destroying the documentation of the inquisitors, especially those powerful repositories of information, the inquisitorial registers, in which the words and deeds of suspected heretics and their networks were recorded. The theft of books and registers is one indication that people wanted to destroy potentially incriminating evidence, as John Arnold has suggested. As noted above, the process of creating an authentic deposition relied heavily on the deponents themselves, who had to agree that the words and account of the inquisitorial questioning were true. Arnold has shown very successfully that the construction of an autonomous subject was fundamental to the inquisitors work for this very reason: they were needed to ratify the truth of what was written about them.[39] The destruction of that truth through the destruction of the written records that housed it was one means by which heretical activity could be masked and concealed.

Finally, some of these tactics of self-censorship might be summarized and illustrated through the tale of one particular individual. The example of Bernard Rival is a singular case, but because of its length it touches on a range of issues around dissimulation. Bernard Rival was sworn in on February 21, 1273, for the second time. It is noted that he had already been incarcerated for some time and now sought to "correct" his former confession and provide more information. Bernard's testimony seems frank and full. In response to the usual opening question, "Have you ever seen a heretic?," Bernard admitted that he had. He told of one instance at Aurin, twenty-five years previously, when he had seen and adored two heretics, and had been blessed by them. Bernard provided their names, and then told of a number of other occasions when he had seen these two men, and greeted them and even "adored" them at times. Bernard was questioned about other people who were there when he interacted with these heretics, and was asked if others also adored them, were blessed by them, or ate bread that had been blessed by them. He offered some names, noting that his own children had witnessed some heretical activity at a young age, and, as mentioned previously, that the "children did not know what sort of people the heretics were," while another boy of twelve "did not adore them." Bernard was also implicated in the transmission of a wax tablet with the name of the "deacon of the heretics" on it. He confessed that he and Pons Rastel had been working in his vineyard when two escaped heretics came by to organize with Pons the exchange of a wax tablet and the carrying of that tablet to some incarcerated heretics. The idea was that the captive heretics could write on the tablet the name of the man they thought should be the new "deacon of heretics," and the tablet could then be circulated to the appropriate people. Finally, Bernard informed the inquisitors, presumably in response to a question about the whereabouts of a particular woman, that he knew that she had left for Lombardy with some family members a year ago. The confession ended with a statement from Bernard attesting to his belief that for fifteen years he thought that heretics were good people and would save him.

On the surface, Bernard's testimony seems to disclose much. However, opacity is present. Above all, his words distance himself from much of the heretical activity he describes. When he saw and adored heretics, it was a quarter of a century ago: those with whom he associated are dead, in Lombardy or elsewhere out of inquisitorial reach, while some names, he does not even remember. Bernard is one deponent who specifically notes that his children were too young to be implicated in heretical activity or association. He does not admit to actively participating in the transmission of the wax tablet to the heretics; he was simply "pruning" his "newly planted vineyard" when the heretics happened to come by. The heretics implicated in the wax tablet affair were themselves burned at Montségur, the famous Cathar fortress that was destroyed in 1244, and cannot verify or disprove Bernard's statement. The woman about whom he is finally questioned is also out of reach in northern Italy. Bernard Rival's testimony thus does not lead to much, from an inquisitorial perspective. We do not know if this was Bernard's intention, of course. Nonetheless, his confession is veiled if not by misinformation or overt lies as by information of limited use. We do know that after his final confession, Bernard was in a bad state. He was found by the notary in the inquisitorial prison with a head wound, and he told the notary that he had tried to kill himself by hitting himself in the head. At this point Bernard was in leg irons, "wishing to die, wishing to kill himself."

Conclusions

Reading inquisitorial testimonies through the lens of self-censorship or dissimulation opens up some directions for considering the nature of both the texts and the meaning of medieval censorship practices. Much of the recent historiography on inquisitorial texts has attempted to challenge a nineteenth-century view of the Inquisition as a monolithic and uniform institution, founded on principles of repression. Indeed, for historians such as Henry Lea, the Inquisition was characterized by coercion and violence: both inquisitorial procedure and the institution of the Inquisition were viewed as oppressive and brutal products of a Catholic Church bent on suppressing difference and dissent through censorship and manipulation.[40] Twentieth- and twenty-first-century historians have, in response to insights drawn from poststructuralist historical methodologies, considered the inquisitorial process in terms of power relationships in order to tease out the agency of the inquisitorial subject. John Arnold's study of the dialogical nature of inquisitorial testimonies is one example of this approach. While recognizing the difficult and frightening situations in which some suspected heretics found themselves, Arnold also found through a close reading of the construction of the inquisitorial depositions that suspects also created opportunities for self-reflection, for dissent, for obstruction through their words and actions. Indeed, the "confessing self" identified by Arnold as a feature of inquisitorial testimonies may also be read as evidence of individual negotiations with the apparatus of inquisitorial power.[41]

As noted above, James Given has also read the depositions for what they might tell us about collective and individual resistance to inquisitorial questioning. Given understands the production of inquisitorial texts to be one part of an overall technology of power relations in medieval Languedoc. The relationship between the questioners and the questioned, the power structures already existing in the stratified social world of thirteenth-century France, and the productive quality of power in a sociological sense are brought together in Given's analysis to suggest a world predicated on much more sophisticated understandings and manifestations of power than a purely repressive model would allow. This is a Foucauldian view to some degree, where power is produced rather than wielded and where self-monitoring constitutes the docile subject.

These ideas are replicated in some of the historiography on censorship, too. Judith Butler argued that censorship is a productive form of power, and that its actions are not solely repressive but also formative or constitutive.[42] Beate Müller proposed that censorship might be understood as a communicative process, where the dialogues and relationships between individuals are as important as the repressive qualities of censorship. As Müller points out, "new censorship" studies can tend to describe almost any form of social control as censorship. But what sets censorship apart is both its historical specificity and its basic quality as a means of controlling communication.[43] Self-censorship is understood both as the product of choice and agency, and as the product of unconscious drives that may not even be prompted by the threat of repression. Dissimulation can take the form of half-truths, ambiguity, speaking in the negative, concealing secrets, offering useless pieces of information, or providing no information at all. Repression, dialogue, agency, speech, and silence are all aspects of modern censorship studies that find echoes in the historiography of the early Inquisition.

We may go a little further than this to consider what self-censorship might have meant in the inquisitorial context. Certainly, if we understand self-censorship to be a conscious strategy, we may agree that a study of medieval self-censorship is a useful and productive means of recovering the voices of those who would otherwise be lost to history. If we follow the prevalent historiographical view, uncovering acts of self-censorship in the inquisitorial record turns up evidence that individual agency existed in what might be perceived as the most repressive of contexts. When deponents in Doat 25–26 were reported as saying time and time again "dixit quod non vidit," "dixit quod non recordatur," "dixit quod nunquam vidit haereticos," it is entirely possible to read those words as being as informative as the more fulsome and descriptive responses that are also recorded by the notaries. Seeking meaning in obstruction and silence within the written record thus bestows a productive and assertive role on the deponent in the production of the inquisitorial text.

At the same time, however, self-censorship could also be seen to serve the inquisitorial project. Inquisitors in the early tribunals were concerned to find evidence of heretical belief, evidence of heretical association, and to uncover the hidden networks of heresy that were thought to exist in the Languedoc. They proceeded from the assumption that not only was heresy present, but that it was insidious, deliberately secretive and hidden from view. Indeed, "secretiveness and heresy became so linked in the clerical imagination . . . that those who were judged to be secretive . . . could also be judged to be heretics on that basis," observes Karen Sullivan.[44] For monastic writers like Henry of Clairvaux, heretics were in hiding like moles, "underground where they can gnaw and destroy the roots of holy places,"[45] and it was the work of the inquisitors to expose these heretics. The dissimulative nature of deponents' responses could be understood to give the inquisitors precisely what they expected to find: half-truths and evasive answers given by people whose very nature was to be concealing. Mark Pegg has pursued this line of argument to suggest that the very construction of the Cathar heresy itself was a product of the historiography of the inquisitorial record: Catharism was a textual fabrication of an organized religious movement in order to justify repressive action against heterodoxy and to affirm orthodoxy.[46] We need not go as far as Pegg to establish that the records of the testimonies also functioned as evidence of inquisitorial success. The wily ambiguity of the deponents' words as we read them can just as easily be interpreted as inquisitorial proof as they can be interpreted as individual agency.

Thus, the evidence of thirteenth-century inquisitorial testimonies indicates that self-censorship can be a useful, if complex, heuristic device for looking at this particular historical process of communication and confrontation. The relationship between suspect and questioner may be exposed as both affirmative and limiting, productive and stifling. Self-censorship reminds us to insist on the symbiotic relationship between historical context, textual construction, and communicative relationships as the foundations of a critical analysis. In so doing, it is the process of inquisition that is illuminated, just as much as it is the words of its earliest adversaries.

NOTES

1. Godman (2000).

2. Thijssen (1998).

3. For the debate, see Pegg (2001b) 181–95 and most recently Moore (2012); see the trenchant review of the latter by Biller (2014).

4. For the subsequent formal bull charging the Dominicans with inquisitorial activities, see Ripoli (1729–40) 1:95 (*Ille humani generis*, May 20, 1237). For useful general overviews of the formation of the early inquisitorial tribunals, see Peters (1988); Lambert (1992).

5. For a useful and accessible outline, see Robinson (2004).

6. Peters (1988); Kieckhefer (1995).

7. The region of Languedoc was known as such from 1271.

8. See Given (1997).

9. Arnold (2001).

10. Bruschi (2003); Given (1997). See also Pegg (2003).

11. Biller et al. (2010).

12. See ibid., 41–48.

13. E.g., ibid., 323, "These things he attested at Toulouse, a captive in the Chateau Narbonnais."

14. For the inquisitorial prison, see Given (1997) 52–65; Peters (1995); Cassidy-Welch (2011).

15. Biller et al. (2010) 199 (for Bernard Rival) and 229 for Gaubert of Aula.

16. Ibid., 961.

17. Ibid., 225.

18. Given (1997) 93–110.

19. Pegg (2003) 112. See also Bueno (2009).

20. Biller et al. (2010) 275.

21. Ibid., 181, 185.

22. Ibid., 221.

23. Ibid., 229.

24. Ibid., 233.

25. Ibid., 209.

26. Ibid., 255.

27. Ibid., 459.

28. Ibid., 201.

29. Ibid., 419.

30. Ibid., 527.

31. Ibid., 239.

32. Ibid., 291.

33. Ibid., 372, 377.

34. Ibid., 291.

35. Ibid., 441.

36. Ibid., 445.

37. Ibid., 465.

38. For an account of this, see Ames (2009) 61–62.

39. Arnold (2001) 82, 99. See also Given (1997) 25–51 on the technology of documentation generally and especially 42–44 on the inquisitorial archives in the Languedocian imagination.

40. Lea (1955).

41. Arnold (2001). For medieval conceptions of the self, see Morris (1972); Zink (1999).

42. Butler (1998) 247–59.

43. Müller (2003) 1–32.

44. Sullivan (2005) 63.

45. Cited in Kienzle (2001) 123.

46. Pegg (2001a).

REFERENCES

Ames, Christine Caldwell. 2009. *Righteous Persecution: Inquisition, Dominicans and Christianity in the Middle Ages.* Philadelphia: University of Pennsylvania Press.

Arnold, John. 2001. *Inquisition and Power: Catharism and the Confessing Subject in Medieval Languedoc.* Philadelphia: University of Pennsylvania Press.

Biller, Peter. 2014. Review of *The War on Heresy: Faith and Power in Medieval Europe.* Review no. 1546. http://www.history.ac.uk/reviews/review/1546.

Biller, Peter, Caterina Bruschi, and Shelagh Sneddon, eds. 2010. *Inquisitors and Heretics in Thirteenth-Century Languedoc: Edition and Translation of Toulouse Inquisition Depositions, 1273–1282.* Leiden: Brill.

Bruschi, Caterina. 2003. "'Magna diligentia est habenda per inquisitorem': Precautions Before Reading Doat 21–26." In *Texts and the Repression of Medieval Heresy*, ed. Caterina Bruschi and Peter Biller, 81–110. York: York Medieval Press.

Bruschi, Caterina and Peter Biller, eds. 2003. *Texts and the Repression of Medieval Heresy.* York: York Medieval Press.

Bueno, Irene. 2009. "Dixit quod non recordatur. Memory as Proof in Inquisition Records (Early Fourteenth Century France)." In *The Making of Memory in the Middle Ages*, ed. Lucie Dolezalova, 365–93. Leiden: Brill.

Butler, Judith. 1998. "Ruled Out: Vocabularies of the Censor." In *Censorship and Silencing: Practices of Cultural Regulation*, ed. Robert C. Post, 247–59. Los Angeles: Getty Research Institute.

Cassidy-Welch, Megan. 2011. *Imprisonment in the Medieval Religious Imagination, c. 1150–1400.* Basingstoke: Palgrave Macmillan.

Courtenay, William. 1989. "Inquiry and Inquisition: Academic Freedom in Medieval Universities." *Church History* 58: 168–81.

Given, James B. 1997. *Inquisition and Medieval Society: Power, Discipline, and Resistance in Languedoc*. Ithaca, NY: Cornell University Press.

Godman, Peter. 2000. *The Silent Masters: Latin Literature and Its Censors in the High Middle Ages*. Princeton: Princeton University Press.

Kieckhefer, Richard. 1995. "The Office of Inquisition and Medieval Heresy: The Transition from Personal to Institutional Jurisdiction." *Journal of Ecclesiastical History* 46: 36–61.

Kienzle, Beverley. 2001. *Cistercians, Heresy and Crusade in Occitania, 1145–1229: Preaching in the Lord's Vineyard*. Woodbridge: York Medieval Press.

Lambert, Malcolm. 1992. *Medieval Heresy: Popular Movements from the Gregorian Reform to the Reformation*. 2nd ed. Oxford: Blackwell.

Lea, Henry Charles. 1955. *A History of the Inquisition of the Middle Ages*. 3 vols. New York: Russell and Russell.

Moore, R. I. 2012. *The War on Heresy: Faith and Power in Medieval Europe*. London: Profile Books.

Morris, Colin. 1972. *The Discovery of the Individual, 1050–1200*. New York: Harper and Row.

Müller, Beate, ed. 2003. *Censorship and Cultural Regulation in the Modern Age*. Amsterdam: Rodopi.

Pegg, Mark. 2001a. *The Corruption of Angels: The Great Inquisition of 1245–1246*. Princeton: Princeton University Press.

———. 2001b. "On Cathars, Albigenses, and Good Men of Languedoc." *Journal of Medieval History* 27: 181–95.

———. 2003. "Questions About Questions: Toulouse 609 and the Great Inquisition of 1245–6." In *Texts and the Repression of Medieval Heresy*, ed. Caterina Bruschi and Peter Biller, 111–25. York: York Medieval Press.

Peters, Edward. 1988. *Inquisition*. New York: Free Press.

———. 1995. "The Prison Before the Prison." In *The Oxford History of the Prison: The Practice of Punishment in Western Society*, ed. Norval Morris and David Rothman, 3–43. Oxford: Oxford University Press.

Ripoli, T., ed. 1729–40. *Bullarium Ordinis Fratrum Praedicatorum*. 7 vols. Rome: Ex Typographia Hieronymi Mainardi.

Robinson, I. S. 2004. "The Papacy. 1122–1198." In *The New Cambridge Medieval History*, vol. 4, pt. 2, ed. David Luscombe and Jonathan Riley-Smith, 337–83. Cambridge: Cambridge University Press.

Sullivan, Karen. 2005. *Truth and the Heretic: Crises of Knowledge in Medieval French Literature*. Chicago: University of Chicago Press.

Thijssen, J. M. M. H. 1998. *Censure and Heresy at the University of Paris, 1200–1400*. Philadelphia: University of Pennsylvania Press.

Zink, Michel. 1999. *The Invention of Literary Subjectivity*. Tr. David Sices. Baltimore: Johns Hopkins University Press.

Chapter 13

Inquisition, Art, and Self-Censorship in the Early Modern Spanish Church, 1563–1834

François Soyer

On December 3 and 4, 1563, bishops and churchmen gathered in the church of Santa Maria Maggiore for the twenty-fifth, and final, session of the Council of Trent. Among the subjects debated was the invocation and veneration of the relics of saints and the proper use of sacred images in churches. The participants were acutely aware of the scorn and ridicule in which Protestant reformers, and particularly Calvinist iconoclasts, held the religious imagery—both paintings and statues—within Catholic churches. They were also conscious of the need to police the orthodoxy of such public images with greater care in order to avoid the spread of heterodox ideas both in the Church and among the wider population:

> And if at times, when expedient for the unlettered people, it should happen that the facts and narratives of sacred Scripture are portrayed and represented then the people shall be taught, that the Divinity is not thereby represented as though it could be seen by the eyes of the body or be portrayed by colours or figures. Moreover, in the invocation of saints, the veneration of relics and the sacred use of images, every superstition shall be removed and all filthy lucre shall be abolished; finally, all lasciviousness shall be avoided in such ways that figures shall not be painted or adorned

> with a beauty exciting lust; nor shall the celebration of the saints and the visitation of relics be perverted into revelling and drunkenness by any person; as if festivals are celebrated to the honour of the saints by luxury and wantonness.
>
> In fine, let great care and diligence be used herein by bishops so that there shall be nothing seen that is disorderly, or that is unbecomingly or confusedly arranged, nothing that is profane, nothing indecorous, seeing that holiness becometh the house of God. And that these things may be the more faithfully observed, the holy synod ordains that no one shall be allowed to place, or cause to be placed any unusual image in any place, or church, howsoever exempted, except that image which has been approved of by the bishop. Also, that no new miracles are to be acknowledged, or new relics recognised, unless the said bishop has taken cognizance and approved of it. [The bishop], as soon as he has obtained some certain information in regard to these matters, shall, after having taken the advice of theologians and of other pious men, act therein as he shall judge to be consonant with truth and piety.[1]

The decree promulgated by the Catholic Church in 1563 effectively ordered the ecclesiastical authorities to embark upon a campaign of self-censorship since it concerned only works of art publicly exposed in churches and the impact of the Council of Trent on the production of sacred art in Southern Europe was enormous. Not only did the spirit of the council influence the subjects and character of religious artworks—most notably with a shift from Mannerism to a more emotionally intense Baroque style—but it also resulted in a climate of suspicion within the church as works of sacred art were subjected to closer scrutiny and churches to (supposedly) regular episcopal inspections of their paintings, statues, and murals. By promoting a campaign of artistic self-censorship within the Church, the hierarchy of the Catholic Church hoped to neutralize the potency of Protestant attacks upon the veneration of religious images or at least minimize its impact in the propaganda war waged by Protestants.

Even in Rome itself, the nudity depicted in the fresco of the *Last Judgment* painted in the Sistine Chapel by Michelangelo in 1537–41 was (in)famously deemed to have fallen foul of Tridentine decorum, and inspection visits were conducted in Roman churches at the behest of the pontiffs.[2] Paolo

Veronese was another artist who found himself offering explanations to the inquisitors in Venice when his painting *Feast in the House of Levi* on the rear wall of the refectory of Basilica di San Giovanni e Paolo was found to be indecorous to the point of irreverence. The impact of the Council of Trent on religious art in Spain was also soon felt, as can be observed in the provincial and diocesan synods of both Spain and its American colonies during the sixteenth and seventeenth centuries.[3] Andrés Pacheco, the bishop of Cuenca (Castile), is reputed to have ordered the destruction of one hundred fifty religious images that apparently failed to meet the criteria set out by Trent.[4]

This chapter explores the extent to which the Catholic Church actively sought to self-censor and destroy images that might inadvertently contradict official dogma. It focuses upon the role of the Inquisition in Spain as an instrument of self-censorship within the church and its action in the policing and censure of religious imagery from the Council of Trent until its abolition in 1834. It would be impossible within this short chapter to offer a comprehensive survey and analysis of the Spanish Inquisition's role in the policing of art during over two and a half centuries, and this is not my intention. Such a project, and the book that it would produce, is still to be written, even though some historians have conducted reviews of parts of the documentary evidence and have tended to minimize the impact of the Inquisition upon early modern Spain's sacred art and its artists.[5]

The specific object of this chapter is to examine the considerations that underpinned moves made by the Spanish Church to self-censor the religious works of art of its churches in the wake of Trent and the manner in which the Inquisition responded when it was called upon to assist with this task. The first section offers a broad appraisal of the impact of the Tridentine decree of 1563 on artistic production in early modern Spain. In its second section, this chapter offers three case studies of the Inquisition's involvement in the policing of religious works of art. The first case study involves an investigation conducted in 1644–45 into a set of paintings representing seven archangels, which were confiscated from an artist's shop in Madrid. The second focuses upon a number of paintings in the Augustinian college of Doña María de Aragón in Madrid, which were the subject of close inquisitorial scrutiny in 1658. The third, and final, case study analyzes the investigation that led to the prohibition of a painting depicting Christ dying on the cross by the inquisitorial tribunal based in the provincial town of Cuenca in 1764. The investigations carried out by the Inquisition in these three instances demonstrate very clearly the extent to which the Council of Trent created an atmosphere of heightened anxiety and suspicion in which religious art was submitted to closer scrutiny and criticism than had hitherto been the case.

Subjects of Self-Censorship

The proper use of religious images had provoked debate and contention within the church before the Council of Trent, but after 1563 the new decree created a climate in which both painters and the commissioners of paintings were aware that works of art would be subject to a greater degree of theological scrutiny.[6] Self-censorship was therefore exercised at a primary level by both artists and patrons. Patrons usually laid out clear specifications for the paintings they commissioned and were therefore unlikely to commission works that could be of suspect orthodoxy. Spanish artists themselves, or at least the artistic elite, actively contributed to this ambience of self-censorship. This can be clearly observed in literature relating to artistic theory that was produced in Spain during the seventeenth century. Various books and pamphlets were written seeking to offer normative guidelines to painters about the approved manner in which religious subjects were to be painted. At the same time, these writings castigated painters who contravened the decree of the Council of Trent on religious images. Crucially, their authors were not ecclesiastical moralists but artists themselves.[7]

The Italian painter Vicente Carducho (1568–1638), who lived and worked most of his life in Madrid, wrote his *Dialogos de la pintura: Su defensa, origen, essencia, definicion, modos y diferencias* in 1634. In this work, Carducho set out the moral purpose of art and the standards of propriety that were to be followed by artists. Another famous example can be found in the *Arte de la Pintura* of the Sevillian artist Francisco Pacheco (1564–1644), the mentor and father-in-law of Diego Velázquez. In the *Arte de la Pintura* (posthumously printed in 1649), Pacheco claimed that he received the title of "overseer of painters" (*veedor del oficio de la pintura*) from the municipal council of Seville and, in 1618, that of "overseer of sacred paintings" (*veedor de pinturas sagradas*) from the tribunal of the Inquisition in Seville. Later on, the artists José García Hidalgo (1645–1717) and Antonio Palomino de Castro y Velasco (1655–1726) both wrote similar books and claimed to have been appointed as censors of sacred art by the Inquisition.[8]

The Council of Trent had made it explicit that the policing of sacred art exposed in churches was the responsibility of bishops and the twenty-fifth session did not refer to the Inquisition. In spite of this, the Spanish Inquisition soon found itself involved in the enforcement of this form of self-censorship, and this new mission was made explicit in the 1583 index of prohibited books published by the Inquisitor General Gaspar de Quiroga: "Moreover, [we] prohibit all and any images, portraits, figures, coins, prints, inventions, masks, representations and medals that are made, printed, painted, drawn, carved, woven or represented in any material whatsoever in such a manner that they ridicule the saints and demonstrate contempt and irreverence towards them, their images, relics or miracles, [ecclesiastical] habit, profession or life. The same shall also apply to those that are contemptuous of the Holy Apostolic See, the Roman pontiffs, cardinals and bishops."[9] As a tribunal whose sole purpose was to extirpate heresy from Spain and its empire, the Inquisition was already involved in the prosecution of those individuals who uttered "heretical propositions" and blasphemed, as well as the censorship and expurgation of books that were deemed to be dangerous to the Catholic faith. Sacred art was widely acknowledged as a form of religious instruction for illiterate men and women, who composed the majority of the population, and the involvement of the Inquisition was a logical development.

> The inquisitors were well aware that like any instrument of religious instruction, sacred art could be deliberately used by the enemies of the Catholic Church to transmit doctrinal errors or that unintentional inaccuracies in such works could mislead the faithful into believing erroneous propositions. During the seventeenth and eighteenth centuries, the Catholic Church actively sought to prevent, and occasionally to pre-empt, works of art that, while not intrinsically erroneous or heretical, were thought to be potentially dangerous. These included depictions of the Holy Trinity as three identical men (the *Trinidad Trilliza*) as well as some works depicting the Virgin Mary lactating and whose representation of her breasts was considered to go against proper decorum to such an extent as to appear to encourage lascivious thoughts and deeds.[10]

The Inquisition actively sought to prevent the circulation within the Iberian Peninsula of Lutheran or Calvinist propaganda in the form of printed illustrations and pamphlets. In some cases, however, inquisitorial tribunals also fulfilled the role of arbiters of orthodoxy and were asked to judge controversial printed images of a very different kind. In 1635, for example, the Supreme Council of the Spanish Inquisition in Madrid was asked to settle a dispute between the monks of the Orders of Saint Benedict and Saint Basil the Great. The controversy revolved around a printed image produced in Flanders that showed Saint Benedict and other founders of monastic orders kneeling at the feet of Saint Basil. The outraged Benedictines demanded that the Inquisition order the prohibition of the print and confiscation of all existing copies that could be found. They vociferously complained that the printed image explicitly made the claim that Saint Basil, rather than Saint Benedict, had been the first creator of a monastic order, a claim they utterly rejected. Moreover, they refused to acknowledge claims that Saint Benedict had been a disciple of Saint Basil and that the Rule of Saint Benedict was derived from that of Saint Basil. The controversy generated a voluminous inquisitorial file as both sides submitted complex memoranda defending their position. The dispute, which led to the intervention of the papacy, was only settled when the Inquisition decided to ban and seize the printed images on October 12, 1635, and the ban was extended to Spain's overseas empire.[11] As late as 1818, the Supreme Council was called to examine a printed image of the temptations of Saint Anthony that was deemed objectionable not only because the representation of the Devil was "ridiculous" but also because the painting centered upon the breasts of a nude woman tempting the saint, which were deemed to be "too conspicuous."[12]

One problem that increasingly concerned the Church, and by extension the Inquisition, was the use of sacred images on profane objects. The depiction of Jesus Christ, the Virgin Mary, or saints on such mundane items as handheld fans for ladies or the handles of cutlery was problematic as it detracted from the reverence in which the church expected the populace to hold such images. In 1649, an edict was issued in January against the inclusion of images of Christ or the Passion on the handles of knives and a second edict was promulgated in August banning the use of religious images (of angels, bleeding hearts, or the apostles) on fans. In the following century, on August 17, 1767, an edict reiterated the prohibition on the use of religious images on profane objects and, more specifically, the placing of crucifixes and depictions of the Virgin on tombstones "where they could be stepped on and spat upon."[13] Documentary evidence exists to prove that such offending mundane objects with sacred imagery were confiscated by the Inquisition in the Canary Islands during the seventeenth and eighteenth centuries, Mexico in the eighteenth century, and Madrid during the late eighteenth and early nineteenth centuries.[14]

The jurisdiction of the Inquisition made it responsible for offenses against the faith that were deemed to be contrary to church dogma and thus heretical. Many of the works of religious art that were brought to the attention of the Spanish Inquisition from the late sixteenth to the eighteenth century were subject to criticism because the theological nature of their content seemed to contravene dogma or because their dubious aesthetic quality was considered irreverent. In its activity relating to suspect works of sacred art, the Inquisition was confronted with the church's own ambiguous position on certain theological subjects, including, as will be discussed in the case study analyzed further below, the Immaculate Conception. The church's position on a number of theological subjects either had not been defined or was so subtle that it created a theological gray area that was exploited (presumably often unintentionally) in popular religious devotion.

By the early nineteenth century, the mainstay of the Inquisition's activity in the policing of art, at least in Madrid, appears to have revolved around the repression of pornographic images and nudes that were perceived to present a danger to public morality. As the activity of the Inquisition waned in the final decades of its existence, and it struggled with the consequences of the French revolution and Napoleonic invasion of Spain, the inquisitors somewhat comically applied themselves in 1803 to an attempt to prevent the sale of fans with pornographic watermarks. Similarly, in 1815, manikins in the premises of various hairdressers of Madrid that were "scandalously nude" (*escandalosamente desnudas*) and "particularly indecent" (*indecentísimas*) with exposed breasts were condemned.[15] The most famous artistic "victim" of the Inquisition at this late stage in its history is without doubt the painter Francisco Goya (1746–1826), whose painting of the reclining and nude *Maja desnuda* was denounced in 1814 as obscene. Although Goya was summoned to explain himself, there is no evidence that any further action was taken against the artist.[16]

Case Studies in Self-Censorship

The Controversial Archangels (Madrid, 1644)

A perfect example of this challenging situation is offered by the questions surrounding the legitimacy of representing the apocryphal archangels with their names and distinguishing attributes. The Supreme Council of the Spanish Inquisition was forced to grapple with this contentious problem on September 27, 1644, when a cleric and commissary of the Inquisition denounced a painter living and working in the Calle Mayor in Madrid, one of the main thoroughfares of the Spanish capital. The commissary stated that, while walking down the Calle Mayor, he had espied six large paintings measuring two *varas* in height (approximately six feet or two meters) that were exposed at the door of the man's residence and presumably for sale. Each of the paintings depicted an angel and beneath each angel was an explanatory inscription (a *rótulo*) providing the names not only of Gabriel and Raphael but also of the *ángeles extraordinarios*: Uriel, Jehudiel, Barachiel, and Selatiel. These were four of the apocryphal archangels who, unlike Michael, Gabriel, and Raphael, were not mentioned in the scriptures officially accepted by the Catholic Church as part of its canon and whose cult had been condemned by Pope Zachary (741–52) at the Council of Rome in 745. The discovery in 1516 of a Byzantine mural of the seven archangels in Palermo (Sicily) led to a rebirth of their veneration, not only in Italy but also in Spain and its overseas American empire, which enjoyed the enthusiastic support of the Spanish monarchy.[17] In this instance, however, the archangels in the paintings on sale were not only identified by name but represented with items designed to distinguish them. That very same day, the Inquisition dispatched one of its officials, who ordered the artist to bring the works to the Supreme Council so that their orthodoxy could be assessed and threatened him with severe punishments if he did not comply.

Once the paintings of the archangels were safely in the possession of the Inquisition, it was discovered that the collection actually included seven paintings as the denunciator had not noticed another painting that depicted the archangel Michael. The paintings were displayed to four theologians acting as theological experts (*calificadores*)—an Augustinian, a Jesuit, and two Franciscans—who reported on October 3, 1644, that there were no grounds to censure such paintings. Citing the work of the respected Jesuit exegete Cornelius a Lapide (1567–1637), they pointed out that similar paintings existed and were tolerated in both Rome and Palermo as well as other Italian cities.[18] This point of view nevertheless irked Fray Francisco de Araújo (1580–1664), a respected Dominican theologian who had also been consulted. On October 23, he submitted a separate report in which he unambiguously condemned the paintings as contravening the decrees of the 725 Council of Rome and the more recent Council of Trent. He also sought to undermine the legitimacy of the paintings exposed in Palermo by asserting that the angelic cult begun in 1516 by the Italian Antonio Ducca, the author of a work titled *Septem principum angelorum*, was a recent (and therefore unwelcome) innovation and was linked to the visions of the fifteenth-century Franciscan Amadeo of Portugal. His conclusion was that "even if they were approved of and permitted in one of the chapels in Palermo, this should nonetheless not serve as an example to the rest."

The Inquisition received another opinion in February 1645, when a third report (*parecer*) was submitted by Dr. Luis Velazco de Villarín. In a carefully worded and well-researched exposition, Villarín attacked the angelic cult and the naming of the apocryphal archangels in paintings as unorthodox. He dismissed the work of Antonio Ducca as lacking in credibility and relying on "superstitious" sources and the work of Hebrew cabbalists. Villarín was nevertheless willing to admit that painters who gave names and distinguishing attributes to apocryphal angels were almost certainly sinning through ignorance rather than malice. Later that month, a panel of theologians from the University of Salamanca, whom the inquisitors had also consulted, sided decisively with Villarín. In a letter sent to the Inquisition, they adopted a seemingly uncompromising position in favor of the expurgation of the paintings:

> They unanimously agreed that the aforesaid [arch]angels cannot be represented or painted in the manner that they have been [by the painter of the works seized in Madrid]. If some have been painted in such a manner then any [distinguishing] colored clothing, insignias, inscriptions or cartouches bearing the names of Uriel, Jehudiel, Barachiel and Selatiel must be erased as such paintings are superstitious and dangerous to the Catholic faith and rites as well as not conforming to the proper usage in the Catholic Church, which does not allow [the creation of] any novel images or paintings nor recognizes the names of any angels except Michael, Gabriel and Raphael.[19]

The inquisitorial investigation ended with the report of the Salamanca theologians, and it appears that, despite the negative opinions of the majority of the theologians consulted, no decisive action was taken to prohibit representations of apocryphal archangels with their names and distinguishing attributes. Such a prohibition would have been extremely delicate as the cult of the archangels, including the apocryphal ones, not only was popular but had powerful followers. In the heart of Madrid itself, representations of the apocryphal archangels dating from the early seventeenth century adorned the walls of the Convent of the Descalzas Reales, which enjoyed the patronage and protection of the Spanish royal family. In this instance, the decrees of the Council of Trent do not appear to have prevailed over the combined influence of established artistic practice and religious devotion.

The Paintings of the College of Doña María de Aragón (Madrid, 1658)

Founded in 1581 by Doña María de Córdoba y Aragón (1539–93) and completed in 1590, the Augustinian College of the Incarnation—which became popularly known as the College of Doña María de Aragón—was situated in the heart of Habsburg Madrid and very close to the royal palace, the Alcázar. Having already suffered from considerable depredations during the Napoleonic occupation of Madrid, the college was expropriated in 1836 and its buildings occupied by the Spanish senate. In the seventeenth century the college acquired a sizeable collection of works of sacred art to adorn the walls of it buildings and particularly its large church. These included paintings of Saint Augustine and Saint Nicolas of Tolentino by the royal artist Juan Pantoja de la Cruz, but the college's crowning glory was without doubt its sublime altarpiece: a polyptych commissioned from El Greco in 1596 and completed by the artist in July 1600.[20]

The sacred images in the College of Doña María de Aragón were first brought to the attention of the Inquisition by an anonymous denunciation sent to the Supreme Council of the Inquisition on August 30, 1658. Although the existing inquisitorial file is not complete and the course of events has to be reconstructed from the limited extant documentation, it offers a fascinating insight into the method and criteria used within the Spanish church to determine the orthodoxy of an image.[21] The denunciation warned the inquisitors of the existence within the Augustinian college of "extraordinary" and "apocryphal" works of religious art whose "novelty" and "extravagance" warranted an urgent explanation. The works of art denounced were as follows:

1. A painting divided into four sections displaying two red crosses, a dove holding on to a branch of *fleurs de lys* along with a text

written in Greek that proclaimed that the crosses had (allegedly) been painted from the blood of Thomas the Apostle. This work was hung on one of the pillars of the chapel of the *Cristo de la Buena Muerte* and referred to the alleged discovery by the Portuguese in Mylapore (India) of a cross that had been miraculously carved in a stone by the blood of the apostle.

2. A painting of the Virgin, kneeling down and holding a consecrated host over a chalice as an offering to God the Father and the Holy Spirit (conventionally represented as a dove). This work was located at the door of the sacristy.
3. The large painting of seven archangels, each painted with their five distinguishing insignias in the chapel of the *Cristo de la Buena Muerte*.
4. Within the same chapel, located in the vault, was also a painting of a crucifix that had allegedly been the property of the father of Saint Catalina. A legend held that the father of the Saint had intended to manufacture a golden idol of the pagan god Jupiter but that the molten metal, when cooled, had miraculously come out of its mold in the form of a crucifix.
5. A large painting of "The Immaculate Conception revealed to Saint Thomas Aquinas after his Death" was hung in the main chapel next to the Gospels. Painted "with extravagance," it bore the Latin verse from John 20:29 as a caption: *Quia vidisti me Thoma, credidisti. Beati qui non viderunt et crediderunt sacramentum hoc.*
6. A painting of the *Santos Auxiliadores* (the fourteen saints who were thought to respond particularly effectively to invocations from the faithful).

The denounced paintings were indeed potentially problematic for a number of different reasons. The author of the denunciation believed that some of them were painted in an unbecoming or indecorous manner, but the absence of the original works renders it impossible to analyze such aesthetic criticisms. Fortunately, sketches of the painting with the two red crosses and of the image of the kneeling Virgin were commissioned by the Inquisition and have survived (Figures 13.1 and 13.2).

Beyond the issue of the aesthetic quality of the paintings, the apocryphal nature of the subject of some of these artworks was theologically contentious

Figure 13.1. Sketch of the painting representing the Virgin, kneeling down and holding a consecrated host over a chalice as an offering to God the Father and to the Holy Spirit, located at the door of the sacristy of the Augustinian college of Doña María de Aragón. Ministerio de Educación, Cultura y Deporte (Spain). Archivo Histórico Nacional, Sección Inquisición, Mapas, Planos y Dibujos, Carpeta 12, no. 164. Printed by the kind permission of the Archivo Histórico Nacional, Madrid

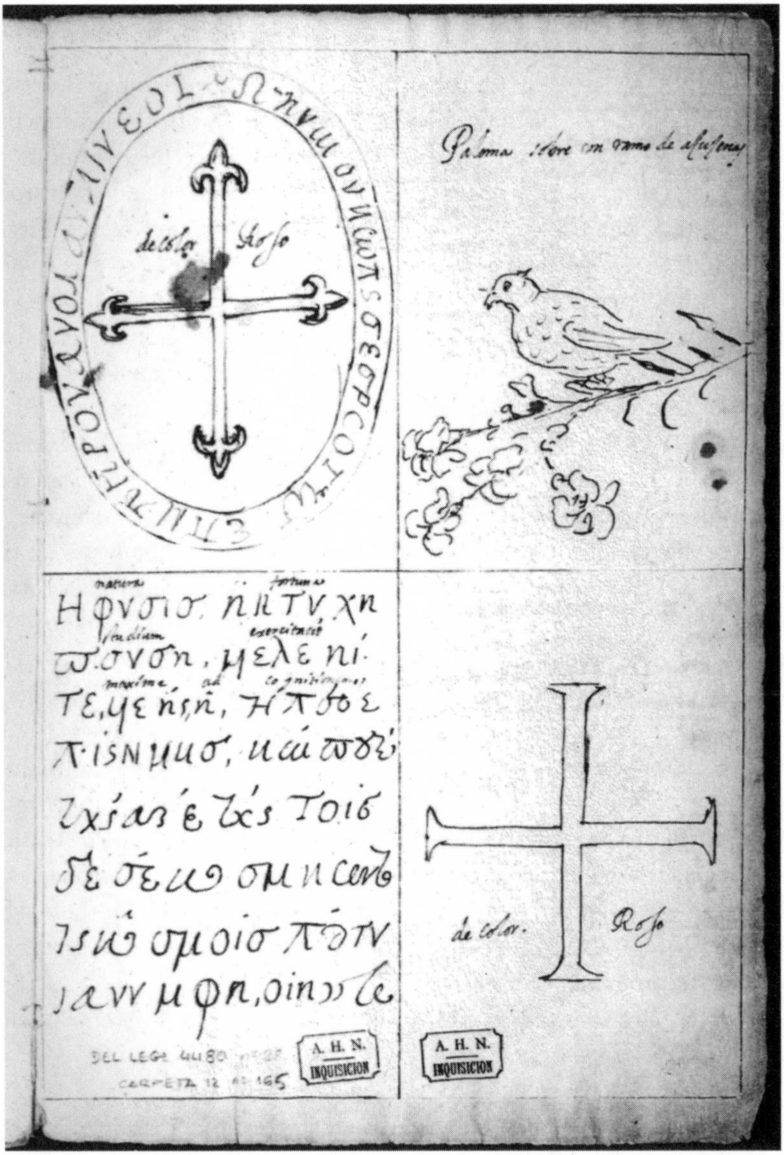

Figure 13.2. Sketch of a painting divided into four sections displaying two crosses, a dove, along with a text in the Greek alphabet that proclaimed that the original cross in India had been painted from the blood of Thomas the Apostle. This work was hung on one of the pillars of the chapel of Cristo de la Buena Muerte in the Augustinian college of Doña María de Aragón Ministerio de Educación, Cultura y Deporte (Spain). Archivo Histórico Nacional, Sección Inquisición, Mapas, Planos y Dibujos, Carpeta 12, no. 165. Printed by the kind permission of the Archivo Histórico Nacional, Madrid

or suspect. As the previous case study has indicated, the painting of the seven archangels, including the four apocryphal archangels, with their distinctive insignia had caused controversy within the church since the pontificate of Zachary and the Spanish Inquisition had already been called upon to investigate the orthodoxy of such paintings.[22] The representation of the Virgin Mary, for its part, potentially ran the risk of being misinterpreted as an endorsement of female ordination. Finally the Latin caption in the painting of the Immaculate Conception pointed to Saint Thomas Aquinas's refusal to accept the concept of the Immaculate Conception in the *Summa Theologica* and made the tendentious claim that the saint had finally been convinced of it when he saw the Virgin after his death. As such, by comparing Thomas Aquinas to the doubting Apostle Thomas, the painting could be viewed as grossly disrespectful of a respected saint and authority within the church.[23]

The content of the painting of the Immaculate Conception was all the more problematic and sensitive as the subject of the Immaculate Conception of the Virgin Mary by her mother Anne had been the cause of much ongoing debate and controversy among theologians since the twelfth century. The debate revolved around whether the sanctification of the Virgin Mary took place *before* the infusion of the soul into the flesh so that her soul was free of original sin or whether, on the contrary, it took place *after* the infusion, a position that excluded the notion of an Immaculate Conception of the Virgin. Proponents of sanctification before infusion in Spain described their position as the *opinión pía*. The Latin caption of the painting of the Immaculate Conception in the Augustinian college was thus an explicit attack on those who did not embrace the *opinión pía*. No clear position on the Immaculate Conception had been adopted during the Council of Trent, and in 1622 Pope Gregory XV had imposed an edict of silence on its critics while the papacy sought to define its position.[24]

The Inquisition responded to the denunciation by asking trusted theologians to examine the artworks involved and to report back. The inquisitorial file contains the detailed report (*parecer*) of one such *calificador*: a Jesuit named José Sánchez who submitted his *parecer*, neatly written in Latin, on September 12. Father Sánchez's report is most notable in that he did not find the painting of the Virgin Mary (Figure 13.1) to be objectionable or unorthodox. He claimed to have seen another very similar painting legitimately circulating elsewhere in Europe and that he understood the Virgin's gesture on the canvas as a representation of her exhibiting or offering the Eucharist, which did not amount to an endorsement of female ordination. Rather, Father

Sánchez drew a careful distinction between the act of exhibiting the Eucharist, which was open to all Christians, and the consecration of the host, which pertained only to the ordained male priesthood.

A defense of the works of art in the college was also submitted by the Augustinian Fray Miguel de Aguirre on September 22. Miguel de Aguirre (c. 1598–1664) stands out not only as an Augustinian friar but also because he was at the time a resident in the very seminary whose paintings were deemed to be suspicious. He was born in the town of La Plata in the viceroyalty of Peru. He joined the Augustinian Order in Lima in 1619 and eventually traveled to Rome and Madrid, settling in the latter city. Described in a later biography as a particularly zealous and austere man, Miguel de Aguirre rose rapidly in the Order and occupied numerous positions of authority and responsibility. Crucially, Aguirre was largely responsible for instituting a program of beautification of the college that had commissioned many new artworks, including the ones that were now subject to investigation.[25]

The inquisitors Juan Santos de San Pedro and Diego García de Trasmiero—both of whom were members of the Supreme Council of the Spanish Inquisition—convened a meeting (*junta*) on September 27 with six consultant theologians: Alonso Vázquez (abbot of Santa Anastasia), Alonso de Herrera (Order of Minims), Alonso Pérez (Tironensian Order), Jerónimo de Salzedo (in minor orders), Bernardo de Ontiveros (Benedictine Order) and Antonio de Riviera (Franciscan Order). Regarding the painting of the two crosses, the dove and the Greek inscription divided into four separate sections (Figure 13.2), these *calificadores* agreed that the Greek inscription should be erased "because it serves no didactic purpose but rather may cause a scandal and ridicule against the religious artwork." They advised that a more convenient caption offering a straightforward narrative of the story of the miraculous creation and discovery of the cross of Saint Thomas the Apostle in India should replace it.

While there was consensus about the painting of the two crosses, this was not the case with that of the Immaculate Conception and Saint Thomas Aquinas. The discussion of the *calificadores* in the *junta* focused particularly upon the painting of the revelation of Saint Thomas Aquinas and its Latin caption, but they failed to agree on a common position. Three of the *calificadores*—Alonso de Herrera, Alonso Pérez, and Bernardo de Ontiveros—expressed the belief that the inscription in the painting of the revelation of Saint Thomas Aquinas should not be erased or altered as any such action would be perceived as a victory by those who contested the *opinión pía* and the Immaculate

Conception. In complete contrast, Alonso Vázquez, Jerónimo de Salzedo, and Antonio de Riviera were convinced that it should be erased either in part or totally. They argued that, at the very least, the Latin inscription should be modified from John 20:29 to the less controversial Daniel 2:30 *sacramentum hoc revelatum* ("this mystery has been revealed"). They justified this position by declaring that any failure to do so would run the risk of angering the Papal *Curia* in Rome by violating the 1622 Edict of Silence and seemingly favoring the proponents of the *opinión pía* in Spain at a time when the papacy was still seeking to officially define its position on the Immaculate Conception and to avoid opening a rift within the church.

The very same day, Fray Antonio de Riviera submitted a personal *parecer* on both the painting of the Immaculate Conception and Saint Thomas Aquinas as well as on that of the Virgin. Regarding the Immaculate Conception, Fray Antonio reiterated his preference for the solution of altering the problematic text to the less offensive Daniel 2:30 and rationalized his position by citing the church's acceptance of the *Revelations* of the fourteenth-century mystic Saint Bridget of Sweden and her vision of a Virgin conceived without original sin. Insofar as the painting of the kneeling Virgin was concerned, Fray Antonio de Riviera took a harsher view and referred to an earlier *junta* whose date is not provided and whose deliberations were either not recorded or not included in the inquisitorial file. He claimed, reiterating his own position in the earlier *junta*, that the painting contravened the decree of the Council of Trent against novel images, served no didactic purpose and risked misleading the ignorant populace into error by encouraging them to believe that the Virgin, by holding a chalice and consecrated host, was acting as an ordained priest. He referred to the commentary on Saint Thomas Aquinas of the Jesuit theologian Gabriel Vásquez (c. 1549–1604), in which female ordination was condemned and presented as a heretical doctrine only espoused by condemned dissenters such as the followers of the Montanism heresy in the history of the early church. Also cited was the rejection of female ordination in the *Panarion* of Saint Epiphanius (c. 320–403). Instead of its destruction, the Franciscan suggested that the chalice and host should be replaced by a representation of the infant Christ in order to remove any trace of the problematic chalice and host.[26]

The ultimate fate of the works of art of the College of Doña María de Aragón is not known. The inquisitorial file does not reveal whether the decisions taken during the *junta* of September 27 were actually implemented. While Natividad Sánchez Esteban has argued that the paintings were probably removed and either altered or destroyed, this was not necessarily the case.[27]

The failure of the *calificadores* to reach a consensus regarding the painting of Saint Thomas and the Immaculate Conception does not, by itself, mean that the Inquisition would necessarily have followed the advice of the three theologians in favor of its alteration. Moreover, Fray Antonio de Riviera's thoughts about the painting of the kneeling Virgin were his own and although he hints at another *junta* when the fate of the painting was debated, he does not reveal what course of action the *calificadores* had actually agreed at that meeting or if they had even agreed upon one. The very fact that he sought to remind the inquisitors of his personal position in favor of altering the painting may suggest that he had found himself in the minority.

"Fantastic Novelties": An Unorthodox Painting of the Death of Christ on the Cross (Cuenca, 1764)

Over a century later, the Inquisition was called upon to consider the theological implications of yet another painting, this time one with the subject of *Jesús Cristo al espirar* (Jesus Christ at the moment of death).[28] The denunciation that opened the investigation was written on May 22, 1764, by a Franciscan named Fray Juan Sanz, who resided in the town of Cuenca. Fray Sanz described a rectangular painting measuring roughly 1.5 meters in height and 1 meter in width with an explanatory inscription in its lower part that identified it as the copy of an image of Jesus Christ, whose original version was said to be venerated in Malta and was reputed to have been painted by the Devil at the behest of a woman enslaved to him who wished to see how the Jews had placed the Savior on the Cross and how he had appeared when he died. The inscription recorded that the Devil had resisted at first because he feared that the woman would convert (back to Christianity) when she beheld it but that she had prevailed upon him. The painting's legend held that the woman had indeed been miraculously moved by the Devil's painting and had converted to Christianity. The offending painting was handed over to the Inquisition by Fray Sanz along with his denunciation.

Fray Sanz noted that the feet of Christ were pierced by a single nail and that, contrary to custom, these did not go through the insteps (*empeines*) but rather sideways through the ankles (*tobillos*). Christ appeared to have a gaping wound on his right side that bled blood and water, while his hands, feet, shoulders, and other parts of his body were torn and bleeding. His right eye was open while the left one was closed "in an unnatural manner," and the fingers of his right hand were retracted, while three fingers of his left hand were extended. Fray Sanz concluded his description by giving his opinion that "the overall posture of the body is irregular, with its twisted members, it is extremely violent and seems to be manifesting spite towards those who see it."[29]

The information that Fray Sanz provides regarding the origin of the painting he denounced offers another very interesting insight into the culture of self-censorship that had developed in post-Tridentine Spain:

> This painting came into the possession of a certain person who is very distinguished and who was displeased by it. He handed it over to me with the explicit order that I should do what appeared best if I judged it to warrant prohibition. He also assured me that the aforesaid painting belonged to Don Francisco Alba, who was a presbyter and prebendary of the Holy Cathedral of Salamanca and is now a resident in the isolated monastery of the Carmelite fathers in Cambrón. It is a copy of a painting privately venerated by the Carmelites in Salamanca and that there are other copies circulating in these kingdoms. With this information in hand, I have resolved to submit to our Catholic Faith and religion and to denounce the described painting to this Holy Office [of the Inquisition] because of the grave reasons that I have set out.[30]

Fray Sanz was therefore not a straightforward denunciator but rather more of an intermediary for another individual who preferred to remain anonymous but obviously considered the painting to be of dubious orthodoxy and feared that possessing it might result in problems with the Inquisition and a public scandal.

Sanz asserted that the painting itself was objectionable because of the unorthodox depiction of Christ's body upon the cross, and that the artist had gone much too far since all the respected Christian authorities were clear that "no bone in the body of Christ was broken" during his ordeal and there was no theological precedent validating the depiction of the nails penetrating Christ's ankles rather than insteps. Finally, he pointed out that the wound made by the lance on Christ's side (John 19:31–37) was made *after* his death and not before it as the painting appeared to suggest. To justify the denunciation, Fray Sanz referred to a battery of precedents and authorities. He pointed to the twenty-fifth session of the Council of Trent as well as a second papal bull, this time issued by Pope Urban VIII (1623–44) on March 15, 1642, reiterating the ban on "obscene, lascivious and immodest" works of art from churches. More concretely, he noted previous instances in which religious images had been censured. These included a papal prohibition promulgated in 1752 by Pope Benedict XIV (1740–58) against depictions of the Holy Spirit in human form and the prohibition that the Papal Curia had inflicted upon a representation of *Santa Maria dello Spasimo* (the "Fainting Madonna") that presented her in a swoon and lying on the ground. To cap it all, Fray Sanz directed the inquisitors to consider the "horrendous blasphemy of the impious Calvin, who claimed and defended [the opinion] that Our Redeemer lost hope when He was on the Cross and manifested his despair" and that, if such a painter were to be tolerated, "uncouth" observers (*rudos*) might well be similarly led astray. No less a person than Pope Benedict XIV had condemned this position in one of the works he had written when he was still a cardinal.[31]

The final objection raised by Fray Sanz concerned the legend detailing the creation of the original painting that was recorded in the inscription. In his comments about this point, Fray Sanz put a number of rhetorical questions to the inquisitors. How was it possible for the painting not to be suspect if the original painter had been the Devil and its commissioner a woman possessed by him? Could the Devil, in his "diabolical craftiness" (*astucia diabólica*), not be attempting to ridicule the crucifixion and undermine the exemplary virtue of Christ through such "fantastic novelties" (*fantásticas novedades*) as the inaccuracies of the painting? Fray Sanz reminded the inquisitors that the Inquisition, as a rule, banned all books written by heresiarchs—arch-heretics such as Luther or Calvin—in its official indexes of banned and censored books. Did it not logically follow that the same should occur with paintings, which were considered "laymen's books" (*libros de los leigos*)? Surely a painting attributed to the Devil, the forerunner of all heretics and heresiarchs, should suffer the same treatment.

On May 23, 1764, the painting was examined by the prosecutor (the *fiscal*) of the inquisitorial tribunal of Cuenca, Don Anguiano. His brief report corroborated all of the points noted by Fray Sanz and he concisely offered his opinion: "It appears to me convenient that it should be prohibited and that it be confiscated, along with any other [paintings] similar to the denounced one that can be found, to thereby avoid the grave prejudice that could be caused by this devilish invention."[32] The prosecutor's colleagues in Cuenca, inquisitors Don Manuel de Ocilla y Estavilla, and Don Diego de Viana, agreed with his judgment. They issued a prohibition against the painting and issued a decree ordering the confiscation of this painting and any others like it that were discovered. The file ends abruptly at this point, and proof of the destruction of the painting handed over to the Inquisition in Cuenca appears to have been sealed, and no other documentary evidence concerning the seizure of similar paintings elsewhere in Spain has yet surfaced.

Conclusion

The Holy Office of the Inquisition was an instrument of religious repression and social control, actively tracking heresy and punishing heretics and those guilty of sexual crimes (bigamy, homosexuality, bestiality, heterosexual anal intercourse). In relation to the world of sacred art in early modern Spain, the Inquisition was, however, just as much an instrument of self-censorship by which the church sought to control its own religious artworks in order to root out potentially problematic works and thereby prevent heresy *before* it happened. One of the most striking aspects of the three case studies analyzed in this chapter is that the Inquisition did not actively seek out the artworks concerned but rather was informed about them by clergymen who denounced them of their own free will. None of the artworks implicated in these case studies were conscious attempts to spread unorthodox ideas but rather unwittingly (or even accidentally) blundered into the blurred and subjective world of the Tridentine prohibition on indecorous and irreverent religious art.

The spirit of the twenty-fifth session of the Council of Trent sought to inspire a wave of self-censorship within the Church by which sacred works of art would be inspected much more closely that had hitherto been the case in order to forestall the spread of unorthodoxy and Protestantism. This decree had particular resonance in early modern Spain as Spanish society felt besieged by enemies. These did not just include its external Protestant and Muslim enemies but also crypto-Judaizing *Conversos* and crypto-Muslim Moriscos: heretics who were believed to be conspiring to undermine the foundations of the Catholic Church and the Habsburg monarchy in order to fulfill the Devil's scheme to destroy them.

It is against this background of heightened anxiety about religious nonconformity that the rise of artistic self-censorship in Spain must be understood. If the body of literature about artistic theory produced in Spain in the seventeenth century and the three case studies analyzed above are anything to go by, the church fathers gathered in Trent can be said to have succeeded in their aims. Self-censorship, by its very nature, leaves few documentary traces, and it is extremely difficult to quantify the extent to which it affected the production of works of art in early modern Spain. Nevertheless, the evidence in the files of the tribunal of the Inquisition does offer testimony of how fear can generate self-censorship. In the wake of the Council of Trent, an atmosphere of fear arose in the early modern Spanish Church regarding the orthodoxy of sacred images: fear of inquisitorial prosecution on the one hand and fear of the spread of Protestant heresy on the other. These fears led to what could be described as a "conspiracy of caution" in which artists, patrons, bishops, and inquisitors all colluded (both consciously and unconsciously). Moreover, the case study from Cuenca, in particular, highlights how, in Herman Roodenburg's words, "the smallest punitive actions rapidly led to the desired self-censorship against a pedagogy of fear."[33] Further research on this topic, and in the archives of the Inquisition and of Spanish dioceses, will doubtless provide a more detailed assessment of the extent of self-censorship in early modern Spain.[34]

NOTES

1. Waterworth (1848) 235–36. I have slightly modified Waterworth's translation.

2. On the censorship of religious images in Rome between 1592 and 1605, see the excellent but sadly unpublished PhD thesis of Mansour (2003).

3. See Saraiva (1960) and Rodríguez Nóbrega (2008) 36–57.

4. Nalle (1992) 152.

5. See Cordero de Ciria (1997) and Sánchez Castro (1996).

6. On the debates and controversies relating to sacred imagery before Trent, see Martínez-Burgos García (1990).

7. For an anthology of such literature, see Calvo Serraller (1991).

8. Carducho (1634); Pacheco (1649); Calvo Serraller (1991) 589–699.

9. De Bujanda (1993) 885–86. General article 12 of the 1583 index: "Assi mesmo se prohiben todas y qualesquier imágenes, retractos, figuras, monedas, empresas, invenciones, maxcaras, representaciones, y medallas, en qualquier materia que esten estampadas, pintadas, debuxadas, labradas, texidas, figuradas, o hechas, que sean en irrision de los sanctos, y en desacato, e irreverencia suya, y de sus imágenes, y reliquias, o milagros, habito, profesión, o vida. Y assi mesmo las que fueren en desacato de la sancta Sede Apostolica, de los Romanos Pontifices, Cardenales, y obispos."

10. Rodríguez Nóbrega (2008) 106–46. Despite its colonial emphasis, this book also touches upon attitudes in the Catholic Church in Europe.

11. AHN, Sección Inquisición, legajo 4456, expedientes 63 and 64. The edict of 1635 was also sent to Mexico, see Archivo General de la Nación, Mexico (AGN), Inquisición, Edictos, vol. 3, expediente 229. See Gruzinski (2010) 156.

12. AHN, Sección Inquisición, legajo 4494, expediente 17.

13. AHN, Sección Inquisición, legajo 4480, expediente 28 and legajo 3740, expediente 85.

14. For a selection of such cases see Archivo de la Inquisición de Canarias, ES 35001; AMC/INQ-215.020, AMC/INQ-021.004; AMC/INQ-298.029; AGN (Mexico), Inquisición, Vol. 1070, expediente 17, fols. 298r–308; AHN, Sección Inquisición, legajo 4494, expediente 38 and legajo 4490, expediente 2.

15. AHN, Sección Inquisición, legajo 4459, expediente 14 and legajo 4494, expediente 35.

16. AHN, Sección Inquisición, legajo 4499, expedientes 3 and 6.

17. *González Estévez* (2012) 111–32.

18. a Lapide (1891) chap. 1.

19. AHN, Sección Inquisición, legajo 4456, document 14: ". . . cada uno de ellos fue de acuerdo que no se podía usar ni pintar en la dicha forma de las imágenes y pinturas de los dichos Ángeles y que si había algunas pinturas en la forma referida se debía borrar dichos vestidos colores insignias letras títulos y tarjetas de todos y los nombres de los cuatro Uriel, Sealthiel, Jeudiel, Barachiel, por ser las dichas pinturas y nombres cosas supersticiosas y peligrosas en la fe cuanto al culto, y rito exterior, y no conforme con el uso de la iglesia católica, la cual no permite imágenes ni pinturas no usadas ni conoce por sus propios nombres mas que tres Ángeles que son Miguel, Gabriel y Rafael."

20. The altarpiece by El Greco is now preserved in the Prado museum. See Andueza Unanua (2010) and Lazcano (2013).

21. AHN, Sección Inquisición, legajo 4480, expediente 28. The original documentation is not foliated.

22. Mujica Pinilla (1992) 3–14.

23. *Summa Theologica*, III, *Quæstione* 27, article 3.

24. It was not until 1661 that Pope Alexander VII decreed that the soul of the Virgin Mary was immune from original sin from the moment that her soul infused her body at conception. The modern definition of the Immaculate Conception was finally formulated by Pope Pius IX in 1854.

25. de San Francisco (1756) 4:67–73; Lazcano (2013) 397–99.

26. Vásquez (1613), disp. 245, cap. I, 952–53; Saint Epiphanius, *Panarion*, 79.

27. Sánchez Esteban (1989).

28. AHN, Sección Inquisición, legajo 2594, expediente 48. The original file has no foliation.

29. AHN, Sección Inquisición, legajo 2594, expediente 48: "Y en fin la postura total del cuerpo crucificado en acción irregular, de sus miembros retorcidos, violentísima, y como manifestando a la vista de ojos algún despecho interior."

30. AHN, Sección Inquisición, legajo 2594, expediente 48: "Cierto sujeto, muy distinguido, a cuya manos llegó este retrato, se desagrado mucho de su pintura y me la remitió con orden expreso, de que se la juzgase digna de alguna prohibición, ejecutase lo que según el Señor me pareciese mas conveniente. Asimismo me aseguró, que la dicha pintura era propia de Don Francisco Alba, presbítero secular, Prebendado, que fue de la Santa Iglesia Catedral de Salamanca, y al presente morador en el desierto del Cambrón de R.R. P.P. Carmelitas es copia de obra, que privadamente se venera en cierta comunidad de Salamanca; y que otras semejantes copias (se dice) andan del mismo modo por estos Reinos. Con estas noticias, y en

vista de todo, he resuelto en obsequio de nuestra católica fe, y religión, delatar el insinuado retrato a ese Santo Oficio, por las graves motivos, que ja expongo."

31. Lambertini (1761) 1:396–98.

32. AHN, Sección Inquisición, legajo 2594, expediente 48: ". . . me parece conveniente que se prohíba, y se mande recoger, con las demás que se hallaren semejantes a esta delatada, para evitar por este medio los gravísimos perjuicios que puede ocasionar esta diabólica invención."

33. Roodenburg and Spierenburg (2004) 1:126.

34. This work is part of a greater project on the Inquisition and (self-)censorship of art in early modern Spain and its empire that I am currently completing and which will eventually result in a monograph.

REFERENCES

Manuscripts

AGN (Archivo General de la Nación, Mexico), Inquisición. Edictos, vol. 3, expediente 229.

———, Inquisición, vol. 1070, expediente 17, fols. 298r–308.

AHN (Archivo Histórico Nacional, Madrid, Spain), Sección Inquisición, legajo 2594, expediente 48.

———, Sección Inquisición, legajo 4456, expedientes 63 and 64.

———, Sección Inquisición, legajo 4459, expediente 14 and legajo 4494, expediente 35.

———, Sección Inquisición, legajo 4480, expediente 28 and legajo 3740, expediente 85.

———, Sección Inquisición, legajo 4494, expediente 17.

———, Sección Inquisición, legajo 4494, expediente 38 and legajo 4490, expediente 2.

———, Sección Inquisición, legajo 4499, expedientes 3 and 6.

Archivo de la Inquisición de Canarias, ES 35001; AMC/INQ-215.020, AMC/INQ-021.004; AMC/INQ-298.029.

Printed Documents

a Lapide, Cornelius. 1891. *Commentarius in Apocalypsin Sancti Joannis Apostoli*. Paris: Ludovicum Vives, Bibliopolam Editorem.

Andueza Unanua, Pilar. 2010. "Nuevos datos documentales sobre el Colegio de Doña María de Aragón de Madrid." *Anuario del Departamento de Historia y Teoría del Arte* 22: 87–102.

Calvo Serraller, Francisco. 1991. *Teoría de la Pintura del Siglo de Oro*. Madrid: Catedra.

Carducho, Vicente. 1634. *Dialogos de la pintura: Su defensa, origen, essencia, definicion, modos y diferencias*. Madrid: Fr. Martinez.

Cordero de Ciria, Enrique. 1997. "Arte e Inquisición en la España de los Austrias." *Boletín del Museo e Instituto "Carmón Aznar"* 70: 29–86.

De Bujanda, Jesús Martínez, ed. 1993. *Index de l'Inquisition Espagnole 1583, 1584*. Sherbrooke: Librairie Droz.

de San Francisco, Fr. Pedro. 1756. *Historia General de los Religiosos Descalzos del Orden de los Hermitaños del Gran Padre y Doctor de la Iglesia San Agustín*. Zaragoza: Francisco Moreno.

González Estévez, Escardiel. 2012. "De fervor regio a piedad virreinal Culto e iconografía de los siete arcángeles." *Semata: Ciencias sociais e humanidades* 24: 111–32.

Gruzinski, Serge. 2010. *La guerra de las imágenes. De Cristóbal Colón a "Blade Runner" (1492–2019)*. Mexico City: Fondo de Cultura Económica.

Lambertini, Prosperus Cardinalis (postea Benedict XIV). 1761. *Commentarius de D. N. Jesu Christi Matrisque ejus festis retractatus atque auctus*. Louvain: Ex Typographia Academica.

Lazcano, Rafael. 2013. "Colegio de doña María de Aragón (Madrid): De los orígenes a la desamortización de Mendizábal." In *La desamortización: El expolio del patrimonio artístico y cultural de la Iglesia en España: Actas del Simposium 6/9-IX-2007*, ed. Francisco Javier Campos and Fernández de Sevilla, 369–411. Madrid: Instituto Escurialense de investigaciones históricas y artísticas.

Mansour, Orpher. 2003. "Offensive Images: Censure and Censorship in Rome Under Clement VIII 1592–1605." PhD thesis, Courtauld Institute of Art, London.

Martínez-Burgos García, Palma. 1990. *Ídolos e imágenes. La controversia del arte religioso en el siglo XVI*. Valladolid: Universidad de Valladolid.

Mujica Pinilla, Ramón. 1992. *Ángeles apócrifos en la América Virreinal*. Lima: Fondo de Cultura Económica (Peru).

Nalle, Sara. 1992. *God in La Mancha: Religious Reform and the People of Cuenca 1500–1650*. Baltimore: Johns Hopkins University Press.

Pacheco, Francisco. 1649. *Arte de la Pintura: Su antiguedad y grandezas*. Seville: Simon Faxardo.

Rodríguez Nóbrega, Janeth. 2008. *Las imágenes expurgadas: Censura del arte religioso en el período colonial*. León: Universidad de León.

Roodenburg, Herman and Pieter Spierenburg, eds. 2004. *Social Control in Europe 1500–1800*. Columbus: Ohio State University Press.

Sánchez Castro, José. 1996. "La censura de la figuración artística en España (1487–1820)." *Boletín del Museo e Instituto Camón Aznar* 65: 37–98.

Sánchez Esteban, Natividad. 1989. "Pinturas en el Colegio de Doña María de Aragón: Problemas inquisitoriales." *Cuadernos de Arte e Iconografía* 2: 106–16.

Saraiva, Crescenciano. 1960. "Repercusión en España del decreto del concilio de Trento sobre las imágenes." *Boletín del Seminario de Estudios de Arte y Arqueología* 26: 129–43.

Vásquez, Gabriel. 1613. *Commentariorum ac Disputationum in Tertiam Partem S. Thomae: Tomus Tertius*. Madrid: Andream Sanchez de Ezpeleta.

Waterworth, James, ed. and tr. 1848. *The Canons and Decrees of the Sacred and Oecumenical Council of Trent*. London: C. Dolman.

Chapter 14

Thomas Hobbes and the Problem of Self-Censorship

Jonathan Parkin

At a time when questions of self-censorship are very much to the fore both in philosophical circles and in the wider public culture, it may be illuminating to consider the circumstances under which modern discourse of self-censorship came into being and to examine the historical development of self-censorship as a term of art in that discourse. Although to do so is to step back into a world that is in some respects very different from our own, not least in perspectives on freedom of speech, the issues dealt with by early modern writers were not so very far removed from those which continue to worry modern philosophers and writers about politics, for whom the tension between free speech and public order and its implications for self-censorship remain great problems.[1]

Self-censorship was an extremely serious issue for early modern political thinkers, faced as they were with deeply conflicted societies. As we shall see, a formal recognition of its political necessity featured prominently in some of the major theoretical responses to the unprecedented religious strife of the sixteenth and seventeenth centuries. Discussions of self-censorship in a political setting drew upon a cluster of concepts that had been designed to cope with new political realities: refurbished classical and Christian notions of selfhood, secularized notions of the political community, and the concomitant identification of public and private spheres with commitments peculiar to each. As this nexus of concepts retains a central importance in modern liberal political theory, to examine its character is not only to engage with thinkers dealing with similar problems in the past, but also to understand something about the terms in which we discuss those issues in the present.

Such an examination is all the more in order if, as some historians and philosophers have persuasively argued, some of the deepest conceptual problems facing modern liberal theorizing are vestigial.[2] By examining the work of one of the most important contributors to its evolution—the English philosopher Thomas Hobbes—we may hope to discover something of interest not only about *his* solution to the problem of self-censorship, but also about our own, sometimes queasy, responses to the problem.

Recent scholarship has drawn attention to the fact that Hobbes was a political philosopher who practiced self-censorship.[3] When it came to publishing his political, religious, and scientific positions, Hobbes deliberately concealed his private views out of a concern for the way that his reading public might respond to them. One perhaps predictable motivation for this form of concealment was self-preservation, in both a narrow and a broader sense. The narrow sense relates to Hobbes's own self-preservation. If he had published his heterodox theological views candidly, it is highly likely that he would have faced prosecution on a capital charge like heresy—or perhaps even treason.[4] But Hobbes's silences were not just about avoiding personal prosecution; he also self-censored even when his immediate personal safety was not in jeopardy.

Hobbes's silences bespeak a broader sense of the threats to peace, and therefore to self-preservation, that could result from the propagation of ideas that might too readily be misunderstood or misapplied. This broader concern to censor the self in the interest of peace was obtrusively present in Hobbes's political theory, in which self-censorship was presented not simply as a matter of anticipating and avoiding legal proscription but rather as one of the natural duties of a responsible citizen, and a duty that played a crucial role in Hobbes's solution to the problem of political conflict.

To understand Hobbes's theory in these terms is to cast doubt upon some influential modern interpretations of it. Recent discussions of Hobbes's use of dissimulative techniques such as self-censorship have pointed to the similarities between his position and that of the renaissance *ragion di stato* (reason of state) writers in the Machiavellian tradition, whose *politique* distinction between the internal self and one's public *persona* offered a pragmatic solution to problems of political and religious pluralism. Self-censorship, in their writings as in Hobbes's theory, is a desirable characteristic of princes and subjects, and an essential condition of civil peace. It has been suggested that

Hobbes's theory has the same essentially pragmatic structure.[5] However, in exploring Hobbes's treatment of self-censorship, I would like to suggest that while Hobbes did indeed see benefits in the practice of censoring the self, as the reason of state theorists recommended, he also saw costs.

In particular, Hobbes recognized the potentially damaging tensions produced by the recommended disjunction between one's public and private beliefs. Hobbes's proposed solution to this problem was an ambitious attempt to eliminate these tensions through a dramatic redefinition of the nature of the self. Hobbes may have self-censored, but, *pace* recent discussions, his ambition was to create a world in which the problems to which self-censorship was the answer were effectively eliminated rather than simply contained.

In what follows I examine Hobbes's views on the problem of self-censorship and the role that it plays within his theory. In the second section I consider the relationship between Hobbes's position on self-censorship and the reason of state tradition with which he has been associated. In the third section I argue that it might be better to think of Hobbes as a perceptive critic of the reason of state writers on this issue, and one who was proposing a distinctive solution to the problem of self-censorship that has been lost to view.

Hobbes and Self-Censorship

It is difficult to find evidence of self-censorship among early modern writers,[6] but Hobbes is an intriguing instance of an author whose doctrine appears to recommend self-censorship, and whose private transactions appear to embody it. To begin with his doctrine: Hobbes's commitment to some form of self-censorship arises from the relationship between his formal commitment to free thought, and his striking claim that individuals have no entitlement at all to freedom of speech or action; not only are subjects formally obliged to profess whatever is required of them by the sovereign, but they also have an obligation to self-censor their speech and acts according to the requirements of peace, even where the sovereign has not commanded them to do so.

Hobbes's defense of free thought begins from the position that such freedom naturally pertains to human beings because beliefs simply cannot be coerced. Hobbes argues that belief can never be coerced because beliefs or opinions are not the products of voluntary action. This means that it is impossible to lay any sort of external obligation upon individuals' mental processes. As Hobbes famously notes, "beleef, and unbeleef never follow mens commands."[7] As the internal sphere of belief is not amenable to coercion, political communities are necessarily committed to the de facto toleration of all private beliefs; for as Hobbes puts it when discussing private religious beliefs in chapter 31 of *Leviathan*, "Private, is in secret Free."[8] With regard to the external sphere of action, however, the story is very different.

Hobbesian subjects have no right to the free public expression of their beliefs, and are obliged to conform their public statements to whatever is required of them by the sovereign. This view is elaborated unapologetically in chapter 42 of *Leviathan*, where Hobbes confronts the potentially hard case of religious believers required by their sovereign to subscribe publicly to beliefs that they privately find intolerable.[9] In response, Hobbes points out that any command to a Christian that forbids *belief* in Christ will simply be ineffective because belief, being involuntary, cannot be subject to commands. On the other hand, if a Christian is required to *say* that he does not believe in Christ, Hobbes counsels that "profession with the tongue is but an externall thing," and is no more than a gesture signifying obedience to the sovereign. Therefore a Christian commanded to repudiate Christ has the same liberty as Naaman the Syrian in the book of Kings who, after he had converted to the God of Israel, was still required to worship in the temple of Rimmon and did so (or so Hobbes claims) with the approval of the prophet Elisha.[10]

The Naaman example became one of the most notorious passages in the book: Hobbes appeared to be recommending nothing short of hypocrisy, violating the true Christian's conscience by asking the believer to fall in with the public conscience instead. Many of Hobbes's critics zeroed in on the Nicodemism of the Naaman passage as an indication not only of Hobbes's approval of dissimulation, but also as damning evidence of the probable insincerity of many of his other views, particularly his religious views.[11] On this basis, they suggested, nothing that Hobbes said could be taken to be a reliable marker of anything more than his willingness to pay lip service to the legal authorities. This willingness was unseemly in itself, but it suggested worse: that his true opinions were so outrageously heterodox that he felt compelled to hide them at all costs. The subtlety of Hobbes's position, as his opponents very quickly realized, was that it made it very difficult to prove that he held unorthodox opinions and almost impossible to convict him for doing so, since his own principles not only allowed but required him to recant any position of which the sovereign disapproved.[12]

Hobbes endorsed the self-censorship of one's views in deference to official orthodoxy. But his interest in self-censorship didn't end there. It carried through into his account of natural moral obligations, contained in his description of natural law. Natural law for Hobbes consisted in a series of linked conclusions or theorems concerning the best means of achieving peaceful coexistence. These theorems are not, he argues, formally obligatory laws like those made by the sovereign, but they are propositions that should be acted upon whenever it is safe to do so. Hobbes envisaged a situation in which the security provided by sovereignty creates an environment in which individuals should naturally seek to put natural law (which is obligatory only *in foro interno*) into effect (*in foro externo*) even if they are not formally commanded to do so by the sovereign.[13]

Traditionally natural law, as a law of God, was as much concerned with the intention that lay behind an action as with the action itself. What is striking about Hobbes's discussion of natural law is how little concerned it is with the intentions of individuals, focusing instead upon how they should present themselves to others if they wish to secure peace. Perhaps the most interesting example of this is Hobbes's discussion of the third law of nature. This law specifies that people should be prepared to "performe their Covenants made." Indicating that you are prepared to keep your promises is an essential precondition of peace.[14]

To underline his point Hobbes introduces a character he calls the "Foole" (alluding to the Foole of the Psalms), who, notwithstanding Hobbes's position, argues that since every man's self-preservation is in his own hands, there is no reason that an individual should not choose to break a promise whenever he judges it advantageous to his preservation to do so. In response to the Foole, one of Hobbes's counterarguments is to say that "he which declares he thinks it reason to deceive those that help him, can in reason expect no other means of safety, than what can be had from his own single Power."[15] If the Foole "declareth" that he may with reason break his covenant, then he "cannot be received into any Society, that unite themselves for Peace and Defence, but by the errour of them that receive him." Individuals who go about advertising their willingness to break covenants are hardly likely to be accepted as trusted members of society: if you want to live peacefully, then you have to indicate to others that you believe it is just to keep your promises.

The interesting point here is that a significant feature of the Foole's foolishness is his willingness to *publicize* his belief that it is acceptable to break promises when it suits. Hobbes's contemporaries and some modern commentators have been quick to note that this point did little to address the problem of the silent "Foole" who self-censors his internal belief that promise breaking is legitimate and present to the world an air of unquestioned respectability. All that Hobbes says is that, regardless of what you really think, if you look like a promise breaker you are not likely to elicit the kind of social response that will promote your self-preservation.[16]

Similar points figure in Hobbes's accounts of the other laws of nature, which codify the kinds of public signal likely to produce peace.[17] With regard to the fourth law, Hobbes states that the giving of gifts should be met with signs of gratitude; with regard to the fifth, Hobbes posits mutual accommodation between men, effectively requiring them to temper the expression of their natural diversity of affections. In discussion of the sixth, pardoning past offenses is explained as a sign of a commitment to future peace, as is the abstinence from revenge required by the seventh law. The eighth law is particularly interesting for its focus upon social signs, as in its requirement that "no man by any deed, word, countenance or gesture, declare Hatred, or Contempt of another."[18] There is no suggestion here that we must genuinely learn to love our fellow citizens, rather the suggestion is that, even if we don't think much of them, we should censor these sentiments in public. Again, the ninth law of nature requires that men regard each other as natural equals regardless of whether it is true that nature has made men so; whether one believes in the equality of men or not is beside the point. What matters is that "because men will not enter into conditions of peace but upon equal terms, such equality must be admitted."[19]

In each of these cases, Hobbes seems to be much less interested in what subjects actually think than in how they appear or present themselves to each other. Hobbes's laws of nature have little to say about the interiority of the subject, that is, about whether and how far the goodness of an action is connected to the intentions or beliefs or dispositions of the would be do-gooder. Instead, Hobbes's attention centers on the outward demeanor of citizens without reference to their internal beliefs. Samantha Frost suggests that this direction of attention is definitive of Hobbes's ethical approach, in which the vital condition of peace is the willingness of individuals to simulate appropriately peaceable qualities in the public sphere. In effect, says Frost, Hobbes's theory is all about the need to "fake" the kind of external commitments required to make individuals legible to each other as peaceable citizens.[20]

The thought that Hobbes endorsed this sort of fakery is reinforced by evidence that we have of his willingness to censor his own views along the lines suggested above. This evidence indicates Hobbes's readiness to suppress what he felt to be true doctrine in line with the demands of self-censorship implied by his account of natural law. Consider Hobbes's views on free will, which were perhaps the least objectionable—certainly from a legal standpoint—and in some ways the most popular items in the Hobbesian range.[21] Even so, there is evidence that Hobbes would have preferred to keep these views private, for fear of the wider implications of publicizing them widely.

In the early summer of 1645, Hobbes acceded to a request from his sometime patron, the Earl of Newcastle, to take part in a private debate at his residence in Paris with John Bramhall, the Bishop of Derry, on the subject of free will.[22] Hobbes's views of free will were the pendant to his materialism. The traditional notion of free will, he argued, was a delusion, because all events were the necessary consequences of prior material causes. Individuals might perceive themselves to be making choices through the exercise of their wills, but this was only because they were unable to identify the causes involved in producing the effect they wrongly attributed to their own choices.[23] Bramhall was predictably outraged by Hobbes's position, not least because it offended traditional assumptions about personal responsibility and implied that God, as the first cause, was (albeit at a distance) the author of sinful acts. Newcastle subsequently asked Bramhall to provide a written account of his position; the bishop agreed on condition that Hobbes was asked to do the same. Hobbes did so, but asked Newcastle to keep the contents of his paper private. He later explained his reasons for doing so:

> I must confess, if we consider the greatest part of Mankinde, not as they should be, but as they are, that is, as men, whom either the study of acquiring wealth, or preferment, or whom the appetite of sensual delights, or the impatience of meditating, or the rash embracing of wrong principles have made unapt to discuss the truth of things, I must say I confess, that the dispute of the question will rather hurt their piety, and therefore if his Lordship had not desired this answer, I should not have written it, nor do I write it but in hopes your Lordship and his will keep it private.[24]

Hobbes wanted to censor his views out of the concern that they could be misinterpreted in a way that would prove prejudicial to piety and moral behavior. This latter possibility had been recognized by Bramhall, who had pointed out that by questioning the concept of personal responsibility Hobbes was effectively undermining the social order.[25] Evidently Hobbes agreed. In a later letter he explained that the men whom he "thought might take hurt thereby" were those who would reason erroneously to the conclusion that the determinism he was discussing reduced to a form of fatalism, "saying with themselves, if I shall be saved, I shall be saved whether I walk uprightly or no, and consequently thereunto shall behave themselves negligently, and pursue the pleasant way of the sins they are in love with."[26] The problem was that unconstrained by its relations to his other doctrines, Hobbes's view of determinism could be used to bolster a number of different positions, some of which might be used to legitimate vice.[27] For this reason Hobbes was extremely reluctant to let the doctrine out un-chaperoned into the public sphere.[28]

The picture that emerges from this discussion of Hobbes's doctrine and the evidence of his practice suggests that, in a variety of forms, self-censorship lay at the heart of the Hobbesian enterprise. Indeed, it might be helpful to think of Hobbes's doctrine as a large-scale exercise in self-censorship. *The* political problem, as described in all of Hobbes's political works, is the unrestrained expression of the beliefs and opinions of autonomous selves pursuing their own goods; the inevitable clash between them results in a state of war. An important part of Hobbes's solution is to create a mechanism, sovereign power, by which those individuals limit themselves to expressions of opinion and belief that do not create political instability. The fact that the *Leviathan* is created through the consent of Hobbesian subjects makes even this formal censorship a form of *self*-censorship, a point that Hobbes was keen to underscore in writing that the sovereign's action is always the subject's own.[29] Add to this the fact that many of the formal requirements of natural law involve censoring the self in the general cause of peace and the extent of the role played by self-censorship in Hobbes's work becomes clear.

Hobbes and Reason of State Theory

This brief exploration of the role of self-censorship in Hobbes's theory raises some interesting questions about both the ambitions of Hobbes's political theory and his place in the history of political thought. Hobbes has been taken to be a proto-enlightenment figure, in the sense that his philosophy is understood to have attempted to deliver ordinary people from the disabling threat of disorder by establishing a transparently rational structure to justify the authority of the state.[30] On the face of it, Hobbes's extensive reliance upon techniques of self-censorship would seem to put him squarely at odds with that enlightenment agenda. Hobbes's technique of self-censorship appears to involve a situation in which a radical distinction between the public and private spheres underwrites an argument in favor of the hypocritical subscription to views adopted simply for their public utility rather than their rational consistency or their truth. On this description, it looks as if Hobbes is asking people, and particularly the wise, to forsake the truth and sign up to a lot of noble lies.

This skeptical and *anti*-utopian aspect of Hobbes's thought has led some commentators to suggest, that in spite of appearances, Hobbes's underlying argument has less to do with modern rationalism than with the Machiavellian statecraft of the late renaissance reason of state tradition—a tradition in which the topic of self-censorship was an essential part of politics.[31] In the second half of this chapter I examine the extent to which this identification makes sense, and suggest that, although Hobbesian self-censorship is undoubtedly informed by the reason of state tradition, Hobbes's ambition was to go beyond this tradition in a way that he thought would ultimately remove the need for self-censorship altogether.[32]

As many historians of political thought have pointed out, reason of state discourse was less a coherent political philosophy than a formal compilation of political techniques. Its form reflects its origins as a self-consciously anti-utopian response to religious and political strife.[33] Machiavelli's *Prince* stands at the beginning of the reason of state tradition in the early modern period, infamously countenancing wrongdoing on the part of princes seeking to secure their states. As the phrase itself suggests, reason of state was a genre of writing that implied that the practice of statecraft, possessing its own logic of security, was exempt from conventional ethical considerations. A favored topic of discussion in the genre was the practice of dissimulation by princes, and the various forms of deception required to maintain one's rule. These included classic Machiavellian stratagems such as the instrumental use of religion and the need to adopt appearances that might be at odds with reality.[34]

These stratagems were predicated on the thought that the prince as a political actor might be required to conceal his true nature behind a public persona that could be used to manipulate and control the populace. Although Machiavelli's name soon became too disreputable to cite openly, his doctrines were too useful to ignore in a Europe riven by religious conflict, and the genre was subtly adapted, sanitized, and made over along classical lines as Neo-Stoic and Tacitean ideas came to be incorporated in it. Justus Lipsius in the Netherlands was one of most prominent of the new generation of writers in the genre, infamous for the elaborating what he called "mixed prudence." This idea arose out of consideration of various levels of fraudulent behavior by rulers, ranging from "light" (dissimulation and the concealment of intentions), through medium (active deception and bribery), to great (the breaking of treaties).[35] For Lipsius, only the last was unacceptable; dissimulation was regarded as advisable and other forms of deception were regarded as tolerable.

Lipsius's political advice was primarily aimed at governors, but the political turmoil of late sixteenth-century Europe soon meant that writers were turning their attention to forms of dissimulation that had become necessary for subjects. This was the case in France especially, where religious civil war pulled French society apart, leaving subjects with increasingly difficult choices, and never more so than when faced with the choice between following conscience and making the kind of *politique* compromises necessary for civil peace. As the Huguenot Agrippa d'Aubigné summarized in his fictionalized representation of the *politique* position, "Know then that almost all men have been reduced to this point: to be on bad terms either with their conscience or with the course of the century."[36] The only solution for many was a categorical divorce between the internal and external spheres, with the prudent man effectively withdrawing into the private sphere in his judgments, while submitting his external actions to judgment of his ruler.[37]

This solution was systematized in the work of the leading French *politique* writers, notably Michel de Montaigne, Pierre Charron, and Guillaume du Vair.[38] These writers translated reason of state's emphasis upon dissimulation not only into recommendations for princes, but also into handbooks for their subjects, offering advice for the wise caught up in an irrational world dominated and driven by opinion rather than reason. The substance of their advice was to stress the importance of distinguishing between the politically necessary presentation of the external self and the identification of an authentic inner self as the only way to remain free from servitude to passion and opinion. As Charron puts it, in the language of a contemporary translation,

> We must know how to distinguish and separate our selues from our publike charges: euery one of vs playeth two parts, two persons; the one strange and apparent, the other proper and essentiall: we must discerne the skinne from the shirt. An actiue man will performe his charge, and yet withall not leaue to iudge of the follie,

> vice, deceit that is therein: he will conforme himselfe to euery thing, because the custome of his countrey requireth it, it is profitable to the weale-publike: the world liues so, and therefore it must be done. A man must serue and make vse of the world such as he findeth it; in the meane time, he must likewise consider it as a thing estranged from it selfe, know how to keepe and carie himselfe apart, and to communicate himselfe to his owne trustie good, howsoeuer things fall out with himself.[39]

The practical necessity of separating internal and external commitments paved the way for an exploration of the essential self, embodied in Charron's slightly relentless demand that the sage "looke therefore into thy selfe, know thy selfe, hold thy selfe to thy selfe; thy spirit and will which is els where imployed, reduce it unto thy selfe . . . gather thy selfe unto thy selfe, and shut up thy selfe within thy selfe: examine, search, know thy selfe."[40] The self here is characterized by its independence from external things; rather than the self being defined by its offices, it stands independently from all its roles, as a judging, reasoning entity, the deliberating actor behind the many masks it is required to wear. This self is a precondition, as Montaigne observed, of any effective performance.[41]

Arguments of this kind effectively prepared the ground for a new preoccupation with questions of self-censorship, in that reason of state discourse created the need to articulate the relationship between a novel formulation of selfhood and new accounts of an autonomous public sphere. In this context, the topic of prudent silence returns again and again in later reason of state discussions of dissimulation. For example, Robert Dallington's *Aphorisms Civil and Military*, continuing the popular theatrical metaphor employed by Montaigne, suggested that those in public employment "must of necessity wear vizards and change them in every scene. Because, the generall good and safety of a State is the Center in which all their actions, and counsailes muste meete: To which men cannot always arrive by plaine pathes, and beaten waies." Openly expressing one's nature, or venting one's purpose, Dallington argued, is a "thing of dangerous consequence."[42] Francis Bacon, another English adapter of continental reason of state discourse with a keen sense of the need for the distinction between public and private, devoted an essay to the topic of simulation and dissimulation, which elaborated the degrees and circumstances of this "hiding and veiling of a man's self."[43]

As Kinch Hoekstra and Noel Malcolm have recently pointed out, Hobbes, a former amanuensis to Bacon, was familiar with reason of state discourse and its obsession with dissimulation and secrecy. Indeed as a secretary to the Earls of Devonshire, Hobbes was, by trade, a keeper of secrets. The art of a secretary, a contemporary advice book stated, "is nothing other than the science of things that must be kept secret and revealed."[44] The library at Hardwick Hall, which Hobbes probably helped to stock, contained nearly all of the canonical authors in the tradition: Machiavelli, Guicciardini, Botero, Lipsius, Mariana, and Charron.[45] Hobbes not only was familiar this continental literature, he had traveled across Europe and knew some of its leading figures personally.[46]

Further evidence of Hobbes's fascination with reason of state comes from his earliest correspondence, which is full of discussion of *arcana imperii*, or mysteries of state.[47] It also comes from works that he was involved in producing and translating for his patrons. A piece written by his patron but sometimes attributed to Hobbes, *A discourse upon the beginnings of Tacitus* (1620) is a study of the classical guru of reason of state writers with an interest in the political use of religion.[48] Noel Malcolm's recently discovered Hobbesian translation of the *Altera secretissima instructio*, a text immersed in reason of state culture, demonstrates that Hobbes's formative years were spent thinking about reason of state ideas.[49] As the brief discussion of Hobbes's work at the beginning of this chapter indicates, Hobbes's later published work uses terms and concepts culled from the tradition: the obsession with the role of opinion, the critical distinction between internal and external spheres, the distinctive reliance upon dissimulation as the solution to political problems, and, most pertinently for present purposes, the critical role played by a systematic application of self-censorship.

The case, then, for seeing Hobbes as a late exponent of reason of state arguments looks unanswerable. And yet if we take this last feature of Hobbes's work seriously and attend to it closely, it turns out to be something of a mistake to reduce Hobbes's work to a variant of the anti-utopian techniques recommended by the reason of state writers. One of the most typical features of Hobbes's work was his ability to take a range of existing ideas familiar to his audience and to subtly transform and assimilate them to his larger project. This was certainly the case with Hobbes's treatments of religion and theology, treatments in which most of the familiar pieces of Protestant Christianity remained in play but the rules of the game had been quietly but fundamentally altered. There is a parallel case with Hobbes's use of the language of reason of state: if for all his deployment of orthodox Christian categories Hobbes was no orthodox Christian, so it is also true that for all his deployment of reason of state categories, Hobbes was no straightforward reason of state theorist.

Hobbes Against Reason of State Theory

It is Hobbes's posture toward the question of self-censorship that reveals most clearly his distance from the reason of state thinkers. This claim may seem odd. Hobbes sometimes sounds as if he is directly paraphrasing Charron's *De la sagesse* in the distinctions that he draws between the internal self and the external performance. This is so not least at the beginning of *Leviathan* where, following Charron, Hobbes argues that what men ought to do is know themselves (*nosce teipsum*).[50] But with Hobbes the conscious echo is sometimes a clue that something fishy is going on, and the familiar is undergoing a decisive change.

Anyone assuming that Hobbes is simply following the reason of state writers when it comes to the matter of self-censorship has failed to grasp the full implications of Hobbes's remarks about the self. Hobbes himself comments that the instruction to know or read oneself is "not of late understood," its having been taken either as an excuse to countenance bad behavior in princes, or, and importantly, to encourage their social inferiors in what he calls "sawcie behaviour" toward their betters.[51] His own understanding of that instruction is elaborated in *Leviathan*; in positioning that instruction prominently at the beginning of his great work, Hobbes is not so much aligning himself with and endorsing the reason of state tradition as drawing his readers' attention to one of its decisive weaknesses.

It is often assumed that Hobbes's distinction between internal and external spheres maps very directly onto the reason of state model, either because he was simply endorsing the *politique* solution to political conflict or because he was endeavoring to reserve a suitably Charronian space for free thought. But the reason of state model generated consequences that Hobbes would have found deeply problematical. Perhaps the best discussion of this problem, which I think may be described not unreasonably as a problem of self-censorship, comes (ironically) from a critique of Hobbes by Carl Schmitt, which presented the English philosopher as the proponent of a novel account of the internal/external dichotomy.[52]

Schmitt argued that Hobbes adopted this dichotomous structure as a solution to the problem of religious and political strife. In doing so, however, Hobbes had sown the seeds of the destruction of his *Leviathan*: he had reduced the political sphere to a morally neutral mechanism for stability, while at the same time creating a privileged and apolitical space for the exercise of conscience that would, in time, reassert its authority over the political sphere with disastrous results.[53] Schmitt's analysis was supplemented by greater historical detail in the work of his follower, Reinhart Koselleck, who argued that what he called the utopian strand of enlightenment thinking (and, through the working out of that strand of thinking over time, of the ideological forces arrayed against the modern state) was the antipolitical progeny of this failed attempt to divide the public and the political.[54] Leaving aside for the moment the broader accuracy of this story, I think that although neither Schmitt nor Koselleck get Hobbes quite right, they do identify what Hobbes himself had recognized as the *damnosa hereditas* of the reason of state tradition.

The recourse to a very sharp distinction between mutually exclusive public and private spheres, no longer policed by an omnicompetent church-based religion, may well have provided a temporary self-censoring solution to the political problems identified by the *politiques*. But the same distinction stored up future trouble by generating a potentially authoritative moral self at odds with the public sphere. Far from being a long-term solution to it, for Hobbes this was yet another species of the problem that *Leviathan* was trying to address, namely the need for the systematic elimination of any source of authority independent of the political realm if a civilized common life were to be possible.

I think that this comes across very clearly from Hobbes's reconfiguration of what it actually means to "know thy self." It certainly does not mean the recovery of some essential and unique self, or the delineation of a private sphere in which the self can act as an autonomous source of authority. Hobbes effectively goes to war against this notion of the self throughout *Leviathan*, subjecting it to a devastating critique.

Hobbes's demolition job involves the redefinition, rewriting, or brute rejection of what were conventionally understood to be the authoritative sources of the self. The underlying logic of that redefinition is supplied by his commitment to materialism, which precludes the possibility that anything identified with an autonomous self might enjoy a mode or manner of existence that could not be explained in material terms. On one side this logic rules out the notion that the self is an immaterial entity (this same logic, of course, had motivated Hobbes's objections to Descartes's *Meditations* and helps to explain the Frenchman's very testy replies); on the other side it removes the standard basis for claiming that its operations are not susceptible to human analysis. The traditional constituents of the self are all systematically reformulated by Hobbes according to this logic, in a way that undermines their potential for acting as independent sources of authority.

Thus Hobbes downgrades reason from the scholastic "right reason" that connects man with God to an instrumental calculating faculty, which enjoys no privileged access to truth.[55] Free will is similarly reduced to an effect of material causes. As I have noted, Hobbes argues that the will has nothing to do with an independent faculty of deliberation; every act of man's will, he explains, "and every desire, and inclination proceedeth from some cause, and that from another cause, in a continuall chaine . . . they proceed from necessity."[56] Hobbes is withering in his treatment of conscience, a word now used, he says, by men "vehemently in love with their own new opinions (though never so absurd)" who being "obstinately bent to maintain them, gave those their opinions also the reverenced name of Conscience, as if they would have it seem unlawfull, to change or speak against them; and so pretend to know they are true, when they know at most, but that they think so."[57] As Johan Tralau has recently discussed, Hobbes dismisses the notion of individual conscience as an improper metaphor, emphasizing instead the idea of conscience as externally shared knowledge.[58]

The aim of Hobbes's rewriting of the self is to leave his readers in little doubt that what they take to be the formal properties of an autonomous entity—the self—with a range of causal powers are in fact merely *effects*, necessary consequences of their embodied material existence. Hobbes's self possesses neither the autonomy nor the private authority that is an essential feature of Charron's self. In effect what Hobbes reveals, and in a manner that is calculated to deflate the dualism that is so dear to the reason of state writers and the clergy alike, is that there is no way that an autonomous self could be isolated and secured inviolably against the intrusions of the outside world in the way they suggest. This is so because there is no "inside" that can be favorably juxtaposed against the outside, no internal world that is categorically separate from the external world, no intelligible world that stands over and above the world of sense. Hobbes's nominalism and his materialism are put to work together, and their cutting effect, like that of a pair of scissors, derives from their mutual interaction. Everything is body, and the names we give to bodies tell us only how we think of them, which opens the possibility that we could learn to think differently about them.[59]

Together, Hobbes's materialism and his nominalism cut through a whole range of putatively authoritative claims made by his predecessors about the self. But Hobbes's aim is positive as well as negative. This destructive work is accompanied by a positive explanation of the kind of practical self-knowledge of which men are capable under these conditions. Hobbes explains that to "know oneself" is to understand and recognize the psychological mechanisms that lie behind and generate all human behavior. The phrase *nosce teipsum* is designed, he says, "to teach us that for the similitude of the thoughts, and Passions of another, whosoever looketh into himself, and considereth what he doth, when he does thinke, opine, reason, hope feare, &c and upon what grounds; he shall thereby read and know, what are the thoughts, and Passions of all other men, upon the like occasions."[60] Understanding the self is no longer a search for an authentic inner self, but rather an attempt to identify the external conditions that cause the thoughts and passions that lead to certain sorts of action, not only in oneself, but also in others—an almost complete externalization of the self, which exposes what individuals conventionally take for self-consciousness as the necessary effect of the operation of one body upon another. It tacitly assumes that the generation of certain sorts of output is dependent on two factors: a given set of sensory inputs and the self-knowledge needed to process those inputs in the appropriate manner to obtain the desired outputs. This metaphysical framework structures the political argument of *Leviathan*, in which the identification of the political conditions required to achieve the self-preservation that Hobbes identifies as the common root of human motivation is matched by an account of how people must understand themselves and act if they are to sustain the conditions that sustain them.[61] With the quest for self-knowledge now entirely reoriented toward the conditions required for the continued existence of the self, the Hobbesian subject and the Hobbesian sovereign alike are in a position to grasp the rational necessity of the political relationships that Hobbes describes. In grasping this necessity, the beliefs, opinions, and actions of subject and sovereign are reshaped accordingly.[62]

In other words, Hobbes's project embodied a *two*-pronged approach to the problem of the divided self: on the one side generating a set of formal requirements designed to pacify the external political sphere, and on the other laying the groundwork for an ambitious materialist reconstitution of the self through which the individual's private understanding and their public *persona* could be brought into alignment. Far from requiring any long-term subscription to noble lies, Hobbes's ambition was to create a situation in which the sovereign's requirements and the subject's opinions and beliefs converged around the imperatives of peace or what he called "natural law." That this ideal of perpetual peace was his ambition appears in his assessment in *De cive* of what a properly realized moral science might do for mankind: "For if the patterns of human action were known with the same certainty as the relations of magnitude in figures, ambition and greed, whose power rests on the false opinions of the common people about right and wrong, would be disarmed, and the human race would enjoy such secure peace that (apart from conflicts over space as the population grew) it seems unlikely that it would ever have to fight again."[63] Hobbes was aware of the need to be careful about the public expression of doctrine and more aware yet of the need to couch his arguments in terms familiar to his audience; but borrowing terms is not the same as borrowing positions. Crucially, Hobbes sought to transform and synchronize diverse forms of doctrine in a single unified system, to generate a mortal God to embody and represent what was essentially unknowable and institutionally fragile: the single, unitary authority without which civilization could not stand.[64]

Conclusion

This brings me back to the question of self-censorship. Hobbes's model, with its mechanism for reconciling people to a natural political necessity, effectively dissolved the potential for tension between an inner self and its external commitments by showing all too clearly that those external commitments were what constituted and sustained that self in the first place. Hobbes's new version of self-knowledge promised to eliminate the need for political self-censorship altogether, for it would do away with the problems that resulted from the attempt to divide the private from the public world. Schmitt and Koselleck were wrong to see Hobbes as the inaugurator of what we might call the political problem of self-censorship; in fact, he saw the problem very clearly and envisaged a radical and enlightened solution. But if their casting was poor, there nevertheless remains something compelling about the story they tell of the Manichaean conflict between the inner world of the self and the external world of the political. Their story does seem to capture very well some of developments in political thought after Hobbes.

Few went as far as Hobbes in deploying a systematically materialist conception of the self. But lacking this conception, or something like it, the tensions introduced by the reason of state discourse persisted in the seventeenth-century natural law thinkers. The most influential European theorists of the post-Westphalian period, particularly thinkers like Samuel Pufendorf and Christian Thomasius, pursued arguments that carried these unresolved tensions at their core.[65] Although Locke attempted his own reconciliatory reformulation of the self, the theological dimension to his solution was soon eclipsed by secular good intentions, only to be recovered to sight, if only as an item of historical interest, in recent times.[66] As Ian Hunter has recently suggested, the persistence of the problem set the scene for a clash between the structures generated by the political and pragmatic thinkers who emerged from the reason of state tradition, and the metaphysical and utopian forces of the Republic of Letters, cultivated in the private sphere created by the early modern state.[67] In this latter tradition of enlightenment, unconstrained by the requirements of the political, self-censorship would become less a necessary political virtue than an unacceptable compromise. This is the legacy that, in various ways, we still live and continue to grapple with today in our own uneasy responses to issues of self-censorship.

NOTES

An early version of this chapter was originally composed for the Morrell Conference on Censorship and Self-Censorship, held at the University of York in 2008. I would like to thank audiences at the Department of Politics and International Relations at the London School of Economics and the Institute of Historical Research in London for helpful comments. I would particularly like to thank Dr. Tim Stanton for discussion of the issues raised here and also for his help in clarifying the presentation of the argument.

1. I should stress at the outset that in this chapter I am mainly concerned with self-censorship understood as a form of *self-constraint*, where individuals adopt values that constrain the expression of their attitudes. This might be distinguished from the other very common discourse of self-censorship in early modern societies (to be considered elsewhere), which arises from consideration of situations where individuals are dominated by others such that they are forced to self-censor in accordance with the dominating agent. This form of *self-censorship by proxy* can be held to be distinct from *self-censorship by self-constraint* insofar as the latter is not dependent upon the existence of a dominating agent external to the individual. The distinction is clearly not absolute but constitutes a useful way to differentiate commonly recognized forms of self-censorship. For discussion of this point, see Cook and Conrad (2010). For discussion of self-censorship in situations of domination, see particularly the work of Skinner (2008) 91–94.

2. Here I have in mind the work of Reinhart Koselleck, particularly his analysis in

(1959), which has recently been revived for an English-speaking audience in Ian Hunter (2001).

3. See particularly Hoekstra (2006).

4. See Parkin (2013). In this piece I show that heresy proceedings against Hobbes were taken seriously in the later 1660s, and that Hobbes's anxieties about such proceedings were not simply the product of paranoia.

5. Hoekstra (2006).

6. For discussion of a variety of self-censoring practices, see particularly Zagorin (1990) chap. 12.

7. Hobbes (1991) 343; see also chap. 26, 198: "for mens beliefe, and interiour cogitations, are not subject to the commands, but only to the operation of God."

8. Hobbes (1991) 249.

9. Ibid., 343–44; see also the example in *De cive* chap. 15, 183–85 where Hobbes considers the case of Christians ordered to perform acts against their faith.

10. The Naaman passage was a classic text associated with "Nicodemism," a term deriving from Calvin's disparaging name for Protestants who conformed outwardly to Catholicism (after Nicodemus, the Christian Pharisee from John 3:1–2 who concealed his faith). Much of the early modern debate over the passage turned on whether Elisha's comment to Naaman "Go in peace" signified the prophet's approval or a simple "goodbye." Hobbes's interpretation, although controversial, was not out of line with other orthodox Christian accounts of the passage.

11. See, for example, Bramhall (1657) 491–92; Tenison (1670) 199; Hyde (1676) 249–51; Whitehall (1679) 63ff.

12. Hobbists would always simply recant any position not approved by the magistrate, a difficulty encountered by those prosecuting the Cambridge Hobbist Daniel Scargill in 1669. A contemporary broadside caught the difficulty quite nicely: "If Justice Catch *Leviathan* in's hook / Will he implore the Benefit of's book?"; Anonymous (1670). For the Scargill affair, see Parkin (2007) 244–52.

13. Hobbes (1991) 110–11.

14. Ibid., 101–3.

15. Ibid., 102.

16. The point was noted by Lucy (1663) 222–23 and more recently has formed the subject of an interesting debate between Kinch Hoekstra and Peter Hayes. See Hoekstra (1997); Hayes (1999); Hoekstra (1999). See also Lloyd (2009) 310–17.

17. Hobbes (1991) 103–11.

18. Ibid., 107.

19. Ibid., 107.

20. Frost (2001).

21. This was because they shadowed a recognizably Protestant understanding of the free will issue. Indeed, Hobbes referred to this fact in the course of his debate with Bramhall, whose account of free will Hobbes attempted to associate with Roman Catholic theology.

22. Parkin (2007) 39ff.

23. Hobbes's (1845) 55 position is set out very clearly (and amusingly) in response to Bramhall: "A wooden top that is lashed by the boys, and runs about sometimes to one wall, sometimes to another, sometimes spinning, sometimes hitting men in the shins, if it were sensible of its own motion, would think it proceeded from its own will, unless it felt what lashed it. And is a man any wiser, when he runs to one place for a benefice, to another for a bargain, and troubles the world with writing errors and requiring answers, because he thinks he doth it without other cause than his own will, and seeth not what are the lashings that cause his will?"

24. Hobbes (1654) 35–36.

25. Hobbes (1999) 4. Bramhall comments, "If there be no liberty, there shall be no day of doom, no last judgement, no rewards nor punishments after death. A man can never make himself a criminal if he be not left at liberty to commit a crime. No man can be justly punished for doing that which was not in his power to shun. To take away liberty hazards heaven, but undoubtedly it leaves no hell": Chappell (1999) 4.

26. Hobbes (1656) 334.

27. We have no record of Hobbes's views being used to underpin justifications of libertinism, although the thought that they might underpin the libertinism of the 1670s was explored in Shadwell (1675), where the serial killer antihero Don John excuses his various crimes by quoting directly from Hobbes. See Parkin (2007) 304–11.

28. Hobbes's views were eventually published in a pirated edition of his manuscript copied by one of his amanuenses, John Davies of Kidwelly. Hoekstra suggests that if this had not happened, we would not know much about Hobbes's views of free will. However, most of Hobbes's position was reproduced very clearly in *Leviathan*; it is the context in which the argument was released that made the difference for Hobbes.

29. Hobbes (1991) chap. 17, 120: The Hobbesian subject promises to "owne, and acknowledge himselfe to be Author of whatsoever he that so beareth their Person, shall Act, or cause to be Acted, in those things which concerne the Common Peace and Safetie; and therein to submit their Wills, every one to his Will, and their Judgements, to his Judgement."

30. See, for example, J. Waldron's (2001) comments.

31. See particularly Hoekstra (2006), but this is also an implication of Collins (2005).

32. In this my argument hopefully supports Noel Malcolm's suggestion (*pace* Hoekstra) that in spite of some obvious similarities, Hobbes's position ultimately goes beyond reason of state theory. See his comments in Malcolm (2007) 121–23.

33. For general surveys of reason of state theory, see Burke (1991) and Tuck (1993) 31–136.

34. See particularly Machiavelli (1988) chap. 18, 62; for the instrumental use of religion see Machiavelli (1970) I.11, 139–42.

35. Lipsius (1589) 204–16. On Lipsius and his influence, see Oestreich (1982); McCrea (1997).

36. D'Aubigné, *La confession du sieur de Sancy*, quoted in Koselleck (1959) 19.

37. It is worth noting that the distinction between internal and external spheres was hardly new in itself, being an integral part of the Christian tradition, and familiar from the work of Augustine and Aquinas. However the changes wrought by the Reformation removed the possibilities for reconciliation traditionally offered by the visible institution of the Church, which held both together. This combined with the increasingly skeptical character of politique thought generated the basis for the novel accounts of subjectivity found in politique writers. See also the discussion in Koselleck (1959) 29n27.

38. For a general account of *politique* philosophy during this period, see Keohane (1980).

39. Charron (1608) 252.

40. Ibid., 2.

41. See also Charron's (1608) Sig A2r comments to this effect: "He that hath an erroneous knowledge of himselfe, that subiecteth his minde to any kinde of seruitude, either of passions or popular opinions, makes himselfe partiall; and by enthralling himselfe to some particular opinion is depriued of the libertie and iurisdiction of discerning, iudging and examining all things." For a helpful discussion of *politique* concepts of selfhood, see Baldwin (2001). Although Charles Taylor does not discuss these writers, or indeed Hobbes in much detail, his comments on Montaigne are also relevant: Taylor (1989).

42. Quoted in McCrea (1997) 57.

43. Bacon (1985) 76–78; see also McCrea (1997) chap. 2.

44. Torquato Tasso, *Il secretario* (1605) 6, quoted in Hoekstra (2006) 43.

45. Malcolm (2007) 109–10.

46. Hobbes was acquainted with the Venetian state counselor Fulgenzio Micanzio, a friend of Paolo Sarpi, and facilitated a correspondence between him and his employer, the Earl of Devonshire.

47. Hobbes (1994) 1:1–4.

48. Hobbes (1995).

49. Malcolm (2007) 105–23.

50. Hobbes (1991) 10.

51. Ibid., 10.

52. Schmitt (1996) esp. chap. 5, 53–63.

53. Ibid., 56–57: "The distinction between private and public, faith and confession, fides and confessio, is introduced in a way from which everything else was logically derived in the century that ensued until the rise of the liberal constitutional state. The modern 'neutral' state, derived from the agnosticism and not from the religiosity of Protestant sectarians, originated at this point. If looked at from the perspective of constitutional history, a dual beginning was made here: first, the juristically . . . constructed beginning of modern, individualistic right of freedom of thought and conscience and thereby the characteristic individual freedoms embodied in the structure of the liberal constitutionalist system; and, second, the evolution of the state from one inherently . . . into a justifiable external power, the *stato neutrale e agnostico* of the nineteenth and twentieth centuries." Schmitt goes on to state that Hobbes "underscores the importance of absorbing the right

of private freedom of thought and belief into the political system. This contained the seed of death that destroyed the mighty Leviathan from within and brought about the end of the mortal god."

54. Koselleck (1959) 38–39: "Pressed by the need for a lasting peace, the State conceded to the individual an inner space that did not much impair the sovereign decision; as a matter of fact, it was essential to that decision. It was essential for the State to be politically neutral if it was to preserve its political form. Moral neutrality was the distinguishing mark of the sovereign decision. . . . The State created a new order, but then—in genuinely historic fashion, fell prey to that order. As evident in Hobbes, the moral inner space that had been excised from the State and reserved for man as human being meant . . . a source of the unrest that was originally exclusive to the Absolutist system. The authority of conscience remained an unconquered remnant of the state of nature, protruding into the formally perfected state."

55. Hobbes (1991) 32–33.

56. Ibid., 146–47.

57. Ibid., 48.

58. Tralau (2011). Tralau's exposition of Hobbes's position on liberty of conscience complements the position argued for in this chapter.

59. I would like to thank Tim Stanton for this compelling explanation of the relationship between Hobbes's materialism and his nominalism.

60. Hobbes (1991) 10.

61. I think that the lack of this extensive political account of the natural necessity of sovereignty was the reason Hobbes self-censored his doctrine of free will in 1646. Presented without it, the argument could be used to legitimize any form of action, and this is why Hobbes felt able to publish it in the broader context of *Leviathan* in 1651.

62. Hobbes's scheme therefore required that *Leviathan*'s doctrine, or at least a summary of key arguments, should be taught in the universities. It should be noted that this was not, as David Wootton has recently suggested, simply a form of brainwashing. Hobbes makes clear, as I have noted, that the beliefs and opinions required for the stability of the political community cannot simply be commanded. Individuals have to be persuaded by the argument. Hobbes thought he had produced a suitably persuasive argument that would prove its worth by delivering peace. For this view, see Parkin (forthcoming). For David Wootton's interpretation of Hobbes as a Machiavellian, see Wootton (1998).

63. Hobbes (1998) 5.

64. Hobbes (1991) 120. It should be noted that this analysis brings Hobbes's position much closer to Spinoza's.

65. Both writers were clearly indebted to Hobbes in their dualism, although this became harder to admit as the reaction to Hobbes gained momentum. However in rejecting Hobbes's materialism and lacking a convincing account of divine obligation, they arguably failed to find a response to the problem.

66. For Locke's reconfiguration of what he calls the "penalized self," see Tully (1993).

67. Hunter (2001) 364–76. See also Malcolm's (2002) 537ff. suggestive comments on the character of the Republic of Letters, which also appear to follow Koselleck's analysis.

REFERENCES

Primary Sources

Anonymous. 1670?. *The Atheist's Help at a Dead Lift*. London.

Bramhall, John. 1657. *Castigations of Mr Hobbes*. London: J. Crook.

Charron, P. 1608. *Of Wisdome: Three Bookes Written in French by Peter Charro[n] Doctr of Lawe in Paris*. Tr. Samson Lennard. London: Eliot's Court Press.

Hobbes, Thomas. 1654. *Of Libertie and Necessitie a Treatise, Wherein All Controversie Concerning Predestination, Election, Free-Will, Grace, Merits, Reprobation, &c. Is Fully Decided and Cleared, in Answer to a Treatise Written by the Bishop of Londonderry, on the Same Subject*. London: Printed by W. B. for F. Eaglesfield.

———. 1656. *The Questions Concerning Liberty, Necessity, and Chance Clearly Stated and Debated Between Dr. Bramhall, Bishop of Derry, and Thomas Hobbes of Malmesbury*. London: Printed for Andrew Crook.

———. 1845. *The English Works of Thomas Hobbes of Malmesbury*. Vol. 5. London: J. Bohn.

———. 1991. *Leviathan*. Ed. R. Tuck. Cambridge: Cambridge University Press.

———. 1994. *The Correspondence*. Ed. Noel Malcolm. Oxford: Oxford University Press.

———. 1995. *Three Discourses*. Ed. N. B. Reynolds and A. W. Saxonhouse. Chicago: University of Chicago Press.

———. 1998. *Hobbes: On the Citizen (De cive)*. Ed. R. Tuck and M. Silverthorne. Cambridge: Cambridge University Press.

Hyde, Earl of Clarendon, Edward. 1676. *A Brief View and Survey of Leviathan*. Oxford: Printed at the Theater.

Lipsius, J. 1589. *Politicorum sive Civilis doctrinae libri sex*. Leiden: C. Plantin.

Lucy, William. 1663. *Observations, Censures and Confutations of Notorious Errours in Mr Hobbes His Leviathan*. London: Printed by J. G. for Nath. Brooke.

Machiavelli, Niccolò. 1988. *The Prince*. Ed. Q. Skinner and R. Price. Cambridge: Cambridge University Press.

———. 1970. *Discourses*. Ed. L. Walker. London: Routledge.

Shadwell, Thomas. 1675. *The Libertine: A Tragedy*. London: Printed by T. N. for Henry Herringman.

Tenison, Thomas. 1670. *The Creed of Mr Hobbes Examined*. London: Printed for Francis Tyton.

Whitehall, John. 1679. *The Leviathan Found Out; or, The Answer to Mr. Hobbes's Leviathan*. London: Printed by A. Godbid and J. Playford.

Secondary Sources

Bacon, Francis. 1985. "Of Simulation and Dissimulation." In *Essays*, ed. J. Pitcher, 76–8. London: Penguin.

Baldwin, Geoff. 2001. "Individual and Self in the Late Renaissance." *Historical Journal* 44: 341–64.

Burke, P. 1991. "Tacitism, Scepticism, and Reason of State." In *The Cambridge History of Political Thought 1450–1700*, ed. J. H. Burns and M. Goldie, 479–98. Cambridge: Cambridge University Press.

Chappell, V. 1999. *Hobbes and Bramhall on Liberty and Necessity*. Cambridge: Cambridge University Press.

Collins, Jeffrey. 2005. *The Allegiance of Thomas Hobbes*. Oxford: Oxford University Press.

Cook, Philip and Conrad Heilman. 2010. "Censorship and Two Types of Self-Censorship: Public and Private." Social Science Research Network, March 20. http://ssrn.com/abstract=1575662.

Frost, S. 2001. "Faking It: Hobbes's Thinking-Bodies and the Ethics of Dissimulation." *Political Theory* 29: 30–57.

Hayes, P. 1999. "Hobbes's Silent Fool: A Response to Hoekstra." *Political Theory* 27: 225–29.

Hoekstra, K. 1997. "Hobbes and the Foole." *Political Theory* 25: 620–54.

———. 1999. "Nothing to Declare? Hobbes and the Advocate of Injustice." *Political Theory* 27: 230–35.

———. 2006. "The End of Philosophy: The Case of Hobbes." *Proceedings of the Aristotelian Society* 106: 23–60.

Hunter, I. 2001. *Rival Enlightenments*. Cambridge: Cambridge University Press.

Keohane, N. O. 1980. *Philosophy and the State in France: The Renaissance to the Enlightenment*. Princeton: Princeton University Press.

Koselleck, Reinhart. 1959. *Critique and Crisis: Enlightenment and the Pathogenesis of Modern Society*. Cambridge, MA: MIT Press.

Lloyd, S. A. 2009. *Morality in the Philosophy of Thomas Hobbes: Cases in the Law of Nature*. Cambridge: Cambridge University Press.

Malcolm, Noel. 2002. *Aspects of Hobbes*. Oxford: Oxford University Press.

———. 2007. *Reason of State, Propaganda, and the Thirty Years' War: An Unknown Translation by Thomas Hobbes*. Oxford: Oxford University Press.

McCrea, A. 1997. *Constant Minds: Political Virtue and the Lipsian Paradigm in England 1584–1650*. Toronto: University of Toronto Press.

Oestreich, G. 1982. *Neostoicism and the Early Modern State*. Cambridge: Cambridge University Press.

Parkin, J. 2007. *Taming the Leviathan*. Cambridge: Cambridge University Press.

———. 2013. "Baiting the Bear: The Anglican Attack on Hobbes in the Later 1660s." *History of Political Thought* 34: 421–58.

Schmitt, C. 1996. *The Leviathan in the State Theory of Thomas Hobbes: Meaning and Failure of a Political Symbol.* Tr. G. Schwab and E. Hilfstein. Chicago: University of Chicago Press.

Skinner, Quentin. 2008. "Freedom as the Absence of Arbitrary Power." In *Republicanism and Political Theory*, ed. C. Laborde and J. Maynor, 83–102. Malden, MA: Wiley-Blackwell.

Taylor, Charles. 1989. *Sources of the Self.* Cambridge, MA: Harvard University Press.

Tralau, J. 2011. "Hobbes contra Liberty of Conscience." *Political Theory* 39: 58–84.

Tuck, Richard. 1993. *Philosophy and Government 1572–1651.* Cambridge: Cambridge University Press.

Tully, James. 1993. "Governing Conduct: Locke on the Reform of Thought and Behaviour." In *An Approach to Political Philosophy: Locke in Contexts*, ed. Tully, 179–241. Cambridge: Cambridge University Press.

Waldron, J. 2001. "Hobbes and the Principle of Publicity." *Pacific Philosophical Quarterly* 82: 447–74.

Wootton, David. 1998. "Thomas Hobbes's Machiavellian Moments." In *The Historical Imagination in Early Modern Britain*, ed. D. Kelley and D. Sacks, 210–42. Washington, DC: Woodrow Wilson Center Press.

Zagorin, P. 1990. *Ways of Lying: Dissimulation, Persecution, and Conformity in Early Modern Europe.* Cambridge, MA: Harvard University Press.

Epilogue

Han Baltussen and Peter J. Davis

The idea that citizens have an inherent right to freedom of thought and expression seems to be a distinctive feature of societies that lay claim to inheriting the politico-cultural traditions of the ancient Greeks and Romans. Central to the essays in this volume is the recognition of two facts: first, that every society imposes formal or informal restrictions on this right and, second, that thinkers, writers, artists, and indeed ordinary people will attempt to evade those restrictions, whether contemporaries regard them as oppressive or not. Despite the great variety of material examined in our essays, certain common strategies have emerged, whether the society concerned is ancient, medieval, or early modern, quasi-democratic or authoritarian, pre-Christian or Christian, whether it is located in Southern or Northern Europe or in the eastern or western Mediterranean.

Democratic Athens and republican Rome set the benchmark for free expression, imposing very few if any legal restraints: Athenians took pride in the equal rights of citizens to speak freely and frankly (*isêgoria*, *parrhêsia*), while Romans prized *libertas*, "freedom," a broad concept that included freedom of speech. There was no such thing as "censorship" in the modern sense in either democratic Athens or republican Rome. But if *legal* restraints in these ancient cities were few or nonexistent, informal constraints, as in all societies that value free speech, were real and considerable. Even these, however, could be circumvented, under particular privileged circumstances whether public or private. In both Athens and Rome critics of contemporary morality and politics could exploit certain physical or cultural sites for free expression, for in both cities the theater, for example, was a place for the exploration of current issues. And we might see Diogenes the Cynic as adopting an analogous strategy, that of self-marginalization: from the edges of respectable society the "new Socrates," unlike the old, was able to mock his fellow citizens with impunity.

In both Athens and Rome we can read self-censorship as a central element in the art of veiled speech. We see self-censorship operating in Athens when poets restrict political subject matter to a purely domestic audience, and in both cities when dramatists avoid the naming of individual politicians. And yet there is no denying that tragic and comic playwrights were vitally concerned with the exploration of issues central to the societies they served.

It is under more autocratic regimes, however, regimes like that of Augustus and his successors at Rome, that the art of veiled speech came into its own, for now we are dealing with rulers who concern themselves with controlling communication. Not surprisingly, self-censorship took on a more drastic form in the early imperial period, when Virgil and Ovid both decided (unsuccessfully) to burn their epics and when Seneca paraded his refusal to include discussion of contemporary politics in his letters. But veiled speech could take other forms, for under the Flavians and Antonines we found writers exploiting the mythological tradition (a tradition already politicized by Ennius and Virgil) and practicing what Quintilian called *emphasis*, the rhetorical art of concealing one's true meaning.

Conversion of the empire to Christianity did not affect this situation, for church authorities in late antiquity and the Middle Ages were no less keen than the Caesars to control communication. Self-censorship continued and new techniques of veiled speech appeared (or perhaps reappeared): those writing letters resorted to careful selection of message-bearers, the issuing of secret instructions, concealment of the names of addressees (in the manner of Ovid's *Tristia*); those confronted with imprisonment and torture proffered claims to a faulty memory and the deliberate provision of information of limited use.

The collection closed with two essays on self-censorship in the early modern period. In the context of this volume, the distinction between late antiquity and the Middle Ages on the one hand and the early modern period on the other is perhaps justified by several major developments that radically altered both the nature of authority and the nature of communication: the creation of nation-states under centralized monarchies, the invention of printing, which enabled the mechanical reproduction of texts and images, and the advent of the Protestant reformation, which broke the monopoly power of the Catholic Church in Western Europe. Both of our early modern chapters address the place of self-censorship in these changed conditions, conditions in which self-censorship can be seen by some at least as a virtue. We saw ecclesiastical officials in Spain, responding to the decrees of the Council of Trent, prompted to censor the visual arts in their churches in order to prevent the inadvertent expression of heretical opinions, and Thomas Hobbes in England espousing freedom of thought but denying the entitlement to freedom of speech and action.

While rejection of the Greco-Roman tradition of free speech is one solution to the difficulty of balancing the need for freedom against the need for order, it does not have universal appeal. The debate continues.

Contributors

Pauline Allen (FAHA) is director of the Centre for Early Christian Studies, Australian Catholic University (Brisbane), and research associate at the University of Pretoria and Sydney College of Divinity.

Han Baltussen (FAHA) is the Hughes Professor of Classics and associate investigator of the ARC Centre of Excellence for the History of Emotions (1100–1800) at the University of Adelaide.

Megan Cassidy-Welch is ARC Future Fellow at the School of Historical, Philosophical and International Studies, Monash University, Melbourne.

Peter J. Davis (FAHA) is adjunct associate professor of classics (Tasmania) and visiting research fellow at the Classics Discipline, University of Adelaide.

Andrew Hartwig is an honorary associate in classics at the University of Sydney.

Gesine Manuwald is professor of Latin at University College London.

Bronwen Neil (FAHA) is senior lecturer in religious studies at the Centre for Early Christian Studies, Australian Catholic University, Brisbane.

Lara O'Sullivan is lecturer in classics and ancient history at the University of Western Australia.

Jonathan Parkin is lecturer (CUF) in early modern history at St Hugh's College, Oxford.

John Penwill is honorary associate (formerly senior lecturer) in humanities at La Trobe University, Bendigo.

François Soyer (FHS) is associate professor of late medieval and early modern history at the University of Southampton.

Marcus Wilson is associate professor in classics at Auckland University, New Zealand.

Ioannis Ziogas is lecturer in classics at the Australian National University, Canberra.

Index

Accius: *Brutus*, 101, 103; *Tereus*, 101
Acolytes, 210, 222 n. 18
Aeetes, 159–64, 168, 171
Aelian, 53
Aeschines, 46
Afranius, 99
Agatho (pope), 243
Agricola, 167, 168–69, 174 n. 34
Agrippa d'Aubigné, 302
Aguirra, Fray Miguel de, 283
aischrologia, 45–46, 48
Albigensian crusade, 253
Alcaeus, 52
Alexander (of Macedon), 6, 48–50, 84
Alexander (pope), 290 n. 24
Ambrose, bishop of Milan, 219
Anacreon, 52
Anastarius the Apocrisiarius, 234, 237, 241–42, 245 n. 25
Anastasius of Sinai, 138, 245 n. 30
Anastasius the Monk, 234, 236–38
Anathema, 216
Anaxarchus, 50
angelic cult, 277. *See also* archangels
Antisthenes, 75–76, 83
antiutopian, 301, 304
Anytus, 75
Apollinaris, bishop of Valence, 211, 220
Apollonius of Rhodes, 157, 164, 166, 172 nn. 1–2
Aquinas, Thomas, 279, 282–84; *Summa Theologica*, 282
archangels, 271, 276–79, 282
Archilochus: blame poetry, 53, 66 n. 39, 67 n. 45; constructed persona, 65 n. 31; Critias's criticism of, 53, 56, 67 n. 46; democratic icon, 67 n. 50; lowly, 63 n. 11; stasis, 66 n. 42
Aristogeiton, 27, 43, 57, 59, 61, 84
Aristophanes, 2, 9, 18, 20–24, 28–33, 37 nn. 63, 65, 72; *Acharnians*, 20–24, 28–29, 32–33; *Babylonians*, 21–22, 33; *Birds*, 28; *Frogs*, 20, 29–33; *Knights*, 23, 29; *Thesmophoriazusae*, 30–31; *Wasps*, 23, 29, 52
Aristotle, 6, 86
Arnobius, *Adversus nationes*, 107
Asinius Pollio, 120–21
Atellana, 101, 104
Athenaeus, 43
Auctor ad Herennium, 100
auctoritas: Augustus, 118–21, 123; Ovid, 120, 124, 129; and *potestas*, 118; Virgil, 117–19, 121, 123, 129
Augustine, bishop of Hippo, 97–98, 212–13, 219–21, 222 n. 18, 225 n. 106, 233, 243 n. 2
Augustinian College of the Incarnation, 278
Augustus, 10–11, 119; *Deeds of the Divine Augustus (Res Gestae)*, 116–17, 122; manuscript burning, 123–24
autocratic regimes, 74

Basil, bishop of Caesarea, 213, 219, 223 n. 43
Benedict, 274
Benedict XIV (pope), 287
blasphemy, 233–34, 236–39, 24–43, 244 n. 2
Book of Kings, 296
books: banned, 287; burning, 6, 123–24, 141–43
boundaries of social tolerance, 75, 87
Bramhall, 299, 311 n. 11
British Museum, 75
burning, 118, 120, 122–24
Burrus, 137, 151 n. 2

Caligula, 104. *See also* Suetonius, *Caligula*
Carducho, Vincente, 272, 289 n. 8
Cassius Dio, 138, 139, 142
Cassius Severus, 142

Castro y Velasco, Antonio Palomino de, 272
Cathars, 252, 263, 265
Catholic Church, 269–71, 273, 276, 286, 288, 289 n. 10
Cato, 107Catullus, 176
Catullus 1 (*Nouum Libellum*), 125–26
Caux, Bernart de, 255
censors, 236, Roman office, 94–95; poets and dramatists in role of, 97–99; intervention of, 100, 116; reactive control, 105
censorship: burning, 116, 123–25; definition and scope, 2–5, 7–12, 95–96, 101; and City Dionysia, 32; and democracy 46, 53, 60–61; informal control 101, 104–5, 107–8; laws, 42–43, 53, 56–58, 60–62, 103; and norms of public discourse, 53, 58, 75, 99; in theater, 94–96, 98–99, 107–8; and power, 130, 132 n. 21, 142, 146, 149, 151, 171–72, 233–34, 236, 240, 252, 264. *See also* book burning; self-censorship
Charron, 302–5, 307
China, 2Christian, 296, 304, 305, 310
Christianity, 304
Cicero, 10, 96, 98, 101–3, 138; *Brutus,* 10, 94; Ep. 118.2–3, 139–40, 142, 151 n. 1, 158, 168–69, 209, 211, 219, 222 n. 1; *For Archias,* 96; *For Sestius (Pro Sestio),* 101; *Letters to Atticus,* 10, 100–101, 103; *Letters to Friends (Epistulae ad Familiares),* 10, 101–3; *On Duties (De Officiis),* 100; *Philippics,* 101, 107; *Republic (De Re Publica),* 97–98, 107
Cicero, 138
City Dionysia, 9, 18–19, 23, 25, 29–33
civic standards, 84
civil war, 157–59, 163–64, 166–67, 170–71
Claudius, 105
Cleitus, 49–51
Clement of Alexandria, *Protrepticus,* 60
Cleon (Kleon), 18, 20–24, 28–29, 31, 33, 46
Coetzee, John, 4
Collection Doat, 255
conception, immaculate, 275, 279, 282–85; defined by Pope Pius IX, 290 n. 24
conscience, 296, 302, 306–7, 313 n. 53, 314 n. 54
conspiracy of caution, 289
Constans II (emperor), 234–35, 237, 239–43, 244 n. 8
Constitution of Athens, 56
Council of Chalcedon, 210, 218
Cremutius Cordus, 142
Critias: blame, 67 n. 46; democracy and sympotic practice, 53, 55–56, 67 n. 49, 68 nn. 58, 60
cuenca, 271, 285, 287, 289
Curiatius Maternus: *Medea,* 104; *Thyestes,* 104
cynics, nihilistic, 80
Cyprian of Carthage, 210
Cyril, patriarch of Alexandria, 215–16

Daniel, 284
deacons, 210–11, 217, 220, 223 n. 24
deceit, 303
Decimus Laberius, 102
defiance of convention, 80–81, 87
delusion, 299
Demades, 54
Demetrios the Besieger, 24, 26–27, 36 nn. 43–44, 46
democracy: and *parrhêsia,* 42, 45–46, and sympotic practice, 53–55, 57–58, 60–62, 62 n. 3, 69 n. 67, 74, 88
Demosthenes, 67 n. 53, 69 n. 71, *Against Conon, 45, 48;* on Athenian *parrhêsia;* on invective 44, 46, 64 n. 16; *Olynthiacs,* 59
denunciation, 278–9, 282, 285–6
Descartes, 307
determinism, 300
deviance, 76, 82; product of social interaction, 83
Devil, 274, 285, 287–88
Diaz, Junot, 115
Dio Cassius, 117, 162, 171, 172, 173 n. 19, 174 nn. 40, 42
Diodorus, 53, 55
Diogenes Laertius, 76; *Lives,* 77
Diogenes the Cynic, 9, 74–76; abrasive,78–79; defiance of convention, 80–83, 87; defacing coinage, 81; dog-like (*kunikos*), 79; exile, 84, 86–87; paradoxes, 86; pretender to wisdom, 84; respected by Athenians, 82; self-control (ἐγκράτεια), 76, 81; self-sufficiency, 80, 87–88; shameless, 81, 87; Socratic philosopher, 83, 86; values, 76, 80–81, 87–88; writing, 78
Dionysius (of Syracuse), 84
Disputatio Bizyae, 235, 239, 244 n. 20
dissenters, 75
dissimulation, 294, 296, 301–2, 303–4. *See also* Nicodemism
Domitian (emperor), 105, 142, 159, 162,

168–69, 177–85, 187–89, 193–95. *See also* Suetonius, *Life of Domitian*
Domitius Ahenobarbus, Cn., 100
Donatists, 220
Donatus: *On Terence's Eunuchus*, 107; *Virgil*, 118, 126
Dyothelitism, 234, 239, 241, 243

edict, 289 n. 11; of silence, 282, 284
Elegiaca Adespota IEG 27, 48
eleutheria, 9, 42, 45
El Greco, 278, 290 n. 20
emphasis, 176, 188–89, 202 n. 57, 204 n. 76
Enlightenment, 300–301, 306, 310
Ennius, 96, 99, 117, 130, 157–58, 172 n. 1; *Annals* (*Annales*), 96
Ennodius, bishop of Pavia, 213–15, 217, 221, 223 n. 40, 224 n. 73, 225 n. 104
Epicureanism, 140, 145–47, 149, 153 nn. 29–30
Epiphanius (patrician), 235, 242
Epiphanius, bishop of Pavia, 215
Epiphanius, Saint, 284, 290 n. 26
Eubulus, 48
Eupolis, 9, 31; *Demoi*, 20, 31; *Marikas*, 29, 31
Euripides, *Phoenician Women*, 1
exile, 138, 140, 142, 144, 150–51, 152 n. 16, 185, 189, 198 n. 27, 200 n. 46, 217–18, 234, 236, 240–41, 245 n. 25; *Diogenes*, 84, 86–87; as an honor, 87; *Ovid*, 119–20; *Meliboeus*, 122, 129
external-internal divide, 295–96, 298, 302, 304–9

fabula praetexta, 97–98, 101, 103, 105
fakery, 298
Felix (pope), 216
Firmus, bishop of Caesarea, 221, 222 n. 18
Foucault, Michel, 264
frank speech, 81. *See also* free speech; *parrhêsia*
freedom, 88
free speech, 1–2, 4–5, 8, 10. See also frank speech; *parrhêsia*
free thought, 293, 295, 305; esp. when private, 296
free will, 299, 307 friendship (*philia/amicitia*), 209, 217, 225 n. 103
Fronto, 100

Gellius, Aulus, *Attic Nights* (NA), 96
Gratian (emperor), 219
Gregory, bishop of Nyssa, 213, 223 n. 29
Gregory I (pope), 212, 218
Gregory IX (pope), 253
Gregory XV (pope), 282

Harmodius, 43, 57, 59, 61, 84
Helvidius Priscus, 177, 179
Heraclius (emperor), 234, 236–37, 242, 244 nn. 7–8
Heresiarchs, 287
heresy, 6, 11–12, 234, 238, 243, 244 n. 2, 252–56, 258–61, 265, 273, 284, 288–89, 294, 311 n. 4
heretics, 253–56, 257–63, 287–88
Hermippos, *Bread Sellers*, 29
Hidalgo, José García, 272
Hobbes, practiced self-censorship, 294. *See also* Leviathan
Homer: speech and status in the *Iliad*, 45–46, 50–51, 63 n. 11; subversive humor in the *Iliad*, 60; literary conventions and criticism, 64 nn. 12, 14, 157, 158
Horace, 102, 116–17,183, 193, 194; *Ars Poetica*, 102; *Epodes* 7.17–20, 163, 168; *Odes*, 116–17; *Satires 1*, 102
Hormisdas (pope), 216–17
humor, 76, 86
Hyperides, *Against Philippides*, 43, 57–59, 63 n. 6
Hypomnesticon, 235, 241

iconoclast, 75
ideology, religious, 4,
Ignatius, bishop of Antioch, 210
images: sacred, 296, 278, 289; on profane objects, 274; pornographic, 275
impiety trials, 75
index, 273, 289 n. 9
informers (*delatores*), 143, 145, 149
inquisition: institution, 251, 263, 269, 271–74, 289, 291 n. 34; procedure, 252–53, 255
inquisitor, 275, 277–78
insincerity, 296
intentions, 298, 310; concealment of, 302
interiority, 298
Iran, 2
isêgoria, 9, 42, 47
isonomia, 42, 47

Jason, 158, 161, 162, 163, 164, 166–69, 171, 172 n. 2

Jerome, 213, 219, 221
Jesus Christ, 274, 285, 293, 296
John (the Baptist), 279
John, bishop of Antioch, 215–16, 218
John IV (pope), 235
John Chrysostom, 218
Juvenal, 11; *Satire 1*, 189–94

Kassandros, 27
know thy self, 303, 306

Lactantius, Divine Institutes (*Institutiones Divinae*), 107
laity, 211
Lapide, Cornelius a, 276
Laurentius, bishop of Milan, 217
law: natural, 297–98, 300, 309; of God, 297
Lenaia, 9, 19, 25, 29–33
Leo (emperor), 216
letters: official, 212–13; private, 210–13
letter-bearers, 209–11, 217, 222 n.14
Leviathan, 296, 300, 305–6, 308, 311 n. 12, 312 n. 28, 314 nn. 53, 62
Lex Oppia, 99
Libanius, 211–12, 218, 223 n. 29
liberal politics, 293–94, 313 n. 53
libertas, 3–4, 9, 141–42, 148, 152 n. 19, 177, 179, 182, 184–85, 189, 193–96, 198 n. 20, 203 n. 65
liberty, 296, 312 n. 25, 314 n. 58
Lipsius, Justus, 302, 304
Livy, 99, 141
Lucan, 158, 163, 164, 168, 171, 172, 177
Lucian, *On How to Write History*, 6
Lucilius, 99, 190–94, 202 n. 55
Lucius Caecilius Metellus Diadematus, 100
Lucretius, 158, 176
Lysias, 53

Machiavelli, 294, 301, 304, 312 nn. 34, 62
Macrobius, *Saturnalia*, 102, 120
Madrid, 271–72, 274, 276, 283
maiestas, 141–44, 146, 149, 150
Maria, de Aragon, 278, 280–81
Mark Antony, 107
Martial, 11; I *Praefatio*, 107; *Epigrams* books 10–12, 179–89
Martin I (pope), 12, 234–36, 238–43, 244 n. 13, 246 n. 41, 247 n. 55
materialism, 299, 306–8
Maximus the Confessor, 12, 234–39, 240–41
Medea, 157, 159, 164, 169, 172 nn. 1–2
Meletus, 75
Metelli, 97
Michelangelo, 270
mime, 101
monks, 211
monoenergism, 234–35, 238, 244 n. 5
monothelitism, 234–35, 238–39, 241–43, 244 n. 5
Montaigne, 302, 303, 313 n. 41
moral deterioration, 79
Muslims, 288
Mylapore (India), 279

Naevius, 96–97, 158
Narrationes de exilio sancti papae Martini, 235, 241, 246 n. 36, 247 n. 55
natural law. See law
Nero, 50, 103–5, 137–39, 143–46, 150, 153 n. 28, 154 n. 44, 181
Nerva, 11, 177–82, 185–86, 188–89, 195
Nicodemism, 296, 311 n. 10. *See also* dissimulation
nominalism, 307–8

obligation: external, 295; moral, 297
offenses, 298
Old Oligarch (Xenophon), *Constitution of Athens*, 56
opinión pía, 282–84
ordination, female, 282, 284
Orthodox(y), 297, 304–5, 311 n. 10
Ovid, 10–11, 115; exile, 119–20, 122; *The Heroines (Heroides)*, 121; *Letters from the Black Sea (Epistulae ex Ponto)*, 120; *The Loves (Amores)*, 116, 128–29; manuscript burning, 122–24; *Sorrows (Tristia)*, 119–28; *Transformations (Metamorphoses)*, 121–27, 130, 142, 157–59, 172 n. 1, 177, 182, 185–86, 189, 198 n. 28, 199 n. 29, 200 n. 43, 201 n. 46, 240

Pacheco, Andrés, 271
Pacheco, Francisco, 272
palliata, 106
Pamfronius, 214
pamphlets, 272–73
parrhêsia (παρρησία): definition and scope, 1–4, 7–11, 42–43, 47, 60–62; moderated by self-censorship, 45; and shame, 45–46, 81, 87; criticism and abuse, 49, 51–52; and norms of public discourse, 53–54;

Diogenes, 81, 87, 172, 210, 212, 216, 218, 220–21, 226. *See also* frank speech; free speech
Paulinus of Nola, 209, 211
peace, 294, 297, 298, 300, 302; requirements of, 295; imperatives of, 309
pedagogy of fear, 289
Pelias, 161–63, 168–69
Persius, 192–94, 196 n. 4
persona, 308
Philip (of Macedon): *parrhêsia*, 54–55, 67 n. 51; and symposium, 48, 58–61, 69 n. 71; tyrant, 69 n. 68
Philip III (king), 256
Philippides, 10, 18, 24–27, 58, 69 n. 70. *See also* Hyperides, *Against Philippides*
Philochorus, 47
philosophy, 140, 145, 147, 148; as action, 76, 86
Plato, 42, 64 n. 13, 79, 84, 86, 88; *Apology*, 81; *Laws*, 32
Plato Comicus, 32; *Hyperbolos*, 29; *Kleophon*, 29; *Skeuai*, 20
Plautus, 97, 99, 106; *Aulularia*, 99; *Captivi*, 106; *Casina*, 106; *Curculio*, 99; *Epidicus*, 99; *Mostellaria*, 99; *Stichus*, 99
Pliny (the Younger), 11, 176, 190, 192–93, 195–96, 196 n. 3, 197 n. 7, 198 nn. 24, 27, 201 n. 50, 203 nn. 62, 65, 204 n. 75, 209
Plutarch, 26; *Alexander*, 50; *Amatorius*, 26; *Demetrios*, 26; *Lycurgus*, 48; *Sulla*, 10
Pollux, 22
Polybius, 7
Pompey, 102
potestas, 118
presbyters, 210
principles, 296, 299
private sphere, 293, 295, 302, 309–10, 313 n. 53, 314 n. 53
prohibition, 286–87; of print, 274; of images, 271, 287–88 (Tridentine)
Propertius, 121
provocation, 86
Ps. Demosthenes, 42
Ps. Seneca, *Octavia*, 103, 105, 151. *See also* Seneca (the Younger)
Ps. Xenophon, 76. *See also* Xenophon
Psalms, 297
public sphere, 300–301, 303, 306, 308
Publilius Syrus, 102–3
Pylamenes, 212
Quintilian, 10, 176–77, 189, 194, 201 n. 50; *Institutes of Oratory (Institutio Oratia)*, 100
Quintus Caecilius Metellus Macedonicus, 99
Quintus Smyrnaeus, *Posthomerica*, 51
Quiroga, Gaspar de, 273

Rabbula, bishop of Edessa, 216
rationalism, 301
readers (church office), 211
reason of state *(ragion di stato)*, 294, 310
religion, 12, 149, 238, 286, 294, 301, 304, 306
repression, 275
Ruricius, bishop of Limoges, 214–15, 222 n. 18
Rushdie, Salman, 115

Sannyrion, *Danae*, 20
satire, 88
Scargill, Daniel, 311 n. 12
schism, 216–17, 220
secrecy, 210, 212, 215–16, 218, 304
self: autonomous, 300; external, 302; internal, 294, 295
self-censorship: definition and scope, 2–3, 5, 7, 9, 11–13, 45, 99, 116; comic poetry, 18–19, 24, 27; at festivals, 29–30, 32–33; to avoid stasis, 51–52; Virgil and Ovid, 116, 120, 124, 126, 128, 130, 145, 210, 214–18, 234, 240–41, 243, 252, 256–63, 271, 293–97, 299–301, 303, 305, 309–10
self-control (ἐγκράτεια), 81
selfhood, 293
self-knowledge, 308–9
self-preservation, 294, 297–98, 308
self-regulation, 83
Seneca (the Elder), 142. *See also* ps. Seneca
Seneca (the Younger), 105; *Moral Epistles (Epistulae Morales ad Lucilium),* 11, 107, 148; *Pumpkinification of the Divine Claudius (Apocolocyntosis),* 105; *On Clemency (De clementia)*, 105; 118.2–3, 139, 209. *See also* ps. Seneca
Servius, 126–127, 129
Severus, patriarch of Antioch, 211, 212, 218, 221, 225 n. 82
sheep with the golden fleece, 84
Sidonius Apolllinaris, 211, 214, 215, 220
silence, 6, 24, 143–44, 178, 233, 237–38, 264, 294; Edict of Silence, 284; prudent, 303
Silius Italicus, 157, 158, 168
Simeon, bishop of Chalcis, 211

Simplicius (early fifth c.), 211
Sinope, 83–84
social control, 288
social order, 298–99
Socrates, 8–9, 15 n.22, 75–76, 81, 86, 88
Solon, *IEG*, 54
Sophronius (bishop of Jerusalem), 234, 235, 244 n. 6
speech act, 84
St Pierre, Jean de, 255
Statius, 157, 158
status, 210–11, 223 n. 24
Stoicism, 140, 145–49, 152 n. 14, 153 n. 30, 154 n. 39
Stratokles, 18, 24–27
subdeacons, 210–11
subversion, 74, 86, 88
Suetonius, 171, 173 n. 18, 174 n. 40, 195, 197 n. 16, 202 n. 55; *Augustus*, 31, 120, 123, 126, 143; *Caligula*, 104; *Domitian*, 10, 105; *Galba*, 104; *Nero*, 104–5; *Tiberius*, 104
Sulpicius Severus, 211
symposium, 9
Synesius, bishop of Cyrene, 212, 213, 214, 220

Tacitus, 11, 104–5, 138, 141–43; *Agricola*, 167–69, 174 n. 34; *Annals*, 10, 104–5, 144, 149–50, 152 n. 12, 153 n. 16, 177, 179, 192, 194–96, 204 n. 74; *Dialogue on Oratory (Dialogus de oratoribus)* 104; *Histories*, 10
Terence, 99, 106, 108; *Adelphoe*, 108; *Andria*, 100; *Eunuchus*, 96, 99, 106–8; *Heauton Timorumenos*, 99; *Phormio*, 99
Tertullian, *De Spectaculis*, 107
Theodore I (pope), 235, 240–41
Theodoret, bishop of Cyrrhus, 217
Theophilus, patriarch of Alexandria, 214
Theophrastus, *Characters, 45*
Theopompus, 6–7
Thersites, 45–46, 50–51, 54, 60; *Aethiopis*, 50–51
Thomas the Apostle, 279
Thrasea Paetus, 138, 143–46, 179
Thucydides, 19
Titinius, *Barbatus*, 99
Titus (emperor), 159, 162–63
Titus Labienus, 146
tolerance, 74, 76
Trajan (emperor), 11, 178–79, 185–89, 193–94, 197 n. 7, 198 nn. 24, 26–28, 199 n. 31, 200 nn. 38, 41, 43–44, 201 nn. 48, 50, 203 n. 65, 204 n. 73, 210
Trent, council of, 282, 284, 286, 288
truth, 86
Twelve Tables, 97–98, 118
typos, 234–35, 238, 241–42
tyranny, 160–63, 168, 169

uirtus, 11, 143, 167–70, 173 nn. 16, 33–34
unlawful, 307
unorthodox, 296
Urban VIII (pope), 286
urban culture, 79
Utopian, 301, 306, 310

Valerius Antias, 141
Valerius Flaccus: *Argonautica*, 11; passages quoted, 170, 160–62, 165, 166, 164, 171, 192
Valerius Maximus, 107
verbal communication, 210, 213–16, 219, 221
Vespasian (emperor), 11, 159, 162, 170, 171, 172, 173 n. 21
vice, 300, 303
Virgil, 10–11; *Aeneid*, 116, 118–22, 127–29; *auctoritas*, 117–19, 121, 123, 129; *Eclogues*, 129, 147; editorial changes, 126, 130; *Epigrams*, 117; *Georgics* 117, 170; manuscript burning, 118, 120, 122–24, 158–60, 165–66, 168, 180, 186, 195, 196 n. 3
Virgin Mary, 272–73, 279–80, 282, 284–85
Vizards, 303

Waldensians, 253
Waterfield, Robin, 75
Williamson, David, 108
women, 211

Xenophanes, 51–52
Xenophon, 56; *Constitution of Athens*, 56; *Cyropaedia*, 47

Zachary (pope), 276
Zanker, Paul, 75

Acknowledgments

We would like to thank the contributors who joined us in exploring the themes related to free speech enthusiastically and with an open mind for interdisciplinary exchange. Early versions of some of the essays were researched with the support of the Australasian Society of Classical Studies.

The editors wish to record their mutual thanks for a pleasant and successful collaboration over the past three and a half years, and their thanks to Ioannis Ziogas and Mark P. Davies for enriching the discussions about censorship in their role as postdoctoral researchers with the project (2011–13). In addition, we thank Ana Silkatcheva for many useful bibliographical searches, and Aisha Mahmood and Sandra Horne, who skillfully assisted us in proof checking, formatting, and editing several versions of the essays.

We are also grateful to the anonymous readers, who gave generously of their time and effort. Last but not least, we warmly thank Deborah Blake, consulting editor of the University of Pennsylvania Press, for responding so positively and expeditiously to the proposal and for guiding the manuscript through the assessment and production process with her sound advice, patience, and efficiency.

HB
PJD